Data Alchemy in Insurance: Revolutionizing the Insurance Industry through Big Data Analytics

Edited by

Sanjay Taneja
Department of Management Studies, Graphic Era Deemed to be University, Dehradun, Uttarakhand, India

Ercan Ozen
Department of Banking and Finance, University of Usak Usak, Turkey

Luan Vardar
University "Ukshin Hoti" Prizren, Kosovo (Serbia)

Mohit Kukreti
University of Technology and Applied Sciences (CAS Ibri), Muscat, Oman

&

Mohammad Kashif
Department of Management Studies, Graphic Era Deemed to be University, Dehradun, Uttarakhand, India

Data Alchemy in Insurance: Revolutionizing the Insurance Industry through Big Data Analytics

Editors: Sanjay Taneja, Ercan Ozen, Luan Vardar, Mohit Kukreti and Mohammad Kashif

ISBN (Online): 978-981-5313-83-3

ISBN (Print): 978-981-5313-84-0

ISBN (Paperback): 978-981-5313-85-7

First published in 2025.

Bentham Science Publishers Pte. Ltd.
80 Robinson Road #02-00
Singapore 068898
Singapore
Email: subscriptions@benthamscience.net

BENTHAM
SCIENCE

CONTENTS

FOREWORD

"**Data Alchemy in Insurance: Revolutionizing the Insurance Industry through Big Data Analytics**" is a book that explores how this tool is changing insurance. It shows how data is now guiding decisions in the insurance world.

Big Data analytics is becoming more than a passing trend for insurance businesses; it is essential to remain competitive and meet clients' demands. This book examines the way data influences how insurance claims are handled, how clients are engaged, and how risks are evaluated.

Big Data analytics is explained simply throughout the book, with studies and examples to aid understanding. This book contains information for everyone interested in how technology affects insurance, whether they are insurance professionals, students studying insurance technology, or simply interested in the subject.

As you read "**Data Alchemy in Insurance: Revolutionizing the Insurance Industry through Big Data Analytics**," you'll learn about the challenges and opportunities of using data in insurance. Each chapter gives a complete picture of how things are changing and guides people in the industry.

This book will be helpful for everyone interested in insurance-related big data analytics. Let it serve as an invitation to explore the future of insurance, one in which data will be the key to improving insurance for all people while we watch this exciting transformation taking place.

Dr Amar Johri
Professor, College of Administrative and Financial Sciences
Saudi Electronic University, Riyadh ,11673
Saudi Arabia

PREFACE

In the dynamic landscape of the 21st century, industries across the globe are experiencing unprecedented transformations, fueled by technological advancements that redefine the way we conduct business. Among these industries, the insurance sector stands at the forefront of change, undergoing a revolutionary evolution driven by the transformative power of Big Data Analytics.

"Data Alchemy in Insurance: Revolutionizing the Insurance Industry through Big Data Analytics" is a comprehensive exploration into the profound impact of data analytics on the insurance landscape. As we navigate through an era defined by data-driven decision-making, this book serves as a beacon, shedding light on the pivotal role that Big Data plays in reshaping the fundamental pillars of the insurance industry.

The integration of Big Data Analytics into insurance operations is not merely a trend but a necessity, as insurers strive to remain competitive, adaptive, and responsive to the ever-shifting demands of the market. This book delves into the intricate ways in which data analytics is reshaping risk assessment, customer engagement, underwriting processes, and claims management within the insurance ecosystem.

Through insightful case studies, expert analyses, and real-world examples, this book aims to demystify the complexities surrounding Big Data Analytics for readers from various backgrounds – be it industry professionals seeking to enhance their practices, scholars delving into the realms of InsurTech, or enthusiasts eager to understand the technological underpinnings of the insurance revolution.

As we embark on this journey through the pages of "Data Alchemy in Insurance: Revolutionizing the Insurance Industry through Big Data Analytics" readers will gain valuable insights into the challenges and opportunities that arise at the intersection of insurance and data. The chapters within this book are crafted to provide a holistic perspective on the ongoing transformation, offering a roadmap for industry stakeholders to navigate the evolving landscape with confidence and foresight.

It is our sincere hope that this book becomes a trusted companion for those seeking to unravel the mysteries of Big Data Analytics in the insurance sector. As we witness the revolution unfold, let this preface serve as an invitation to explore the future of insurance – a future where data is not just a commodity but the driving force behind a more resilient, efficient, and customer-centric industry. Following are the abstracts of the chapters included in this book:

Chapter 1

In the realm of motor insurance, customer retention has become a critical focus for companies, given the high cost of acquiring new customers. This study proposes a machine learning model to predict customer churn in the motor insurance sector. The objective is to develop a high-accuracy prediction model, identify significant factors for customer attrition, and create customer segments using machine learning algorithms. The literature review highlights the challenges faced by motor insurance providers, such as annual policy renewals and intense competition. Existing research emphasizes the importance of predicting customer churn to improve service quality and gain new users. Various methods, including under-sampling and neural network models, have been explored to address the issue. The study utilizes a hybrid classifier, GWO-KELM, to predict churn and evaluates its performance through confusion matrices and ROC curve analysis. The results demonstrate the algorithm's ability to characterize test data and its overall accuracy. Data processing involves the Expectation Maximization technique, enhancing decision-making transparency and outcomes.

Chapter 2

In the changing corporate landscape, the combination of Artificial Intelligence (AI) and data analytics has altered the insurance industry, resulting in a customer-centric paradigm through data-driven operations. AI-powered data analytics plays a critical role in helping clients understand, engage with, and select insurance services. This chapter delves into the detailed uses of AI-powered data analytics in the insurance sector, including AI assessment, problems, and ramifications, with a particular emphasis on product customization. The goal is to demonstrate how AI-powered data analytics is altering the industry, meeting customer requests, and investigating disruptive implications. The process entails analyzing secondary sources such as research publications and industry reports to better comprehend the impact on customer choices and service provider tactics. Findings reveal a notable shift in the insurance landscape, emphasizing AI-powered data analytics' profound impact on personalized experiences, data-driven insights, risk assessment, claims processing, premium decisions, and policy customization. This technological evolution signifies a significant transformation in the insurance sector.

Chapter 3

Robo Advisors are ushering in a new era of automated health guardianship, which is ushering in a new era of automated health guardianship in the ever-evolving environment of healthcare, which has seen an explosion in the integration of technology. This article goes into the paradigm change brought about by these sophisticated algorithms in the field of insurance planning, specifically with regard to health coverage. The purpose of this paper is to investigate the revolutionary effect that Robo Advisors have had on the process of insurance planning. Specifically, the article will shed light on the functionalities of Robo Advisors as well as the consequences that these features have for consumers as well as the insurance sector. Additionally, the ethical and regulatory considerations that surround the use of Robo Advisors in insurance planning are covered in this article. Concerns around data privacy, bias mitigation, and openness in algorithmic capabilities become critical as the use of artificial intelligence in decision-making processes becomes more widespread. Also, the changing role of insurance experts in connection with Robo Advisors is investigated in this article. Although these automated technologies simplify and improve the decision-making process, there is still no substitute for the human element when it comes to reading preferences down to the most detailed level and offering individualized guidance.

Chapter 4

Insurance is a healing ointment for every person, but it's better to go for insurance as a shock absorber for different types of shock in life.

People also take insurance to plan their lives, which helps them reduce tensions throughout life, but so many people also try to avoid taking insurance due to the long time and time-consuming operational procedures at various stages of their insured life. They need an assistant to reduce or resolve the operational problems related to buying policy, claim filing, and renewal of the policy. Traditional practices to resolve issues related to such problems include interaction with men either in the form of physical meetings or by communication through emails and telephones. The advent of the 21st century is the growth of automation in businesses, and the insurance industry is also adopting technology to reduce the issues related to claim settlement policy selling and understanding consumer behavior, which assists in policy selling. This chapter will visualize the growth of technology in the Indian insurance industry.

Chapter 5

The post-COVID era has accelerated the growth of the health insurance sector drastically. Nowadays, the public is focussing on taking health insurance to mitigate the sudden expenses of health services. However, finding the best health scheme for people is still considered challenging. Hence, the present study attempts to solve the issue by developing a framework that considers a range of essential factors of the health insurance plan. The identified factors were ranked by using the integrated Delphi and best-worst methods. The study helps consumers choose their policy effectively using the proposed framework.

Chapter 6

The landscape of the insurance industry is undergoing a profound transformation propelled by the integration of advanced data analytics. This paper explores the evolving role of data analytics in reshaping critical aspects of insurance, ranging from traditional risk assessment to customer-centric practices. Against the backdrop of exponential data growth and technological advancements, insurers are increasingly relying on analytics to inform strategic decision-making, enhance risk modeling, and optimize customer engagement. The abstract provides a concise summary of the primary themes covered in this paper, underscoring the pivotal role of data analytics in navigating the challenges and leveraging the opportunities that lie ahead for the insurance sector. The exploration encompasses current trends, technological advancements, ethical considerations, and regulatory landscapes, aiming to provide a comprehensive understanding of the dynamic future that awaits the intersection of data analytics and insurance.

Chapter 7

After the e-tail and the e-travel industries, the insurance industry has likewise begun its computerized development in India. The Web aggregators have reformed the web-based insurance industry under the permit of the Insurance Regulatory and Development Authority of India. There are currently around 16 authorized web aggregators in India, and some of them have moved forward to try and do online deals with their imperative licenses. Indeed, even insurance organizations have begun to sell online through their immediate channels, yet not all arrangements are suitable for online transactions. The insurance renewal business gradually moves onto the digital platform with basic ECS and auto-debit mandates, even for offline policies. The Boston Consulting Group report anticipates an extreme development in renewals. The organization benefits more because the specialist payout goes down fundamentally, and the operational costs of writing and giving the policy are not there. The online insurance industry is quickly rising, and just 30% of the insurance purchasers in India are non-digitalized, and that number is quickly diminishing, as per the BCG examination. The digitalization of the insurance industry speeds up development and brings down costs. The cost of sales and dispersion of insurance products in India through absolutely advanced channels is close to one-sixth that of physical channels. The computerized impact on insurance sales is growing, with pre- and post-deal advanced impact playing a significant role. E-insurance is quickly catching up to e-wallets and internet banking, which are now well-established trends. The present paper aims to study the growth of life insurance in India and its challenges. The present paper found that the growth of the private sector life insurance company has continuously increased compared to the public life insurance companies in India.

Chapter 8

This study critically examines the multifaceted impact of artificial intelligence (AI) on contemporary societal dynamics. Exploring economic, social, ethical, and cultural dimensions, our research sheds light on the unprecedented opportunities and challenges that accompany the rapid integration of AI technologies. Assessing the transformative potential of AI in diverse industries, we delve into economic implications, highlighting efficiency gains and innovation. Socially, we investigate evolving employment patterns, educational paradigms, and interpersonal relationships shaped by AI. Ethical considerations, including algorithmic bias and transparency, are scrutinized. Additionally, we explore how cultural factors influence AI perceptions and adaptation. This interdisciplinary analysis aims to provide a nuanced understanding of the intricate relationship between AI and society, offering insights for responsible AI development, policy-making, and fostering a harmonious coexistence in the evolving technological landscape.

Chapter 9

This study intricately explores the ethical landscape surrounding data analytics within the insurance sector, aiming to untangle the intricacies and quandaries arising in the pursuit of data-driven insights. In an era dominated by technological strides, the insurance industry increasingly relies on data analytics to bolster risk assessment, optimize operations, and tailor services to individual needs. However, the widespread use of data introduces ethical challenges pertaining to privacy, equity, and openness. The principal objective of this research is to traverse and critically examine the ethical considerations woven into the fabric of applying data analytics within the insurance sector. To accomplish this, a methodology centered on the case study is employed, delving into the real-world scenario and their practical implication. By closely analyzing specific instances within the insurance industry, the research aims to provide a nuanced comprehension of how ethical concerns manifest during the implementation of data analytics. The methodology encompasses the selection of diverse case studies representing various aspects of data analytics in insurance, encompassing customer profiling, risk assessment algorithms, and claims processing. Through a thorough analysis of these cases, the study seeks to uncover patterns, confront challenges, and propose potential solutions related to ethical considerations. Ethical frameworks, industry guidelines, and stakeholder perspectives will be leveraged to assess the ramifications of data analytics practices in the insurance domain. In conclusion, this research adds to the ongoing dialogue on responsible data analytics in the insurance sector. By unraveling the ethical tapestry and offering insights gleaned from real-world cases, the study aspires to present actionable recommendations for industry professionals, policymakers, and stakeholders to navigate the ethical quandaries associated with data analytics in insurance responsibly.

Chapter 10

In this article, we explore the emerging trend of integrating health insurance data into life insurance policies in the Indian context. This innovative approach aims to revolutionize risk management in India's rapidly evolving insurance sector. By leveraging detailed health data, insurance providers can offer more accurate risk assessments, leading to tailored insurance products that better meet the diverse needs of the Indian populace. However, this integration raises critical issues around data privacy, regulatory compliance, and infrastructural challenges, especially in rural areas. We will analyze the potential benefits, such as enhanced risk prediction and promotion of healthier lifestyles, against these challenges, drawing insights from early adopters and regulatory guidelines from IRDAI. The article aims to provide a comprehensive overview of this integration's impact on India's insurance landscape.

Chapter 11

In India, LIC of India is the one and only public insurance company that introduced micro-insurance (MI) policies with effect from 28th September 2006. This study has made an attempt to examine the micro-insurance schemes and distribution channels of LIC of India, the growth and development of the microinsurance business, and the claims and settlements of LIC of India. The LIC of India micro insurance agents gradually increased, maturity claims were more than the total death claims, and the number of microinsurance policies continuously increased. Later, the number of policies had fallen down drastically. This study concluded that the LIC of India should conduct revival campaigns in both rural and urban areas and create more awareness of revival campaigns among the existing micro insurance policyholders for developing business and reducing lapsation.

Chapter 12

Life insurance provides financial security to families in case of the unfortunate death of the policyholder. In this chapter, a bibliometric analysis of 144 papers published between 1973 and 2022 in the Scopus database was performed to identify key themes and trends in the literature on Life Insurance. The analysis included citation analysis for leading countries, organizations, and authors. It was found that there has been significant growth in research on Life Insurance since 2019, the duration of covid 19. Three dominant themes were identified: customer satisfaction with insurance, the efficiency of insurance, and the relationship between economic growth and insurance. This chapter provides important insights for Life Insurance companies and other stakeholders to promote life insurance growth in India.

Chapter 13

The current study delves into the advancing field of robo-advisors, an evolving business model revolutionizing investment advisory services through full automation. Examining 299 research papers from the Scopus database, spanning from 2002 to January 2024, this study employs bibliometric analysis to uncover key research topics, annual publication trends, subject areas, leading countries, geographic distribution, and co-occurrence and citation network of this scientific exploration. The keywords applied to the study were "robo-advising" OR "robo-advisors" OR "smart wealth management" OR "artificial intelligence in finance". The data were subjected to analysis using the VOSviewer tool, and the 299 selected papers were examined through descriptive, tabular, and visual presentations within the framework discussion. The results indicated that the concept of robo-advising has evolved as an emerging concept in relation to smart wealth management from 2016 onwards. The United States has emerged as the leading country in contributing the maximum number of publications to this concept, and the subject area is computer science. Furthermore, there is a limited exploration of the concept of robo-advising and sustainability as the authors found nil manuscripts for the two together. Finally, at the end of the research, limitations, and suggestions are stated regarding the need for integrated research efforts on this subject.

Chapter 14

The radical shift observed in industries from physical to digital platforms has escalated the implications of data depositories. The extent to which data is growing is exponential. The insurance industry is no exception. The availability of data on various digital platforms has contributed to an enormous amount of repositories in a short span of time. The present study is focused on performance analysis of research constituents that contributed to the domain of insurance industry and big data. An analysis of 541 research publications from 2012 to 2023 retrieved from the WoS database from more than 2000 authors is performed using the bibliophily app, highlighting trends and contributions by authors, universities, and countries. The findings showed that big data has improved the process of database management and profiling in the insurance sector, further easing the claim process. This study will assist researchers and practitioners in understanding the past and present research trends in the area.

Chapter 15

This book chapter explores the profound impact of machine learning and robo-advisors on the insurance industry, ushering in a transformative era characterized by heightened efficiency and innovation. Through an in-depth analysis of their ascendance, we delve into how these technologies are revolutionizing traditional practices within the insurance sector. The utilization of machine learning algorithms is examined across various facets of the industry, including fraud detection, underwriting automation, claims processing optimization, and risk management through predictive analytics. Additionally, the integration of IoT, telematics, and other emerging technologies further amplifies the potential for enhanced customer experiences and streamlined operations. Ethical considerations, regulatory compliance, and the imperative need for explainable AI in decision-making processes are also addressed. The study underscores the collaborative efforts between insurers and InsurTech startups, illustrating how such partnerships leverage the power of machine learning to navigate and thrive in an evolving landscape. As the insurance industry undergoes this significant metamorphosis, the book chapter concludes by highlighting key trends and implications for the future trajectory of the sector.

Sanjay Taneja
Department of Management Studies
Graphic Era Deemed to be University
Dehradun, Uttarakhand, India

Ercan Ozen
Department of Banking and Finance
University of Usak, Usak, Turkey

Luan Vardar
University "Ukshin Hoti" Prizren
Kosovo (Serbia)

Mohit Kukreti
University of Technology and Applied Sciences
(CAS Ibri), Muscat, Oman

&

Mohammad Kashif
Department of Management Studies
Graphic Era Deemed to be University
Dehradun, Uttarakhand, India

List of Contributors

Abdullah Malik	Department of Commerce (Jain Online), Jain University, Bengaluru, India
Abhishek Singh Chauhan	Graphic Era deemed to be University, Dehradun, India
Arokiaraj David	Swiss Business School, Ras AI Khaimah, Ras Al Khaimah, UAE
Ashish C. Pius	Karpagam Academy of Higher Education, Coimbatore, Tamil Nadu, India
Aastha Agarwal	Graphic Era Deemed to Be University, Dehradun, India
Ankit Srivastava	School of Management, IMS Unison University, Dehradun, India
Chouturu Manoj Kumar	Department of Humanities & Sciences (Management), KSRM College of Engineering, Kadapa, Andhra Pradesh, India
Harshi Garg	IIMT University, Meerut, Uttar Pradesh, India
Jaspreet Kaur	University School of Business, Chandigarh University, Gharuan, Punjab, India
Luan Vardari	University "Ukshin Hoti" Prizren, Kosovo (Serbia)
Mohammad Kashif	Department of Management Studies, Graphic Era deemed to be University, Dehradun, Uttarakhand, India
Mohit Kukreti	University of Technology and Applied Sciences, (CAS Ibri), Muscat, Oman
Manish Singh	Swami Rama Himalayan University, Uttarakhand, India
Mohd Amir	Uttaranchal Institute of Management, Uttaranchal University, Dehradun, India
Muskan Singh	Graphic Era Deemed to Be University, Dehradun, India
Mandeep Singh	AIT-APEX, Chandigarh University, Mohali, Punjab, India
Mukul Bhatnagar	Graphic Era deemed to be University, Dehradun, India
Nikita Singhal	IIMT University, Meerut, Uttar Pradesh, India
Neeraj Saxena	Sandip University, Nashik, Maharashtra, India
Prayank Sharma	Swami Rama Himalayan University, Uttarakhand, India
Pawan Kumar	Graphic Era deemed to be University, Dehradun, India
Pooja Sharma	Amity University, Noida, Uttar Pradesh, India
Pooja Sharma	IMT University, Meerut, Uttar Pardesh, India
Reepu	University School of Business, Chandigarh University, Gharuan, Punjab, India
Ritik Joshi	Department of Management, IES Institute of Technology & Management, IES University, Bhopal, Madhya Pradesh, India
R. Velmurugan	Karpagam Academy of Higher Education, Coimbatore, Tamil Nadu, India
Rajesh Tiwari	Graphic Era Deemed to Be University, Dehradun, India
Rajwinder Kaur	University School of Business, Chandigarh University, Punjab, India
Rajeev Srivastava	School of Management, IMS Unison University, Dehradun, India

Sanjay Taneja	Department of Management Studies, Graphic Era Deemed to be University, Dehradun, Uttarakhand, India
Supriya Hazra	Uttaranchal University, Uttarakhand, India
Shikha Goyal	Amity University, Noida, Uttar Pradesh, India
S. Raghunatha Reddy	Department of Humanities & Sciences (Management), KSRM College of Engineering, Kadapa, Andhra Pradesh, India
Sneha Badola	School of Management, IMS Unison University, Dehradun, India
Sangeet Vashishtha	IMT University, Meerut, Uttar Pardesh, India
Shruti Saxena	Sandip University, Nashik, Maharashtra, India
Vijay Prakash Gupta	Institute of Business Management, GLA University, Mathura, India
Vijay Lahri	University of Petroleum and Energy Studies, Dehradun, India
Varnesh Ghildiyal	H.N.B. Garhwal Central University, Uttarakhand, India
Vanshika Kakkar	Graphic Era Deemed to Be University, Dehradun, India
Vartika Bisht	University School of Business, Chandigarh University, Punjab, India
Zelhuda Shamsuddin	Faculty of Business Management and Accounting, Universiti Sultan Zainal Abidin, Terengganu, Malaysia

CHAPTER 1

A Machine Learning Algorithm for Forecasting Customer Churn in the Motor Insurance Industry

Reepu[1], **Sanjay Taneja**[2,3,*] and **Zelhuda Shamsuddin**[3]

[1] *University School of Business, Chandigarh University, Gharuan, Punjab, India*

[2] *Department of Management Studies, Graphic Era Deemed to be University, Dehradun, Uttarakhand, India*

[3] *Faculty of Business Management and Accounting, Universiti Sultan Zainal Abidin, Terengganu, Malaysia*

Abstract: In the realm of motor insurance, customer retention has become a critical focus for companies, given the high cost of acquiring new customers. This study proposes a machine learning model to predict customer churn in the motor insurance sector. The objective is to develop a high-accuracy prediction model, identify significant factors for customer attrition, and create customer segments using machine learning algorithms. The literature review highlights the challenges faced by motor insurance providers, such as annual policy renewals and intense competition. Existing research emphasizes the importance of predicting customer churn to improve service quality and gain new users. Various methods, including under-sampling and neural network models, have been explored to address the issue. The study utilizes a hybrid classifier, GWO-KELM, to predict churn and evaluates its performance through confusion matrices and ROC curve analysis. The results demonstrate the algorithm's ability to characterize test data and its overall accuracy. Data processing involves the Expectation Maximization technique, enhancing decision-making transparency and outcomes. The dataset, collected from a motor insurance company, comprises relevant features for training the classifier. The study identifies nine influential parameters affecting churn, including customer type, policy benefits, claims history, branch continuity, renewal premium, car size, sum insured, renewal timing, and the number of policies. These insights provide actionable recommendations for insurers to improve customer retention strategies. In conclusion, the research addresses challenges in customer churn prediction for motor insurance companies. The developed machine learning model, GWO-KELM, proves effective in characterizing test data and provides valuable insights into factors influencing customer attrition. The identified parameters offer practical implications for insurers to tailor retention efforts and enhance customer satisfaction. The study underscores the significance of machine learning in real-time applications for organizational growth in the dynamic motor insurance market.

* **Corresponding author Sanjay Taneja:** Department of Management Studies, Graphic Era Deemed to be University, India and Faculty of Business Management and Accounting, Universiti Sultan Zainal Abidin, Terengganu, Malaysia; E-mail: drsanjaytaneja1@gmail.com

Sanjay Taneja, Ercan Ozen, Luan Vardar, Mohit Kukreti & Mohammad Kashif (Eds.)

Keywords: Customer retention, GWO-KELM, Machine learning, Motor insurance.

INTRODUCTION

In the realm of motor insurance, companies often dedicate a significant portion of their resources, time, and energy to acquiring new business. While it is crucial to replace lost clients and expand into new markets, the primary objective remains maintaining relationships with existing or past customers. In today's landscape, where consumers are more discerning and competition is fierce, retaining customers has become paramount for motor insurance organizations (Singhal, Goyal & Singhal, 2022). Through literature review, it has been found that the cost of acquiring new customers can be up to five times greater than that of retaining current ones. Furthermore, even a small increase in customer retention can have a positive impact on an organization's revenue. Therefore, while seeking new business opportunities is important, it should not come at the expense of neglecting existing customer relationships (Singh *et al.*, 2020).

How having multiple insurance policies with the same organization increases the chances of renewing policies. When a customer cancels their policies, it is called "churning." Predicting when customers might churn can help motor insurance companies take steps to keep them as customers. It is important for companies to retain their existing customers because getting new ones is difficult and expensive. Losing customers means losing revenue, which harms the company's reputation and growth. The study proposes using churn prediction to help with retention efforts (Datta *et al.*, 2016).

With the intensifying competition in the motor insurance market, insurance companies have become increasingly aware of the need to put forth more effort into retaining existing clients and preventing them from switching to other competitors. Acquiring new customers is a complex process, making it essential for motor insurance organizations to maintain a low churn rate by keeping their old clients satisfied (Jnawali *et al.*, 2016). This has prompted researchers to develop methods for predicting customer churn in order to improve company performance. The consistent decline in retention rates within the motor insurance industry has been identified as a key factor motivating research on customer churn prediction. By identifying users who are likely to switch providers beforehand, motor insurance companies can focus their resources on retaining these individuals rather than contacting every policyholder indiscriminately. It is this motivation that drives our proposed research project.

Research Challenges

Insurance companies, specifically vehicle insurance, struggle with retaining customers due to policies being renewed annually and competition from other providers. Predicting customer churn is important for improving service quality and gaining new users. However, it is difficult to predict unless customers directly contact the organization with complaints. The attrition of customers, or the rate at which they switch to competitors, is a major issue that results in declining revenue. To address this, organizations use various methods for forecasting attrition and building better customer relationships. Retaining existing high-risk customers is a vital issue in insurance segments and requires identifying risk parameters and analyzing time until the churn event (Chowdhury *et al.*, 2022).

Motor insurance providers face increasing competition and struggle to retain customers due to factors like service quality and benefits offered. High churn rates make it difficult to keep customers, who often switch for better offers from other providers. Developing effective methods to overcome these challenges is a difficult task, as customer behaviors and intentions vary greatly (Poongodi *et al.*, 2020).

Research Aim

Our work aims to create a machine-learning model to predict customer churns for motor insurance companies. We designed an accurate prediction model using an optimization strategy. This study highlights the importance of machine learning in real-time applications for organizational growth.

Objectives of the Study

- To develop a model with high accuracy in prediction when compared to the existing data mining algorithms.
- To apply the developed machine learning model to determine the most significant factors for the customer attrition of the motor insurance sector.
- To develop customer segments using the developed model by applying the machine learning algorithm for prediction of attrition rate of customers in the vehicle insurance sector.

Review of Literature

Research focuses on framework structure and uses multiple datasets to investigate potential expansions in findings. Under-sampling method accidentally selects a record set suitable for predicting attrition. Neural network models show high scores, prompting exploration of hyperparameter tuning to improve prediction accuracy (Scriney, Nie, *et al.*, 2020).

OCSVM under-sampling improves classifier performance by extracting support vectors from the majority class and combining them with the minority class. Multiple kernels were used to test its impact on unstable datasets. Projected

under-sampling simplified system construction and produced significant results when compared to other works (Sunderkumar, Ravi *et al.*, 2015).

Educated customers churn due to insurer attitude, industry workers care about the brand name, and low-importance customers prioritize policy timeframes. Insurer-customer relation affects churn. Dropping churn customers is possible. Results help managers prevent client attrition and switching to competitors (Soeini & Rodpysh, 2012).

Reducing churn customers is a major concern in client relationship management and advertising, especially in fields like telecommunications, finance, and insurance. Researchers are studying how to create an index formula to understand why customers leave. They developed a formula using six classification methods (Decision tree QUEST, Decision tree C5.0, Decision tree CHAID, Decision tree CART, Bayesian network, and Neural network (Rodpysh, 2013).

A new system called BaYcP has been developed to address customer churn behavior. It uses a two-phase approach: first, the data is collected and a risk profiling score is generated based on decision trees and associated with a threshold value. Then, a prediction model is created using the Bayesian classifier method on suitable topographies based on scores above the threshold. The model has an accuracy of 97.89%, outpacing other models and frameworks (Bhattacharya, Ladha *et al.*, 2020).

Data Reprocessing

Transparency of data is one of the vital qualities of the collected data. It explores the perceptible rate of the data acquisition process. It also assists in making a better decision process. Moreover, it also looks to obtain similar decision outcomes (Kashif *et al.*, 2024). The preprocessing of the data brings drastic changes in deriving decisions about the data perceptibly

In this study, the researchers have come up with a way to sample data using something called the Expectation Maximization technique. This process has two stages: the E-Step and M-Step. It helps us figure out how likely it is that certain data points belong to certain groups by exploring their probability distributions and learning parameters. This approach works well with different machine learning algorithms, but sometimes it can be difficult if there are variables that we don't know about (called latent variables). By estimating values for these latent variables, we can improve our estimates of maximum likelihood estimation until we get an accurate answer (Kashif, David, Gupta, & Alam, 2024). The researchers also used this approach to estimate missing data in a dataset where some of the information was not observable. They did this by assuming that each process relied on the Gaussian probability distribution and then estimated parameters for those distributions so they could combine and distribute the given points effectively as shown in Fig. (**1**).

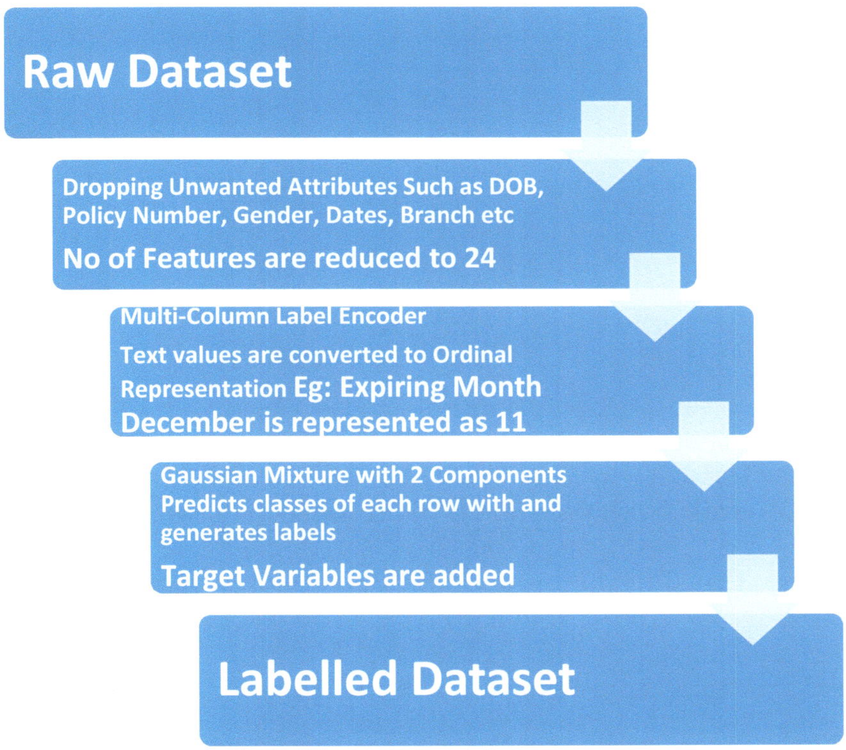

Fig. (1). Data Processing. (Source: Author calculations).

Dataset Description

An insurance dataset is collected from a motor insurance company. This is used for experimental purposes. The dataset has the details of each customer recorded throughout the one-and-a-half-month period. It consists of 37 columns and 1,000 rows in which only relevant features are taken to create the training classifier as mentioned in the Fig. (**2**).

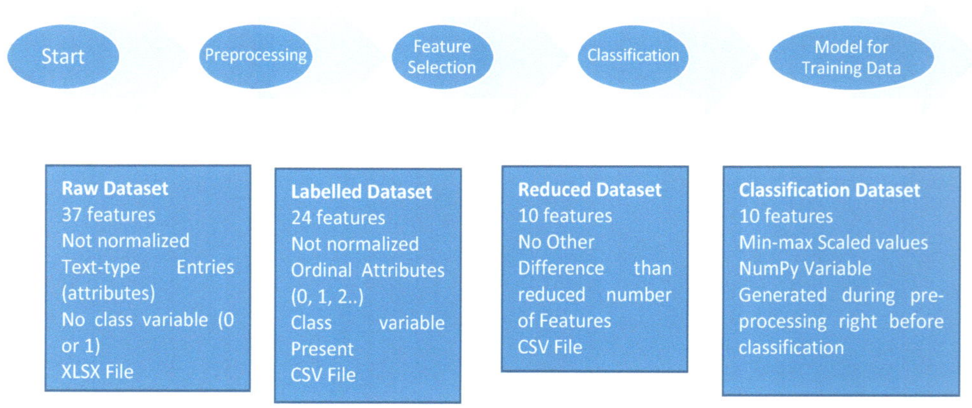

Fig. (2). Overall view of Algorithm. (Source: Author calculations).

Algo

1. **Start**
2. **Preprocessing** - Basic Transformations on Dataset before applying any ML algorithm
    a. **Import Raw Dataset**
    b. **Remove Obvious Irrelevant Features** (manual process) present in the Dataset
    c. Apply **Data transformation** to applicable features (Text to Nominal Conversion).
    d. If Dataset has Target Variables, go to step e
        i. As the Data present is assumed to be in Gaussian Distribution, Apply Gaussian Mixture to generate probabilistic model
        ii. Classify and Label the dataset
    e. Save Transformed dataset as **Labelled Dataset**
3. **Feature Selection**
    a. Create a Feed Forward Neural Network (**Extreme Learning Machine**) with initial params
    b. Import **Labelled Dataset**
    c. Use the **Grey Wolf Optimization Algorithm** to identify features and train network such that:
        i. **Least Entropy** in Softmax, KNN, and K-Means algorithms
        ii. **Best of Multiple Argument Partitions** are selected
        iii. **Cross-validation score** is the highest for the chosen argument partition
    d. Generate weights of ELM Kernel and save it as a NumPy file

   e. From the results of step (2c), get the names of Features; remove other features
   f. Save dataset as **Reduced Dataset**
4. **Classification**
   a. **Pre-processing**: Do min-max scaling to all variables; Perform train-test split on the DS
   b. Import **Labelled Dataset** and Weights of network generated in the previous step
   c. **Train Network** using the Train-Split of Labelled Dataset and **Test Network** using Test-DS
   d. Replace the original target variables with predicted labels
   e. Save Dataset as **Classification Dataset**
5. **Model Generation**
LR_Model=**Logistic Regression**(reduced_dataset, target_variables = predicted_labels).
6. **End**

RESULTS AND DISCUSSION

The hybrid classifier is evaluated for its ability to characterize test data sources using various optimal constraints. The accuracy of the algorithm in characterizing test data is also demonstrated. Parameters are set for GWO-KELM to mine similar patterns, utilizing iterative methods such as penalty function, reward function, and feasibility to derive an optimal solution among other complex methods available (Fariya, Saini, & Kashif, 2024). A population size of 40 grey wolves is used, with 150 iterations performed on all constrained benchmark functions. Additionally, 30 Monte Carlo (Krauth W., 2006) runs are executed on each constrained benchmark function for effective validation of the proposed GWO algorithm compared to existing machine learning classifiers. Impartial comparison between these algorithms requires parameter settings, which can be a challenging task during execution. For GWO and KELM algorithms, two random vectors r~1 and r~2 are taken from a range of (0,1) while controlling parameters ~a have linearly decreasing values ranging from 2 to 0 over the course of iterations; chaotic function variables a=0.5 and b=0.2 are utilized as well.

The study objected to detecting 2 classes, namely, churners and non-churners. Thus, a confusion matrix is displayed as follows.

The above Fig. (**3**) presents the confusion matrix for hybrid GWO-KELM techniques. It contains two dimensions wherein the X-dimension relates to the predicted label, and the Y-dimension relates to the true label.

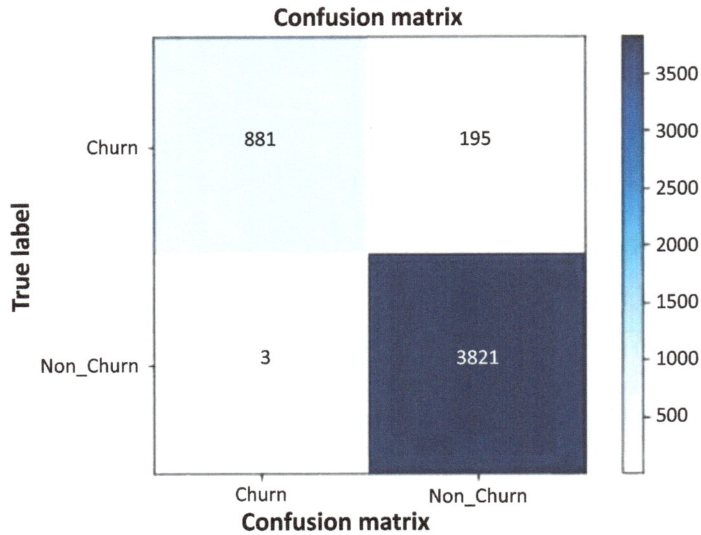

Fig. (3). Confusion matrix for hybrid GWO-KELM. (Source: Author calculations).

The above Fig. (**4**) presents the confusion matrix for hybrid GWO-KELM techniques. It contains two dimensions wherein the X-dimension relates to the predicted label and the Y-dimension relates to the True label.

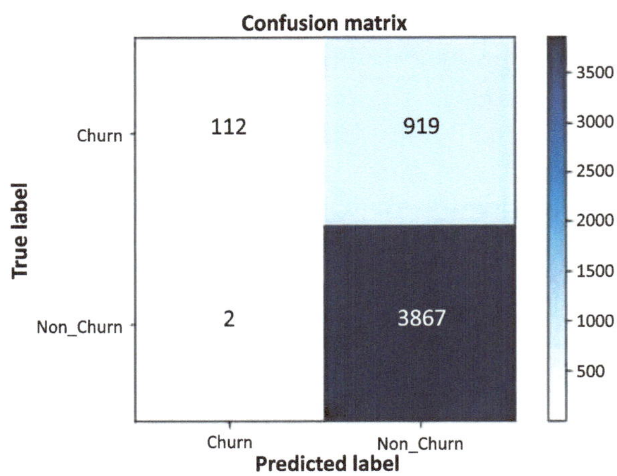

Fig. (4). Confusion matrix for existing, KELM. (Source: Author calculations).

Receiver Operating Characteristics (ROC) is a performance measure investigated in this study. ROC graphs are useful tools for organizing classifiers and visualizing their performance (Egan, 1975; Swets *et al.*, 2000). These graphs have traditionally been used in medical decision-making, but more recently, they have become increasingly popular in machine learning and data mining research. Although seemingly straightforward, there are several common misconceptions and pitfalls that can arise when using ROC graphs.

The classification problems addressed in this study involve two classes: positive and negative labels assigned to each instance I. A classifier maps instances to these labels by predicting the appropriate class membership based on continuous output values associated with different thresholds.

ROC graphs in Fig. (**5**) are 2D plots that depict the tradeoff between true positive rates (tp rate) plotted along the y-axis and false positive rates (fp rate) plotted along the x-axis. Each classifier generates an fp rate-tp rate pair corresponding to a single point on the graph representing its overall accuracy or error rates.

The lower left point of the graph represents perfect classification where no errors occur, whereas the upper right point depicts inequality constraints for positive classifications only. Finally, the arrival rate of perfect classification is represented at point (0,1).

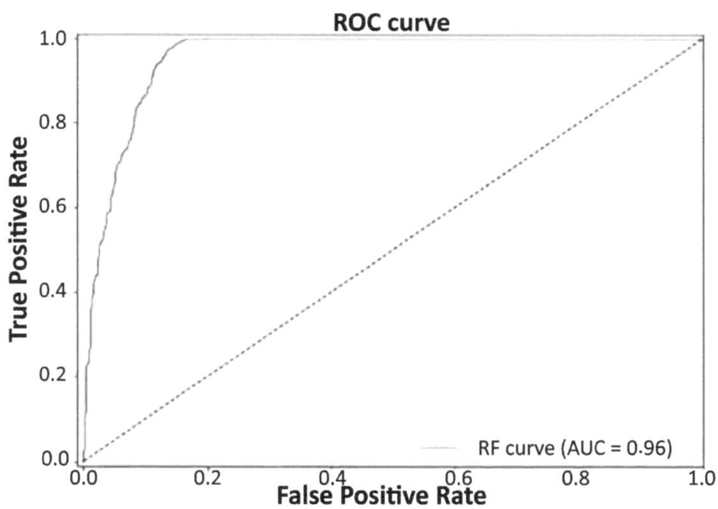

Fig. (5). 5 ROC curve analysis for hybrid GWO-KELM. (Source: Author calculations).

The concept of an optimal solution is more straightforward than that of single objective optimization. The majority of the solution lies in Pareto optimally, whereby a point is deemed Pareto optimal only if it cannot be moved from while reducing at least one objective function without increasing any other. Typically, several Pareto optimal points are used to settle objectives and articulate preferences. There are two types of preferences utilized: a prioritization of preferences and a posterior articulation of preferences. Prioritization assists users in specifying their relative importance for the objectives or runs of optimization algorithms. Scalarization methods entail merging objectives into a single scalar function by incorporating method parameters such as components, weights, or exponential functions with a prior articulation of preferences.

The business interpretation of this can be detailed as follows:

Among the XX influencing parameters initially thought of in the data set, it has now been filtered down to the nine most influencing parameters.

- Individual Customers tend to renew the policy more than Corporate customers.
- Policies without benefit Nil Depreciation tend to renew more compared with other addon benefits in the policy. Typically in the market, this cover is available for the first 3 years of the policy only and hence this cover may be non-existent in the policies with age more than three years.
- It is noted that when there are no claims made on the existing policy, they tend to renew more compared to policies that had a claim during the year. The higher churn observed in policies with claims may provide some indicators of the "Customer Experience" during the claim process itself.
- It is to be noted that when the customer continues with the same branch of the company, they tend to renew their policy more than compared to those whose servicing branch was changed during the tenure of the policy.
- Churn is much less in cases where the renewal Premium is less than the current premium. Where it has gone –up due to various reasons, like loss of NCB, Break-in, Rate revision, Location change, *etc*., customers tend to churn more.
- It is interesting to note that the small car owners tend to stay with the insurer and renew viz a viz customers owning cars with high engine capacity.
- Similarly, the churn is much less in cases where the policy sum insured is in the lower bands (again, smaller cars or aged cars with fewer IDVs) compared to customers who own cars with a sum insured in the higher bands.
- It is observed that the policies coming up for renewal in the last quarter of the financial year (Jan, Feb, Mar) tend to churn less compared to policies expiring in other months.
- It is also to be noted that the churn is less for customers who have up to two policies with the same insurer. Insurers can take a cue from these findings and plan the retention efforts accordingly. A few examples of additional customer retention initiatives that can be taken up by the insurance companies based on the results observed are listed below:
- Increase efforts to retain good and profitable corporate customer policies
- Improve "Customer Experience" during claims
- Keep customer servicing branch the same as far as possible
- On a case to case basis, look at additional offers to good customers for whom

the Renewal Premium has gone up compared to the expiring policy premium.
- Increase efforts to retain good customers with cars with higher engine sizes or where the sum insured falls in higher sum insured bands.

Increase efforts to retain good and profitable customer policies in the period Q1 to Q3 of the financial year. Another challenge in Customer Churn Prediction (CCP) is the unavailability of relevant information. Undoubtedly, for CCP, a vast amount of information is being gathered, but sometimes, the actual or desired data required for analysis will be unavailable. In our study, tocollect data samples, for the preprocessing stage, optimal constraints are taken. After the model is prepared with astounding exactness, the model must have the capacity to anticipate the rundown of churners from the genuine dataset, which excludes irrelevant information. This results in a loss of profit for the company. Sometimes, for predicting customer actions, information from multiple sources is explored and integrated to derive a specific result. As this information is multifarious in nature, during information transfer, a vast amount of noisy information might be added, thus creating problems (Kashif, Shajar, Singhal, & Kumar, 2023). Therefore, information gathered must be reprocessed by discarding the noisy information. The pre-processing step usually consumes a lot of time. In CCP, customers' privacy is also at risk. Customers get into trouble while providing their details to companies. As companies use customers' personal details for their personal interests, customers' privacy will be at greater risk. This refrains customers from giving their strategic data and thus significantly hinders CCP procedure. While studying or realizing the customer actions, generally, the transactional or purchasing actions are considered, whereas the deep analysis of customers/users and their situations is greatly ignored. The transactional activities of customers are dependent on their attitudinal, social, physiological, and many other unjustifiable factors which are considered. However, consideration of all possible factors affecting CCP is explored. Many prediction frameworks employ customer's transactional data alone for CCP. However, the information captured while performing numerous transactions by customers is inadequate for CCP, as it does not provide sufficient proof for predicting the churn action of customers. Thus, the available raw information must be converted into optimal knowledge for acquiring required inferences.

CONCLUSION

In the dynamic landscape of motor insurance, the challenge of retaining customers is formidable, given annual policy renewals and fierce competition. This research, aiming to predict customer churn using a machine learning model, has yielded valuable insights and practical recommendations for motor insurance companies.

The hybrid classifier, GWO-KELM, demonstrated its effectiveness in characterizing test data, as evidenced by confusion matrices and ROC curve analysis. The study identified nine influential parameters affecting customer churn, providing a nuanced understanding for insurers to refine their retention strategies.

The findings reveal that individual customers tend to renew policies more than corporate customers. Policies without benefits, like Nil Depreciation, witness higher renewal rates. The absence of claims in the existing policy correlates with higher renewal rates, emphasizing the importance of positive customer experiences during the claims process. Additionally, factors like continuity with the same branch, lower renewal premiums, smaller car sizes, and lower sum insured contribute to higher customer retention.

The identified parameters offer actionable insights for insurers:

- Focus on retaining good and profitable corporate customer policies.
- Enhance the customer experience during claims to improve satisfaction.
- Maintain consistency in customer servicing branches where possible.
- Offer additional incentives to customers facing increased renewal premiums.
- Tailor retention efforts for customers with higher engine sizes or higher sum insured.
- Intensify retention efforts for policies expiring in the first three quarters of the financial year.

Despite the success of the GWO-KELM model, challenges in customer churn prediction persist. The unavailability of relevant information, potential privacy concerns, and the need for comprehensive data integration remain hurdles. The study emphasizes the importance of data preprocessing in addressing these challenges and highlights the potential risks to customer privacy.

In conclusion, the research contributes significantly to the field of customer churn prediction in motor insurance. The developed model and identified parameters provide a foundation for insurers to optimize their retention efforts, ultimately fostering growth and customer satisfaction in a competitive market. The study underscores the importance of ongoing research and innovation in addressing evolving challenges within the motor insurance industry.

REFERENCES

Abdelhadi, S., Elbahnasy, K., Abdelsalam, M. (2020). A proposed model to predict auto insurance claims using machine learning techniques. *J. Theor. Appl. Inf. Technol., 98*, 3428-3437.

Kumar, D.A., Ravi, V. (2008). Predicting credit card customer churn in banks using data mining. *International Journal of Data Analysis Techniques and Strategies, 1*(1), 4-28.

[http://dx.doi.org/10.1504/IJDATS.2008.020020]

Bagheri, M., Valipour, M., Amin, V. (2012). The bankruptcy prediction in Tehran share holding using neural network and it's comparison with logistic regression. *Journal of Mathematics and Computer Science, 5*(3), 219-228.
[http://dx.doi.org/10.22436/jmcs.05.03.10]

Baicker, K., Chandra, A. (2006). The labour market effects of rising health insurance premiums. *J. Labor Econ., 24*(3), 609-634.
[http://dx.doi.org/10.1086/505049]

Bhattacharya, P., Ladha, A., Kumar, A., Verma, A., Bodkhe, U. (2020). BaY cP: A novel Bayesian customer Churn prediction scheme for Telecom sector. *Sixth International Conference on Parallel, Distributed and Grid Computing (PDGC),* 260-265.
[http://dx.doi.org/10.1109/PDGC50313.2020.9315766]

Coussement, K., Van den Poel, D. (2008). Integrating the voice of customers through call center emails into a decision support system for churn prediction. *Inf. Manage., 45*(3), 164-174.
[http://dx.doi.org/10.1016/j.im.2008.01.005]

Dasgupta, K., Singh, R., Viswanathan, B., Chakraborty, D., Mukherjea, S., Nanavati, A.A., Joshi, A. (2008). Social Ties and their Relevance to Churn in Mobile Telecom Networks. *Proceedings of the 11th International Conf. Extending Database Technology: Advances in Database Technology (EDBT 08),* 668-677.
[http://dx.doi.org/10.1145/1353343.1353424]

Egan, J.P. (1975). *Signal Detection Theory and ROC Analysis. Series in Cognitition and Perception.* New York: Academic Press.

Fariya, Saini, A., & Kashif, M. (2024). Exploring the Influence of Factors Driving Financial Accessibility, Financial Activities, and Financial Education on Sustainable Development. In Artificial Intelligence and Machine Learning-Powered Smart Finance, pp. 23-49.

General Insurance Council. (2020). Yearbook 2019–20. https://www.gicouncil.in/yearbook.

Insurance Regulatory and Development Authority of India. (2020). Annual report 2019–20..

Kashif, M., Shajar, S.N., Singhal, N., Kumar, P. (2023). Achieving sustainable investment practices through green finance: Challenges and opportunities. *Sustainable Investments in Green Finance.*
[http://dx.doi.org/10.4018/979-8-3693-1388-6.ch016]

Kashif, M., David, A., Gupta, V.P., Alam, S. (2024). Integration of Artificial Intelligence in the Financial Sector. *Artificial Intelligence and Machine Learning-Powered Smart Finance.,* 96-108.
[http://dx.doi.org/10.4018/979-8-3693-3264-1.ch005]

Kashif, M., Singhal, N., Goyal, S., Singh, S.K. (2024). Foreign Exchange Reserves and Economic Growth of Brazil: A Nonlinear Approach. *Finance: Theory and Practice, 28*(1), 145-154.

Krauth W., (2006). Introduction to Monte Carlo algorithms. Summer school in Beg-Rohu (France) and Budapest 1996. Available from: https://cel.hal.science/cel-00092936.

Kaur, M., Kang, S. (2016). Market Basket Analysis: Identify the changing trends of market data using association rule mining. *Procedia Comput. Sci., 85*, 78-85.
[http://dx.doi.org/10.1016/j.procs.2016.05.180]

Lalwani, P., Mishra, M.K., Chadha, J.S., Sethi, P. (2022). Customer churn prediction system: a machine learning approach. *Computing, 104*(2), 271-294.
[http://dx.doi.org/10.1007/s00607-021-00908-y]

Larivière, B., Vandenpoel, D. (2005). Predicting customer retention and profitability by using random forests and regression forests techniques. *Expert Syst. Appl., 29*(2), 472-484.
[http://dx.doi.org/10.1016/j.eswa.2005.04.043]

Rodpysh, K.V. (2013). Providing a Method for Determining the Index of Customer Churn in Industry. *International Journal of Information Technology, Control and Automation, 3*(1), 61-70.

[http://dx.doi.org/10.5121/ijitca.2013.3105]

Singhal, N., Goyal, S., Singhal, T. (2022). Demand Following Hypothesis: Empirical Evidence from Insurance Sector of Emerging Asian Markets. *Finance India, XXXVI*(2), 777-798.

Soeini, R.A., Rodpysh, K.V. (2012). Applying data mining to insurance customer churn management. *International Proceedings of Computer Science and Information Technology, 30*, 82-92.

Swets, J.A., Dawes, R.M., Monahan, J. (2000). Better decisions through science. *Sci. Am., 283*(4), 82-87. a Available from: http://www.psychologicalscience.org/newsresearch/publications/journals/ [http://dx.doi.org/10.1038/scientificamerican1000-82] [PMID: 11011389]

Singh, S., Kumar, V., Dhanjal, D.S., Datta, S., Bhatia, D., Dhiman, J., Samuel, J., Prasad, R., Singh, J. (2020). A sustainable paradigm of sewage sludge biochar: Valorization, opportunities, challenges and future prospects. *J. Clean. Prod., 269*, 122259. [http://dx.doi.org/10.1016/j.jclepro.2020.122259]

Datta, S., Singh, J., Singh, S., Singh, J. (2016). Earthworms, pesticides and sustainable agriculture: a review. *Environ. Sci. Pollut. Res. Int., 23*(9), 8227-8243. [http://dx.doi.org/10.1007/s11356-016-6375-0] [PMID: 26951221]

Jnawali, P., Kumar, V., Tanwar, B. (2016). Celiac disease: Overview and considerations for development of gluten-free foods. *Food Sci. Hum. Wellness, 5*(4), 169-176. [http://dx.doi.org/10.1016/j.fshw.2016.09.003]

Chowdhury, S., Yadaiah, N., Prakash, C., Ramakrishna, S., Dixit, S., Gupta, L.R., Buddhi, D. (2022). Laser powder bed fusion: a state-of-the-art review of the technology, materials, properties & defects, and numerical modelling. *J. Mater. Res. Technol., 20*, 2109-2172. [http://dx.doi.org/10.1016/j.jmrt.2022.07.121]

M, P., Sharma, A., v, V., Bhardwaj, V., Sharma, A.P., Iqbal, R., Kumar, R. (2020). Prediction of the price of Ethereum blockchain cryptocurrency in an industrial finance system. *Comput. Electr. Eng., 81*, 106527. [http://dx.doi.org/10.1016/j.compeleceng.2019.106527]

CHAPTER 2

Ai-Powered Data Analytics for Customer-Centric Insurance Experience

Vijay Prakash Gupta[1] and **Mohammad Kashif** [2,*]

[1] *Institute of Business Management, GLA University, Mathura, India*

[2] *Department of Management Studies, Graphic Era deemed to be University, Dehradun, Uttarakhand, India*

Abstract: In the changing corporate landscape, the combination of Artificial Intelligence (AI) and data analytics has altered the insurance industry, resulting in a customer-centric paradigm through data-driven operations. AI-powered data analytics plays a critical role in helping clients understand, engage with, and select insurance services. This chapter delves into the detailed uses of AI-powered data analytics in the insurance sector, including AI assessment, problems, and ramifications, with a particular emphasis on product customization. The goal is to demonstrate how AI-powered data analytics is altering the industry, meeting customer requests, and investigating disruptive implications. The process entails analyzing secondary sources such as research publications and industry reports to better comprehend the impact on customer choices and service provider tactics. Findings reveal a notable shift in the insurance landscape, emphasizing AI-powered data analytics' profound impact on personalized experiences, data-driven insights, risk assessment, claims processing, premium decisions, and policy customization. This technological evolution signifies a significant transformation in the insurance sector.

Keywords: Artificial Intelligence (AI), Advanced technology, Customer-centric paradigm, Customer relationship, Data analytics, Insurance, Predictive behaviors, Service sector.

INTRODUCTION

The current insurance industry is undergoing a radical transformation in the digital era, which is driven by the integration of data analytics and artificial intelligence (AI). This integration of technologies has transformed the operations of insurers, exploiting the vast amount of data to extract valuable insights, manage risks effectively, and uplift customer service experiences. The convergence of artificial intelligence (AI) and data analytics brings disruptive change and reshapes the engagement of the client and service offerings. This cutting-edge

* **Corresponding author Mohammad Kashif:** Department of Management Studies, Graphic Era Deemed to be University, Dehradun, Uttarakhand, India; E-mail: mkashif69@gmail.com

technology has resulted in a major change, transformed customer-centric personalized experiences, and leveraged data-driven approaches in insurance products.

The integration of AI and data analytics in the insurance industry has emerged as a foundational pillar and connection between insurers and their clients. Nowadays, insurers are no longer limited by the enormous amount of data; they can now leverage their great power.

With the help of artificial intelligence (AI) and data analytics, insurers can explore complicated data landscapes by seamlessly integrating advanced data analysis tools, discovering complex patterns anticipating consumer behaviors, and developing personalized solutions suitable to individual consumer demands (Haldhar *et al.*, 2018).

This chapter includes a thorough examination of AI-powered data analytics in insurance services and investigates the various applications and far-reaching consequences of this technological convergence. The combined influence of AI and data analytics also helps improve risk assessment models, accelerate claims processing, and foster proactive consumer involvement. In the current digital era, customer-centricity emerges as the foundation of insurance services, drastically disrupting current paradigms (Kashif, Shajar, Singhal, & Kumar, 2023).

This chapter has explored the fundamental implications of this technological collaboration and demonstrates the disruptive potential of AI-powered data analytics in reconsidering insurers' understanding, connectedness, and service strategies concerning their clients (Khamparia *et al.*, 2019).

This chapter also explained how insurers transition from reactive service providers to proactive partners, adeptly aligning their products with consumer demands and preferences by emphasizing the strategic integration of AI and data analytics.

EVOLUTION OF AI AND DATA ANALYTICS IN INSURANCE

The Transition from Traditional to Advanced Systems

In the current insurance industry, the shift from manual operations toward innovative AI-driven systems has completely transformed insurance services, increasing productivity, improving risk assessment, and refining overall client experiences.

Innovations for Profitability

Using innovative algorithms in data analytics for more accurate insurance premium pricing to enhance risk management and financial viability.

Beginning of Online Sales of Insurance Policy

After the economic reforms in India, the beginning of direct online policy was started by marketers and insurers and shifted to the insurance industry. This course of action increased customer loyalty and retention by streaming new revenue.

Integration of Digital Technology

In recent years, there has been a greater integration of digital tools with data analytics, which are playing a major role in the transformation of offering insurance services to clients. Understanding the client's needs, seeing growth opportunities, and quickly responding to changing preferences are all made easier with the help of this integration (Kashif, David, Gupta, & Alam, 2024).

Important Change Agents

With the continuous development and reform and growing digital environment, the introduction of technologies such as the Internet of Things is constantly shifting demands of consumers. The current goals are improving customer experiences, putting data-centric strategies into practice, and launching cutting-edge products designed for the digital age.

Sustained Evolution

For insurers to stay competitive in a market that is changing quickly, it is expected that this revolutionary trend will continue as they adopt more advanced procedures and technologies.

NEED FOR DIGITAL TRANSFORMATION IN THE INSURANCE INDUSTRY

The current insurance industry is facing increased competition, which is displaying a digital shift from traditional methods to innovative methods to keep up with a rapidly changing market as shown in Table **1**.

- Insurance companies are being forced to offer online services, easily accessible information, and expedited claims processes due to shifting customer demands, which demand smooth digital interactions across industries.

- Switching to a digital experience is essential to satisfying consumer needs and encouraging greater participation through customized services as well as effective channels of communication.
- Digitization has brought improvements in insurance services and operations by using AI for underwriting and claims, streamlining procedures, and employing data analytics to decrease costs and boost efficiency.
- Digital transformation results in statistics, which promote well-informed decision-making by offering an extensive understanding of market trends, risk profiles, and customer behavior.
- By adopting digital technology, insurers can strengthen cybersecurity protocols, provide new services, and adapt to transforming regulatory requirements.
- By becoming flexible, responsive, and relevant, insurers are able to respond quickly to market dynamics and ensure long-term viability in an increasingly digital landscape.

Table 1. Key developments in ai-powered data analytics.

Period	Key Developments
Pre-2000s	**Manual Procedures:** In the insurance industry, manual data collection, risk assessment, and underwriting. **Basic Statistical Models:** Statistical models are first applied to risk assessment.
The early 2000s	**Digitization:** Data began being digitized for storage and retrieval. **Emergence of Predictive Modeling:** Initial use of predictive modeling for risk assessment using historical data.
Mid-2000s	**Introduction of Machine Learning:** Insurers started using machine learning for advanced risk analysis. **Focus on Customer Segmentation:** Data analytics used for personalized customer offerings.
Late 2000s - Early 2010s	**Expansion of Predictive Analytics:** AI-driven predictive analytics for claims forecasting. **Introduction of Telematics:** Adoption of telematics for real-time driving data in auto insurance.
Mid-2010s	**Enhanced Customer Experience:** AI-powered chatbots for customer service. **IoT Integration:** Integration of IoT devices for data collection from various sources.
Late 2010s	**Fraud Detection and Prevention:** Extensive use of AI for fraud detection. **Personalization in Offerings:** Further refinement of personalized insurance offerings based on detailed customer profiles.
Early 2020s	**Automation and Process Optimization:** Increased use of AI for automating underwriting, claims processing, and risk assessment. **AI Advancements:** Progress in AI technologies impacting insurance operations.
Mid-2020s - Present	**Emphasis on Explainable AI:** Focus on making AI decisions transparent and understandable. **AI-driven Underwriting:** Greater reliance on AI-driven underwriting processes.

(Table 1) cont.....

Period	Key Developments
Future Trends	**Further Personalization:** Deeper personalization of insurance products using AI. **Enhanced Risk Prediction:** AI advancements for more accurate risk prediction and mitigation.

TRANSFORMATIVE IMPACTS IN KEY AREAS IN THE INSURANCE INDUSTRY

Risk Assessment and Underwriting

For insurers, risk assessment and underwriting have changed as a result of the confluence of data analytics and AI. Insurers may now rapidly examine real-time data that includes demographics, market trends, previous claims, and even unstructured data from social media sites by using sophisticated algorithms. This abundance of data allows for accurate risk assessments, tailored coverage options, and pricing model refinement through AI-driven prediction models that identify patterns and correlations to better understand risk factors (Singhal, Goyal & Singhal, 2022).

Claims Management and Fraud Detection

The fields of data analytics and artificial intelligence (AI) have revolutionized the way that claims are managed. Automation has made the once labor- and time-intensive claims processing process more efficient, leading to quicker payouts and more satisfied consumers. By analyzing claim and policy data, AI systems find anomalies that can be used to identify fraudulent activities. In the end, actual policyholders gain from this since it protects system fairness and safeguards the interests of insurers (Sharma *et al.*, 2010).

Personalized Customer Experiences

In order to tailor products and services to individual needs, insurers employ artificial intelligence and data analytics to delve into consumer preferences and behavior. Customer relationships are strengthened, and client satisfaction and retention rates rise as a result of this personalization. Additionally, by reducing operating costs and offering prompt assistance, process guidance, and personalized experiences, AI-powered chatbots, and virtual assistants facilitate smooth interactions (Saxena *et al.*, 2018).

Fraud Prevention and Risk Mitigation

AI and data analytics are becoming strong allies in fighting against fraud. These algorithms continually learn from historical data to identify suspicious patterns and behaviors that hint at fraud. This proactive approach increases industry trust while safeguarding money.

OBJECTIVES AND SIGNIFICANCE OF AI-POWERED DATA ANALYTICS IN CUSTOMER-CENTRIC INSURANCE.

AI-powered data analytics in the insurance industry promises to transform client experiences by utilizing technology to address customer needs more effectively and efficiently. Following are the objectives and importance:

OBJECTIVES

- ***Tailoring Insurance Products:*** Insurance companies can customize insurance plans to each customer's needs by using AI technology to evaluate a variety of client data, such as risk indicators, behavioral patterns, and demographics. This customized strategy significantly boosts customer satisfaction and fosters greater loyalty by customizing insurance policies to each client's unique needs and preferences (Kaswan & Rathi, 2019).
- ***Risk Assessment and Pricing:*** Insurance companies can offer more competitively priced plans with fair rates that are based on individual risk profiles thanks to artificial intelligence (AI)-powered analytics that more accurately evaluate risk variables.
- ***Claims Processing:*** Claims processing can be streamlined and expedited with AI. This includes quicker evaluations, automatic payouts, and fraud detection—all of which reduce processing times and increase client satisfaction.
- ***Customer Service Improvement:*** Use Chabot's and virtual assistants driven by AI to improve customer service by offering real-time help, responding to inquiries, and assisting clients with policy information.
- ***Predictive Analytics for Customer Behavior:*** AI systems examine historical data to predict client behavior, including potential policy lapses or adjustments to coverage requirements. This enables proactive communication to lower attrition.

SIGNIFICANCE OF AI-POWERED DATA ANALYTICS

- **Enhanced Risk Management:** Artificial Intelligence (AI) helps insurers make more accurate risk assessments by helping them comprehend the risks connected with certain clients. This improves the overall financial health of insurance organizations by reducing losses.
- **Fraud Detection and Prevention:** Insurance companies may be able to lower losses while still charging reasonable premiums to upstanding customers by employing advanced analytics.

- **Efficiency and Cost Reduction:** For insurance companies, automation of processes such as underwriting, claims processing, and customer support saves a significant amount of money and improves operations.
- **Competitive Advantage:** Companies can gain a significant competitive edge in the market by offering better services, competitive pricing, and enhanced customer experiences through the effective application of AI-powered data analytics.
- **Regulatory Compliance:** Businesses may guarantee regulatory compliance by utilizing AI-driven analytics, which provides precise data analysis and reporting capabilities.

IMPLICATIONS OF AI AND DATA ANALYTICS IN THE INSURANCE SECTOR

Artificial intelligence (AI) and DA Analytics help in improving risk assessment as well as enable insurers to identify new hazards and modify their approaches appropriately.

- **Advanced Risk Management:** AI will continue to advance risk assessment, allowing insurers to recognize new risks and adjust their strategies accordingly.
- **Personalized Insurance Products:** The rise of insurance coverage tailored to individual behavior and tastes will boost customer loyalty.
- **Enhanced Fraud Detection:** Artificial intelligence will be crucial to spotting and preventing fraudulent conduct, protecting both clients and insurers.
- **Automation and Efficiency:** Additional process automation leads to cost savings and operational simplification.

TECHNOLOGICAL INTEGRATION IN THE INSURANCE INDUSTRY

Advanced technological innovations referred to as “insurtech” possess the capacity to profoundly transform the insurance sector and the regulations that oversee it. These cutting-edge technologies could bring about novel concepts, creative solutions, or even the alteration of established insurance practices.

The financial industry has been changing constantly, adjusting to new technological developments in order to increase productivity. Often called “FinTech,” this movement uses technology to speed up and reduce the cost of providing intangible financial services. The sector has undergone changes due to advancements in internet connectivity, personal computers, and mobile devices, which have increased market share and heightened competition.

To describe innovation as purely disruptive, however, would be oversimplifying, given its dynamic and continuous advancement. Technology also has an impact on the insurance sector; this is called “InsurTech,” and it prioritizes improving customer service over business expansion. Consumers will benefit from technology that supports this trend, which includes speedier payment processing *via* updated networks, online insurance claims and product comparisons, and 24-hour ATM access.

It is imperative to adjust to technology advancements that impact society and the economy, particularly in the context of risk management specific to businesses.

When the insurance industry relied on paper-based systems, human data entry resulted in processing backlogs and inaccurate policy and claim data. On the other hand, technological innovations like machine learning, blockchain, and artificial intelligence (AI) have improved customer service and increased efficiency.

Progressive, a well-known US insurance company, demonstrates a seamless digital connection with its usage-based insurance program. This innovation has increased revenue, improved customer retention, and drawn in new business, setting the company apart from its rivals as a progressive, customer-focused leader.

Insurance companies face difficulties in implementing a modernization strategy for technology despite numerous examples of successful implementations, such as Progressive's. Using insurance technologies could go wrong if there is not a well-thought-out, long-term plan in place.

TECHNOLOGY REVOLUTIONIZING CUSTOMER SERVICE IN INSURANCE

Insurtech Digital offers a comprehensive analysis of the transformative effects of AI and machine learning on customer service within the insurance sector. Special focus is placed on the advancements in automated phone conversations and chatbots, which have a significant positive impact on customized sales approaches and streamline intricate claims regarding management processes. Many facets of insurance operations are integrated by them, thereby optimizing the speed and accuracy of quote generation, claims processing, and policy administration.

Chatbot deployment is a critical component that provides continuous and conveniently accessible assistance, particularly for regular issues, ensuring customer service 24 hours a day. This strategic integration recognizes and safeguards the inherent necessity of human interaction in addition to technology, especially when dealing with complex and emotionally draining claims scenarios. This delicate balancing act improves automation efficiency while maintaining a courteous and sympathetic service delivery paradigm.

Artificial intelligence (AI) and machine learning have totally revolutionized the claims processing paradigm, increasing the speed and accuracy of data collection, analysis, and usage. The instant assessment of losses, accurate estimation of restoration costs, and prompt reimbursements indicate the tangible impact of these technologies on the insurance claim process. This advancement in service standards, which incorporate automation without losing the basic ideals of openness, speed, and user-centricity, redefines the customer-agent connection (Fariya, Saini, & Kashif, 2024).

Furthermore, the adoption of conversational AI platforms improves consumer experience by delivering seamless self-service options across digital platforms. These platforms employ complicated algorithms to tailor user experiences based on subtle criteria such as intent, tone, and user profiles. Furthermore, AI-powered support during live calls enables operators to navigate and address complex inquiries effectively and sympathetically, ensuring a first-rate client experience across all touchpoints.

ROLE OF TECHNOLOGY TO IMPROVED SPEED IN INSURANCE PROCESSES

Streamlined Policy Creation

Insurance policy management software makes use of AI capabilities to automate policy formulation and tailor policies based on consumer data research. As a result, processes are streamlined, reducing errors and time. AI, for example, swiftly generates customized policies based on historical and demographic data, ensuring successful service delivery.

Data-driven Underwriting

Automated underwriting, which employs a range of data sources for risk appraisal and policy approvals, allows insurance businesses to adapt to changing client demands. Using data from sources such as social media makes it easier to make educated underwriting decisions and match policies to consumer demands.

Intelligent Policy Administration

By automating policy issuance, renewal, and revisions, smart systems increase operational accuracy and real-time data communication. For example, automated systems quickly update policy changes across databases, ensuring smooth stakeholder communication.

Efficient Policy Documentation

Technological advancements make digital migration easier, assure safe and easy-access storage, and streamline policy paperwork. Digitizing documents ensures that policy-related information is easily accessible, reduces burden, and enhances document management.

Real-time Policy Changes

Through self-service portals, policyholders can instantaneously alter policy details, with changes taking effect almost immediately. Online systems, for example, increase flexibility by enabling users to update personal information or change coverage options in real time.

Personalized Customer Engagement

By enabling tailored interactions in underwriting, sales, and marketing, insurance technology increases enjoyment and loyalty. Chatbots enabled by AI, for example, provide personalized information to boost customer engagement and service standards.

Automated Renewals and Notifications

Renewal notices are automated, which reduces friction points and makes the process more efficient. Insurers make customers' renewal processes easier by offering automated renewal alternatives and reminders.

Claims Processing Efficiency

Modern technologies automate claim filing, verification, and analysis, hence expediting the claims process. Fast payouts and fraud detection reduce claim settlement times while increasing customer satisfaction. AI technologies, for example, assess claim data quickly, which speeds up the verification process.

Enhanced Compliance and Reporting

Policy management systems provide automated solutions that ensure proper documentation and adherence to industry regulations. Non-compliance risks are mitigated, and regulatory standards are adhered to by automating reporting and compliance inspections.

Thus, technology is transforming insurance policy management by reducing operations and improving client relations. Insurers can gain a competitive advantage in the market by offering streamlined processes, improved client satisfaction, and efficient services by leveraging these innovations.

CUSTOMER-CENTRIC APPROACH IN INSURANCE SERVICES

Customer centricity is based on a strategic strategy that aims to match a company's product and service development with the needs of its most significant customers, both now and in the future. The primary goal is to optimize the long-term financial value of these consumers to the organization.

An insurance company that wants to implement a customer-centric strategy must be able to personalize the products and services it offers and must focus on the mentioned areas:

- **Understanding Customers Deeply:** Understanding clients' fundamental demographics is not enough to gain an in-depth understanding of them; customer centricity demands more. It involves investigating their preferences, brand loyalty tendencies, and future development potential inside the company environment.
- **Foresight and Proactivity:** A customer-focused approach necessitates initiative. Businesses can leverage their deep customer awareness to anticipate needs in order to stay ahead of the curve and fulfill evolving consumer demands.
- **Differential Treatment of Customers:** Realizing that not every client is worth the same amount of money is crucial. Comprehending the different consumer groups, tailoring tactics to them, and attending to their specific requirements are all components of successful customer-centric strategies.
- **Data Analytics and Personalization:** Making use of advanced data analytics is crucial. It makes it easier to create precise consumer profiles with factual information combined with humanistic and subtle subtleties. This data allows for the customization of products, services, and the complete client journey.
- **Customized Offerings and Experiences:** A high degree of personalization is required when implementing a customer-focused strategy. Businesses should try to tailor their offers in terms of products, services, and customer interactions to each individual client's specific needs and preferences.

Customer-Centric Evolution in Insurance

The future direction of the insurance sector is moving in the direction of a customer-centric paradigm. In addition to process improvement, AI integration and data analytics portend a significant change in how insurers interact with their clients (Kashif *et al.*, 2024). By utilizing data analytics, insurers can enhance client experiences by means of tailored communication, anticipatory risk reduction, and expedited claim handling. This progress goes beyond technology;

in a more digitalized world, it is an essential undertaking in building long-term connections, trust, and the ability to adapt to changing client needs.

All things considered, the history of artificial intelligence and data analytics in the insurance industry is one of continuous innovations. The key for insurers will be embracing new technologies and utilizing data-driven insights to push industry standards in the direction of a customer-focused, operationally effective, and environmentally progressive future.

Digital Transformation in the Insurance Industry

Digital transformation is the process of using technology to innovate current business processes or to develop new products, services, or procedures. Facilitating this progress involves putting cutting-edge technologies into practice, such as robotics, big data, the Internet of Things (IoT), and artificial intelligence (AI). As consumer purchasing shifts into emerging technical sectors, the insurance industry is seeing an increasing number of issues. Simultaneously, InsurTech companies are revolutionizing the insurance industry by streamlining the search and digital channel purchase process. In order to thrive in this dynamic landscape, insurers need to be adaptable and fully embrace change.

THE IMPACT OF DIGITAL TRANSFORMATION ON THE INSURANCE INDUSTRY

Numerous examples highlight the significant improvements that the insurance industry has experienced as a result of the digital revolution. Examples of this include improved process efficiency, the growing use of automated claim processing, chat interfaces for customer communications, and brokers' capacity to merge data for quicker and more accurate operations. On the other hand, the following four key benefits perfectly encapsulate the essence of the digital transformation's influence on the insurance industry:

Numerous improvements have been brought about by digital transformation in the insurance sector, which is most notable for its efficacy, personalization, scalability, and agility.

- **Efficient:** The first and most obvious result of digital transformation for the insurance sector is the increased efficiencies it brings about. Artificial intelligence (AI) and its allied technologies, machine learning, and predictive analytics have played a major role in streamlining nearly every aspect of insurance operations for velocity. Instantaneous claim processing through an app and faster insurance drafting are made possible by machine learning skills.

Customer service is also being expedited by digital transformation, as live chat and digital assistants assist customers with their most urgent requirements.

- **Personalization:** Consumers today demand individualized service that is catered to their unique needs, and this expectation cuts across all business sectors. The digital shift has given insurers better tools to deliver exceptional service without overstretching their resources. A more individualized experience for brokers and consumers is made possible by AI and machine intelligence. Customers can access policies, file claims, and pay bills using applications, and brokers can effectively manage information under a single system. Digital technologies decrease waiting times by giving customers rapid feedback and enabling brokers to work more productively. Moreover, insurance's digital revolution makes it possible to conduct targeted marketing campaigns using AI-strong data analytics and social media to connect with key audiences efficiently.
- **Scalability:** Scalability is a key component of the digital growth of insurance because it permits flexibility in both front-end and back-end operations. Technology has changed the once complex insurance market into a more flexible structure that can accommodate changing needs. Self-service dashboards and apps make it simple for customers to access services these days, and insurers are able to obtain vital customer data by using wearables and IoT-enabled devices. In turn, this data helps brokers and insurers make more accurate choices about product creation, underwriting, and policy design.
- **Agility:** One of the main advantages of digital transformation in insurance is still agility, or the capacity to future-proof processes. Analytics, blockchain data, AI, and machine learning set the stage for insurers to advance with new technology. This technology base makes it possible for insurers to smoothly incorporate new developments into the insurance market, encouraging expansion and capacity to adjust to new opportunities.

AI AND DATA ANALYTICS IMPACT ON INSURANCE

The insurance industry has seen revolutionary developments as a result of AI and data analytics. They have radically changed conventional methods, enhancing consumer connections, streamlining operational processes, and refining risk management techniques. These technologies have completely changed the way that insurers do business and interact with their clients. They include predictive modeling and tailored services.

Through the use of AI-powered data analytics, insurers have successfully tapped into vast data volumes, leading to more accurate risk assessments, efficient claims processing, and the development of customized insurance solutions. In addition to boosting operational effectiveness, the use of data-driven decision-making has ushered in a new period of proactive response and greater industry agility.

Implications of AI and Data Analytics in the Insurance Sector

- **Risk Assessment and Underwriting:** By evaluating vast volumes of data from several sources, artificial intelligence (AI) and data analytics help insurers evaluate risk more precisely. As a result, underwriting decisions become more accurate, enabling insurers to set policy prices according to the risk profiles of specific individuals.
- **Fraud Detection and Prevention:** Artificial intelligence systems are able to identify trends that point to possible fraud. Through real-time data analysis, insurers can avert financial losses brought on by fraudulent activity.
- **Personalized Customer Experience:** Insurance companies may learn more about the preferences and actions of their clients with AI-driven data. This allows for more effective customer service, tailored offerings, and recommendations for policies.
- **Claims Processing and Automation:** Claims processing is streamlined by artificial intelligence (AI), which automates repetitive processes. Claims papers can be understood and categorized more quickly and accurately with the use of natural language processing (NLP).
- **Predictive Analytics for Decision Making:** Data analytics models help insurers make well-informed business decisions by forecasting market movements, customer behavior, and trends. This forecasting skill raises profitability while lowering hazards.
- **Product Development and Innovation:** The creation of new insurance products that better meet the needs of the market and evolving consumer demands is made possible by insights from artificial intelligence and data analytics. These goods are adaptable to shifting risk settings and can be made with greater customization.
- **Operational Efficiency and Cost Reduction:** Through process simplification, cost savings, and increased productivity, automation boosts operational effectiveness and lowers expenses. This covers risk assessment, document processing, and customer service.
- **Regulatory Compliance and Risk Management:** Artificial Intelligence helps insurers stay compliant with constantly changing rules by evaluating and understanding regulatory requirements. It also helps identify and manage hazards more successfully.
- **Health and Wellness Programs:** Insurance companies offer wellness programs through the use of data analytics and artificial intelligence. These initiatives promote healthier lives among policyholders, which eventually lowers claims and enhances general well-being.
- **Cybersecurity and data protection:** AI is essential for protecting sensitive client data and identifying any cyber threats. It makes proactive cyber-security measures possible, protecting customer trust and data integrity.

CONCLUSION

The integration of AI-powered data analytics into the insurance industry represents a transformative leap toward a customer-centric approach. By harnessing the power of AI, insurers are equipped to offer tailored solutions that address diverse customer needs, enhancing engagement and satisfaction. This chapter has demonstrated how AI facilitates product customization, data-driven insights, and efficient processes, reshaping traditional insurance models. Key applications of AI-powered data analytics include personalized premium decisions, streamlined claims processing, accurate risk assessment, and innovative policy customization. These advancements not only improve operational efficiency but also empower customers with greater transparency and control over their insurance decisions. As customers demand more personalized and seamless experiences, the role of AI in predicting preferences, identifying trends, and responding proactively becomes indispensable. However, the adoption of AI in insurance also presents challenges, such as data privacy concerns, ethical dilemmas, and the need for regulatory compliance. Addressing these issues will require a collaborative effort among insurers, regulators, and technologists to establish frameworks that ensure trust and fairness. The findings of this chapter underscore the disruptive potential of AI-powered data analytics in transforming the insurance industry. As this technology continues to evolve, its role in fostering deeper customer connections and enabling adaptive business strategies will remain pivotal. In conclusion, the convergence of AI and data analytics offers not only a competitive edge for insurers but also a future where insurance is more intuitive, inclusive, and aligned with customer expectations.

REFERENCES

Ali Albasheir, K. A. M. (2023). The Impact of IT on Insurance of the Technological Industry. *Journal of Advanced Zoology, 44.*

Fariya, Saini, A., & Kashif, M. (2024). Exploring the Influence of Factors Driving Financial Accessibility, Financial Activities, and Financial Education on Sustainable Development.

Guzmán-Ortiz, C.V., Navarro-Acosta, N.G., Florez-Garcia, W., Vicente-Ramos, W. (2020). Impact of digital transformation on the individual job performance of insurance companies in Peru. *International Journal of Data and Network Science, 4*(4), 337-346.
[http://dx.doi.org/10.5267/j.ijdns.2020.9.005]

Herrmann, H., Masawi, B. (2022). Three and a half decades of artificial intelligence in banking, financial services, and insurance: A systematic evolutionary review. *Strateg. Change, 31*(6), 549-569.
[http://dx.doi.org/10.1002/jsc.2525]

Ho, C.W.L., Ali, J., Caals, K. (2020). Ensuring trustworthy use of artificial intelligence and big data analytics in health insurance. *Bull. World Health Organ., 98*(4), 263-269.
[http://dx.doi.org/10.2471/BLT.19.234732] [PMID: 32284650]

Kacar, M. (2023). Application of AI in Customer Experience Management. *Marketing and Sales Automation: Basics, Implementation, and Applications.* (pp. 409-430). Cham: Springer International Publishing.
[http://dx.doi.org/10.1007/978-3-031-20040-3_26]

Kashif, M., David, A., Gupta, V.P., Alam, S. (2024). Integration of Artificial Intelligence in the Financial Sector. *Artificial Intelligence and Machine Learning-Powered Smart Finance.,* 96-108.
[http://dx.doi.org/10.4018/979-8-3693-3264-1.ch005]

Kashif, M., Shajar, S.N., Singhal, N., Kumar, P. (2023). Achieving sustainable investment practices through green finance: Challenges and opportunities. *Sustainable Investments in Green Finance.,* 234-244.
[http://dx.doi.org/10.4018/979-8-3693-1388-6.ch016]

Kashif, M., Singhal, N., Goyal, S., Singh, S.K. (2024). Foreign Exchange Reserves and Economic Growth of Brazil: A Nonlinear Approach. *Finance: Theory and Practice, 28*(1), 145-154.

Lissy, N. S., Bhuvaneswari, V., Krupa, M. E. Impact of digital transformation in the insurance industry. *Digitalization of the insurance sector, 71.*

Moodley, T., Govender, K.K. (2020). Collaborative leadership and customer-centricity: the case of an insurance service provider. *Journal of Public Value and Administrative Insight, 3*(3), 66-81.
[http://dx.doi.org/10.31580/jpvai.v3i3.1487]

Moturi, C.A., Okemwa, V.O., Orwa, D.O. (2022). Big data analytics capability for digital transformation in the insurance sector. *International Journal of Big Data Management, 2*(1), 42-59.
[http://dx.doi.org/10.1504/IJBDM.2022.119435]

Moturi, C.A., Okemwa, V.O., Orwa, D.O. (2022). Big data analytics capability for digital transformation in the insurance sector. *International Journal of Big Data Management, 2*(1), 42-59.
[http://dx.doi.org/10.1504/IJBDM.2022.119435]

Musaigwa, M., Mutula, S. (2022). Impact of digital transformation on strategy in the insurance sector. *International Journal of Research in Business and Social Science, 11*(4), 69-76.

Paruchuri, H. (2020). The impact of machine learning on the future of insurance industry. *Am. J. Trade Policy, 7*(3), 85-90.
[http://dx.doi.org/10.18034/ajtp.v7i3.537]

Pugnetti, C., Seitz, M. (2021). Data-driven services in insurance: Potential evolution and impact in the Swiss market. *Journal of Risk and Financial Management, 14*(5), 227.
[http://dx.doi.org/10.3390/jrfm14050227]

Rahmani, F. M., Zohuri, B. (2023). The Transformative Impact of AI on Financial Institutions, with a Focus on Banking. *Journal of Engineering and Applied Sciences Technology. SRC/JEAST-279, 192*(5), 2-6.

Riikkinen, M., Saarijärvi, H., Sarlin, P., Lähteenmäki, I. (2018). Using artificial intelligence to create value in insurance. *Int. J. Bank Mark., 36*(6), 1145-1168.
[http://dx.doi.org/10.1108/IJBM-01-2017-0015]

Satuluri, R.K. (2021). Digital transformation in Indian insurance industry. *Turkish Journal of Computer and Mathematics Education, 12*(4), 310-324.

Silvello, A. (2017). IoT and Connected Insurance Reshaping The Health Insurance Industry. A Customer-centric "From Cure To Care" Approach. *EAI Endorsed Transactions on Ambient Systems, 4*(15).

Singh, S. (2021). Adoption and Implementation of AI in Customer Relationship Management. *IGI Global.*

Singhal, N., Goyal, S., Singhal, T. (2022). The relationship between insurance and economic growth in Asian countries: a regional perspective. *Macroeconomics and Finance in Emerging Market Economies, 15*(3), 301-322.
[http://dx.doi.org/10.1080/17520843.2021.1957599]

Śmietanka, M., Koshiyama, A., Treleaven, P. (2021). Algorithms in future insurance markets. *International Journal of Data Science and Big Data Analytics, 1*(1), 1-19.
[http://dx.doi.org/10.51483/IJDSBDA.1.1.2021.1-19]

Kaswan, M.S., Rathi, R. (2019). Analysis and modeling the enablers of green lean six sigma implementation using interpretive structural modeling. *J. Clean. Prod., 231*, 1182-1191.

[http://dx.doi.org/10.1016/j.jclepro.2019.05.253]

Saxena, A., Prasad, D., Haldhar, R., Singh, G., Kumar, A. (2018). Use of Sida cordifolia extract as green corrosion inhibitor for mild steel in 0.5 M H2SO4. *J. Environ. Chem. Eng., 6*(1), 694-700. [http://dx.doi.org/10.1016/j.jece.2017.12.064]

Sharma, P., Kaur, R., Baskar, C., Chung, W.J. (2010). Removal of methylene blue from aqueous waste using rice husk and rice husk ash. *Desalination, 259*(1-3), 249-257. [http://dx.doi.org/10.1016/j.desal.2010.03.044]

Khamparia, A., Gupta, D., Nguyen, N.G., Khanna, A., Pandey, B., Tiwari, P. (2019). Sound classification using convolutional neural network and tensor deep stacking network. *IEEE Access, 7*, 7717-7727. [http://dx.doi.org/10.1109/ACCESS.2018.2888882]

Haldhar, R., Prasad, D., Saxena, A. (2018). Myristica fragrans extract as an eco-friendly corrosion inhibitor for mild steel in 0.5 M H_2SO_4 solution. *J. Environ. Chem. Eng., 6*(2), 2290-2301. [http://dx.doi.org/10.1016/j.jece.2018.03.023]

CHAPTER 3

The Dawn of Automated Health Guardianship: Robo Advisors in Insurance Planning

Jaspreet Kaur[1], **Sanjay Taneja**[2,*] and **Mohit Kukreti**[3]

[1] *University School of Business, Chandigarh University, Gharuan, Punjab, India*

[2] *Department of Management Studies, Graphic Era deemed to be University, Dehradun, Uttarakhand, India*

[3] *University of Technology and Applied Sciences, (CAS Ibri), Muscat, Oman*

Abstract: Robo Advisors are ushering in a new era of automated health guardianship, and in the ever-evolving environment of healthcare, an explosion has been seen in the integration of technology. This article delves into the paradigm change brought about by these sophisticated algorithms in the field of insurance planning, specifically with regard to health coverage. The purpose of this paper is to investigate the revolutionary effect that Robo Advisors have had on the process of insurance planning. Specifically, the article will shed light on the functionalities of Robo Advisors as well as the consequences that these features have for consumers as well as the insurance sector. Additionally, the ethical and regulatory considerations that surround the use of Robo Advisors in insurance planning are covered in this article. Concerns around data privacy, bias mitigation, and openness in algorithmic capabilities become critical as the use of artificial intelligence in decision-making processes becomes more widespread. Also, the changing role of insurance experts in connection with Robo Advisors is investigated in this article. Although these automated technologies simplify and improve the decision-making process, there is still no substitute for the human element when it comes to reading preferences down to the most detailed level and offering individualized guidance.

Keywords: Automated health guardianship, Algorithmic insurance solutions, Artificial intelligence, Health insurance automation, Healthcare, Insurance, Insurance planning, Machine learning, Risk assessment automation.

INTRODUCTION

The process of navigating the complex web of health insurance plans may be a demanding undertaking, leaving individuals often bewildered and uncertain about

* **Corresponding author Sanjay Taneja:** Department of Management Studies, Graphic Era Deemed to be University, Dehradun, Uttarakhand, India; E-mail: drsanjaytaneja1@gmail.com

the coverage option that is most suited to their requirements (Nijhawan & Jain, 2018). Enter the idea of Robo Advisors, a technological innovation that is positioned to completely transform the process of preparing for health insurance. Robo Advisors, which have their origins in the world of finance, have recently expanded their operations into the medical industry (Srivastava *et al.*, 2024). Automated platforms like this make use of algorithms and data analytics to provide individualized guidance and solutions to users. In the context of planning for health insurance, they function as essential instruments, offering direction and comprehension amidst the muddled landscape of available insurance choices, as depicted in Fig. (**1**) below:

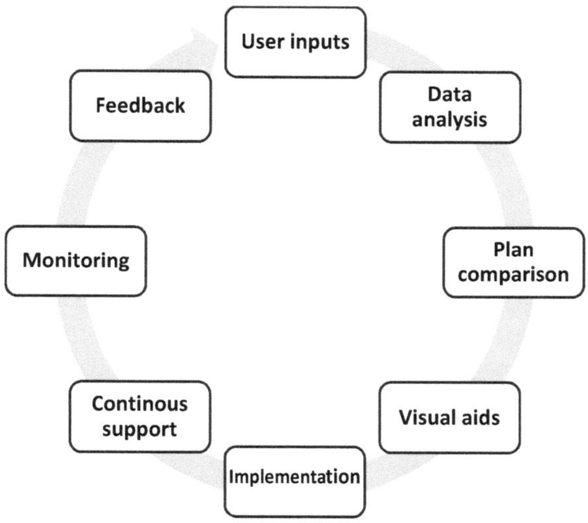

Fig. (1). Incorporating Robo Advisors into the planning process for health insurance flowchart. Source: Waliszewski *et al.* (2020).

Robo Advisors in the field of health insurance planning have as their primary focus the accomplishment of a number of essential goals. To begin, one of their primary goals is to make health insurance more accessible to customers by leveling the playing field between them and the complex insurance industry (G. Singh *et al.*, 2024; Yashu *et al.*, 2024). They make the insurance language understandable by giving individuals intuitive interfaces and simplified explanations, which enables individuals to make choices based on accurate information. The application of Robo Advisors in the process of planning one's health insurance can potentially cover a wide range of different aspects. They analyze an individual's demands, financial capabilities, and healthcare requirements before streamlining the process of selecting insurance policies (Badawy *et al.*, 2024; S. Gupta *et al.*, 2021; Mangla *et al.*, 2019). Furthermore, these platforms have the potential to teach customers about various coverage alternatives, deductibles, and subtleties within insurance policies, which equips them with the knowledge necessary to make decisions with self-assurance (Debasis *et al.*, 2020; Ojha, Thapliyal, *et al.*, 2024; Samantaray *et al.*, 2024).

It is important to stress the importance of incorporating Robo Advisors into the planning process for health insurance. These digital assistants are incredibly helpful in this day and age because medical expenditures are skyrocketing, and there is a greater variety of insurance policies available than ever before. They have the ability to demystify the complexities of insurance, which could result in cost reductions and improved coverage (Pargaien *et al.*, 2021; Rajput *et al.*, 2024; Rawat, Singh, Ray, & Szabo, 2020; Sar *et al.*, 2024). The integration of technology and the management of healthcare finances is a critical component in the development of an approach to insurance planning that is both more effective and customer-focused. Robo Advisors, by virtue of the algorithms they use and the data-driven insights they provide, are able to respond to individual preferences, thereby ensuring that health insurance plans are in line with particular requirements and inclinations (Juyal & Sharma, 2021; Pargaien *et al.*, 2024; A. P. S. Yadav *et al.*, 2024). Recognizing the revolutionary potential of Robo Advisors is necessary for comprehending the role that they play in the process of health insurance planning. Individuals are able to obtain access to tailored assistance through the utilization of these technological breakthroughs, which has the effect of transforming, what was formerly a laborious chore, into a process that is streamlined and informed decision-making (V. Kumar, Banerjee, *et al.*, 2024a; Mitra *et al.*, 2022; Semwal *et al.*, 2020).

In the following subsections, we will conduct an in-depth investigation into the capabilities and functionalities of Robo Advisors that have been specifically tailored for the health insurance industry. The purpose of this investigation is to determine how effective they are in educating consumers, easing the decision-making process, and eventually improving the efficiency with which health insurance plans are chosen. In order to provide a full understanding of how Robo Advisors can improve health insurance planning, case studies, industry trends, user experiences, and relevant regulatory considerations will be analyzed (Agarwal *et al.*, 2024; R. Jain *et al.*, 2024b; Kunwar *et al.*, 2021; Rajora *et al.*, 2024; Y. K. Sharma *et al.*, 2018). In addition, the study will emphasize the necessity of ongoing innovation in this field to ensure the smooth incorporation of technology into healthcare financial management (Dhawan, Sharma, Rana, *et al.*, 2024; I. Jain *et al.*, 2024; Pal *et al.*, 2024; Shakya *et al.*, 2018; Walia *et al.*, 2024).

The way in which individuals interact with and make the most of their health insurance coverage is undergoing a fundamental transition, and Robo Advisors are at the vanguard of this shift. These platforms have enormous promise in not just simplifying insurance planning but also ensuring that healthcare coverage becomes more personalized and efficient, which will ultimately lead to improved healthcare outcomes (Kamal, Shobha, *et al.*, 2022; A. Kaur, Kukreja, Kumar, *et al.*, 2024; Rawat, Singh, Ray, Szabó, *et al.*, 2020; H. Sharma *et al.*, 2024). As technology continues to advance, this promise will only increase as these platforms become more widely used.

THE DEVELOPMENT OF ROBOTIC ADVISORS IN THE MEDICAL INDUSTRY

Robo Advisors had their beginnings in the financial advice services industry, but they have steadily expanded their skills to change the healthcare industry by providing patients and healthcare practitioners with individualized assistance, predictive analytic, and personalized suggestions. Robo Advisors were initially rooted in the financial advisory services industry (R. Jain *et al.*, 2024a).

In the beginning phases of the application of Robo Advisors in the healthcare industry, the primary attention was placed on fundamental capabilities, such as appointment scheduling and reminders, with the intention of improving patient involvement and adherence to treatment programs. These elementary computer programs laid the groundwork for the development of more complex applications that make use of artificial intelligence (AI) and machine learning methods. Robo Advisors are now able to efficiently examine enormous volumes of healthcare data thanks to the integration of artificial intelligence (AI) and machine learning techniques. This skill has shown to be very useful in predictive analytic, in the prevention of disease, and even in the suggestion of individualized treatment options based on individual health profiles.

The application of Robo Advisors in the management of chronic diseases is one of the most significant developments in the history of this technology in the healthcare industry. These advisers provide continuous monitoring, individualized food suggestions, and medication adherence reminders in order to aid clients in managing illnesses such as diabetes, hypertension, and heart disease. This preventative approach helps in reducing the risk of problems while also enhancing the patient's general health. In addition to this, Robo Advisors have made major contributions to the development of telemedicine (Mudholkar *et al.*, 2022; Shashikala *et al.*, 2022).

They make remote consultations, symptom assessments, and triage possible, which ultimately leads to an increase in access to healthcare services, particularly in places that are either under-served or remote. These advisors not only connect patients with healthcare providers but also collect relevant medical history and symptoms to assist healthcare professionals in making more educated judgments during virtual consultations. In addition to connecting patients with healthcare providers, these advisors also gather this information [6]. The development of Robo Advisors in the healthcare industry has expanded to include the function that these advisors play in increasing the operational efficiency of healthcare organizations. These advisers help streamline administrative activities, optimize resource allocation, and provide assistance with inventory management. As a result, overhead expenses are reduced, and healthcare providers are able to focus more on patient care (Mahajan *et al.*, 2024; Upadhyay *et al.*, 2024).

In a nutshell, the introduction of Robo Advisors into the healthcare industry represents the beginning of a paradigm shift away from the conventional approaches to patient care and health management and toward an approach that is more tech-integrated and data-driven, as depicted in Fig. (**2**) below:

Additionally, Robo Advisors have extended their services to include support for mental health issues. These advisers provide assistance, therapy sessions, and mood-tracking tools in response to the growing awareness of concerns relating to mental health. This ensures that individuals who are seeking mental wellness have access to constant support and resources.

Ethical concerns, data privacy, and regulatory compliance are going to become increasingly important as the use of Robo Advisors in the healthcare industry continues to advance. In order to preserve confidence and credibility in these technological breakthroughs, it is essential to ensure the safe management of sensitive patient data and to comply with all applicable healthcare legislation (Alemu *et al.*, 2024; Kamal, Shende, *et al.*, 2022; V. Kumar, Banerjee, *et al.*, 2024b).

When looking into the future, the trajectory of Robo Advisors in the healthcare industry appears to hold a lot of promise. The combination of Robo Advisors with wearable devices, the Internet of Things (Io-T) in healthcare, and genomics holds the possibility of more individualized and data-driven approaches to medical care. These technological advances have the potential to completely transform preventative care, early illness detection, and precision medicine that is personalized to an individual's genetic predispositions (R. R. Kumar *et al.*, 2024).

In a nutshell, the development of Robo Advisors in the healthcare industry is a huge step toward the creation of a healthcare ecosystem that is increasingly interconnected and driven by data. These advisers have transformed the landscape of healthcare delivery in a variety of ways, from the most fundamental patient engagement tools to the most advanced predictive analytic and individualized treatment suggestions. Robo Advisors are positioned to play an increasingly important role as technology continues to advance and data analytics become increasingly complex. This will open up previously unimaginable avenues for the improvement of patient outcomes, the enhancement of healthcare delivery, and the disruption of the entire healthcare business (Gusain *et al.*, 2022; Tomar & Sharma, 2021).

Early Stages:

- Basic patient engagement tools (Appointment scheduling, reminders)
- Limited functionalities, primarily administrative support

Integration of AI and Machine Learning:

- Utilization of AI algorithms for data analysis
- Predictive analytics for disease prevention
- Personalized treatment recommendations based on health data

Chronic Disease Management:

- Continuous monitoring for conditions like diabetes, hypertension
- Personalized dietary and medication adherence guidance
- Focus on proactive health management and prevention

Telemedicine Advancements:

- Remote consultations and symptom assessment
- Triage support for virtual healthcare services
- Increased access to healthcare in remote or underserved areas

Operational Efficiency:

- Streamlining administrative tasks
- Resource allocation optimization
- Inventory management for cost reduction

Mental Health Support:

- Guidance, therapy sessions, mood tracking tools
- Continuous support for mental wellness

Ethical and Regulatory Considerations:

- Data privacy and security
- Compliance with healthcare regulations and ethical guidelines

Future Trajectory:

- Integration with wearable devices and IoT in healthcare
- Advancements in precision medicine and personalized healthcare
- Potential for preventive care and early disease detection

Fig. (2). Evolution of robo-advisors. Source (Adhikari *et al.*, 2021).

THE CAPABILITIES AND WORKINGS OF ROBOTIC ADVISORS

The use of advanced technical mechanisms to process data, apply algorithms, and provide individualized suggestions is what Robo Advisors in the health insurance industry do. This has revolutionized the way in which individuals negotiate the complexity of insurance coverage. In order to provide individualized direction, these computerized systems rely on a multi-pronged strategy that incorporates data examination, machine learning, and user participation (Garg *et al.*, 2024).

The processing of data is the fundamental activity that underpins the technical operations of Robo Advisors. These systems take in huge amounts of data, which may include user demographics, health history, financial information, and facts regarding insurance plans. This data acts as the cornerstone for their analytical capabilities, which enables them to generate individualized profiles for each individual user (A. Kaur, Sharma, Thapliyal, *et al.*, 2024).

The functionality of Robo Advisors is entirely dependent on the algorithms that power them. The gathered data is processed by machine learning techniques such as decision trees, clustering, and neural networks in order to extract patterns, correlations, and insights from the data. The recommendations provided by these algorithms are continuously improved as a result of ongoing learning and adaptation in response to activity from users. Robo Advisors make use of predictive analytics in order to make predictions on possible healthcare requirements and dangers. These systems are able to identify prospective health issues or prescribe preventative measures by doing an analysis of historical data as well as information that is particular to the individual. For instance, the adviser may suggest wellness programs or screenings to a user based on the user's health profile and lifestyle in order to reduce the user's exposure to potential future health hazards (Tanwar *et al.*, 2024).

Robo Advisors in the field of health insurance planning place a significant emphasis on individualization. These systems provide customized recommendations for insurance policies based on the actions taken by users and analyses of the data they collect. In order to provide recommendations for insurance plans that are the most appropriate fit for the user's situation, a number of considerations, including but not limited to the individual's preferences, requirements for coverage, financial limitations, and health care needs, are given careful attention.

Robo Advisors equipped with capabilities in natural language processing (NLP) are able to interact with users in a manner that is friendly to users. Conversational user interfaces, in which individuals can seek advice, ask questions, or clarify doubts regarding insurance plans, are made possible by these systems because they can understand and interpret user inquiries. The user's comprehension can also be improved with the help of NLP by presenting difficult insurance jargon in a language that is simple to understand (A. Kaur, Sharma, Upadhyay, *et al.*, 2024).

Robo Advisors consistently improve their recommendations by incorporating the input and feedback of their users. The advisers will make dynamic adjustments to their recommendations whenever users interact with the system, provide feedback, or update their information. Because of this iterative approach, the recommendations are guaranteed to continue to be useful and to appropriately reflect the user's ever-evolving requirements (Banerjee, Sharma, Chauhan, *et al.*, 2024).

In addition, Robo Advisors facilitate the user's decision-making process by providing comparisons of the various insurance policies. They present important features, coverage particulars, deductibles, and estimated prices in a format that is easy to understand, so empowering users to make choices based on accurate information (A. Kaur, Sharma, Rana, *et al.*, 2024).

The protection of sensitive health and financial data as well as its confidentiality is of the utmost importance in robo advisors. These systems incorporate sophisticated encryption methods, secure data storage procedures, and compliance mechanisms to preserve user privacy and meet severe regulatory requirements (Gusain *et al.*, 2023).

One example of such a requirement is the Health Insurance Portability and Accountability Act (HIPAA), which is a law that applies in the United States (Govindharaj *et al.*, 2024). When it comes to preparing for health insurance, the incorporation of Robo Advisors does not serve to replace human competence but rather to supplement it. These systems act as decision support tools, enhancing the capacities of insurance professionals while also providing individuals with the ability to make educated decisions about their healthcare coverage (Banerjee, Sharma, Upadhyay, *et al.*, 2024).

In essence, the technical workings of Robo Advisors in health insurance planning require sophisticated data processing, advanced algorithms, predictive analytic, tailored suggestions, user-friendly interfaces, continuous learning, and severe data security measures. Robo Advisors can also learn on their own. Automated systems that make advantage of these skills have as their goals the simplification of the process of selecting an insurance plan, the enhancement of user comprehension, and the optimization of healthcare coverage to successfully match individual requirements (Ojha, Upadhyay, Aeri, *et al.*, 2024).

THE INFLUENCE OF ARTIFICIALLY INTELLIGENT ADVISORS ON INSURANCE DECISION-MAKING

The introduction of Robo Advisors into the world of insurance decision-making has been revolutionary, fundamentally altering the way in which individuals navigate the insurance landscape and choose among various coverage options.

These automated systems have had a considerable impact on a variety of areas of decision-making processes, including accessibility, rationalization, data analysis, and user empowerment, to name a few, as represented in Fig. (**3**) below:

1. Data Processing & Analysis:
- AI algorithms analyze vast datasets, including user information, health records, and insurance options.
- Processing historical data to identify patterns, trends, and risks.

2. Personalized Recommendations:
- Based on data analysis, AI generates tailored insurance recommendations for individuals.
- Considers individual needs, risk profiles, and preferences to suggest suitable coverage.

3. User Interaction & Guidance:
- Interactive interfaces engage users, providing guidance and explanations about insurance plans.
- Offers insights, comparisons, and explanations regarding recommended options.

4. Continuous Learning & Adaptation:
- AI systems continuously learn from user feedback and interactions, refining recommendations over time.
- Adapts to changing user needs, ensuring relevance and accuracy in suggestions.

5. Human Oversight & Ethical Considerations:
- Human professionals review AI-generated recommendations, applying nuanced judgment and ethical considerations.
- Ensures alignment with ethical standards, addresses complexities, and offers personalized advice.

6. Streamlined Decision-Making:
- Combining AI insights with human expertise streamlines decision-making processes.
- Reduces time and effort required for users to evaluate multiple insurance options.

Fig. (3). Impact of artificially intelligent advisors on insurance decision-making. Source: Pisoni and Díaz-Rodríguez (2023).

The Provision of Access and the Spread of Information

The accessibility of insurance information has been completely transformed by Robo Advisors. They function as platforms that are easy to access, friendly to users, and that demystify complicated insurance language while presenting information in a manner that is understandable (Ojha, Upadhyay, Manwal, *et al.*, 2024). People who, in other circumstances, might find making decisions about their insurance to be intimidating or burdensome benefit from this accessibility. These advisers serve as teaching tools, distributing important information regarding insurance plans, policy specifics, deductibles, and prices to their clients.

They make complicated insurance policies easier to grasp by reducing technical details into content that is simple to take in. As a consequence of this, people have a better awareness of the choices available to them, which leads to a decision-making process that is more informed (Kukreti *et al.*, 2024).

Personalized Content and Specifically Catered Suggestions

The capacity of Robo Advisors to generate individualized suggestions is one of the factors that contribute most to the significant influence they have. These systems provide customized recommendations for insurance plans by doing an analysis of user data, which may include health history, demographic information, and preferences. Because of this customization, the proposed programs are guaranteed to be in close accordance with the specific criteria, budget, and demands of the client being referred. In order to curate insurance alternatives that are the most appropriate for the user's situation, the advisers take into consideration a variety of aspects, including the user's family size, health problems, risk tolerance, and financial capacities. This amount of customization improves the relevance and appropriateness of the recommendations, which has a substantial impact on the user's trust in their ability to make decisions (A. Kaur, Kukreja, Thapliyal, *et al.*, 2024).

Data Analysis and Insights into Possible Futures

Robo Advisors make use of cutting-edge data analysis methods and predictive analytic in order to make predictions regarding possible healthcare requirements and dangers. These systems are able to forecast prospective health issues by assessing historical data as well as individual health profiles and then making recommendations for preventative measures (Dhawan, Sharma, Chattopadhyay, *et al.*, 2024). For instance, the adviser may suggest particular wellness programs, screenings, or insurance add-ons that are aligned with projected future health concerns based on the user's health history and lifestyle choices. Individuals are given the ability to better anticipate and respond to prospective medical requirements as a result of this proactive approach to decision-making around insurance coverage (R. Kaur, Gupta, Tripathi, *et al.*, 2024).

Efforts Made to Simplify the Decision-Making Process

The decision-making process can be streamlined with the help of these automated tools, which provide users with full comparisons of different insurance plans. They include in-depth information on the characteristics of the plan, as well as the coverage specifics, deductibles, and expected costs (V. Kumar, Raj, *et al.*, 2024). Because of this simplification, individuals are now able to examine many possibilities side by side, which facilitates a decision-making process that is more time and effort-efficient. Individuals will spend less time and effort as a result of the streamlined decision-making process, which decreases the amount of time they need to spend researching and analyzing the various insurance plans on their own. It speeds up the choosing process and enables consumers to make efficient judgments based on accurate information more quickly (Adelodun *et al.*, 2024).

Empowerment of Users and Engagement of Users

Users are given more agency thanks to Robo Advisors because they encourage more active participation in the decision-making process. Individuals are encouraged to seek assistance, ask questions, and clear up any uncertainties they have regarding insurance policies through the use of interactive user interfaces and user-friendly experiences. In addition, these systems are able to learn from the input and feedback provided by users and continue to develop over time. The more the users engage with the advisors, provide comments, or update their information, the more polished and specific the recommendations become to each individual user's requirements. This iterative method not only guarantees that recommendations continue to be relevant, but also encourages continuous participation (A. Joshi *et al.*, 2024).

Enhancing the Expertise of Humans Instead of Trying to Replace Them

It is essential to keep in mind that Robo Advisors are intended to work in conjunction with human expertise rather than to replace it. These systems act as decision support tools, providing assistance to insurance experts as they steer individuals toward appropriate insurance solutions. They provide data-driven insights and make it easier to make more personalized recommendations, both of which are ways in which they boost the capabilities of professionals. By incorporating Robo Advisors into the process of making decisions about insurance, experts are freed up to concentrate on duties with a higher potential return on investment. These tasks may include providing specialized advice, responding to complex inquiries, or providing extra context or explanations in addition to automated suggestions (Naik *et al.*, 2024).

Conquering Obstacles While Building Trust in One Another

The utilization of Robo Advisors in the process of decision-making within the insurance industry does present some difficulties. Obtaining the users' faith and confidence in these automated systems is a big obstacle that must be overcome. Robo Advisors have a responsibility to emphasize measures of openness, privacy, and safety in order to address this issue. It is essential to ensure clear information about how data is used, implement effective data security measures, and comply with regulatory requirements in order to create and sustain user confidence.

Examples of such standards include GDPR and HIPAA. The provision of channels through which users can reach human support on demand can also help boost users' levels of confidence in the aforementioned automated technologies (D. Singh *et al.*, 2024).

THE PROSPECTIVE PATHWAY AND ITS POTENTIAL IMPACT

If we look to the future, we can see that the influence of Robo Advisors on insurance decisions will continue to grow. As artificial intelligence (AI), machine learning, and data analytics continue to progress, these technologies are likely to become more proficient at user engagement, professionalization, and predictive insights (Tomar *et al.*, 2024).

The integration of Robo Advisors with upcoming technologies like wearable devices, the Internet of Things in healthcare, and genetic profiling has the potential to change the decision-making process in the insurance industry. This connection has the potential to offer even more tailored recommendations by utilizing real-time health data and genetic information to precisely adapt insurance plans to the requirements of a specific individual. In addition, the continued development of these systems will probably center on resolving issues about trust, privacy, and ethical considerations as they arise. Robo Advisors will need to find a way to strike a balance between technological innovation and user-centrist design if they are to continue to have a beneficial impact on the decision-making process in the insurance industry while also retaining the trust and confidence of their users (Ray *et al.*, 2024).

Robo Advisors have had a considerable impact on the insurance decision-making process due to the following factors: increased accessibility, the provision of individualized advice, the utilization of data analysis and predictive insights, the streamlining of processes, the empowerment of users, and the augmentation of human expertise. While they provide tremendous potential for increasing the efficiency and efficacy of insurance choices, resolving difficulties related to trust, privacy, and ethical considerations will be vital for their future success and progress in the field of insurance decision-making (N. C. Joshi & Gururani, 2023; Rather *et al.*, 2023).

ETHICAL CONCERNS AS WELL AS REGULATORY HURDLES INVOLVED WITH THE USE OF ROBOT ADVISORS IN THE INSURANCE PLANNING PROCESS

When it comes to insurance planning, the use of Robo Advisors raises a wide variety of ethical concerns and regulatory hurdles, all of which need to be carefully considered and managed. In spite of the fact that the installation of these automated systems creates a number of concerns relating to data privacy, algorithmic biases, transparency, and regulatory compliance, these systems offer a multitude of benefits in terms of improving decision-making processes (G. Kumar *et al.*, 2023).

Privacy and Protection of Sensitive Data

The management of sensitive personal data presents one of the most significant challenges for Robo Advisors in the field of insurance planning from an ethical standpoint. These systems rely on huge volumes of personal information, which may include demographic characteristics, financial data, and health records. It is essential to implement stringent data privacy protections in order to prevent unwanted access, data breaches, or inappropriate use of this information (Mir *et al.*, 2024). Data management and privacy protection are subject to stringent standards thanks to laws such as the General Data Protection Regulation (GDPR) in the European Union and the Health Insurance Portability and Accountability Act (HIPAA) in the United States. To protect the personal information of persons and to preserve their faith in these systems, compliance with these standards is absolutely necessary (Harbola *et al.*, 2024).

The Problem with Algorithmic Fairness and Its Solutions

The possibility of biases being built into the algorithms that are utilized by Robo Advisors is yet another serious ethical concern. Machine learning algorithms, despite their capacity, have the potential to unintentionally reinforce biases that are already present in the data used for training. Because of these prejudices, the decisions that are made, particularly regarding insurance, could end up being unjust or discriminatory. For instance, if the historical data that is utilized to train these algorithms has prejudices relating to gender, color, or socioeconomic position, then the suggestions that are provided by the Robo Advisors could reflect and perpetuate these biases. Because of this, it might be difficult to provide fair and equal treatment to all of the people who are looking for insurance coverage. In order to address the biases introduced by algorithms, continual monitoring, evaluation, and mitigation measures are required. Essential steps in mitigating these ethical problems include incorporating fairness metrics into the design of algorithms and conducting routine audits of algorithms to check for biases (Santoyo *et al.*, 2024).

Transparency as well as an Ability to Explain

The opaque nature of algorithms creates difficulties in terms of transparency and the capacity to explain their workings. Users may have a difficult time comprehending the process by which Robo Advisors make their recommendations because the software frequently relies on intricate algorithms and machine learning models. A lack of openness can erode confidence and make it more difficult for users to appreciate the reasoning behind recommendations. Improving these systems' levels of transparency and explainability is absolutely necessary if user acceptance and ethical requirements are to be met. Concerns about transparency can be alleviated by giving users access to and explanations of the decision-making process, as well as by providing explicit explanations of how data is used and how recommendations are made (Semwal *et al.*, 2023).

Compliance with Regulations and the Establishment of Legal Frameworks

The adoption of Robo Advisors in insurance planning faces substantial obstacles due to the complicated terrain of regulatory compliance that they must navigate. The legislative frameworks and laws that regulate insurance, data protection, and financial services can differ significantly from one location to the next. It is of the utmost importance to ensure compliance with these regulations, the most important of which are the General Data Protection Regulation (GDPR), the Health Insurance Portability and Accountability Act (HIPAA), and the requirements imposed by the Insurance Regulatory and Development Authority (IRDA) in India. In order to maintain compliance with the applicable legal requirements, continuous monitoring, adaptation to ever-changing rules, and the implementation of effective compliance systems are all required (Kholiya *et al.*, 2023).

Oversight and Accountability Provided by Humans

An important factor to examine from an ethical point of view is the part that human supervision and responsibility play in the operation of Robo Advisors. Even if these technologies automate decision-making processes, there is still a significant need for human input, mainly when dealing with complicated or sensitive instances. It is essential to determine clear lines of accountability for the decisions that Robo Advisors make and to ensure that there are channels for human intervention in situations that call for nuanced judgment or ethical considerations. Maintaining ethical standards and ensuring that judgments are made in accordance with ethical norms and regulatory requirements can be accomplished by striking a balance between automation and human oversight (Ganesan *et al.*, 2023).

ADDRESSING THE CONCERNS ABOUT ETHICS AND DIFFICULTIES IN MEETING REGULATORY REQUIREMENTS

Several different approaches and models of best practice can be utilized in order to overcome these ethical and regulatory difficulties, including the following:

Approach Called "Ethics by Design"

It is important to incorporate ethical considerations and fairness standards into the design and development of Robo Advisors from the very beginning.

Transparency and Explainability

Increase the amount of transparency by giving users access to information about how data is being used and by providing them with explanations that make it easy to grasp how recommendations are created.

Conducting Regular Audits and Attempting to Reduce Biases

It is important to conduct regular audits of algorithms in order to identify and attempt to reduce biases. Put in place procedures that will guarantee that the decision-making processes are fair. Consent and control of the user empower users by giving them control over their data and ensuring that they give informed consent on the use of their data and how it is processed.

Regulatory Compliance Frameworks

Maintain an awareness of the ever-changing regulatory landscapes and strictly adhere to the pertinent legal frameworks in order to guarantee compliance with all applicable data protection and financial requirements. Establishing clear procedures for human oversight and responsibility in decision-making processes is especially important in cases that are either critically important or ethically sensitive.

Overall, Robo Advisors in the field of insurance planning have a tremendous amount of promise to streamline decision-making procedures and improve user experiences. However, its implementation poses ethical concerns and legal obstacles linked to data privacy, algorithmic biases, and transparency. To effectively handle these difficulties, it is essential to take the following important steps: adopting ethical-by-design principles, assuring openness, minimizing biases, complying with rules, and incorporating human oversight. Building confidence, upholding integrity, and ensuring the responsible and ethical deployment of Robo Advisors in insurance planning all require striking a balance between technological innovation and ethical issues (Khosravi *et al.*, 2024).

COLLABORATION BETWEEN HUMANS AND ALGORITHMS IN THE PROCESS OF INSURANCE PLANNING

The synergy that may be achieved when humans and computers work together to develop insurance policies offers an innovative strategy that capitalizes on the qualities that set each component apart. Human knowledge provides sophisticated judgment, empathy, and ethical concerns to the decision-making process, in contrast to the superior performance of algorithms and Robo Advisors in the processing of data, analysis, and generation of suggestions. This partnership re-imagines insurance planning by drawing on the skills of both humans and algorithms to improve ethics while also boosting productivity and effectiveness (A. K. Yadav *et al.*, 2024).

Processing and Evaluation of Data are the Purview of lgorithms

Processing enormous amounts of data quickly and effectively is a strength of both algorithms and robotic advisors. They provide individualized suggestions based on user information, historical data, and insurance options by analyzing all of these factors. These automated systems make use of machine learning and predictive analytics in order to recognize patterns, trends, and potential dangers. As a result, they contribute to decision-making that is more data-driven (Duong *et al.*, 2024).

Judgment and Ethical Considerations in Regards to Humans

The human expert possesses sophisticated judgment, sensitivity, and the ability to take ethical considerations into account. Insurance experts have the capacity to comprehend intricate user demands, solve particular problems, and overcome ethical conundrums that algorithms may miss. They add a human element to the decision-making process by taking into account intangible characteristics, such as emotional facets or specific circumstances, that computers may not be able to grasp (Banerjee *et al.*, 2023).

Individualization and Pinpoint Accuracy

A greater degree of customization and accuracy in insurance planning can be achieved through the combined efforts of humans and algorithms. While algorithms make use of data analysis to provide specialized recommendations, human specialists have the ability to fine-tune these recommendations based on individual preferences, specific circumstances, and ethical considerations (Saikumar *et al.*, 2024; Sunori *et al.*, 2023).

Ethical Considerations, as well as an Understanding of the Context

When it comes to insurance planning, humans bring a contextual understanding and ethical issues to the table. They are able to handle critical situations, evaluate the bigger picture of a user's predicament, and factor ethical standards into decision-making. Because of this human intervention, judgments are more likely to conform to ethical standards and to address the comprehensive requirements of persons (Elbagory *et al.*, 2022; P. Gupta *et al.*, 2023; Kaushik *et al.*, 2024).

Trust and a Better Overall Experience for Users

The user experience can be improved through the collaboration of humans and algorithms. Human specialists are able to provide more individualized assistance, explanations, and empathy, while computers are able to efficiently process data and provide recommendations. Users who feel understood, supported, and reassured as a result of human connection are more likely to trust the service being provided (Jaswal *et al.*, 2023; Tina *et al.*, 2024; Vashishth *et al.*, 2023).

CASES AND SCENARIOS FOR THEIR APPLICATION

Advisory Services that Make Use of Algorithms to Complement Them

Insurance consulting services that are reinforced by algorithms capitalize on the capabilities possessed by both of the companies. User data is processed, various insurance choices are analyzed, and initial suggestions are generated by algorithms. After that, human experts examine and modify these recommendations based on their knowledge, taking into account ethical considerations and having a profound comprehension of the requirements of particular users (Bhatnagar *et al.*, 2022; A. K. Gupta *et al.*, 2024).

Making Moral Determinations Amidst Difficult Circumstances

Human intervention is essential in circumstances that are either extremely complicated or highly ethically charged. It may be difficult for algorithms to take into account the nuances of ethical considerations or emotional elements. Human specialists are called upon to evaluate these intricacies, use ethical frameworks, and provide individualized assistance that is in line with the moral and psychological requirements of users (P. Singh *et al.*, 2024).

Continual Accumulation of Knowledge and Progress

The partnership between humans and algorithms creates an environment that is conducive to ongoing learning and progress. Human input, the behaviors of users, and the knowledge of experts all contribute to an algorithm's growth and development. Human experts, on the other hand, learn from the insights provided by algorithms. They incorporate data-driven approaches into their decision-making processes and work to improve their comprehension of user requirements (Chakravorty *et al.*, 2022).

THE OBSTACLES FACING AND HOW WE PLAN TO OVERCOME THEM

Both Trust and Openness are Essential

It is essential to preserve the trust of users and to practice transparency in decision-making processes. In order to overcome this issue, businesses should ensure that there is transparent information regarding the roles that algorithms and humans play in the decision-making process. Trust may be increased by providing users with explanations for the recommendations that are created by algorithms and by allowing them to contact human support when it is required (Barthwal *et al.*, 2024).

The Problem with Algorithmic Fairness and Its Solutions

It is crucial to ensure fairness in decision-making that algorithmic biases are mitigated whenever possible. It is essential to have human oversight in order to detect and correct biases that are built into algorithms. Strategies to address biases and promote fairness include conducting regular audits, incorporating fairness metrics into the design of algorithms, and ensuring diversity in the data used for training (Pokhariya *et al.*, 2022).

Compliance with Regulations and the Establishment of Ethical Frameworks

It is absolutely necessary to behave ethically and in accordance with the regulations that are in place. Organizations must comply with regulations governing data privacy and ethical standards. Responsible and ethical business practices can be ensured by incorporating ethical principles into the process of designing algorithms, going through decision-making steps, and staying in accordance with legislation.

The Prospective Pathway and Its Potential Impact

The combination of humans and algorithms has the potential to make great progress in insurance planning. This partnership is expected to develop further in the future as artificial intelligence, machine learning, and design prioritize user advancement.

Assistance Powered by Advanced AI

Future developments may incorporate more advanced forms of AI-powered support. These tools might provide real-time insights, predictive capabilities, and greater professionalization, effectively assisting human decision-making processes (Verma *et al.*, 2024).

The Development of Ethical AI

It will be essential to develop artificial intelligence with a higher focus on ethics and openness. In insurance planning, striking a balance between data-driven efficiency and ethical considerations will facilitate the development of more reliable and responsible AI systems (M. Sharma & Singh, 2023).

Giving Users and Professionals the Ability to Do More

It will be easier for people to work together if users are given the tools they need to comprehend and interact with algorithms and if experts are given insights that are driven by artificial intelligence. Because of this, decision-making will be improved, user experiences will be enhanced, and consumers' trust in the process of insurance planning will increase. In the process of insurance planning, the partnership between humans and algorithms constitutes a symbiotic connection that capitalizes on the skills possessed by both parties. Human knowledge adds judgment, ethical considerations, and a human touch to decision-making, whereas algorithms excel in data processing, analysis, and the generation of recommendations (Dhayal *et al.*, 2024).

When it comes to insurance planning, taking a collaborative approach improves not only professionalization but also ethical decision-making and the user experience. Transparent communication, fairness measures, and a strict commitment to ethical standards are required because of the difficulties associated with trust, prejudices, and regulatory compliance. It is expected that as time goes on, the evolution of this relationship will encompass more advanced support for AI, a deeper focus on the creation of ethical AI, and the empowerment of both user's and experts' power. In order to develop an approach to insurance planning that is more responsible, effective, and user-centrist, it is necessary to strike a balance between data-driven efficiency and human-centrist ethics (Rani *et al.*, 2024).

THE PATH THAT WILL BE TAKEN IN THE NEAR FUTURE BY AUTOMATED HEALTH GUARDIANSHIP

The trajectory of automated health guardianship holds a great deal of potential and is well-positioned to change healthcare by merging cutting-edge technology into personalized, proactive, and preventative health management. The term "automated health guardianship" refers to systems and devices driven by artificial intelligence (AI) that continually monitor an individual's health, analyze their health data, provide recommendations, and make it easier to take proactive measures to preserve and improve their health. This transformation will have a profound effect on the delivery of healthcare, the empowerment of patients, and the overall approach to health management (Bisht *et al.*, 2024).

Make the Transition to Personalized and Preventive Healthcare

The provision of individualized and preventative medical care is where the field of automated health guardianship is headed. These systems will make use of artificial intelligence (AI) and machine learning in order to process massive volumes of individual health data, such as genetic information, bio-metrics, lifestyle patterns, and medical history. These watchdogs will deliver personalized insights, predictive analytics, and individualized recommendations for preventative steps after reviewing this data (A. Sharma *et al.*, 2024).

Continuous Monitoring and Detection at an Early Stage

Automated health guardianship will make it possible to perform continuous health monitoring in contexts other than those typically associated with healthcare. Wearable gadgets equipped with artificial intelligence algorithms will monitor vital signs, evaluate data in real-time, and identify small changes that may be symptomatic of possible health problems. When abnormalities or shifts in health patterns are identified early on, timely interventions and preventative actions can be taken, which will ultimately lead to improved health outcomes.

Management and Interventions of One's Health That Are Proactive

Individuals will be actively engaged in the management of their health by these guardians, which are powered by AI (Tamta *et al.*, 2024). These systems will enable individuals to take proactive actions toward maintaining their well-being. They will provide them with individualized recommendations for changes in lifestyle and food habits, exercise routines, and preventive screenings. This preventative strategy tries to head off any health problems before they become serious, with the dual benefits of lowering overall healthcare expenses and boosting overall quality of life (Chauhan *et al.*, 2023).

The Use of Artificial Intelligence in Telemedicine and Remote Care

The development of telemedicine and remote care will be significantly aided by the implementation of automated health guardianship systems. Virtual assistants powered by AI will make it easier to conduct remote consultations, evaluate symptoms, and prioritize patients (Sneha *et al.*, 2023). These technologies will not only connect patients with healthcare practitioners but also help with early assessments and data collecting, which will improve access to healthcare, particularly in places that are currently under-served or located in remote areas.

Decision Support Powered by AI for Professionals Working in the Healthcare Industry

In the not-too-distant future, AI will play an important role as a potent decision-making aid for medical professionals. Automated health guardianship systems will scan huge information, provide diagnostic insights, suggest treatment alternatives, and provide predictive analytic, all with the goal of assisting healthcare providers in making educated decisions (Katyal *et al.*, 2024). The diagnostic processes and treatment strategies that are developed as a result of this cooperative effort between AI and medical practitioners will be more precise and time-effective. The development of automated health guardianship offers obstacles and ethical problems despite the fact that it has the potential to revolutionize healthcare. It is necessary to address concerns related to privacy with the gathering and utilization of sensitive health data. It is essential to find a middle ground between the utility of data and the privacy of patients in order to preserve confidence and remain in compliance with regulatory norms. In addition, mitigating biases and ensuring fair and equitable healthcare delivery requires making certain that AI algorithms are accurate, reliable, and transparent. In order to ensure that decisions are made in an ethical and unbiased manner, these systems need to go through extensive testing, validation, and constant monitoring (Patil *et al.*, 2021).

CHANGING THE WAY WE THINK ABOUT HEALTHCARE WHILE EMPOWERING INDIVIDUALS

Individuals being given the ability to become active participants in the management of their own health is going to be a major focus of future developments in automated health guardianship. These systems will move the focus from reactive sick care to proactive healthcare by providing patients with individualized insights, actionable recommendations, and continuous monitoring. People will have a greater degree of autonomy and control over their own health, which will enable them to make decisions based on accurate information and take preventative actions. This transition toward an approach that is more patient-centered and preventive will lessen the strain on healthcare systems, improve health outcomes, and lead to healthcare delivery that is more sustainable and efficient (Malhotra *et al.*, 2021).

INTEGRATION OF ARTIFICIAL INTELLIGENCE AND PROFESSIONALS WORKING IN HEALTHCARE

The future of automated health guardianship will place an emphasis on a cooperative approach between AI and professionals working in healthcare. These systems will not be able to take the place of human expertise; rather, they will enhance the capacities of healthcare practitioners. The combination of insights generated by AI with those derived from human experience will result in more precise diagnoses, more individualized treatment plans, and overall better patient care. A revolutionary step toward individualized, preventative, and healthcare that is centered on the individual patient is represented by automated health guardianship. In order to empower individuals, provide continuous monitoring, promote early interventions, and change healthcare paradigms toward preventive measures, the future trajectory entails harnessing AI and modern technologies. It will be essential to find solutions to problems relating to data protection, algorithmic biases, ethical considerations, and maintaining a collaborative approach between AI and healthcare experts. In the end, the development of automated health guardianship has the potential to change healthcare, making it possible for individuals to live healthier lives while also revolutionizing the way in which healthcare is provided and experienced (Uniyal *et al.*, 2022).

CONCLUDING REMARKS

When it comes to the field of healthcare, the incorporation of Robo Advisors into the process of insurance planning constitutes a big step forward. This is because it makes it possible to develop automated health guardianship programs that are not only effective but also have the ability to be customized to the specific needs of each individual. It is becoming increasingly clear that the union of cutting-edge technology and medical insurance is not only a fleeting trend but rather a fundamental shift in the way that we protect our health. This realization is becoming more and more apparent as we get closer to the end of this period of upheaval. Specifically, this is due to the fact that medical insurance also covers the costs of medical conditions.

Robo Advisors provide a variety of benefits in the realm of insurance planning, one of the most significant of which is the unparalleled level of precision and accuracy that they boast. Robo Advisors offer a number of advantages. It is possible for these automated systems to do analysis on a substantial amount of data because they make use of complex algorithms and artificial intelligence. They are able to develop judgments that are founded on facts in a manner that is not only exceptionally quick but also reliable. This is because of the fact that they are experts in the field. As a consequence, this leads to increased precision in risk assessment, tailored insurance plans, and fast interventions in the field of healthcare. Another obvious consequence of this is the development of tailored insurance plans. Additionally, the efficiency of Robo Advisors offers a significant contribution to the lowering of costs for all parties concerned, comprising policyholders as well as the organizations that are responsible for providing insurance. Not only does this result in lower insurance rates, but it also makes it possible for insurers to manage their resources in a more efficient manner, which is a significant benefit. In order to achieve success, it was necessary to streamline operations and cut down on administrative costs. These are the components that led to the success. The gaps that currently exist in terms of access to healthcare will be reduced as a result of this better cost-effectiveness, which will ultimately lead to a higher number of individuals having access to high-quality medical coverage. This will ultimately lead to a reduction in the gaps that currently exist.

Robo Advisors are becoming an increasingly crucial component in the process of modernizing insurance planning. This is mostly due to the fact that they are able to be customized. By analyzing personal health data, lifestyle trends, and medical history, these automated systems have the ability to modify insurance plans so that they are tailored to meet the specific requirements of each policyholder. Utilizing statistical analysis is the means by which this objective is realized. As a consequence of this characteristic, it is possible to personalize the products so that they correspond to the particular needs of each and every unique policyholder. Individuals are motivated to take a greater level of responsibility for their own health when this method is implemented, which not only ensures that all individuals are involved but also guarantees that they are included. According to Robo Advisors, one of the most essential components of insurance is the emphasis that is placed on wellness programs and preventative medical care. This is one of the most significant aspects of insurance. As a direct result of this, the healthcare industry has moved away from a reactive approach to patient care and has instead adopted a proactive approach.

Given that we are getting closer and closer to the conclusion of this revolutionary journey, it is of the utmost importance to acknowledge and address issues surrounding the privacy and security of client data. This is especially true in light of the fact that we are getting closer and closer to the finish of this voyage. It is of the utmost importance to put in place stringent measures in order to prevent other people from gaining unauthorized access to personal information for the purpose of protecting it. The reason for this is that there is a significant reliance on considerable health measures. It is of the utmost importance that the necessary steps be taken in order to safeguard the privacy of individuals while simultaneously making the most of the advantages that Robo Advisors provide in the realm of insurance planning. The establishment of robust cyber security frameworks, tough encryption methods, and ethical norms for the utilization of data are all included in these steps. Additionally, the utilization of Robo Advisors calls for the installation of a concentrated effort to educate policyholders as well as insurers regarding the technology. This is a requirement that must be met. With that being said, it is of the utmost need to have communication that is both open and honest regarding the operation of these systems, the advantages that they provide, and the ethical considerations that are involved. Individuals are able to make well-informed decisions on their healthcare coverage as a result of this, which not only helps to establish confidence in the automated procedures but also contributes to the process of ensuring that the procedures are carried out correctly.

It is feasible to arrive at the conclusion that the adoption of automated health guardianship through the utilization of Robo Advisors in the process of insurance planning represents an essential and transformative step in the progression of healthcare. This conclusion can be reached after thorough analysis. Not only can the combination of technology and insurance lead to a significant gain in terms of both efficiency and cost, but it also ushers in a new era of care that is both individualized and preventative in nature. A huge step forward in the field of healthcare has been taken by this endeavor. It is of the utmost importance that we continue to be cautious when dealing with moral problems, ensuring the protection of data, and developing public knowledge of the possibilities and constraints of these automated systems. At the same time that we are in the process of accepting this fundamental shift in thinking, it is absolutely necessary that we continue to be cautious because it contains the promise of a healthcare system that is not only responsive but also proactive and focused on the individual, this path towards a future in which technology is seamlessly integrated with health guardianship is a promising path to follow. This path is a promising path to take because it carries the promise of a hopeful future. It is really interesting to think about the possibilities of this happening.

REFERENCES

Adelodun, B., Agbelusi, O.O., Soma, T., Odey, G., Adeyi, Q., Kumar, P., Ajibade, F.O., Goala, M., Silva, L.F.O., Mostafa, Y.S., Singh, R., Choi, K.S., Eid, E.M. (2024). Rethinking food loss and waste to promote sustainable resource use and climate change mitigation in agri-food systems: A review. *Waste Manag. Res.,* 0734242X241257655.
[http://dx.doi.org/10.1177/0734242X241257655] [PMID: 39078041]

Adhikari, P., Jain, R., Sharma, A., Pandey, A. (2021). Plant Growth Promotion at Low Temperature by Phosphate-Solubilizing Pseudomonas Spp. Isolated from High-Altitude Himalayan Soil. *Microb. Ecol., 82*(3), 677-687.
[http://dx.doi.org/10.1007/s00248-021-01702-1] [PMID: 33512536]

Agarwal, M., Gill, K.S., Upadhyay, D., Devliyal, S. (2024). International Conference on Intelligent Systems for Cybersecurity, ISCS *Institute of Electrical and Electronics Engineers Inc.*
[http://dx.doi.org/10.1109/ISCS61804.2024.10581100]

Alemu, W.K., Worku, L.A., Bachheti, R.K., Bachheti, A., Engida, A.M. (2024). Exploring Phytochemical Profile, Pharmaceutical Activities, and Medicinal and Nutritional Value of Wild Edible Plants in Ethiopia. *Int. J. Food Sci., 2024*(1), 6408892.
[http://dx.doi.org/10.1155/2024/6408892] [PMID: 39105166]

Badawy, A.A., Husen, A., Salem, S.S. (2024). Use of nanobiotechnology in augmenting soil–plant system interaction for higher plant growth and production. *Essential Minerals in Plant-Soil Systems: Coordination, Signaling, and Interaction under Adverse Situations.*
[http://dx.doi.org/10.1016/B978-0-443-16082-0.00006-0]

Banerjee, D., Kukreja, V., Sharma, V., Manwal, M., Jindal, V. (2023). An Ensemble Approach of CNN and SVM for Precise Classification of Sweet Corn Leaf Diseases. *14th International Conference on Computing Communication and Networking Technologies, ICCCNT.* [http://dx.doi.org/10.1109/ICCCNT56998.2023.10306754]

Banerjee, D., Sharma, N., Chauhan, R., Singh, M., Kumar, B.V. (2024). A Deep Dive into Precision Horticulture: Unravelling Olive Peacock Spot Intensity with Hybrid Deep Learning. *5th International Conference for Emerging Technology, INCET.* [http://dx.doi.org/10.1109/INCET61516.2024.10593619]

Banerjee, D., Sharma, N., Upadhyay, D., Singh, M., Chythanya, K.R. (2024). Decoding Sunflower Downy Mildew: Leveraging Hybrid Deep Learning for Scale Severity Analysis. *5th International Conference for Emerging Technology, INCET.* [http://dx.doi.org/10.1109/INCET61516.2024.10592879]

Barthwal, R., Kathuria, D., Joshi, S., Kaler, R.S.S., Singh, N. (2024). New trends in the development and application of artificial intelligence in food processing. *Innov. Food Sci. Emerg. Technol., 92*, 103600. [http://dx.doi.org/10.1016/j.ifset.2024.103600]

Bhatnagar, P., Gururani, P., Bisht, B., Kumar, V., Kumar, N., Joshi, R., Vlaskin, M.S. (2022). Impact of irradiation on physico-chemical and nutritional properties of fruits and vegetables: A mini review. *Heliyon, 8*(10), e10918. [http://dx.doi.org/10.1016/j.heliyon.2022.e10918] [PMID: 36247116]

Bisht, B., Begum, J.P.S., Dmitriev, A.A., Kurbatova, A., Singh, N., Nishinari, K., Nanda, M., Kumar, S., Vlaskin, M.S., Kumar, V. (2024). Unlocking the potential of future version 3D food products with next generation microalgae blue protein integration: A review. *Trends Food Sci. Technol., 147*, 104471. [http://dx.doi.org/10.1016/j.tifs.2024.104471]

Chakravorty, M., Nanda, M., Arora, N., Singh, S., Kumar, V., Deshwal, S. (2022). CRISPR-Cas9 mediated genome tailoring to improve nutritional quality and shelf life in crops: A review. *Plant Gene, 31*, 100369. [http://dx.doi.org/10.1016/j.plgene.2022.100369]

Chauhan, M., Rani, A., Joshi, S., Sharma, P.K. (2023). Role of psychrophilic and psychrotolerant microorganisms toward the development of hill agriculture. *Advanced Microbial Technology for Sustainable Agriculture and Environment.* [http://dx.doi.org/10.1016/B978-0-323-95090-9.00002-9]

Debasis, M., Ganeshamurthy, A.N., Komal, S., Radha, T.K., Rupa, T.R. (2020). Plant growth promotion and biocontrol activity of some typical harsh environment rhizo-microbes and their effects on Amaranthus cruentus plants. *Res. J. Biotechnol., 15*(1), 35-45.

Dhawan, N., Sharma, R., Chattopadhyay, S., Choudhary, A., Jain, V. (2024). Enhancing Green Bean Anthracnose Severity Detection via Integrated CNN-LSTM Models. *4th International Conference on Intelligent Technologies, CONIT.* [http://dx.doi.org/10.1109/CONIT61985.2024.10626282]

Dhawan, N., Sharma, R., Rana, D.S., Garg, A. (2024). Precision Agricultural Classification of Indian Turnip Varieties: CNN and Naive Bayes Methodologies. *5th International Conference for Emerging Technology, INCET.* [http://dx.doi.org/10.1109/INCET61516.2024.10593527]

Dhayal, K.S., Agrawal, S., Agrawal, R., Kumar, A., Giri, A.K. (2024). Green energy innovation initiatives for environmental sustainability: current state and future research directions. *Environ. Sci. Pollut. Res. Int., 31*(22), 31752-31770. [http://dx.doi.org/10.1007/s11356-024-33286-x] [PMID: 38656717]

Duong, L., Kumar, V., Van Binh, T. (2024). Supply chain collaboration in the food industry: a literature review. *Future Food Systems: Exploring Global Production, Processing, Distribution and Consumption.* [http://dx.doi.org/10.1016/B978-0-443-15690-8.00007-2]

Elbagory, M., El-Nahrawy, S., Omara, A.E.D., Eid, E.M., Bachheti, A., Kumar, P., Abou Fayssal, S., Adelodun, B., Bachheti, R.K., Kumar, P., Mioč, B., Kumar, V., Širić, I. (2022). Sustainable Bioconversion of Wetland Plant Biomass for Pleurotus ostreatus var. florida Cultivation: Studies on Proximate and Biochemical Characterization. *Agriculture, 12*(12), 2095.
[http://dx.doi.org/10.3390/agriculture12122095]

Ganesan, R., Manjula, G., Chandan, M., Thamarai, I., Rajavelu, S., Bhatt, U.M., Sarkar, S. (2023). Application of Deep Neural Networks for Weed Detection and Classification. *Proceedings of the 2nd International Conference on Applied Artificial Intelligence and Computing, ICAAIC 2023,* 1014-1024.
[http://dx.doi.org/10.1109/ICAAIC56838.2023.10140235]

Garg, S., Nain, P., Kumar, A., Joshi, S., Punetha, H., Sharma, P.K., Siddiqui, S., Alshaharni, M.O., Algopishi, U.B., Mittal, A. (2024). Next generation plant biostimulants & genome sequencing strategies for sustainable agriculture development. *Front. Microbiol., 15*, 1439561.
[http://dx.doi.org/10.3389/fmicb.2024.1439561] [PMID: 39104588]

Govindharaj, I., Thapliyal, N., Aeri, M., Kukreja, V., Sharma, R. (2024). Onion Purple Blotch Disease Severity Grading: Leveraging a CNN-VGG16 Hybrid Model for Multi-Level Assessment. *International Conference on Innovations and Challenges in Emerging Technologies, ICICET 2024.*
[http://dx.doi.org/10.1109/ICICET59348.2024.10616332]

Gupta, A.K., Kumar, V., Naik, B., Mishra, P. (2024). Edible Flowers: Health Benefits, Nutrition, Processing, and Applications. *Edible Flowers: Health Benefits, Nutrition, Processing, and Applications.*
[http://dx.doi.org/10.1016/C2022-0-02601-5]

Gupta, P., Gopal, S., Sharma, M., Joshi, S., Sahani, C., Ahalawat, K. (2023). Agriculture Informatics and Communication: Paradigm of E-Governance and Drone Technology for Crop Monitoring. *9th International Conference on Smart Computing and Communications: Intelligent Technologies and Applications, ICSCC,* 113-118.
[http://dx.doi.org/10.1109/ICSCC59169.2023.10335058]

Gupta, S., Verma, D., Tufchi, N., Kamboj, A., Bachheti, A., Bachheti, R.K., Husen, A. (2021). Food, fodder and fuelwoods from forest. *Non-Timber Forest Products: Food, Healthcare and Industrial Applications..* Springer International Publishing.
[http://dx.doi.org/10.1007/978-3-030-73077-2_17]

Gusain, R., Vidyarthi, A., Prakash, R., Shukla, A.K. (2022). Statistical Analysis of Positional Variations of NavIc Receiver. *International Conference on Advances in Computing, Communication and Materials, ICACCM 2022.* Institute of Electrical and Electronics Engineers Inc..
[http://dx.doi.org/10.1109/ICACCM56405.2022.10009498]

Gusain, R., Vidyarthi, A., Prakash, R., Shukla, A.K. (2023). Assessing Seasonal Variations in CEP for NavIC Positioning in Dehradun Region. *5th International Conference on Energy, Power, and Environment: Towards Flexible Green Energy Technologies, ICEPE.*
[http://dx.doi.org/10.1109/ICEPE57949.2023.10201493]

Harbola, G., Rawat, M.S., Gupta, A., Gupta, R. (2024). Intelligent Diagnosis of Potato Leaf Diseases using Deep Learning. *Proceedings - 2024 4th International Conference on Pervasive Computing and Social Networking, ICPCSN,* 372-377.
[http://dx.doi.org/10.1109/ICPCSN62568.2024.00065]

Jain, I., Kaur, R., Kumar, A., Paul, M., Singh, N. (2024). Emerging protein sources and novel extraction techniques: a systematic review on sustainable approaches. *Int. J. Food Sci. Technol., 59*(10), 6797-6820.
[http://dx.doi.org/10.1111/ijfs.17466]

Jain, R., Kukreja, V., Chattopadhyay, S., Verma, A., Sharma, R. (2024). Hierarchy in Disease Severity Classification in Banana Leaves through the Integration of Convolutional Neural Network and Decision Tree Models. *5th International Conference for Emerging Technology, INCET.*
[http://dx.doi.org/10.1109/INCET61516.2024.10593446]

Jain, R., Kukreja, V., Chattopadhyay, S., Verma, A., Sharma, R. (2024). Hybrid CNN-RNN Modelling for

Precisely Classifying the Seriousness of Mustard White Rust Disease at Five Levels. *5th International Conference for Emerging Technology, INCET.*
[http://dx.doi.org/10.1109/INCET61516.2024.10593033]

Jaswal, N., Kukreja, V., Sharma, R., Chaudhary, P., Garg, A. (2023). Citrus Leaf Scab Multi-Class Classification: A Hybrid Deep Learning Model for Precision Agriculture. *4th IEEE Global Conference for Advancement in Technology, GCAT.*
[http://dx.doi.org/10.1109/GCAT59970.2023.10353507]

Joshi, A., Gupta, A.K., Mansi, , Semwal, S., Deoli, N., Rather, M.A., Naik, B., Kumar, V., Jha, A.K., Rustagi, S., Preet, M.S. (2024). Sustainable solutions for food security: Evaluating pre-treatment technologies in the growing fruits and vegetables industry of India. *Sustain. Chem. Pharm., 39*, 101580.
[http://dx.doi.org/10.1016/j.scp.2024.101580]

Joshi, N.C., Gururani, P. (2023). A mini review on heavy metal contamination in vegetable crops. *Int. J. Environ. Anal. Chem.*
[http://dx.doi.org/10.1080/03067319.2023.2210058]

Juyal, P., Sharma, S. (2021). Strawberry Plant's Health Detection for Organic Farming Using Unmanned Aerial Vehicle. *Proceedings of the 2021 IEEE International Conference on Innovative Computing, Intelligent Communication and Smart Electrical Systems, ICSES.*
[http://dx.doi.org/10.1109/ICSES52305.2021.9633825]

Kamal, S., Shende, V.G., Swaroopa, K., Bindhu Madhavi, P., Akram, P.S., Pant, K., Patil, S.D., Sahile, K. (2022). FCN Network-Based Weed and Crop Segmentation for IoT-Aided Agriculture Applications. *Wirel. Commun. Mob. Comput., 2022*, 1-10.
[http://dx.doi.org/10.1155/2022/2770706]

Kamal, S., Shobha, K.R., Francis, F., Khilar, R., Tripathi, V., Lakshminarayana, M., Kannadasan, B., Sahile, K. (2022). IOT Automation with Segmentation Techniques for Detection of Plant Seedlings in Agriculture. *Wirel. Commun. Mob. Comput., 2022*, 1-10.
[http://dx.doi.org/10.1155/2022/6466555]

Katyal, M., Thakur, S., Singh, N., Khatkar, B.S., Shishodia, S.K. (2024). A review of wheat chapatti: Quality attributes and shelf stability parameters. *Food Chem. Adv., 4*, 100736.
[http://dx.doi.org/10.1016/j.focha.2024.100736]

Kaur, A., Kukreja, V., Kumar, M., Choudhary, A., Sharma, R. (2024). A Fine-tuned Deep Learning-based VGG16 Model for Cotton Leaf Disease Classification. *5th International Conference for Emerging Technology, INCET.*
[http://dx.doi.org/10.1109/INCET61516.2024.10593164]

Kaur, A., Kukreja, V., Thapliyal, N., Thapliyal, S., Sharma, R. (2024). Bridging Precision in Severity Classification: Siamese CNN Model for Sequoia Cypress Canker in Five Degrees. *5th International Conference for Emerging Technology, INCET.*
[http://dx.doi.org/10.1109/INCET61516.2024.10593359]

Kaur, A., Sharma, R., Rana, D.S., Garg, A. (2024). Unveiling Kale Diversity in Indian Agriculture: CNN-Logistic Regression Classification. *5th International Conference for Emerging Technology, INCET .*
[http://dx.doi.org/10.1109/INCET61516.2024.10593127]

Kaur, A., Sharma, R., Thapliyal, N., Manwal, M. (2024). Broccoli Classification: A Fusion of CNN and AdaBoost. *1st International Conference on Electronics, Computing, Communication and Control Technology, ICECCC.*
[http://dx.doi.org/10.1109/ICECCC61767.2024.10593946]

Kaur, A., Sharma, R., Upadhyay, D., Aeri, M. (2024). Integrating Convolutional Neural Networks and Random Forest for Accurate Grading of Rice Spot Disease Severity. *5th International Conference for Emerging Technology, INCET.*
[http://dx.doi.org/10.1109/INCET61516.2024.10593360]

Kaur, R., Gupta, S., Tripathi, V., Bharadwaj, A. (2024). Unravelling the secrets of soil microbiome and climate change for sustainable agroecosystems. *Folia Microbiol. (Praha).* [http://dx.doi.org/10.1007/s12223-024-01194-9] [PMID: 39249146]

Kaushik, P., Jain, E., Gill, K.S., Upadhyay, D., Devliyal, S. (2024). Comparative Analysis of Cassava Leaf Disease Prediction Using the Deep Learning Approach. *2nd International Conference on Sustainable Computing and Smart Systems, ICSCSS 2024 - Proceedings,* 1369-1373. [http://dx.doi.org/10.1109/ICSCSS60660.2024.10625585]

Kholiya, D., Bagla, P., Mishra, A.K., Tripathi, N., Pandey, N.K. (2023). Sustainable Development of Smart Farming and Agriculture Business using Data Mining. *ICSCCC 2023 - 3rd International Conference on Secure Cyber Computing and Communications,* 75-80. [http://dx.doi.org/10.1109/ICSCCC58608.2023.10176431]

Khosravi, H., Khoshru, B., Nosratabad, A.F., Mitra, D. (2024). Exploring the landscape of biofertilizers containing plant growth-promoting rhizobacteria in Iran: Progress and research prospects. *Curr. Res. Microb. Sci., 7,* 100268. [http://dx.doi.org/10.1016/j.crmicr.2024.100268] [PMID: 39569074]

Kukreti, B., Chaudhary, P., Sharma, A. (2024). Visualization of synergistic interaction between inorganic nanoparticle and bioinoculants. *Vegetos.* [http://dx.doi.org/10.1007/s42535-024-01022-y]

Kumar, G., Kumar, A., Singhal, M., Singh, K.U., Kumar, L., Singh, T. (2023). Revolutionizing Plant Disease Management Through Image Processing Technology. *Proceedings of International Conference on Computational Intelligence and Sustainable Engineering Solution, CISES,* 521-528. [http://dx.doi.org/10.1109/CISES58720.2023.10183408]

Kumar, R.R., Jain, A.K., Sharma, V., Midha, M., Das, P. (2024). Enhancing Crop Health, A Novel CNN-SVM Hybrid Model for Litchi Disease Detection. *5th International Conference for Emerging Technology, INCET.* [http://dx.doi.org/10.1109/INCET61516.2024.10593343]

Kumar, V., Banerjee, D., Upadhyay, D., Singh, M., Chythanya, K.R. (2024). Hybrid CNN & Random Forest Model for Effective Fenugreek Leaf Disease Diagnosis. *International Conference on E-Mobility, Power Control and Smart Systems: Futuristic Technologies for Sustainable Solutions, ICEMPS.* [http://dx.doi.org/10.1109/ICEMPS60684.2024.10559333]

Kumar, V., Banerjee, D., Upadhyay, D., Singh, M., Chythanya, K.R. (2024). Hybrid CNN & Random Forest Model for Effective Marigold Leaf Disease Diagnosis. *International Conference on E-Mobility, Power Control and Smart Systems: Futuristic Technologies for Sustainable Solutions, ICEMPS.* [http://dx.doi.org/10.1109/ICEMPS60684.2024.10559285]

Kumar, V., Raj, R., Verma, P., Garza-Reyes, J.A., Shah, B. (2024). Assessing risk and sustainability factors in spice supply chain management. *Oper. Manage. Res. Adv. Pract. Through Res., 17*(1), 233-252. [http://dx.doi.org/10.1007/s12063-023-00424-6]

Kunwar, S., Bhatt, S., Pandey, D., Pandey, N. (2021). Field Application of the Microbial Technology and Its Importance in Sustainable Development. *Microbial Technology for Sustainable Environment..* Springer Nature. [http://dx.doi.org/10.1007/978-981-16-3840-4_20]

Mahajan, M., Upadhyay, D., Aeri, M., Kukreja, V., Sharma, R. (2024). Advancing Agricultural Health: Hybrid CNN-SVM Framework for Classifying Tomato Diseases. *IEEE 9th International Conference for Convergence in Technology, I2CT.* [http://dx.doi.org/10.1109/I2CT61223.2024.10544232]

Malhotra, R.K., Ojha, M.K., Gupta, S. (2021). A study of assessment of knowledge, perception and attitude of using tele health services among college going students of Uttarakhand. *Journal of Medical pharmaceutical and allied sciences, 10,* 113-116. [http://dx.doi.org/10.22270/jmpas.VIC2I1.2020]

Mangla, S.K., Sharma, Y.K., Patil, P.P., Yadav, G., Xu, J. (2019). Logistics and distribution challenges to

managing operations for corporate sustainability: Study on leading Indian diary organizations. *J. Clean. Prod., 238*, 117620.
[http://dx.doi.org/10.1016/j.jclepro.2019.117620]

Mir, T.A., Banerjee, D., Aggarwal, P., Rawat, R.S., Sunil, G. (2024). Improved Potato Disease Classification: Synergy of CNN and SVM Models. *5th International Conference for Emerging Technology, INCET.*
[http://dx.doi.org/10.1109/INCET61516.2024.10593106]

Mitra, D., Saritha, B., Janeeshma, E., Gusain, P., Khoshru, B., Abo Nouh, F.A., Rani, A., Olatunbosun, A.N., Ruparelia, J., Rabari, A., Mosquera-Sánchez, L.P., Mondal, R., Verma, D., Panneerselvam, P., Das Mohapatra, P.K., Guerra Sierra, B.E. (2022). Arbuscular mycorrhizal fungal association boosted the arsenic resistance in crops with special responsiveness to rice plant. *Environ. Exp. Bot., 193*
[http://dx.doi.org/10.1016/j.envexpbot.2021.104681]

Mudholkar, M., Mudholkar, P., Dornadula, V.H.R., Sreenivasulu, K., Joshi, K., Pant, B. (2022). A Novel Approach to IoT based Plant Health Monitoring System in Smart Agriculture. *Proceedings of 5th International Conference on Contemporary Computing and Informatics, IC3I 2022,* 113-116.
[http://dx.doi.org/10.1109/IC3I56241.2022.10072603]

Naik, B., Kumar, V., Rizwanuddin, S., Mishra, S., Kumar, V., Saris, P.E.J., Khanduri, N., Kumar, A., Pandey, P., Gupta, A.K., Khan, J.M., Rustagi, S. (2024). Biofortification as a solution for addressing nutrient deficiencies and malnutrition. *Heliyon, 10*(9), e30595.
[http://dx.doi.org/10.1016/j.heliyon.2024.e30595] [PMID: 38726166]

Nijhawan, R., Jain, K. (2018). Glacier terminus position monitoring and modelling using remote sensing data. *Commun. Comput. Inf. Sci., 906*, 11-23.
[http://dx.doi.org/10.1007/978-981-13-1813-9_2]

Ojha, N.K., Thapliyal, N., Aeri, M., Kukreja, V., Sharma, R. (2024). CNN-VGG16 Hybrid Model for Onion Purple Blotch Disease Severity Multi-Level Grading. *5th International Conference for Emerging Technology, INCET.*
[http://dx.doi.org/10.1109/INCET61516.2024.10593453]

Ojha, N.K., Upadhyay, D., Aeri, M., Kukreja, V., Sharma, R. (2024). Optimizing Anthracnose Severity Grading in Green Beans with CNN-LSTM Integration. *5th International Conference for Emerging Technology, INCET.*
[http://dx.doi.org/10.1109/INCET61516.2024.10593573]

Ojha, N.K., Upadhyay, D., Manwal, M., Kukreja, V., Sharma, R. (2024). Implementing CNN and RF Models for Multi-Level Classification: Deciphering Beetroot Aphid Disease Severity. *5th International Conference for Emerging Technology, INCET.*
[http://dx.doi.org/10.1109/INCET61516.2024.10593519]

Pal, A.K., Patro, B.D.K., Chaudhary, P. (2024). An Improved Analysis of Weed Prediction in Precision Agriculture using Deep Learning. *Proceedings of International Conference on Communication, Computer Sciences and Engineering, IC3SE 2024,* 936-941.
[http://dx.doi.org/10.1109/IC3SE62002.2024.10593570]

Pargaien, S., Pargaien, A. V. (2024). Deep Learning Inclusion in Plant Diseases, Inflicting a Disparate Insight. *Lecture Notes in Networks and Systems, 1020 LNNS,* 209-226.
[http://dx.doi.org/10.1007/978-981-97-3588-4_18]

Pargaien, S., Prakash, R., Dubey, V.P. (2021). Wheat Crop Classification based on NDVI using Sentinel Time Series: A Case Study Saharanpur Region. *International Conference on Computing, Communication and Green Engineering, CCGE.*
[http://dx.doi.org/10.1109/CCGE50943.2021.9776445]

Patil, S.P., Singh, B., Bisht, J., Gupta, S., Khanna, R. (2021). Yoga for holistic treatment of polycystic ovarian syndrome. *Journal of Medical Pharmaceutical and Allied Sciences, 10*, 120-125.
[http://dx.doi.org/10.22270/jmpas.VIC2I1.2035]

Pokhariya, H.S., Singh, D.P., Prakash, R. (2022). Investigating the impacts of urbanization on different land

cover classes and land surface temperature using GIS and RS techniques. *International Journal of System Assurance Engineering and Management, 13*(S2), 961-969.
[http://dx.doi.org/10.1007/s13198-021-01512-1]

Rajora, R., Gupta, H., Malhotra, S., Devliyal, S., Sunil, G. (2024). Deep Learning for Precise Rice Multi-Class Classification:Unveiling the Potential of CNNs. *International Conference on E-Mobility, Power Control and Smart Systems: Futuristic Technologies for Sustainable Solutions, ICEMPS.*
[http://dx.doi.org/10.1109/ICEMPS60684.2024.10559367]

Rajput, K., Manwal, M., Chauhan, R. K., Kukreja, V., & Mehta, S. (2024). Transforming Sugarcane Leaf Diseases Pathology with Convolutional Neural Networks and SVM. In S. B., A. R., K. S.K., S. K.M., S. A.V., J. S., S. N., C. A., & G. R. (Eds.), *11th International Conference on Reliability, Infocom Technologies and Optimization (Trends and Future Directions), ICRITO*. Institute of Electrical and Electronics Engineers Inc.
[http://dx.doi.org/10.1109/ICRITO61523.2024.10522214]

Rani, A., Pundir, A., Verma, M., Joshi, S., Verma, G., Andjelković, S., Babić, S., Milenković, J., Mitra, D. (2024). Methanotrophy: A Biological Method to Mitigate Global Methane Emission. *Microbiol. Res. (Pavia), 15*(2), 634-654.
[http://dx.doi.org/10.3390/microbiolres15020042]

Rather, M.A., Thakur, R., Hoque, M., Das, R.S., Lima Miki, K.S., Teixeira-Costa, B.E., Mishra, P., Gupta, A.K. (2023). Sorghum (Sorghum bicolor): Phytochemical Composition, Bio- Functional, and Technological Characteristics. *Nutri-Cereals: Nutraceutical and Techno-Functional Potential.*
[http://dx.doi.org/10.1201/9781003251279-3]

Rawat, K. S., Singh, S. K., Ray, R. L., Szabo, S. (2020). Parameterization of the modified water cloud model (MWCM) using normalized difference vegetation index (NDVI) for winter wheat crop: a case study from Punjab, India. *Geocarto International,* 1-14.
[http://dx.doi.org/10.1080/10106049.2020.1783579]

Rawat, K.S., Singh, S.K., Ray, R.L., Szabó, S., Kumar, S. (2020). Parameterizing the modified water cloud model to improve soil moisture data retrieval using vegetation models. *Hungarian Geographical Bulletin, 69*(1), 17-26.
[http://dx.doi.org/10.15201/hungeobull.69.1.2]

Ray, A., Kundu, S., Mohapatra, S.S., Sinha, S., Khoshru, B., Keswani, C., Mitra, D. (2024). An Insight into the Role of Phenolics in Abiotic Stress Tolerance in Plants: Current Perspective for Sustainable Environment. *J. Pure Appl. Microbiol., 18*(1), 64-79.
[http://dx.doi.org/10.22207/JPAM.18.1.09]

Saikumar, A., Singh, A., Dobhal, A., Arora, S., Junaid, P.M., Badwaik, L.S., Kumar, S. (2024). A review on the impact of physical, chemical, and novel treatments on the quality and microbial safety of fruits and vegetables. *Syst. Microbiol. Biomanuf., 4*(2), 575-597.
[http://dx.doi.org/10.1007/s43393-023-00217-9]

Samantaray, A., Chattaraj, S., Mitra, D., Ganguly, A., Kumar, R., Gaur, A., Mohapatra, P.K.D., Santos-Villalobos, S., Rani, A., Thatoi, H. (2024). Advances in microbial based bio-inoculum for amelioration of soil health and sustainable crop production. *Curr. Res. Microb. Sci., 7*, 100251.
[http://dx.doi.org/10.1016/j.crmicr.2024.100251] [PMID: 39165409]

Santoyo, G., Orozco-Mosqueda, M.C., Afridi, M.S., Mitra, D., Valencia-Cantero, E., Macías-Rodríguez, L. (2024). *Trichoderma and Bacillus* multifunctional allies for plant growth and health in saline soils: recent advances and future challenges. *Front. Microbiol., 15*, 1423980.
[http://dx.doi.org/10.3389/fmicb.2024.1423980] [PMID: 39176277]

Sar, A., Goel, A., Choudhury, T., Kotecha, K., Bhattacharya, A. (2024). A Novel Framework for Automatic Plant Disease Detection Using Convolutional Neural Networks. *Lecture Notes in Networks and Systems, 1025*, 483-497.
[http://dx.doi.org/10.1007/978-981-97-3594-5_40]

Semwal, P., Painuli, S., Jamloki, A., Rauf, A., Rahman, M.M., Olatunde, A., Hemeg, H.A., Abu-Izneid, T., Naz, S., Punia Bangar, S., Lorenzo, J.M., Simal-Gandara, J. (2023). Himalayan Wild Fruits as a Strong Source of Nutraceuticals, Therapeutics, Food and Nutrition Security. *Food Rev. Int., 39*(9), 6500-6536. [http://dx.doi.org/10.1080/87559129.2022.2121407]

Semwal, P., Painuli, S., Jugran, A., Palni, L.M.S., Verma, S., Thapliyal, A., Tewari, D. (2020). Genetic Diversity of Scanty Available Himalayan Saussurea obvallata (DC.) Edgew. *Iran. J. Sci. Technol. Trans. A Sci., 44*(3), 587-594. [http://dx.doi.org/10.1007/s40995-020-00862-y]

Shakya, A.K., Ramola, A., Sawant, K., Tiwari, S., Aarfin, S., Mittal, P. (2018). Visual Representation of Change in Vegetation Area of Dehradun, Uttarakhand, India using Normalized Difference Vegetation Index (NDVI). *2nd IEEE International Conference on Power Electronics, Intelligent Control and Energy Systems, ICPEICES,* 1087-1092. [http://dx.doi.org/10.1109/ICPEICES.2018.8897376]

Sharma, A., Kumar, V., Musunur, L.P. (2024). The Good, The Bad and The Ugly: An Open Image Dataset for Automated Sorting of Good, Bad, and Imperfect Produce Using AI and Robotics. *Sustainability (Basel), 16*(15), 6411. [http://dx.doi.org/10.3390/su16156411]

Sharma, H., Kukreja, V., Mehta, S., Nisha Chandran, S., Garg, A. (2024). Plant AI in Agriculture: Innovative Approaches to Sunflower Leaf Disease Detection with Federated Learning CNNs. *5th International Conference for Emerging Technology, INCET.* [http://dx.doi.org/10.1109/INCET61516.2024.10592966]

Sharma, M., Singh, P. (2023). Newly engineered nanoparticles as potential therapeutic agents for plants to ameliorate abiotic and biotic stress. *J. Appl. Nat. Sci., 15*(2), 720-731. [http://dx.doi.org/10.31018/jans.v15i2.4603]

Sharma, Y.K., Patil, P.P., Mangla, S.K. (2018). Analyzing risks in safety and security of food using grey relational analysis. *International Journal of Mechanical Engineering and Technology, 9*(12), 9-19.

Shashikala, R., Singh, B.P., Azam, M., Magesh, C.R. (2022). IoT Engineering Nanomaterial's Approach To Sustainable Advance Crop Production Management. *2nd International Conference on Advance Computing and Innovative Technologies in Engineering, ICACITE,* 2284-2288. [http://dx.doi.org/10.1109/ICACITE53722.2022.9823573]

Singh, D., Chand, K., Sahal, A., Kumar, S., Hussain, A. (2024). Optimization of fermentation parameters and their impact on the final properties of the cereal-legume-based fermented product. *J. Stored Prod. Res., 106*, 102302. [http://dx.doi.org/10.1016/j.jspr.2024.102302]

Singh, G., Aggarwal, R., Bhatnagar, V., Kumar, S., & Dhondiyal, S. A. (2024). Performance Evaluation of Cotton Leaf Disease Detection Using Deep Learning Models. In G. S.C., G. A.B., M. S., & L. U. (Eds.), *Proceedings - 2024 International Conference on Computational Intelligence and Computing Applications, ICCICA*, pp. 193 – 197. Institute of Electrical and Electronics Engineers Inc. [http://dx.doi.org/10.1109/ICCICA60014.2024.10584990]

Singh, P., Gargi, B., Semwal, P., Verma, S. (2024). Global research and research progress on climate change and their impact on plant phenology: 30 years of investigations through bibliometric analysis. *Theor. Appl. Climatol., 155*(6), 4909-4923. [http://dx.doi.org/10.1007/s00704-024-04919-5]

Sneha, S. (2023). Optimizing Cloud-Based Smart Agriculture. *International Conference on Computer Science and Emerging Technologies, CSET.* [http://dx.doi.org/10.1109/CSET58993.2023.10346687]

Srivastava, A., Rawat, B.S., Bajpai, P., Dhondiyal, S.A. (2024). Potato Leaf Disease Detection Method Based on the YOLO Model. *IEEE International Conference on Data Engineering and Communication Systems, ICDECS.*

[http://dx.doi.org/10.1109/ICDECS59733.2023.10502511]

Sunori, S.K., Kant, S., Agarwal, P., Juneja, P. (2023). Development of Rainfall Prediction Models using Linear and Non-linear Regression Techniques. *4th IEEE Global Conference for Advancement in Technology, GCAT.*
[http://dx.doi.org/10.1109/GCAT59970.2023.10353508]

Tamta, S., Vimal, V., Verma, S., Gupta, D., Verma, D., Nangan, S. (2024). Recent development of nanobiomaterials in sustainable agriculture and agrowaste management. *Biocatal. Agric. Biotechnol., 56,* 103050.
[http://dx.doi.org/10.1016/j.bcab.2024.103050]

Tanwar, V., Anand, V., Chauhan, R., Singh, M. (2024). A Standardized Method for Identifying and Categorizing Ladyfinger Diseases. *4th International Conference on Intelligent Technologies, CONIT.*
[http://dx.doi.org/10.1109/CONIT61985.2024.10626980]

Tina, P., Pant, M., Pant, K., Chauhan, A., Negi, A.S., Nainwal, P., Srivastava, A., Kumar, V. (2024). Molecular marker-assisted genetic diversity analysis in soybean cultivars from Himalayan region of Uttarakhand, India. *Ecol. Genet. Genom., 31*, 100237.
[http://dx.doi.org/10.1016/j.egg.2024.100237]

Tomar, S., Sharma, N. (2021). A systematic review of agricultural policies in terms of drivers, enablers, and bottlenecks: Comparison of three Indian states and a model bio-energy village located in different agro climatic regions. *Groundw. Sustain. Dev., 15*, 100683.
[http://dx.doi.org/10.1016/j.gsd.2021.100683]

Tomar, S., Sharma, N., Kumar, R. (2023). Effect of organic food production and consumption on the affective and cognitive well-being of farmers: analysis using prism of NVivo, etic and emic approach. *Environ. Dev. Sustain., 26*(5), 11027-11048.
[http://dx.doi.org/10.1007/s10668-023-03195-z] [PMID: 37363037]

Uniyal, A. K., Kanojia, P., Khanna, R., Dixit, A. K. (2022). Quantitative Analysis of the Impact of Demography and Job Profile on the Organizational Commitment of the Faculty Members in the HEI'S of Uttarakhand. *Communications in Computer and Information Science, 1742 CCIS,* 24-35.
[http://dx.doi.org/10.1007/978-3-031-23647-1_3]

Upadhyay, D., Aeri, M., Kukreja, V., Sharma, R. (2024). Improving Anthracnose Severity Grading in Green Beans through CNN-LSTM Integration. *International Conference on Innovations and Challenges in Emerging Technologies, ICICET.*
[http://dx.doi.org/10.1109/ICICET59348.2024.10616330]

Vashishth, D.S., Bachheti, A., Bachheti, R.K., Husen, A. (2023). Allelopathic effect of *Callistemon viminalis* 's leaves extract on weeds, soil features, and growth performance of wheat and chickpea plants. *J. Plant Interact., 18*(1), 2248172.
[http://dx.doi.org/10.1080/17429145.2023.2248172]

Verma, A., Zaheer, A., Ahsan, A., Anand, A., Abu Serhan, H., Nazli Khatib, M., Syed Zahiruddin, Q., Gaidhane, A.M., Kukreti, N., Rustagi, S., Satapathy, P., Sharma, D., Arora, M., Kumar Sharma, R. (2024). Noma in the WHO's list of neglected tropical diseases: A review of its impact on undeveloped and developing tropical regions. *Prev. Med. Rep., 43*, 102764.
[http://dx.doi.org/10.1016/j.pmedr.2024.102764] [PMID: 38826589]

Walia, N., Sharma, R., Kumar, M., Choudhary, A., Jain, V. (2024). Optimized VGG16 Model for Advanced Classification of Cotton Leaf Diseases. *4th International Conference on Intelligent Technologies, CONIT.*
[http://dx.doi.org/10.1109/CONIT61985.2024.10627057]

Yadav, A.K., Yadav, V., Malik, H., Khargotra, R., Singh, T. (2024). Design of novel IoT-based solar powered PV pumping systems for agricultural applications in diverse climatic zones of India. *Results Eng., 23*, 102584.
[http://dx.doi.org/10.1016/j.rineng.2024.102584]

Yadav, A. P. S., Thapliyal, N., Aeri, M., Kukreja, V., & Sharma, R. (2024). Advanced Deep Learning

Approaches: Utilizing VGG16, VGG19, and ResNet Architectures for Enhanced Grapevine Disease Detection. In S. B., A. R., K. S.K., S. K.M., S. A.V., J. S., S. N., C. A., & G. R. (Eds.), *11th International Conference on Reliability, Infocom Technologies and Optimization (Trends and Future Directions), ICRITO*, Institute of Electrical and Electronics Engineers Inc.
[http://dx.doi.org/10.1109/ICRITO61523.2024.10522276]

Yashu, S. (2024). From Field to Data: A Machine Learning Approach to Classifying Celery Varieties. *1st International Conference on Electronics, Computing, Communication and Control Technology, ICECCC 2024.*
[http://dx.doi.org/10.1109/ICECCC61767.2024.10593956]

CHAPTER 4

Rise of Robo Advising in Insurance

Prayank Sharma[1] and **Manish Singh**[1,*]

[1] *Swami Rama Himalayan University, Uttarakhand, India*

Abstract: Insurance is a healing ointment for every person, but it's better to go for insurance as a shock absorber for different types of shock in life.

People also take insurance to plan their lives, which helps them reduce tensions throughout life, but so many people also try to avoid taking insurance due to the long time and time-consuming operational procedures at various stages of their insured life. They need an assistant to reduce or resolve the operational problems related to buying policy, claim filing, and renewal of the policy. Traditional practices to resolve issues related to such problems include interaction with men either in the form of physical meetings or by communication through emails and telephones. The advent of the 21st century is the growth of automation in businesses, and the insurance industry is also adopting technology to reduce the issues related to claim settlement policy selling and understanding consumer behavior, which assists in policy selling. This chapter will visualize the growth of technology in the Indian insurance industry.

Keywords: Digitalization, Insure tech, Insure tech models, Insurance, Robo advising.

INTRODUCTION

The written traces of insurance in India can be seen in Manusmrithi, Dharmasastra, and Arhasastra. The concept of pooling resources to be redistributed in times of natural calamities was a precursor of modern-day insurance. The oldest medium of transport used by businesses was the sea. Therefore, marine insurance was the first type of insurance. The year 1818 was the year in which the Oriental Life Insurance Company in Calcutta was established, and later on, it failed in 1834. The Madras Equitable began its business in 1829. The British Insurance Act was enacted in 1870 (IRDA, 2007).

In Bombay residency, the Bombay Mutual (1871), Empire of India (1897), and Oriental 1874 were started. The period of the last three decades in the 19th century

* **Corresponding author Manish Singh:** Swami Rama Himalayan University, Uttarakhand, India;
E-mail: manishkrsingh79@rediffmail.com

Sanjay Taneja, Ercan Ozen, Luan Vardar, Mohit Kukreti & Mohammad Kashif (Eds.)

was the strong presence of foreign insurance offices, which did a profitable business in India. Companies like Albert Life Assurance, Royal Insurance, Liverpool, and London Globe Insurance were providing tough competition to Indian companies (IRDA, 2007).

In 1914, the government of India started publishing the returns of insurance companies. The Insurance Amendment Act of 1950 abolished principal agencies, and in 1955, the Life Insurance Company was incorporated (IAS, 2020).

The insurance industry is one of the various growing sectors of the economy. This growth is primarily due to the growth in incomes, increasing awareness among the people, and the pandemic. The Indian insurance sector is the fifth among the world's emerging life insurance markets; the growth rate is approx. 32-34 percent each year. Some major variables of the growth are the Introduction of foreign direct investment, the launch of innovative products by private players, and the liberal licensing policy by the Insurance Regulatory and Development Authority of India (IBEF, 2023).

The Indian insurance industry comprises 57 companies, out of which 24 are life insurers, and 33 are non-life insurers. Some of these are government companies, and some are private players. All these companies are regulated by the Insurance and Regulatory Development Authority of India (IRDAI). Apart from insurance companies, there are various other intermediaries in the industry, like brokers, surveyors, and third-party administrators servicing health insurance claims.

The year 2000 was the year of the advent of the Indian insurance industry, which gained momentum due to factors like the liberal policy of FDI and the Introduction of new private companies. It is expected that the Indian Insurance market will reach US$ 222 billion by 2026.

Digitalization of Insurance

Changing consumer behavior is a challenge that can be addressed through the integration of digital strategy. In the studies, seven variables were identified for a successful digital transformation. A multi-stage model is also required to formulate a digitization strategy.

Indian Insurance Industry: Structure

The insurance industry is governed by the Ministry of Finance as shown in Fig. (**1**). The Ministry of Finance framed a body named the Insurance Regulatory and Development Authority of India in the year 2000 with the aim of protecting policy holder's interests. It is an autonomous body that regulates the industry by registering /licensing insurance, reinsurance, and insurance intermediaries. The major objectives of the body are to ensure speedy claim settlement and prevent insurance fraud and other malpractices (Barthwal *et al.* 2024).

The Life Insurance Corporation was established on 1 September 1956 with the objective of spreading insurance across the nation and providing financial cover to the maximum population of the country. General Insurance Corporation was formed on 22 November 1972 as a private limited company. The objective of the General Insurance Council was to supervise, regulate, and control the general insurance business.

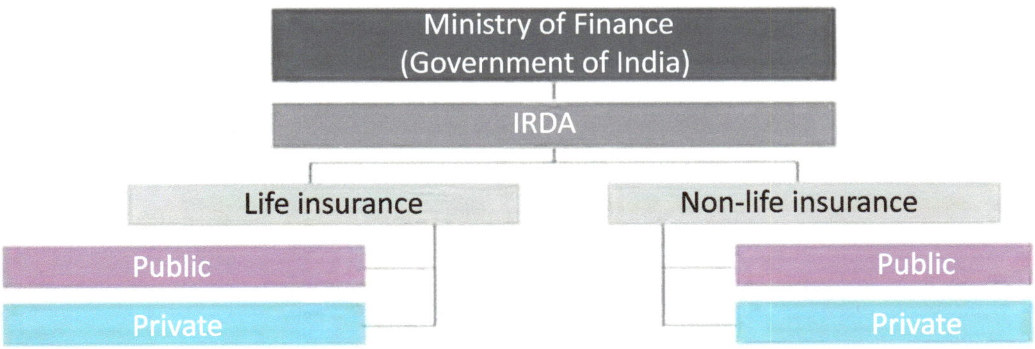

Fig. (1). Insurance industry structure. Source: Insurance regulatory and development authority of india

Market Size

The market size of the insurance industry comprises new business premiums and renewal premiums presents in Fig. (**2**). New business premium refers to the premium earned by insurance companies by selling their products. On the other hand, the renewal premium refers to the premium earned by retaining the customers (NR, 2017).

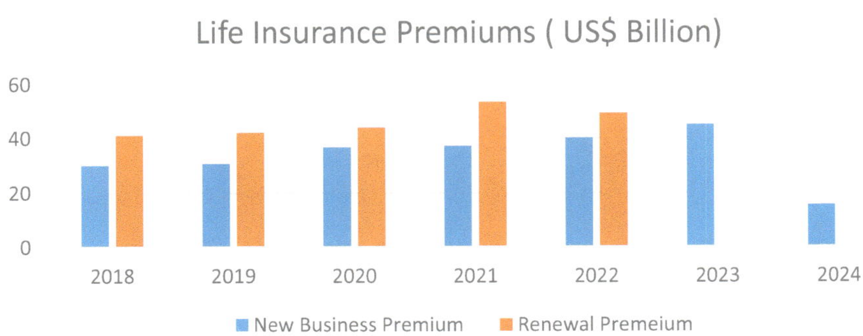

Fig. (2). Industry size. Source: IBEF: Life insurance premiums (US$ billion).

The (Fig. **3**) reveals that in the life insurance business, the premium earned by new business premium is approx. Forty-five billion dollars in the year 2022-23, and the premium earned through renewal business is approx. 49.2 million dollars in the year. It also reveals the rising trend from the financial year 2018. The same figures were 30.1 billion US$ and 41 US$ in 2018, which increased to 30.7 and 42 billion dollars in 2019. The rising premium trends led to the contribution of the insurance industry to the gross domestic product of approximately 2.9%.

Insurance Sector's Share Of Gross Domestic Product (GDP), 2018-2021 ($billions)			
Insurance carriers and related activities			
Year	**Gross Domestic Product**	**Gross Domestic Product**	**Percent of total Gross Domestic Product**
2018	20527.20	590.7	2.9
2019	21372.60	604.5	2.8
2020	20893.70	640.3	3.1
2021	22,996.10	674.2	2.9

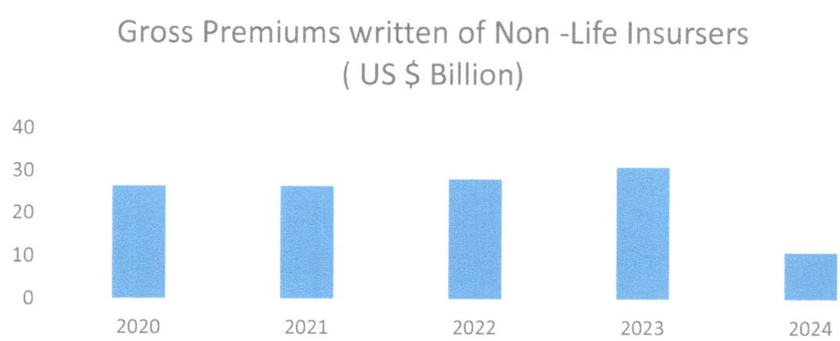

Fig. (3). Industry size general insurance. Source: IBEF: Gross Premiums Written off Non-Life Insurers (US$ Billion).

The non-life business is also showing a growing trend and reached 31 billion US dollars in the year 2022-23. In comparison, 26.49 billion US $ was spent in the year 2019-20.

The non-life insurance business is categorized under health insurance, motor insurance, fire insurance, personal accident, and marine insurance.

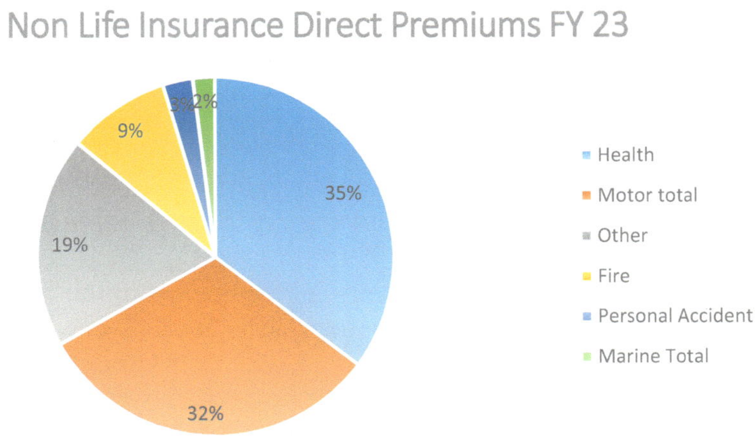

Fig. (4). Industry size general insurance. Source: IBEF: Non-Life Insurance Gross Direct Premiums

The (Fig. **4**) presents that majority of premiums come from health insurance, which is about 35.29 percent of the total, and the second contributor is motor insurance, which contributes up to 31.64 percent of general insurance business in total, both motor and health insurance, which contribute approximately 67 percent of the total non-life insurance gross direct premiums (Singhal, Goyal & Singhal, 2020).

INSURE TECH

The Indian insurance industry is on the rise and showing an increasing trend in the economy. In this growth, information and technology play an important role (Kour *et al.*, 2021). The dominance of technology in the sector led to the invention of the new sector named insure tech, which is the dimension of the use of technology in insurance (Joshi, *et al.*, 2022).

Insure tech controls the various aspects of business like product generation, product distribution, and administration. It also generates leads for sale promotion in the business. The larger proportion of the population of the country is tech savvy, and the increased use of smartphones and the internet are the triggers for the insure tech companies to create an attractive market for insure tech companies. These companies are also providing innovative insurance solutions (Kashif *et al.*, 2024). Estimates value India's insurance tech market opportunity as high as $339 billion. The scope of insurance tech companies becomes wider, which is beyond the telematics and customer risk assessment (Mehra *et al.* 2023). Currently, more than 110 insurance tech startups are operating in India. Some prominent trends in insurance tech are digital distribution channels, data analytics and artificial intelligence, the Internet of Things, health and wellness programs, peer-to-peer insurance, and regulatory sandboxes (Chauhan *et al.*, 2018).

ROBO ADVISING MEANING

The term robo advisory refers to a digital platform that offers robotic, algorithm-driven investment and financial planning facilities. Robo advising means taking the help of robots to assist customers and prospective customers with various pre and post-purchase queries, which help them in purchase decisions (Guo *et al.*, 2020). This technology is used by various companies in the form of a chat box. It started in the form of IVR services there, after it advanced to chat box services, and now it is robo advising (Avikal *et al.* 2023). It combines advanced software algorithms with machine learning and AI to assist investors in investment advice and portfolio services. These services provide assistance to customers to resolve basic queries and reduce the time and workforce needed to take care of customer queries.

Working Methodology of ROBO Advisors

The robo-advisors collect information on financial status and insurance goals through online questionnaires. This information is analyzed through software processes and applied to the financial planning models (Mahate *et al.* 2023). There, it matches the preferences of customers with the products available with the company and suggests the best-suited product for the prospective customer.

Types of ROBO Advisory

Automated Investments

In this category, the customer has to select among the predesigned packages. Scrip Box is one such platform that provides customers with their products, and the customers have to select among those products only (Badhotiya *et al.* 2022).

Direct Plan Based

In this category of robo advising, the companies charge convenience fees and charge transaction charges for the availing services. Companies like bharosaclub.com, orowealth.com, and invezta.com offer direct plan-based advice to customers.

Goal-Based Advisory

In this category of advising, the companies offer asset allocation on the basis of the information provided by the investor (Avikal *et al.* 2021). The advisory is of a basic nature, and the decision to choose a product is totally dependent on the customer.

Full Service

In this category, the full service, as requested by the customer, is provided by the advisor. Information like risk appetite, saving pattern, investment, and expenditure is collected through a questionnaire and processed through software, and investment suggestions are provided.

All types of robo-advising services are in use in the mutual fund industry and portfolio services (Singh *et al.*, 2023).

Robo Advisory Models

Robo-advising is not a new concept in developed economies. Some of the prevailing models in different countries by different companies can be categorized in the areas of software development, machine learning, distribution, technology providers, and risk carriers. Some of the models through which the insurance tech companies are working can be categorized on the basis of the insurance tech matrix. The matrix is created on two dimensions, *i.e.*, Availability of capital and type of innovation presents in Fig. (**5**). These two dimensions are further bifurcated into two subcategories. The first dimension, Availability of capital, is divided into ample capital and limited capital, and the second dimension, type of innovation, is divided into sustaining and disruptive innovation (Kashif, Shajar, Singhal, & Kumar, 2023). For example, many companies in the organization of United Kingdom fall under this matrix; capital is limited, and innovation is disruptive. Similarly, tech c, companies working in different countries can be categorized on the basis of these dimensions. Such models can be adopted in the Indian context, too.

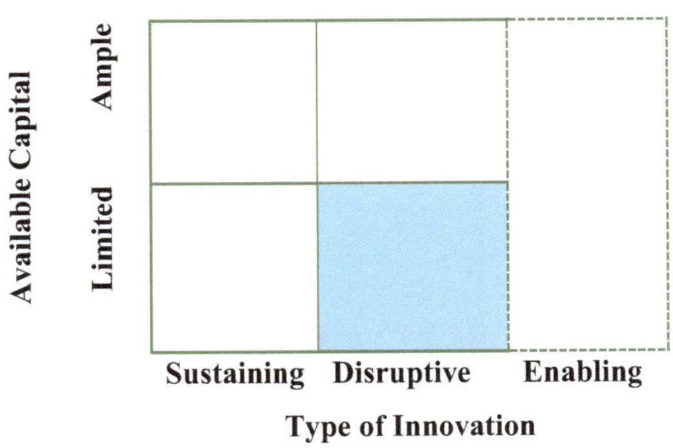

Fig. (5). Insure tech model. Source: Current insure tech landscape: A.

Companies Working on Distribution Innovation Model

Bought by Many, founded in the year 2013 in the United Kingdom, is a free member-only service that helps customers find the right insurance. Their business model is peer-to-peer and E-commerce.

Technology Innovation

Companies Working on Technology Innovation Model

Backbase, founded in the year 2013 in the Netherlands, develops and delivers portal software solutions for financial and large enterprises. Their business model is subscription and layer pattern.

Bigml is a machine learning origination in the USA that provides software as a service for data manipulation and analysis. Their business model is subscription and layer pattern.

MONAX is an open platform for developers that build, ship, and run blockchain-based applications. Their business model is Licensing and subscription. The company was formed in 2014 in the USA.

NEST The company was founded in 2010 and manufactures security systems. Their business model is to Leverage customer data and layer players. (Braun, 20107).

Benefits of ROBO Advisors

The robo advisors are very cost-effective as they are an integral part of their sales channels. It will lead to less of a sales force, and the savings in the form of a low sales force are passed on to the customers through more affordable insurance products (Singh *et al.* 2021). The robo advisers are proven as tech-customized advisors on the basis of their better and more efficient data analysis and interpretation. Besides recommendations, they are automated in activities like follow-ups, reminders, and Automated correspondence, which lead to improved customer engagement. These virtual intermediaries accelerate the application review process (Singh *et al.* 2020). These instantly assess risk levels and apply premium loading factors in real time. It removes the delay in document processing and underwriting. Thus, these algorithms reduce policy issuance time (Avikal *et al.* 2020).

Challenges of ROBO Advisors

In traditional investment, human advisors create a faith system, which is totally missing in robo-advising.

Limited flexibility as against traditional insurance models.

The issue of data privacy issues is also here due to cyber-attacks and data breaches. Faith in technology is still a hard task for Indian insurance consumers.

In a country like India, where private companies hardly cater to the rural economy and such advancements like robo advising are offered by private companies only, the technology adoption rate is very slow in rural areas, and the low literacy rate is also a challenge for dissemination of such technology in the rural areas of the country.

Robo advisors generally make decisions for the customers on the basis of algorithms, which can be biased or unethical.

Compliance with various regulations like mandatory disclosures, anti-money laundering, data protection, and privacy is also a challenge in the adoption of robo-advising technology in the insurance sector.

Future of Robo Advisors

Robo advisors are successfully working in portfolio management and the mutual fund industry. Research states that assets under management in the robot advisors' market are projected to be US$14.87 Billion in 2023. This will grow at an average annual growth rate (CAGR 2023-27) of 14.70 percent, which will reach 25.74 billion US$ in the year 2027. It is also expected that robo-advising will reach 3.250 million users by 2027.

These statistics are very motivating and urge us to implement robo-advisors in the insurance sector, too.

CONCLUSION

The chapter concludes that the Robo advisory is the new concept in insurance, and we can see that the companies that are using this technology in other sectors are not able to make it a human-free technology. Robo advising is a very effective technology for handling frequently asked questions or general queries, but for specific and typical queries and new types of queries, human intervention is required.

Robo-advising has brought about significant changes in the financial advisory landscape. While it offers many benefits such as accessibility, efficiency, and automation, investors should carefully consider their individual preferences, risk tolerance, and the level of human interaction they desire when choosing between robo-advisors and traditional financial advisors. Additionally, ongoing advancements in technology, regulatory developments, and market dynamics will likely shape the future trajectory of robo-advising.

REFERENCES

Administration, I. T. (2023). India insurance sector. Retrieved from Trade.gov: Available from: https://www.trade.gov/market-intelligence/india-insurance-sector.

Braun, A. (20107). The Current InsurTech Landscape: Business Models and Disruptive Potential. St. Gallen: Institute of Insurance Economics I.VW-HSG, University of St. Gallen.

IAS, D. (2020). Available from: https://www.drishtiias.com/daily-news-editorials/insurance-sector-in-india; Available from: www.drishtiiasa.com/daily-news-editorials/insurance-sector-in-India.

BEF. (2023). Insurance Industry Report. New Delhi: Indian Brand Equity Foundation. Available from: https://www.ibef.org/uploads/industry/Infrographics/large/insurance-infographic-august-2023.pdf.

IRDA. (2007). Available from: https://irdai.gov.in/evolution-of-insurance; Available from: irda.gov.in; Available from: https://irdai.gov.in/evolution-of-insurance.

Joshi, K., Kumar, V., Anandaram, H., Kumar, R., Gupta, A., Krishna, K.H. (2023). A review approach on deep learning algorithms in computer vision. *Intelligent Systems and Applications in Computer Vision.,* 1-15. [http://dx.doi.org/10.1201/9781003453406-1]

Kashif, M., Shajar, S.N., Singhal, N., Kumar, P. (2023). *Achieving sustainable investment practices through green finance: Challenges and opportunities. Sustainable Investments in Green Finance.,* 234-244. [http://dx.doi.org/10.4018/979-8-3693-1388-6.ch016]

Kashif, M., Singhal, N., Goyal, S., Singh, S.K. (2024). Foreign Exchange Reserves and Economic Growth of Brazil: A Nonlinear Approach. Finance. *Theory Pract., 28*(1), 145-154.

NR, R. (2017). Rise of Robo Advising in Insurance Companies. Available from: https://rapidvalue.medium.com/the-rise-of-robo-advice-in-insurance-companies-ef21d2ed8a0.

Ramnath Balasubramanian, D. M. (2021). Insurance 2030—The impact of AI on the future of insurance. Available from: https://www.mckinsey.com/industries/financial-services/our-insights/insurance-2030-the-impact-of-ai-on-the-future-of-insurance#/.

Research, G.V. (2020). Robotic Process Automation Market Size, Share & Trends Analysis Report By Type, By Application, By Deployment, By Organization, By Region, And Segment Forecasts, 2023 - 2030. California: Available from: www.Grandviewresearch.com.

Singh, A., Taneja, S., Kumar, P. (2023). Algorithmic approaches to financial technology: Forecasting, trading, and optimization. *Algorithmic Approaches to Financial Technology..* Forecasting, Trading, and Optimization.

Singhal, N., Goyal, S., Singhal, T. (2020). Insurance–growth nexus: empirical evidence from emerging Asian markets. *Transnatl. Corp. Rev., 12*(3), 237-249. [http://dx.doi.org/10.1080/19186444.2020.1756170]

Kour, D., Kaur, T., Devi, R., Yadav, A., Singh, M., Joshi, D., Singh, J., Suyal, D.C., Kumar, A., Rajput, V.D., Yadav, A.N., Singh, K., Singh, J., Sayyed, R.Z., Arora, N.K., Saxena, A.K. (2021). Beneficial microbiomes for bioremediation of diverse contaminated environments for environmental sustainability: present status and future challenges. *Environ. Sci. Pollut. Res. Int., 28*(20), 24917-24939.

[http://dx.doi.org/10.1007/s11356-021-13252-7] [PMID: 33768457]

Chauhan, C.C., Kagdi, A.R., Jotania, R.B., Upadhyay, A., Sandhu, C.S., Shirsath, S.E., Meena, S.S. (2018). Structural, magnetic and dielectric properties of Co-Zr substituted M-type calcium hexagonal ferrite nanoparticles in the presence of α-Fe2O3 phase. *Ceram. Int., 44*(15), 17812-17823. [http://dx.doi.org/10.1016/j.ceramint.2018.06.249]

Guo, H.H., Zhou, D., Du, C., Wang, P.J., Liu, W.F., Pang, L.X., Wang, Q-P., Su, J-Z., Singh, C., Trukhanov, S. (2020). Temperature stable $Li_2Ti_{0.75}(Mg_{1/3}Nb_{2/3})_{0.25}O_3$-based microwave dielectric ceramics with low sintering temperature and ultra-low dielectric loss for dielectric resonator antenna applications. *J. Mater. Chem. C Mater. Opt. Electron. Devices, 8*(14), 4690-4700. [http://dx.doi.org/10.1039/D0TC00326C]

Barthwal, A., Bhatt, M., Avikal, S., Prakash, C. (2024). Machine learning-based prediction models for electoral outcomes in India: a comparative analysis of exit polls from 2014–2021. *Qual. Quant.,* •••, 1-26. [http://dx.doi.org/10.1007/s11135-024-01937-3]

Mehra, A., Gupta, O., Avikal, S. (2023). Finding the combined effect of academic and non-academic performance on management students' placement: A fuzzy logic approach. *Int. J. Manag. Educ., 21*(3), 100837. [http://dx.doi.org/10.1016/j.ijme.2023.100837]

Avikal, S., Pant, R., Kumar, K.N., Kumar, V., Ram, M. (2023). Prioritizing the barriers of manufacturing during Covid-19 using fuzzy AHP. *Advances in Soft Computing Applications.* River Publishers. [http://dx.doi.org/10.1201/9781003425885-11]

Badhotiya, G.K., Avikal, S., Soni, G., Sengar, N. (2022). Analyzing barriers for the adoption of circular economy in the manufacturing sector. *Int. J. Prod. Perform. Manag., 71*(3), 912-931. [http://dx.doi.org/10.1108/IJPPM-01-2021-0021]

Avikal, S., Singh, A.R., Ram, M. (2021). Sustainability in Industry 4.0: Challenges and Remedies. *CRC Press.* [http://dx.doi.org/10.1201/9781003102304]

Singh, A.K., Verma, R.P., Avikal, S., Mehra, K.S. (2021). Mechanical characterization of epoxy composite reinforced with alkali treated walnut shell powder. *Mater. Today Proc., 46*, 10642-10646. [http://dx.doi.org/10.1016/j.matpr.2021.01.383]

Singh, R., Avikal, S., Rashmi, R., Ram, M. (2020). A Kano model, AHP and TOPSIS based approach for selecting the best mobile phone under a fuzzy environment. *Int. J. Qual. Reliab. Manage., 37*(6/7), 837-851. [http://dx.doi.org/10.1108/IJQRM-01-2020-0022]

Avikal, S., Singh, R., Rashmi, R. (2020). QFD and Fuzzy Kano model based approach for classification of aesthetic attributes of SUV car profile. *J. Intell. Manuf., 31*(2), 271-284. [http://dx.doi.org/10.1007/s10845-018-1444-5]

CHAPTER 5

Assessment of Key Drivers for Selecting Sustainable Health Insurance Schemes: Using the BWM Approach

Vijay Lahri[1,*], **Mohd Amir**[2] and **Abdullah Malik**[3]

[1] *University of Petroleum and Energy Studies, Dehradun, India*

[2] *Uttaranchal Institute of Management, Uttaranchal University, Dehradun, India*

[3] *Department of Commerce (Jain Online), Jain University, Bengaluru, India*

Abstract: Post-covid Era has accelerated the growth of the health insurance sector drastically. Nowadays, public is focussing on taking health insurance to mitigate the sudden expenses of health services. However, finding the best health scheme for the people is still considered challenging. Hence, the present study attempts to solve the issue by developing a framework that considers a range of essential factors of the health insurance plan. The identified factors were ranked by using the integrated Delphi and best-worst methods. The study helps consumers to choose their policy effectively using the proposed framework.

Keywords: Best worst method, Delphi method purchase decision, Health insurance scheme, Insurance purchasing intentions, Sustainable.

INTRODUCTION

The health of the people is uncertain, and they may face gradual or drastic medical risks. These medical risks can affect their social life severely (Li *et al.*, 2022). Therefore, medical risk can be reduced by planning a proper health-saving plan. Currently, government and insurance companies are providing various types of health insurance products to mitigate medical risks. The high cost of inpatient medical treatment can drastically affect the person's financial situation and be brought down by a suitable health insurance plan (Vitikainen *et al.*, 2010). The health insurance industry has gained significant attention after the covid 19 outbreak (Heck & Schmidt, 2010). The COVID-19 disaster has proved that medi-

* **Corresponding author Vijay Lahri:** University of Petroleum and Energy Studies Dehradun, India; E-mail: vijay.lahri07@gmail.com

cal expenses have risen beyond the limits of people's expenditure. Hence, the insurance sector has experienced a drastic development post-COVID-19, and people are willing to buy health insurance plans (Webster, 2020). According to (C. *et al*., 2017), around 170 million citizens around the globe have dealt with financial issues due to unexpectedly high medical expenses, which results in them being pushed into poverty to meet their health overheads. This sudden medical expenditure increases the demand for health insurance so that any kind of unplanned medical expenses can be met with a health policy. Commercial health insurance is considered essential for social stability. The rising price of health expenditure can be met with these types of commercial products (Yu *et al*., 2021, Dihom *et al*., 2022, Avikal *et al.* 2023).

Currently, the health industry has been growing at a faster pace. Research and market report shows that the Indian health insurance sector is growing at a compound annual growth rate of 10.2% and has captured the market up to USD 198.45. A health insurance policy acts as a financial safety net for you and your family in a medical emergency. It has several advantages, including paying your medical bills, including pre- and post-hospitalization expenses, protecting your savings, and receiving tax benefits (Bhat *et al*., 2018). Health insurance is critical to the nation's overall well-being, and it must be made more affordable for the vast majority of the population. This sector is a crucial segment of the economic system of a country, as it offers many advantages: it mobilizes savings, contributes to capital formation, promotes productive investments and employment generations, acts as a stabilizer, and more. Medical expenses are among the most critical considerations for the people of the nations.

Developing countries like India, offer several types of health schemes for their people. Such plans are government-backed subsidized health schemes, Social Health schemes provided by the organized sector for their employees, and Private voluntary health insurance, which is a type of retail type of products for individuals and families (C. S. Yadav & Sudhakar, 2017, Singh *et al.* 2021)

Researchers have confirmed that the health insurance sector not only helps in socioeconomic activities but also contributes to the economic development of the country (Trinh *et al*., 2023, Sharma & Saharan, 2016, Avikal *et al.* 2022). Health and its population are directly associated with the growth of a country's GDP. The opportunity cost of healthcare schemes is enormous. Interestingly, the penetration of health insurance products in developing nations is still early, and this is because of lower awareness levels and misleading information about the products.

Presently, several companies offer various health insurance products, and choosing the most suitable products among them is a challenging task for customers. There is still a massive challenge from the customer's perspective in selecting the best health insurance product among the several plans offered by the various companies (Blumberg *et al.*, 2013, Srivastava *et al.*, 2014, Singh *et al.* 2020). Buying health products is based on multiple factors that affect the buying intention of customers for health insurance (NURSIANA *et al.*, 2021a). So far, researchers have studied various factors for buying health insurance products. Bhat *et al.*, (2018) show that the number of children in families, the age, and awareness of future medical care costs affect insurance purchases. (Kashif *et al.*, (2024); Browne *et al.*, (1999); Chaudhry *et al.* (2020) identify macroeconomic factors in health insurance demand. Nowadays, the continuously growing cost of outpatient medical treatment also envisages insurers to consider these factors in their health scheme (Vitikainen *et al.*, 2010). A study revealed that literacy among adults regarding health insurance is an essential factor(Waters *et al.*, 2022). A study conducted on the health purchasing framework identified some benchmarks (benefits, service, quality standards, payments, information) for practical purchasing (Cashin & Gatome-Munyua, 2022; Kc *et al.* 2020).

Bhattacharjee, (2021) conducted an empirical study to examine customers' buying behavior toward health insurance products. They found that factors like recommendations, feedback, and suggestions are essential for choosing a health plan. Similarly, (Ha *et al.*, 2020; Singh *et al.* 2019) studied consumer buying intention for private health insurance in Vietnam. They found that after-sales service or customer care is an essential factor in increasing customer intention for the health product. Some authors performed empirical analysis to understand the influence of product quality, service, the reputation of an insurance company, risk, and purchase intention (NURSIANA *et al.*, 2021a; Rashmi *et al.* 2019). Though many studies have been conducted so far, there is still a considerable gap in understanding the critical factors for buying a health insurance product. In addition, the studies are based on empirical and literature-based, and very few examinations have been conducted to prioritize the essential factors of health insurance products using the MCDM approach. Therefore, there is a growing need for the health insurance sector to bridge this gap. The present work has the following objectives:

- What are the essential factors that influence the selection of the health insurance products?
- To prioritize the essential factors.

To achieve oversaid objectives, a two-phase methodology is applied in this study. In the first phase, literature review and the Delphi method are used to identify and finalize the essential factors of health insurance products. Subsequently, in the second phase Novel best worst method is used to find the weights of the identified factors for selecting the best health insurance products. The unique contribution of the study is that it is the first study that proposed an integrated framework consisting of a range of factors for selecting the best health insurance product by customers. From a methodology perspective, this is the first study that uses the BWM MCDM technique to weigh health insurance indicators (Chaithra, *et al.*, 2023).

The rest of the paper is organized as follows: The second section is dedicated to the literature review, in which we have thoroughly reviewed the literature concerning health insurance products. Section 3 provides the framework development. Further, section 4 illustrates the methodology adopted for this paper. Section 5 presents the results and analysis. Finally, section 6 delivers the conclusion and future scope of the study.

LITERATURE REVIEW

Health insurance has been among the fastest-growing sectors during the last few years. Extensive literature reviews have been carried out to make the theoretical background of the present study. To examine the essential factors that influence health insurance products and the effect of socioeconomic factors, product perception, purchase intention of health policy, and individual's personality traits on the health insurance products plan. Previous studies have shown the various factors affecting the intent to purchase health insurance products. A study identifies the macroeconomic factors in health insurance demand (Browne *et al.*, 1999). The study focused on national income, inflation, government spending, and demographics that are important factors in creating health insurance needs. A study highlighted that most of the factors affecting the Intention of purchasing private health insurance were approached in many ways and views but mainly from the classical economy view with micro and macroeconomics (Ha *et al.*, 2020) . Likewise, someauthors argued that the demand of households had been transformed, and they concluded that household demand for health insurance relies on demographic profile and economic factors (Lee *et al.*, 2010). (Bhat & Jain, 2006) demonstrate that the awareness and purchase intention of health insurance policies significantly impact the number of children in families, the age, and the costs of the policy. The study by (Yamada *et al.*, 2009) revealed that those families having a high income are more implied to purchase a health insurance policy and have positive relationships instead of the low-income group (Singh *et al.*, 2023). The anomalies in the insurance market, where people tend to buy insurance when they should not and vice versa, tend to refuse when they need to acquire health insurance policies, may be explained by risk aversion (Rabin & Thaler, 2001).

Macmillan & Aassve, (2022) asserts that this must be proven to measure how modern welfare states will be affected by the growing awareness of social risks. It focuses on advancements in the pension, health, and unemployment insurance industries. The idea of adverse selection, persons in poorer health had a lower likelihood of receiving insurance than those in good health conditions. The study (Hofer *et al.*, 2022) examines Chile's private health insurance options and how they affect the use of medical services. The findings highlight the significance of various demographic factors, including age, gender, and marital status, in decision-making related to insurance. Socioeconomic variables like education, earnings, employment status, and region of residence all have an impact on the likelihood of buying private insurance (Aggarwal, 2011). This study examines equity in enrollment, renewal of registration, and utilization of community-based health insurance. During the COVID-19 pandemic, most individuals have been more concerned and attentive about getting health insurance to cover the costs of treating diseases brought by COVID-19. Most of them are also first-time insurance customers. Carlsten *et al.*, (2021) investigated the impact of COVID-19 on China Qian's 2021 need for health insurance. However, because the pandemic is not a locally focused event, the insurance market cannot completely cover it. According to a study (Jeffery, 2021 and Singh *et al.*, 2022), health is a critical issue in India, where most people in different states are impoverished. So, the health insurance policy will be a crucial decision for the well-being of families (Fariya, *et al.*, 20).

From all the said studies, it has been found that none of the studies has proposed an integrated framework for the decision-making of the best health insurance product according to the customer's choice. Most of the studies have argued that health insurance is essential for people. However, there had been fewer studies carried out to select which product should be opted for by the customers. In this view, we have identified a range of parameters from past studies and developed a generalized integrated model. Table **1** shows the essential factors in choosing the best health insurance product. In Table **1**, we have provided 18 health factors from past studies.

Table 1. Factors with their description.

S. No.	Factors	Description	Source
1	Waiting period / locking period	It is the period during which a policyholder cannot claim health insurance or may not receive all of the policy's benefits. This period varies from company to company. Customers are more uncertain when a scheme's locking or waiting period is longer.	(Gruber & Kubik, 2002)

(Table 1) cont.....

S. No.	Factors	Description	Source
2	Type of disease covered	This will provide information on the diseases covered by the health insurance product (such as acute and chronic diseases).	(Dong *et al.*, 2008)
3	Claim settlement ratio	It is a crucial indicator of high customer satisfaction. It informs customers about the percentage of claims approved by the insurer company in a given year. It is the ratio of claims filed to claims received each year.	(Ashturkar, 2015; R. K. Yadav, 2014)
4	Payment options or payment mechanism	It provides customers with flexible payment options, such as installments, one-time payments with discounts, and other advantages.	(Blumberg *et al.*, 2013; Khalifa *et al.*, 2022)
5	Legal aspects /regulations	The government imposed coercive rules to protect consumers' long-term benefits from health insurance products.	(Bali *et al.*, 2022; Ezat *et al.*, 2022; Khetpal *et al.*, 2022)
6	Cashless / non-cashless	Insurers have enough ties with hospitals to cover cash-less hospital expenditures.	(Kautish & Arorazb, 2022; Yusoff *et al.*, 2022)
7	IVR calling/ Relationship manager	Iterative voice response empowers customer support for the ease of claim procedure and other queries, as well as time-to-time policy updates.	(Bazyar *et al.*, 2022; Burch, 2022)
8	Local support for claim settlement	It provides customers with a simple claim operation for customer satisfaction.	(Bhattacharjee, 2021a; Ridde *et al.*, 2022; van Eijk *et al.*, 2022)
9	Motivation of purchase	Customers in uncertain medical situations may face substantial medical expenses for medical examination and treatment that exceed their ability to pay, such as dengue fever, covid 19, and other accidents.	(Kitcharoen1, 2022; Nundy *et al.*, 2022; Olaniran *et al.*, 2022)
10	Risk cover	It allows for the coverage of unforeseeable health issues or harmful diseases that endanger persons.	(Douven *et al.*, 2022)
11	Tax benefits	Countries like India, where customers can deduct tax benefits received from medical insurance premiums under Section 80D.	(Bhattacharjee, 2021b; Zare *et al.*, 2022)
12	Accidental coverage	It covers all medical expenses incurred due to road accidents (ambulance charges, inpatient hospitalization, consultation fee, post-hospitalization, compensation for partial or permanent disability, and more).	(Charles, 2021; Sachs, 2022; Taylor & Friedson, 2022; ten Brink *et al.*, 2022)
13	Impatient and outpatient coverage	Coverage of medical expenses when a customer claims health expenses and is either formally admitted to or visits a hospital (Such as medical consultations, laboratory tests, medicines, *etc.*).	(Shaqura *et al.*, 2022; Vitikainen *et al.*, 2010)

(Table 1) cont.....

S. No.	Factors	Description	Source
14	No claim bonus	If the customer does not file a claim for the current year, the insurer will provide an additional discount when renewing the health policy for the following year.	(Bhattacharjee, 2021b; Ejiyi *et al.*, 2022)
15	Outside country claim	It allows for the coverage of health benefits if the customer claims outside of the country's borders.	(Bhattacharjee, 2021b)
16	Pre-existing disease cover	It informs the customer that the health product should cover their existing illnesses.	(Bhattacharjee, 2021b; Liu *et al.*, 2022)
17	Portability	Customers have the right under IRDA to switch to another insurer if they are dissatisfied with the services of their current insurer.	(Bhattacharjee, 2021b; Shetty *et al.*, 2022)
18	Company reputation	It is an intangible attribute for customers to perceive a company's reputation positively.	(NURSIANA *et al.*, 2021b)

MODEL DEVELOPMENT

The health insurance industry is becoming increasingly important to healthcare systems. Several studies have been conducted to identify the critical factors influencing customer purchasing decisions (Singh *et al.*, 2022). However, there is still a wide range of scope available that can be extended with more critical factors for the decision-making of various health plans available in the market. As a result, as shown in Fig. (**1**), we proposed an integrated model in this research work. The proposed model includes nine critical health insurance factors among 18 identified factors shown in Table **1**. Using the Delphi method, we considered nine factors from the identified range of factors in this model.

METHODOLOGY

There is a wide range of techniques available in the literature for the assessment of factors. Among such techniques, multicriteria decision-making techniques are the preferable approaches. So far, various MCDM techniques have been proposed (Cheraghalipour *et al.*, 2018), such as AHP (Saaty, 2008), VIKOR (Demir *et al.*, 2018), ELECTRE (Corrente *et al.*, 2022), TOPSIS (Lai *et al.*, 1994), and Best worst method (Rezaei, 2015). All the techniques are well efficient for decision-making. However, among the available methods, the best-worst method is one of the best techniques for assessing critical factors in decision-making.

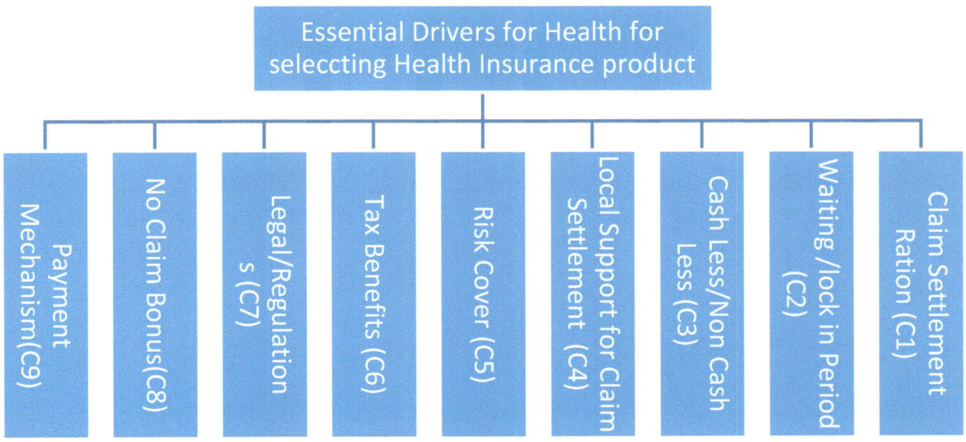

Fig. (1). Decision-making model for health insurance plans.

Best-Worst Method was proposed by (Rezaei, 2015); it works on the principle of pairwise comparison by using a scale of 1 to 9. More specifically, the computation of this method is based on two vectors called best and worst. A decision-maker has to perform pairwise comparisons based on the Best-Worst factors. The BWM has several benefits over AHP, which is a prevalent technique in management studies. AHP method requires n(n-1)/2 pairwise comparisons, while BWM needs only (2n-3) pairwise comparisons. BWM requires fewer data and provides higher consistency (Lahri *et al.*, 2021).

To fulfill research gaps mentioned above, this study has applied two two-stage methodologies. In the first stage, qualitative approach is applied to identify factors associated with decision-making in selecting the health insurance plan. In this study, the authors have considered Scopus and Science Direct databases to achieve the first objective. We have identified 18 factors related to health insurance plans from the literature. These identified factors are shown in Table **1**. Further, in the second stage, we applied Delphi and BWM methods to reduce the 18 identified factors up to 9 factors and provided weights to them using the BWM method.

Proposed Hybrid Solution Approach

The current study proposes a two-stage problem to identify and rank the potential health insurance factors. The details of the proposed solution methodology are given below.

Stage 1: Identification of health insurance factors

- Conducted extensive literature review using the terms: health products, health schemes, essential factors of health insurance selection, and Intention to purchase health insurance.
- Segregated identified research papers in three ways: literature review papers, empirical studies, and quantitative studies using MCDM approaches.
- Identified factors that are common in multiple studies in the available literature.
- Finally, listed all the tables in tabular form and provided their literature support with a summary.

Stage 2: Quantification of identified health insurance factors

- The first 18 identified factors have been reduced to 9 factors using the Delphi method.
- A hierarchical decision-making structure is developed using identified factors.
- The BWM method is applied to obtain the weights of the factors.

RESULTS AND DISCUSSION

To determine potential factors for choosing the best health scheme from the customer's perspective, we have proposed the model shown in Fig. (**1**). Fig. (**1**) shows significant factors with respect to health insurance products. To attain the primary objective, this study has applied a two-stage method. In the first stage, we utilize the qualitative approach. At the start, we conducted literature review and collected 145 papers. From the collected papers, we identified 18 factors related to health insurance schemes, shown in Table **1**. In the second research stage, we applied the Delphi method to identify 9 essential factors among the 18 identified factors. The Delphi method is conducted with eight experts from academia and industry, the respondent profile is shown in Table **2**.

Table 2. Responders profile (Age- 25-35).

S. No.	Sex (F/M)	Type of Profession
1	F	Insurance advisor
2	M	Insurance advisor
3	M	Insurance advisor
4	M	Insurance advisor
5	F	Random person who owns health insurance
6	F	Random person who owns health insurance
7	M	Random person who owns health insurance
8	M	Random person who owns health insurance

Further, we applied the novel best-worst method to rank these nine crucial factors. The best-worst method is a type of multicriteria decision-making approach, and it is easy to implement and provides greater consistency than the other MCDM methods. In the BWM rating process, it is essential to first identify the best and worst factors from the total number of factors. After identifying the best and worst factors, pairwise comparisons were conducted among the remaining factors. Detailed steps for performing the BWM analysis are given in Appendix A. A total of 8 experts have been considered for the study. In the BWM process, consistency was checked, and the (λ) value nearer to zero was considered the best rating by the responders. Lingo 10 optimization solver was used to solve the BWM linear programming problem. Table **3** and **4** show the pairwise comparison for the identified health criteria. The weights of the criteria, calculated using the BWM methodology, are represented in Table **5**. In this study, consistency was observed between 0.088 – 0.168 for the eight responses. The values (λ) are near zero, and the pairwise comparison can be considered consistent.

Table 3. Most essential criteria over other criteria.

Best Other Criteria Criteria		(C1)	(C2)	(C3)	(C4)	(C5)	(C6)	(C7)	(C8)	(C9)
Res 1	(C1)	1	7	4	3	5	4	3	2	4
Res 2	(C5)	2	5	4	6	1	9	4	5	3
Res 3	(C5)	1	4	5	2	1	8	7	4	5
Res 4	(C1)	1	2	4	8	4	3	7	6	4
Res 5	(C3)	2	8	1	1	4	6	3	7	5
Res 6	(C5)	1	8	4	3	1	7	2	5	6
Res 7	(C1)	1	6	4	2	1	5	3	8	7
Res 8	(C1)	1	8	3	1	2	5	4	6	7

Table 4. Other criteria over least critical Criteria.

Respondent	Res 1	Res 2	Res 3	Res 4	Res 5	Res 6	Res 7	Res 8	Res 9
(C1)	8	9	7	7	1	5	7	5	9
(C2)	1	6	1	9	1	8	4	4	6
(C3)	7	3	4	2	2	6	3	2	5
(C4)	5	4	6	5	7	7	5	3	8
(C5)	6	2	2	3	4	3	5	1	2
(C6)	4	1	1	1	3	1	2	6	3
(C7)	7	4	2	2	4	5	6	7	4

(Table 4) cont.....

Respondent	Res 1	Res 2	Res 3	Res 4	Res 5	Res 6	Res 7	Res 8	Res 9
(C8)	2	2	4	5	6	7	7	8	1
(C9)	4	1	3	2	5	3	1	1	3

Table 5. Final matrix for criteria weights for eight responses.

-	λ	C1	C2	C3	C4	C5	C6	C7	C8	C9
Respondent 1	0.088	0.265	0.025	0.088	0.118	0.071	0.088	0.118	0.139	0.088
Respondent 2	0.168	0.252	0.210	0.084	0.105	0.070	0.047	0.105	0.084	0.042
Respondent 3	0.113	0.200	0.313	0.044	0.063	0.156	0.039	0.045	0.078	0.063
Respondent 4	0.147	0.265	0.206	0.103	0.052	0.103	0.039	0.059	0.069	0.103
Respondent 5	0.125	0.181	0.153	0.028	0.305	0.076	0.051	0.102	0.044	0.061
Respondent 6	0.135	0.202	0.246	0.042	0.084	0.112	0.022	0.168	0.067	0.056
Respondent 7	0.099	0.242	0.057	0.085	0.171	0.201	0.068	0.114	0.043	0.020
Respondent 8	0.094	0.228	0.040	0.107	0.273	0.139	0.064	0.080	0.022	0.046

Results depicted in Fig. (**2**) show the average weights of 8 experts for the identified essential health insurance factors. We have given equal importance to each expert, and based on that, we calculated the final optimal weights by deriving an arithmetic average of obtained weights by eight experts. This method was adopted from the study by You *et al*., (2017). From Fig. (**2**), it can be observed that experts have given more emphasis to C1 (Claim Settlement Ratio), followed by C4 (Local support for claim settlement), and C5 (Risk cover). Factor C6 (Tax Benefits) has come out as the least important selection criterion according to the experts with respect to the other criteria (Kashif *et al*., 2023).

The managerial implications of this proposed model are significant from customers' and companies' perspectives. From the proposed model, any Insurance industry providing health coverage can adopt this model and, according to the customer requirement, they can conduct a rating survey that helps them achieve high product impact in the market to become the leading insurance company. This model also allows the customers to decide the factors that are important according to their requirements. This particular model will lead to a competitive environment among health firms.

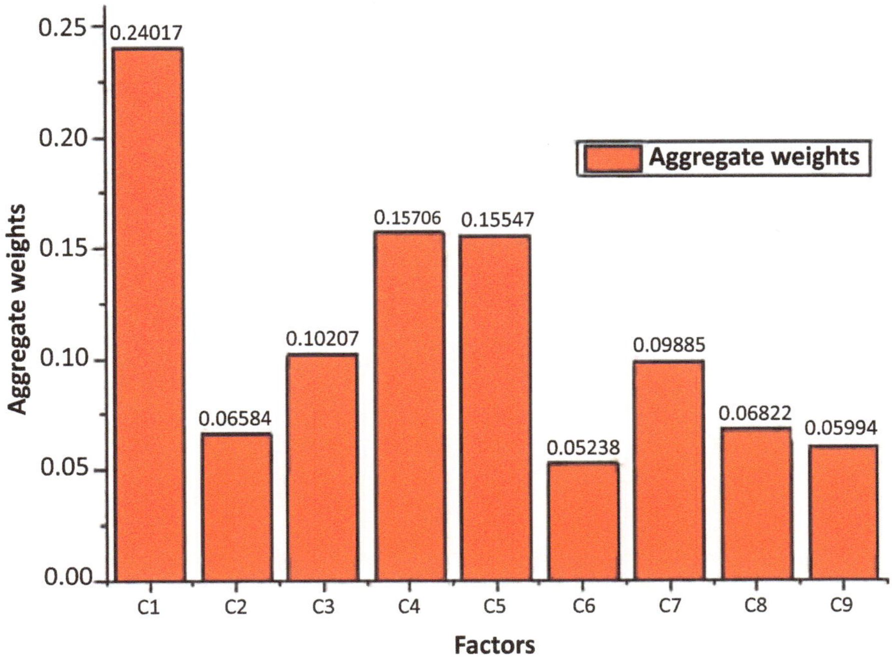

Fig. (2). Aggregate weights for the health factors.

CONCLUSION AND FUTURE RESEARCH

The high cost of medical expenses raises the demand for health products. However, from the customer's perspective, selecting the best health plan may be the most difficult task. As a result, the proposed study addresses health plan selection issues by developing a comprehensive framework. A two-stage method was used to conduct the research in this study. Extensive literature review was conducted in the first stage to identify a variety of health insurance factors using qualitative techniques. A total of eighteen essential factors were identified and then reduced to nine factors using the Delphi method. Following that, in the second stage, the nine essential factors were weighted by expert opinion using the BWM method.

The results show that Claim Settlement Ratio, followed by Local support for claim settlement, and Risk Coverage are the most important health factors to consider when selecting a health plan. Furthermore, Tax Benefits emerged as the least important selection criterion. This study's generalized model aids in focusing on the key factors of health insurance companies. The proposed study is extensively helpful for customers and health insurance companies. The model can be adopted by health insurance companies to emphasize their stakeholders and policymakers by using the identified health factors in the model.

The limitation of the study is the validation of the model, as the model analysis had few respondents. Furthermore, the study only provides the weights of the identified factors and can be further extended to rank the various health insurance plans with respect to the weighted factors in the study using the ranking approach (such as TOPSIS and PROMETHEE methods). Furthermore, the analysis can employ the fuzzy BWM and Fuzzy AHP approaches to deal with respondent biases.

APPENDIX: A

Steps associated with the BWM analysis:

Step 1: Identify a set of G.I. factors $\{F_1, F_2, \ldots F_m\}$ through literature review.

Step 2: Among the identified G.I. factors (F_m) fix the best (F_B) and the worst (F_w) G.I. factor, respectively.

Step 3: *Ask the experts to perform the preference of the best G.I. factor over other G.I. factors using a 1 – 9 scale. On the scale, 1 denotes equal importance between the best to other G.I. factors, and 9 expresses the extreme importance of the best G.I. factor over the other G.I. factors. The resultant vector equation Best-to-Other (B.O.) is articulated as* $A_B = (\alpha_{B1}, \alpha_{B2}, \ldots \alpha_{Bm})$, *and* $(\alpha_{BB} = 1)$. *Similarly, using a scale 1 to 9, the preference of Others-to-Worst (O.W.) G.I. factors is performed. The resultant vector for other to worst would be articulated as:* $A_W = (\alpha_{1W}, \alpha_{2W}, \ldots \alpha_{mW})^T$ *and* $(\alpha_{WW} = 1)$. *Whereas* α_{Bm} *specifies the preference of the B.O. and* α_{mW} *specifies the preference O.W.*

Step 4: Calculate the optimal weights $\{F_1, F_2, \ldots F_m\}$ for all G.I. factors (F_m). The optimal weights (F_m) can be calculated by solving the Minmax model proposed by Rezaei (2016), as shown below:

$$\min \max_m = \left\{ \left| \frac{F_B}{F_m} - \alpha_{Bm} \right|, \left| \frac{F_m}{F_W} - \alpha_{mW} \right| \right\} \text{s.t.} \sum_m^M F_m = 1\ F_m \geq 0, \quad \text{for all m} \qquad \textbf{(Model 1)}$$

The above Minmax *Model (1) can be transformed into a linear programming problem:*

$$\min \quad \varphi^* \ \text{s.t.} \ |F_B - \alpha_{Bm} F_m| \leq \varphi^*, \text{for all m} |F_m - \alpha_{mW} F_W| \leq \varphi^*, \text{for all m} \sum_m^M F_m = 1\ F_m \geq 0, \text{for all m} \qquad \textbf{(Model 2)}$$

Whereas (φ^*) indicates the consistency of the pairwise comparison of G.I. factors.

Step 5: Solve the model (2) to get the optimal weights (F_m) of the G.I. factors and consistency value (φ^*). According to (Rezaei, 2016), the value of (φ^*) nearer to zero depicts the high level of consistent solution.

Table A1. BWM rating scale.

Rating scale	The meaning of the rating scale 1 - 9
1	**Equal** importance
2	Somewhat between Equal and Moderate
3	**Moderately** more important than
4	Somewhat between Moderate and Strong
5	**Strongly** more important than
6	Somewhat between Strong and Very Strong
7	**Very strongly** important than
8	Somewhat between Very strong and Absolute
9	**Absolutely** more important than

REFERENCES

Aggarwal, A. (2011). Achieving Equity in Health through Community-based Health Insurance: India's Experience with a Large CBHI Programme., *47*(11), 1657-1676.
[http://dx.doi.org/10.1080/00220388.2011.609586]

Ashturkar, P.B. (2015). An Examination into claim settlement ratios of public and private life insurance companies in India. *Int. J. Manag. Soc. Sci.,* *3*(8), 322-331. Available from: https://www.indianjournals.com/ijor.aspx?target=ijor:ijmss&volume=3&issue=8&article=030

Bali, A.S., He, A.J., Ramesh, M. (2022). Health policy and COVID-19: path dependency and trajectory. *Policy Soc.,* *41*(1), 83-95.
[http://dx.doi.org/10.1093/polsoc/puab014]

Bazyar, M., Alipouri Sakha, M., Gordeev, V.S., Mousavi, B., Karmi, A., Maniei, R., Attari, S., Ranjbar, M. (2022). Criteria for the selection of complementary private health insurance: the experience of a large organisation in Iran. *BMC Health Serv. Res.,* *22*(1), 1377.
[http://dx.doi.org/10.1186/s12913-022-08777-7] [PMID: 36403056]

Bhat, R., Holtz, J., Avila, C. (2018). Reaching the Missing Middle: Ensuring Health Coverage for India's Urban Poor., *4*(2), 125-135.
[http://dx.doi.org/10.1080/23288604.2018.1445425]

Bhat, R., Jain, N. (2006). Factoring Affecting the Demand for Health Insurance in a Micro Insurance Finance. *Blackwell Publishing,* 206.

Bhattacharjee, I. (2021a). A Study of Factors Influencing Consumer's choice while purchasing Health Insurance Policy in India., *20*(5), 1893-1901.

Bhattacharjee, I. (2021b). A Study of Factors Influencing Consumer's choice while purchasing Health Insurance Policy in India, *20*(5), 1893-1901.

Blumberg, L.J., Long, S.K., Kenney, G.M., & Goin, D. (2013). Factors Influencing Health Plan Choice among the Marketplace Target Population on the Eve of Health Reform.

Browne, M.J., Carson, J.M., Hoyt, R.E. (1999). Economic and Market Predictors of Insolvencies in the Life-Health Insurance Industry. *J. Risk Insur., 66*(4), 643. [http://dx.doi.org/10.2307/253868]

Burch, A.E. (2022). Factors responsible for healthcare avoidance among rural adults in the Eastern Region of North Carolina. *J. Community Health, 47*(5), 737-744. [http://dx.doi.org/10.1007/s10900-022-01106-3] [PMID: 35675005]

Carlsten, C., Gulati, M., Hines, S., Rose, C., Scott, K., Tarlo, S.M., Torén, K., Sood, A., de la Hoz, R.E. (2021). COVID-19 as an occupational disease. *Am. J. Ind. Med., 64*(4), 227-237. [http://dx.doi.org/10.1002/ajim.23222] [PMID: 33491195]

Cashin, C., Gatome-Munyua, A. (2022). The Strategic Health Purchasing Progress Tracking Framework: A Practical Approach to Describing, Assessing, and Improving Strategic Purchasing for Universal Health Coverage. *Health Syst. Reform, 8*(2), e2051794. [http://dx.doi.org/10.1080/23288604.2022.2051794] [PMID: 35446186]

Charles, A. (2021). Health Insurance and Economic Development in Nigeria. *ATBU Journal of Accounting and Finance, 2*, 27143929. Available from: https://www.researchgate.net/publication/358271141

Cheraghalipour, A., Paydar, M.M., Keshteli, M.H. (2018). Applying a hybrid BWM-VIKOR approach to supplier selection: a case study in the Iranian agricultural implements industry. *International Journal of Applied Decision Sciences, 11*(3), 274-301. [http://dx.doi.org/10.1504/IJADS.2018.092796]

Chaithra, N., Jha, J., Sayal, A., Gupta, V., Gupta, A. (2023). A Paradigm Shift towards Computer Vision. *International Conference on Device Intelligence, Computing and Communication Technologies, (DICCT)*, 54-58.

Corrente, S., Rui Figueira, J., Greco, S. (2022). ELECTRE Methods: A Survey on Roman Słowiński Contributions. *Multiple Criteria Decision Making,* 37-58.

Demir, L., Akpınar, M.E., Araz, C., Ilgın, M.A. (2018). A green supplier evaluation system based on a new multi-criteria sorting method: VIKORSORT. *Expert Syst. Appl., 114*, 479-487. [http://dx.doi.org/10.1016/j.eswa.2018.07.071]

Dong, H., Gbangou, A., De Allegri, M., Pokhrel, S., Sauerborn, R. (2008). The differences in characteristics between health-care users and non-users: implication for introducing community-based health insurance in Burkina Faso. *Eur. J. Health Econ., 9*(1), 41-50. [http://dx.doi.org/10.1007/s10198-006-0031-4] [PMID: 17186201]

Douven, R., Kauer, L., Demme, S., Paolucci, F., van de Ven, W., Wasem, J., Zhao, X. (2022). Should administrative costs in health insurance be included in the risk-equalization? An analysis of five countries. *Eur. J. Health Econ., 23*(9), 1437-1453. [http://dx.doi.org/10.1007/s10198-022-01436-y] [PMID: 35129731]

Ejiyi, C.J., Qin, Z., Salako, A.A., Happy, M.N., Nneji, G.U., Ukwuoma, C.C., Chikwendu, I.A., Gen, J. (2022). Comparative Analysis of Building Insurance Prediction Using Some Machine Learning Algorithms. *International Journal of Interactive Multimedia and Artificial Intelligence, 7*(3), 75-85. [http://dx.doi.org/10.9781/ijimai.2022.02.005]

Ezat, S., Puteh, W., Aizuddin, A.N., Abdullah, A., Salem, A. (2022). Feasibility of National Health Insurance for Saudi Healthcare Services: Qualitative Study. *Information Sciences Letters, 11*(2), 427-437. [http://dx.doi.org/10.18576/isl/110213]

Fariya, Saini, A., & Kashif, M. (2024). Exploring the Influence of Factors Driving Financial Accessibility, Financial Activities, and Financial Education on Sustainable Development. In *Artificial Intelligence and Machine Learning-Powered Smart Finance*, pp. 23-49.

Gruber, J., & Kubik, J. (2002). Nber Working Paper Series Health Insurance Coverage and The Disability Insurance Application Decision. Available from: http://www.nber.org/papers/w9148.

Ha, N., Duong, N.T.H., Son, N.T. (2020). Level of Factors impact on the Buyers' Intention in Buying Private Health Insurance with the Case of Vietnam Non-Life Insurance Companies. *Eur. J. Bus. Manag.* [http://dx.doi.org/10.7176/EJBM/12-27-06]

Heck, M., Schmidt, G. (2010). Lot-size planning with non-linear cost functions supporting environmental sustainability. *Communications in Computer and Information Science, 88*(2), 1-6. [http://dx.doi.org/10.1007/978-3-642-14306-9_1]

Hofer, J., Kerpen, E., Busch, H., Lehmann, M., Menon, A. (2022). The Implicit Affiliation Motive, Evaluations of Social Life Events, and Life Satisfaction: Findings from a Cross-Cultural Study with German and Zambian Adolescents. *J Happiness Stud., 23*(8), 4073-4089. [http://dx.doi.org/10.1007/s10902-022-00596-1]

Jeffery, R. (2021). Health policy and federalism in India. *Territory, Politics, Governance, 10*(1), 67-85. [http://dx.doi.org/10.1080/21622671.2021.1899976]

Kashif, M., Kumar, P., Ghai, S., Kumar, S. (2023). Disruptive Technologies in Computational Finance. *Algorithmic Approaches to Financial Technology: Forecasting, Trading, and Optimization,* 46-60.

Kashif, M., Singhal, N., Goyal, S., Singh, S.K. (2024). Foreign Exchange Reserves and Economic Growth of Brazil: A Nonlinear Approach. *Finance: Theory and Practice, 28*(1), 145-154.

Kautish, P., Arorazb, N. (2022). Health insurance in India: an exploratory study to understand customer service and satisfaction. *Building Resilient Organizations,* 1-22. [http://dx.doi.org/10.4324/9781003313663-1]

Khalifa, A.Y., Jabbour, J.Y., Mataria, A., Bakr, M., Farid, M., Mathauer, I. (2022). Purchasing health services under the Egypt's new Universal Health Insurance law: What are the implications for universal health coverage? *Int. J. Health Plann. Manage., 37*(2), 619-631. [http://dx.doi.org/10.1002/hpm.3354] [PMID: 34725863]

Khetpal, V., Roosevelt, J., Jr, Adashi, E.Y. (2022). A Federal Indian Health Insurance Plan: Fulfilling a solemn obligation to American Indians and Alaska Natives in the United States. *Prev. Med. Rep., 25,* 101669. [http://dx.doi.org/10.1016/j.pmedr.2021.101669] [PMID: 34976706]

Kitcharoen, K. (2022). Factors Influencing Consumer Purchase Decision of Insurance towards Word of Mouth: A Case Study of Foreigners Liveing in Thailand. *Journal of Global Business Review, 24*(1), 34-50. Available from: https://so02.tci-thaijo.org/index.php/JGBR/article/view/251693

Lahri, V., Shaw, K., Ishizaka, A. (2021). Sustainable supply chain network design problem: Using the integrated BWM, TOPSIS, possibilistic programming, and ε-constrained methods. *Expert Syst. Appl., 168,* 114373. [http://dx.doi.org/10.1016/j.eswa.2020.114373]

Lai, Y.J., Liu, T.Y., Hwang, C.L. (1994). Topsis for MODM. *Eur. J. Oper. Res., 76*(3), 486-500. [http://dx.doi.org/10.1016/0377-2217(94)90282-8]

Lee, S.Y.D., Tsai, T.I., Tsai, Y.W., Kuo, K.N. (2010). Health literacy, health status, and healthcare utilization of Taiwanese adults: results from a national survey. *BMC Public Health, 10*(1), 614. [http://dx.doi.org/10.1186/1471-2458-10-614] [PMID: 20950479]

Li, Z., Wang, D., Abbas, J., Hassan, S., Mubeen, R. (2022). Tourists' Health Risk Threats Amid COVID-19 Era: Role of Technology Innovation, Transformation, and Recovery Implications for Sustainable Tourism. *Front. Psychol., 12,* 769175. [http://dx.doi.org/10.3389/fpsyg.2021.769175] [PMID: 35465147]

Liu, W., Yang, C., Liao, Y., Wan, F., Lin, L., Huang, X., Zhang, B.H., Yuan, Y., Zhang, P., Zhang, X.J., She, Z.G., Wang, L., Li, H. (2022). Risk factors for COVID-19 progression and mortality in hospitalized patients without pre-existing comorbidities. *J. Infect. Public Health, 15*(1), 13-20. [http://dx.doi.org/10.1016/j.jiph.2021.11.012] [PMID: 34861603]

Macmillan, R., & Aassve, A. (2022). On the new socioeconomics of life satisfaction: How exposure to precarious work explains class differences in satisfaction across Europe. Available from: https://www.researchgate.net/publication/358617811.

Nundy, S., Cooper, L.A., Mate, K.S. (2022). The Quintuple Aim for Health Care Improvement. *JAMA, 327*(6), 521-522. [http://dx.doi.org/10.1001/jama.2021.25181] [PMID: 35061006]

Nursiana, A., Budhijono, F., Fuad, M. (2021). Critical Factors Affecting Customers' Purchase Intention of Insurance Policies in Indonesia. *Journal of Asian Finance. Economics and Business, 8*(2), 123-133. a [http://dx.doi.org/10.13106/jafeb.2021.vol8.no2.0123]

Nursiana, A., Budhijono, F., Fuad, M. (2021). Critical Factors Affecting Customers' Purchase Intention of Insurance Policies in Indonesia. *Journal of Asian Finance. Economics and Business, 8*(2), 123-133. b [http://dx.doi.org/10.13106/jafeb.2021.vol8.no2.0123]

Olaniran, A., Madaj, B., Bar-Zeev, S., Banke-Thomas, A., van den Broek, N. (2022). Factors influencing motivation and job satisfaction of community health workers in Africa and Asia—A multi-country study. *Int. J. Health Plann. Manage., 37*(1), 112-132. [http://dx.doi.org/10.1002/hpm.3319] [PMID: 34476842]

Rabin, M., Thaler, R.H. (2001). Anomalies: Risk Aversion. *J. Econ. Perspect., 15*(1), 219-232. [http://dx.doi.org/10.1257/jep.15.1.219]

Rezaei, J. (2015). Best-worst multi-criteria decision-making method. *Omega, 53*, 49-57. [http://dx.doi.org/10.1016/j.omega.2014.11.009]

Ridde, V., Kane, B., Mbow, N.B., Senghor, I., Faye, A. (2022). The resilience of two departmental health insurance units during the COVID-19 pandemic in Senegal. *BMJ Glob. Health, 7* (Suppl. 9), e010062. [http://dx.doi.org/10.1136/bmjgh-2022-010062] [PMID: 36526299]

Saaty, T.L. (2008). Decision making with the analytic hierarchy process. *Int. J. Serv. Sci., 1*(1), 83. [http://dx.doi.org/10.1504/IJSSCI.2008.017590]

Sachs, R. (2022). The Accidental Innovation Policymakers. *SSRN Electronic Journal.*

Shaqura, I.I., Jaafaripooyan, E., Ahmadi, B., Akbari Sari, A. (2022). Responsiveness of hospitals to inpatient and outpatient services in the low- and middle-income countries: A systematic review. *Int. J. Health Plann. Manage., 37*(1), 78-93. [http://dx.doi.org/10.1002/hpm.3328] [PMID: 34535906]

Shetty, S. R., Chatterjee, D., & Pai, Y. P. (2022). Performance of Third Party Administrators in Indian Healthcare. [http://dx.doi.org/10.1177/09720634221128385]

Singh, A., Taneja, S., Kumar, P. (2023). Algorithmic approaches to financial technology: Forecasting, trading, and optimization. *In Algorithmic Approaches to Financial Technology: Forecasting, Trading, and Optimization.*

Singh, B., Chattu, V.K., Kaur, J., Mol, R., Gauttam, P., Singh, B. (2022). COVID-19 and Global Distributive Justice: 'Health Diplomacy' of India and South Africa for the TRIPS waiver. *J. Asian Afr. Stud.* [http://dx.doi.org/10.1177/00219096211069652/ASSET/IMAGES/LARGE/10.1177_00219096211069652-FIG2.JPEG] [PMID: 37461426]

Taylor, R., Friedson, A. (2022). The Interplay Between Health Insurance and Auto Insurance: Lessons from the ACA. *SSRN Electronic Journal.*

ten Brink, T., Müller, A., & Liu, T. (2022). The Introduction of Pension, Accident, and Health Insurance in Urban China. 33–66. [http://dx.doi.org/10.1007/978-3-030-91088-4_2]

Trinh, C.T., Chao, C.C., Ho, N.Q. (2023). Private health insurance consumption and public health-care provision in OECD countries: Impact of culture, finance, and the pandemic. *N. Am. J. Econ. Finance, 64*, 101849.
[http://dx.doi.org/10.1016/j.najef.2022.101849]

van Eijk, M.S., Prueher, L., Kett, P.M., Frogner, B.K., Guenther, G.A. (2022). Financial Instability of Federal Navigator Program Challenges Organizations to Help Uninsured Enroll in Health Insurance Coverage. *J. Health Care Poor Underserved, 33*(3), 1555-1568.
[http://dx.doi.org/10.1353/hpu.2022.0129] [PMID: 36245180]

Vitikainen, K., Linna, M., Street, A. (2010). Substituting inpatient for outpatient care: what is the impact on hospital costs and efficiency? *Eur. J. Health Econ., 11*(4), 395-404.
[http://dx.doi.org/10.1007/s10198-009-0211-0] [PMID: 20037768]

Waters, A.R., Mann, K., Warner, E.L., Vaca Lopez, P.L., Kaddas, H.K., Ray, N., Tsukamoto, T., Fair, D.B., Lewis, M.A., Perez, G.K., Park, E.R., Kirchhoff, A.C. (2022). "I thought there would be more I understood": health insurance literacy among adolescent and young adult cancer survivors. *Support. Care Cancer, 30*(5), 4457-4464.
[http://dx.doi.org/10.1007/s00520-022-06873-2] [PMID: 35107600]

Webster, P. (2020). Virtual health care in the era of COVID-19. *Lancet, 395*(10231), 1180-1181.
[http://dx.doi.org/10.1016/S0140-6736(20)30818-7] [PMID: 32278374]

Yadav, C.S., Sudhakar, A. (2017). Personal Factors Influencing Purchase Decision Making: A Study of Health Insurance Sector in India. *Bimaquest, 17*(1-A) Available from: http://bimaquest.niapune.org.in/index.php/bimaquest/article/view/9

Yadav, R.K. (2014). Impact of Claim Settlement on Sales of Life Insurance Policies - A Case Study of LIC of India. *International Letters of Social and Humanistic Sciences, 23*, 1-6.
[http://dx.doi.org/10.18052/www.scipress.com/ILSHS.23.1]

Yamada, T., Chen, C.C., Yamada, T., Noguchi, H., Miller, M. (2009). Private health insurance and hospitalization under Japanese national health insurance. *Open Economics Journal, 2*(1), 61-70.
[http://dx.doi.org/10.2174/1874919400902010061]

You, P., Guo, S., Zhao, H., Zhao, H. (2017). Operation performance evaluation of power grid enterprise using a hybrid {BWM}-{TOPSIS} method. *Sustainability, 9*(2329).

Yu, W., Wang, Q., Guan, G., Huang, Y. (2021). Factors affecting the purchase of commercial health insurance: Based on personal health status and the substitution effect of social insurance.
[http://dx.doi.org/10.21203/rs.3.rs-1033408/v1]

Yusoff, N.H., Sarifin, M.R., Zainal Abidin, A. (2022). Factors Influencing Practice of Cashless Purchase During COVID-19 Movement Control Order (MCO) in Malaysian Society. *Int. J. Acad. Res. Bus. Soc. Sci., 12*(1), 702-714.
[http://dx.doi.org/10.6007/IJARBSS/v12-i1/11613]

Zare, H., Eisenberg, M.D., Anderson, G. (2022). Comparing the value of community benefit and Tax-Exemption in non-profit hospitals. *Health Serv. Res., 57*(2), 270-284.
[http://dx.doi.org/10.1111/1475-6773.13668] [PMID: 33966271]

Dihom, H. R., Al-Shaibani, M. M., Mohamed, R. M. S. R., Al-Gheethi, A. A., Sharma, A., & Khamidun, M. H. B. (2022). Photocatalytic degradation of disperse azo dyes in textile wastewater using green zinc oxide nanoparticles synthesized in plant extract: A critical review. *Journal of Water Process Engineering, 47*, 102705.

Sharma, D., Saharan, B.S. (2016). Functional characterization of biomedical potential of biosurfactant produced by *Lactobacillus helveticus. Biotechnol. Rep. (Amst.), 11*, 27-35.
[http://dx.doi.org/10.1016/j.btre.2016.05.001] [PMID: 28352537]

Srivastava, G., Das, C.K., Das, A., Singh, S.K., Roy, M., Kim, H., Sethy, N., Kumar, A., Sharma, R.K., Singh, S.K., Philip, D., Das, M. (2014). Seed treatment with iron pyrite (FeS_2) nanoparticles increases the

production of spinach. *RSC Advances, 4*(102), 58495-58504.
[http://dx.doi.org/10.1039/C4RA06861K]

Avikal, S., Singh, R., Barthwal, A., Ram, M. (2023). COVID-19: a Kano model and AHP-based classification of preventive activities under Fuzzy environment. *International Journal of Quality & Reliability Management.*

Avikal, S., Nigam, M., Ram, M. (2022). A hybrid multi criteria decision making approach for consultant selection problem in ERP project. *International Journal of System Assurance Engineering and Management, 13*(S2) (Suppl. 2), 941-950.
[http://dx.doi.org/10.1007/s13198-021-01505-0]

Singh, R., Avikal, S. (2021). An AHP-Based Approach to Determine the Effects of COVID-19 on Industrial Sustainability. *Sustainability in Industry 4.0.* CRC Press.
[http://dx.doi.org/10.1201/9781003102304-11]

Singh, R., Avikal, S. (2020). COVID-19: A decision-making approach for prioritization of preventive activities. *Int. J. Healthc. Manag., 13*(3), 257-262.
[http://dx.doi.org/10.1080/20479700.2020.1782661]

Chaudhry, V. (2020). Static structural analysis of humerus bone to find out the load at which fracture occurs and predict suitable alternative materials for bone implants. *Mater. Today Proc., 26*, 1701-1706.
[http://dx.doi.org/10.1016/j.matpr.2020.02.359]

Kumar, K. C. N., Chavadaki, S., Shaikh, A., Singh, D. P., & Avikal, S. (2020). Weight optimization of a hat stiffened panel of a typical transport aircraft composite wing. Materials Today: Proceedings, 26, 471–474.
[http://dx.doi.org/10.1016/j.matpr.2019.12.087]

Singh, R., Avikal, S. (2019). A MCDM-Based approach for selection of a sedan car from indian car market. *Harmony search and nature inspired optimization algorithms, 741*, 569-579.

Rashmi, R., Singh, R., Chand, M., Avikal, S. (2019). An MCDM-based approach for selecting the best state for tourism in India. *Harmony Search and Nature Inspired Optimization Algorithms: Theory and Applications, ICHSA,* 17-26.

CHAPTER 6

The Future of Data Analytics in Insurance: A Comprehensive Exploration

Varnesh Ghildiyal[1,*], **Supriya Hazra**[2] and **Muskan Singh**[3]

[1] *H.N.B. Garhwal Central University, Uttarakhand, India*

[2] *Uttaranchal University, Uttarakhand, India*

[3] *Graphic Era Deemed to Be University, Dehradun, India*

Abstract: The landscape of the insurance industry is undergoing a profound transformation propelled by the integration of advanced data analytics. This paper explores the evolving role of data analytics in reshaping critical aspects of insurance, ranging from traditional risk assessment to customer-centric practices. Against the backdrop of exponential data growth and technological advancements, insurers are increasingly relying on analytics to inform strategic decision-making, enhance risk modeling, and optimize customer engagement. The abstract provides a concise summary of the primary themes covered in this paper, underscoring the pivotal role of data analytics in navigating the challenges and leveraging the opportunities that lie ahead for the insurance sector. The exploration encompasses current trends, technological advancements, ethical considerations, and regulatory landscapes, aiming to provide a comprehensive understanding of the dynamic future that awaits the intersection of data analytics and insurance.

Keywords: Artificial intelligence, Customer engagement, Data analytics, Ethical considerations, Insurance, Machine learning, Predictive modeling, Risk management, Regulatory landscape, Telematics.

INTRODUCTION

The insurance industry, traditionally rooted in actuarial models and statistical methods, is currently standing at the precipice of a transformative era fueled by data analytics (Malhotra & Gupta, 2021). In recent years, the exponential growth of data, coupled with advancements in technology, has propelled the insurance sector into uncharted territories of innovation (Upreti & Malhotra, 2024). This introduction sets the stage for a comprehensive exploration of the future of data

* **Corresponding author Varnesh Ghildiyal:** H.N.B. Garhwal Central University, Uttarakhand, India; E-mail: vgpawan1@gmail.com

Sanjay Taneja, Ercan Ozen, Luan Vardar, Mohit Kukreti & Mohammad Kashif (Eds.)

analytics in insurance, emphasizing its pivotal role in revolutionizing key facets of the industry (Mary Joshitta *et al.*, 2023).

Historically, insurance operations have been inherently risk-focused, relying on historical data and statistical models to assess and manage uncertainties (Kanojia *et al.*, 2022). However, the advent of big data has ushered in a paradigm shift, providing insurers with an unprecedented wealth of information. This influx of data, when harnessed effectively through advanced analytics, holds the promise of reshaping fundamental processes within the industry (J. Kaur *et al.*, 2024).

The integration of data analytics into insurance practices extends beyond mere efficiency gains (Neha *et al.*, 2023). It encompasses a profound re-evaluation of traditional underwriting methodologies, claims processing, and overall risk management. This shift is not only driven by technological capabilities but is also a response to the changing expectations of consumers and the need for insurers to remain competitive in a rapidly evolving market (R. Kumar, Singh, *et al.*, 2023).

Furthermore, as the insurance landscape becomes increasingly complex, with emerging risks and dynamic customer expectations, the role of data analytics becomes paramount (P. Sharma *et al.*, 2022). The ability to extract actionable insights from vast datasets empowers insurers to make informed decisions, adapt to market trends, and enhance the overall customer experience (Cavaliere *et al.*, 2024).

It further acknowledges the challenges inherent in this transformative journey, such as concerns surrounding data privacy, regulatory compliance, and the ethical implications of algorithmic decision-making (P. Gupta *et al.*, 2023). However, it also underscores the multitude of opportunities presented by leveraging data analytics for personalized offerings, targeted risk assessment, and improved operational efficiency (Caiado *et al.*, 2023).

Even Public sector entities, including governments, now own extensive datasets that hold the potential to address diverse challenges within their geopolitical frameworks (Juneja *et al.*, 2022). Cities, states, municipalities, and organizations operating at federal or international levels are increasingly identifying pertinent data analytics applications. These applications address evolving business priorities and adapt to the ever-changing market trends (Arora *et al.*, 2022).

The convergence of big data and analytics has emerged as a disruptive force in a variety of disciplines, providing unprecedented opportunities to address core causes and extract deeper insights for informed decision-making (Diddi *et al.*, 2022). This adaptability is especially visible in the government sector, where big data analytics plays a critical role in streamlining operations and improving public services. Fig. (**1**) below depicts the various scopes of big data analytics in government, while Table **1** below shows the various applications on different scopes of big data analytics in government, illuminating how these technologies contribute to advancements in healthcare, education, poverty eradication, taxation, open government initiatives, smart cities, agriculture, transportation, weather forecasting, national security, crime detection and prevention, cybersecurity, and service delivery/public welfare services (Rakhra *et al.*, 2022). Each sector showcases how data-driven insights pave the way for more efficient, equitable, and secure governance, exemplifying the broad impact of big data analytics across various facets of governmental operations (M. A. Kumar *et al.*, 2022).

In the subsequent sections, this paper will conduct a thorough exploration, drawing on existing literature, industry reports, and emerging trends to provide a nuanced understanding of the future trajectory of data analytics in the insurance sector (Matta & Pant, 2020). From predictive modeling to artificial intelligence, this analysis aims to shed light on the dynamic landscape that insurers are navigating and the profound implications this journey holds for the future of the industry (R. Kumar, Kandpal, *et al.*, 2023).

Fig. (1). (Scope of Government Application on Big Data and Data Analysis). The Source: Author calculation from infosyspublicservices.com

Table 1. Application of big data and data analysis in government.

Area	Applications
Healthcare	- Revolutionizing healthcare for equity and value-based services, minimizing costs, and ensuring high-quality care.
	- Enhancing understanding of high-risk patient groups, facilitating evidence-based prevention, and improving overall population health management.
	- Predicting healthcare service usage patterns for effective resource allocation during public health crises or epidemics.
Agriculture	- Implementing precise and sustainable agricultural practices.
	- Utilizing advanced technologies like computer vision and deep learning to identify crop diseases and pests, providing timely alerts to farmers.
	- Improving efficiency in distribution networks through intelligent insights, managing crops, and increasing production to meet growing population and food demands.
Transport	- Obtaining real-time insights into traffic conditions.
	- Identifying and addressing potential threats to road safety.
	- Modeling traffic conditions to optimize transportation infrastructure development.
Education	- Understanding educational needs at local and federal levels.
	- Enhancing evaluation and progress tracking of students.
Poverty Eradication	- Utilizing data analysis on spending patterns, and GIS data on electricity for estimating income indicators.
	- Tackling hunger risk through the analysis of food access data, household surveys on nutrition, online food prices, and health records.
Taxation	- Ensuring information accuracy to detect potential fraud.
	- Maximizing tax collection through predictive analytics.
Open Government	- Segmenting citizens for customized public services.
	- Employing sentiment analysis to understand citizens' interests, opinions, and needs.
	- Improving financial forecast accuracy.
	- Enhancing cybersecurity measures.
	- Understanding voter preferences for effective election campaigns.
Smart Cities	- Automating processes for improved citizen services
	- Encouraging public participation in government initiatives.
	- Fostering economic growth.
	- Enhancing energy efficiency and reducing greenhouse gas emissions.
	- Improving emergency service response for citizen security.
Weather Forecasting	- Analyzing data from various sensors for accurate natural event forecasting.

(Table 1) cont.....

Area	Applications
National Security	- Integrating data from diverse sources to identify and address potential internal or external threats
Crime Detection and Prevention	- Effectively combating illegal activities such as money laundering or terrorism financing.
	- Anticipating crime trends and taking preventive actions using predictive analytics.
Cybersecurity	- Detecting and responding to malware and access attempts from malicious agents.
	- Monitoring internet traffic to identify anomalies and suspicious behavior.
Service Delivery/Public Welfare Services	- Analyzing data (*e.g.*, mobile networks) to forecast population density, urbanization, and migration patterns, guiding the deployment of services like water, schools, health posts, fire safety, and managing infection spread risks.
	- Assessing trends/outcomes in development programs to predict future challenges, such as medical needs, food assistance requests, and education requirements; translating data into actionable insights.

The Source: infosyspublicservices.com

LITERATURE REVIEW

The literature on data analytics in the insurance industry reflects a dynamic and evolving landscape, mirroring the transformative impact that advanced analytics has had on traditional insurance practices (Bhamangol *et al.*, 2022). This section presents a comprehensive review of existing studies, research papers, and industry reports, categorizing findings into key themes that capture the importance of the ongoing paradigm shift (F. Ahmad *et al.*, 2021).

Evolution of Analytics in Insurance

Historically rooted in actuarial models and statistical techniques, the insurance industry has witnessed a notable evolution in its analytical approaches. Early studies focused on the application of statistical methods for risk assessment, paving the way for the integration of more sophisticated analytics techniques. The literature traces the progression from conventional methods to the current era dominated by machine learning algorithms (Barthwal *et al.*, 2023; S. Sharma *et al.*, 2020), predictive modeling (Hajoary *et al.*, 2023), and artificial intelligence (Belwal *et al.*, 2023).

Impact on Risk Management

A substantial body of literature explores how data analytics has reshaped risk management strategies within the insurance sector. Traditional risk models, while valuable, are increasingly complemented and, in some cases, supplanted by predictive analytics. Studies delve into the efficacy of machine learning algorithms in predicting and mitigating risks, offering insights into the enhanced accuracy and responsiveness that analytics brings to risk assessment processes (Mishra *et al.*, 2021).

Fraud Detection and Claims Processing

Data analytics plays a pivotal role in fraud detection and claims processing. The literature highlights the application of anomaly detection algorithms, pattern recognition, and predictive modeling in identifying potentially fraudulent activities. Insights from studies showcase how advanced analytics not only expedites claims processing but also significantly improves accuracy by identifying potentially fraudulent claims, thereby reducing financial losses for insurers (Akana *et al.*, 2023; N. M. Kumar, Islam, *et al.*, 2023; Suresh *et al.*, 2023).

Personalized Pricing and Customer Engagement

The advent of data analytics has enabled insurers to move beyond one-size-fits-all pricing models. Literature reveals the increasing adoption of personalized pricing strategies based on individual risk profiles, driving more accurate premium calculations. Moreover, analytics is leveraged to enhance customer engagement through targeted marketing, personalized recommendations, and improved customer service experiences (Ram & Xing, 2023; Salama *et al.*, 2023).

Ethical and Regulatory Considerations

As insurers embrace advanced analytics, the literature scrutinizes the ethical considerations associated with the use of algorithms in decision-making. Questions of bias, fairness, and transparency in model outcomes are explored, emphasizing the importance of ethical frameworks in data-driven practices (Gaurav *et al.*, 2023). Additionally, the literature reviews the evolving regulatory landscape, including data protection laws and guidelines governing the ethical use of analytics in the insurance sector (Godbole *et al.*, 2023; A. Das Gupta *et al.*, 2022; Praveenchandar *et al.*, 2022).

This comprehensive literature review sets the stage for a nuanced understanding of the current state of data analytics in insurance, providing a foundation for the subsequent analysis of the future landscape. The synthesis of existing knowledge allows for a deeper exploration of emerging trends, challenges, and opportunities that will shape the trajectory of data analytics in the insurance industry (Ansari & Afzal, 2022; A. Kumar, Saxena, *et al.*, 2023).

METHODOLOGY

The methodology employed in this exploration of the future of data analytics in the insurance sector encompasses a qualitative approach, drawing insights from a synthesis of information derived from academic publications, industry reports, and relevant case studies. This section outlines the systematic process undertaken to analyze current trends, technological advancements, and industry practices, providing a robust foundation for the subsequent discussion (Umamaheswaran *et al.*, 2023).

Literature Review and Data Collection

The first phase involves an extensive review of existing literature spanning academic research articles, peer-reviewed journals, conference proceedings, and industry reports. This comprehensive literature review serves as a knowledge base, providing a historical context, and identifying key themes, trends, and challenges in the intersection of data analytics and the insurance industry (N. K. Singh *et al.*, 2023).

Identification of Key Themes

Through a systematic analysis of the literature, key themes emerge, including the evolution of analytics in insurance, the impact on risk management, fraud detection, personalized pricing, customer engagement, and the ethical and regulatory considerations associated with data analytics. These themes provide a structured framework for understanding the multifaceted role of data analytics in the insurance sector (Ram & Xing, 2023).

Synthesis and Analysis

The gathered information is synthesized to distill key insights and trends. The analysis involves identifying patterns, correlations, and disparities in the literature to offer a nuanced understanding of the current state of data analytics in insurance. This phase is crucial for developing a cohesive narrative that informs the exploration of the future landscape.

Case Study Examination

To supplement the findings from academic literature, relevant case studies from the insurance industry are examined. Real-world applications of data analytics in different insurance domains, such as underwriting, claims processing, and customer engagement, provide practical insights into the implementation and impact of analytics strategies (Akberdina *et al.*, 2023; Mohamed *et al.*, 2023; S. K. Singh *et al.*, 2023).

Technological Trends Exploration

The analysis extends to an exploration of current and emerging technological trends shaping data analytics in insurance. This includes advancements in predictive modeling, artificial intelligence, telematics, and the integration of external data sources. Understanding the technological landscape is essential for forecasting the trajectory of data analytics in the future (16).

Ethical and Regulatory Landscape Review

A focused review of the ethical considerations and regulatory frameworks associated with data analytics in insurance is conducted. This encompasses examining the literature on algorithmic fairness, transparency, and compliance with data protection laws. Understanding the ethical and regulatory landscape is crucial for anticipating challenges and ensuring the responsible use of analytics in the insurance sector (Chandna *et al*., 2022; Saini *et al*., 2022).

Conclusion and Future Trajectory Synthesis

The findings from the literature review, case studies, and technological trends exploration are synthesized to draw informed conclusions about the future of data analytics in insurance. This synthesis forms the basis for projecting the trajectory of the industry, highlighting opportunities and challenges that insurers are likely to encounter in the evolving landscape (Komkowski *et al*., 2023).

By employing this comprehensive qualitative methodology, this paper aims to provide a holistic and insightful exploration of the future of data analytics in the insurance sector. The integration of academic literature, real-world case studies, and technological trends ensures a multifaceted understanding of the dynamic forces shaping the intersection of data analytics and insurance (Thapa *et al*., 2022; Verma *et al*., 2022).

THE FUTURE LANDSCAPE

The future landscape of data analytics in the insurance industry is characterized by a convergence of technological advancements, evolving consumer expectations, and a continual shift toward data-driven decision-making. This section delves into the anticipated trajectory, exploring key components that are poised to shape the future of data analytics within the insurance sector (AL-Huqail *et al*., 2022; Unhelkar *et al*., 2022).

Predictive Modeling and Artificial Intelligence

One of the defining features of the future landscape is the escalating prominence of predictive modeling and artificial intelligence (AI). Insurers are increasingly harnessing the power of machine learning algorithms to analyze vast datasets, enabling more accurate risk prediction, fraud detection, and customer segmentation. The integration of AI not only refines existing processes but also opens avenues for novel applications, such as dynamic underwriting and adaptive pricing models (Babu *et al.*, 2022; Dixit *et al.*, 2022).

Real-time Data Processing

The future of data analytics in insurance envisions a paradigm shift towards real-time data processing. With the proliferation of Internet of Things (IoT) devices and telematics, insurers can access a continuous stream of data, allowing for immediate risk assessment and more responsive policy adjustments. Real-time analytics not only enhances operational efficiency but also facilitates proactive risk management and timely interventions, minimizing losses.

Integration of Telematics and IoT Devices

Telematics and IoT devices emerge as integral components of the future insurance landscape. The widespread adoption of connected devices, including those embedded in vehicles, homes, and wearables, provides insurers with granular data on individual behavior and risks. This data-driven approach enables the development of usage-based insurance, where premiums are dynamically adjusted based on real-time behavioral patterns, promoting a more personalized and fair pricing model (Kohli *et al.*, 2022).

Blockchain Technology for Secure Data Sharing

The future landscape anticipates the increased adoption of blockchain technology for secure and transparent data sharing among insurers, reinsurers, and other stakeholders. Blockchain enhances data integrity, reduces fraud, and streamlines processes like claims verification and settlement. As a decentralized and tamper-resistant ledger, blockchain contributes to building trust in the insurance ecosystem while addressing concerns related to data privacy and security (I. Ahmad *et al.*, 2023; R. Kumar, Saxena, *et al.*, 2023).

Ethical Implications of AI-driven Decision-making

The ethical considerations associated with AI-driven decision-making become more pronounced in the future landscape. Insurers face the challenge of ensuring fairness, transparency, and accountability in algorithmic models. Ethical frameworks and guidelines will be essential to navigate issues related to bias, discrimination, and the explainability of AI models, ensuring that the benefits of data analytics are realized without compromising ethical standards (Rajbalaji *et al.*, 2023).

Holistic Customer Experience

The future landscape sees data analytics playing a pivotal role in crafting a holistic customer experience. Insurers leverage customer data to provide personalized services, anticipate needs, and enhance engagement. Customer-centric analytics not only aids in tailoring products but also streamlines the claims process, fostering trust and loyalty among policyholders (Badhotiya *et al.*, 2022; A. Gupta *et al.*, 2022; Josphineleela *et al.*, 2023).

Regulatory and Compliance Challenges

As data analytics becomes more ingrained in insurance practices, regulatory bodies are facing several challenges and they likely to adapt and introduce new frameworks to govern the ethical and responsible use of data. Insurers will need to navigate evolving regulatory landscapes, ensuring compliance with data protection laws, privacy regulations, and guidelines governing algorithmic decision-making (Bansal *et al.*, 2023; Dahiya & Taneja, 2023; Taneja, Gupta, Bhushan, Bhatnagar, *et al.*, 2023).

The future landscape of data analytics in the insurance industry is characterized by a transformative integration of advanced technologies, a heightened focus on real-time data processing, and an emphasis on ethical considerations (Kour *et al.*, 2025; A. Singh *et al.*, 2024; Taneja, Gupta, Singh, Bhatnagar, *et al.*, 2023; TANEJA *et al.*, 2024). As insurers navigate these changes, embracing innovation while addressing challenges, the landscape is poised to redefine industry norms and elevate the role of data analytics in shaping the future of insurance (Dangwal *et al.*, 2022; M. Gupta *et al.*, 2023; Reepu *et al.*, 2023; Taneja & Özen, 2023; Taneja & Sharma, 2023).

CHALLENGES AND OPPORTUNITIES

The dynamic landscape of data analytics in the insurance sector presents a spectrum of challenges and opportunities, influencing the trajectory of the industry. This section provides an in-depth exploration of the multifaceted aspects that insurers must navigate to harness the full potential of data analytics.

Challenges

- **Data Privacy and Security Concerns:** The extensive collection and utilization of sensitive customer data raise significant concerns about privacy and security. Insurers must grapple with evolving data protection regulations and implement robust cybersecurity measures to safeguard against data breaches and unauthorized access (Bhatnagar, Taneja, *et al.*, 2024; P. Kumar, Taneja, & Ozen, 2024; P. Sharma *et al.*, 2024).
- **Ethical Dilemmas in Algorithmic Decision-Making:** The use of algorithms in decision-making processes introduces ethical challenges, including issues of bias, fairness, and transparency. As insurers rely more on artificial intelligence, ensuring ethical practices in algorithm design and implementation becomes crucial to maintain trust and avoid unintended consequences (Bhatnagar, Rajaram, *et al.*, 2024; P. Kumar, Verma, *et al.*, 2023; P. Kumar, Reepu, *et al.*, 2024; Taneja, Bhatnagar, Kumar, & Grima, 2023).
- **Regulatory Compliance Complexity:** The evolving regulatory landscape adds complexity to the deployment of data analytics in insurance. Insurers need to stay abreast of changing regulations, such as GDPR, and develop strategies to comply with both existing and emerging frameworks, which may vary across regions (Bhatnagar *et al.*, 2023; P. Kumar, Bhatnagar, *et al.*, 2023; Taneja, Bhatnagar, Kumar, & Rupeika-apoga, 2023).
- **Interpretability of Advanced Models:** Advanced machine learning models, while powerful, often lack interpretability. Insurers face the challenge of explaining model outcomes to regulators, customers, and internal stakeholders. Ensuring transparency in model predictions is essential for building trust and compliance (Bhatnagar, Kumar, *et al.*, 2024; P. Kumar, Taneja, Bhatnagar, *et al.*, 2024).
- **Integration of New Technologies:** The integration of emerging technologies like blockchain, telematics, and IoT devices requires substantial investment in infrastructure and expertise. Insurers need to navigate the complexities of adopting and integrating these technologies seamlessly into existing operational frameworks (Upadhyay, Manwal, Yadav, *et al.*, 2024; Yashu, Kukreja, Srivastava, Garg, *et al.*, 2024).

Opportunities

- **Enhanced Risk Prediction and Management:** Data analytics enables insurers to move beyond traditional risk assessment models, providing a more nuanced understanding of individual risks. Advanced analytics techniques, including predictive modeling, empower insurers to enhance risk prediction accuracy, leading to more precise underwriting and pricing strategies (M. Pant & Thakur, 2021).

- **Fraud Detection and Prevention:** The increased sophistication of analytics algorithms offers insurers powerful tools for fraud detection and prevention. Machine learning can analyze patterns and anomalies in data to identify potentially fraudulent claims, reducing financial losses and preserving the integrity of insurance systems (Chattopadhyay *et al.*, 2024; Nayak *et al.*, 2024).
- **Personalized Products and Pricing:** The wealth of customer data facilitates the creation of personalized insurance products and pricing models. Insurers can tailor offerings based on individual risk profiles, driving customer satisfaction and loyalty. This personalization also contributes to a more competitive and adaptive market (J. Pant *et al.*, 2024).
- **Improved Customer Engagement:** Data analytics enhances customer engagement by providing insights into customer preferences, behaviors, and needs. This enables insurers to deliver targeted marketing, personalized recommendations, and streamlined customer experiences, ultimately fostering stronger relationships with policyholders (Banerjee *et al.*, 2024).
- **Operational Efficiency and Cost Reduction:** The automation and optimization capabilities of data analytics contribute to operational efficiency, reducing manual efforts and associated costs. Insurers can streamline claims processing, underwriting, and other operational aspects, leading to cost savings and improved overall efficiency (Upadhyay, Manwal, Kukreja, *et al.*, 2024).
- **Innovation and Product Development:** The integration of data analytics stimulates innovation in product development. Insurers can explore new, innovative insurance products that align with emerging risks and market demands. This agility in product development positions insurers as proactive players in a rapidly evolving industry (Joshi *et al.*, 2024; A. Kaur *et al.*, 2024a; Shreshtha *et al.*, 2024; V. P. Singh *et al.*, 2024).
- **Competitive Advantage:** Embracing data analytics provides insurers with a competitive advantage. Those who can effectively harness the power of data will be better positioned to adapt to market changes, stay ahead of competitors, and meet the evolving expectations of consumers (A. Kaur *et al.*, 2024b; V. Kumar *et al.*, 2021; Yashu, Kukreja, Srivastava, & Garg, 2024).

In navigating these challenges and capitalizing on the opportunities presented by data analytics, insurers have the potential to reshape their industry, drive innovation, and deliver enhanced value to both their businesses and the customers they serve. The successful integration of data analytics will require a strategic, adaptive approach that balances technological advancement with ethical considerations and regulatory compliance.

CONCLUSION

In conclusion, this paper has undertaken a comprehensive exploration of the future of data analytics in the insurance industry, revealing a landscape shaped by technological innovation, evolving consumer expectations, and the imperative for data-driven decision-making. The synthesis of existing literature, examination of case studies, and exploration of technological trends provided insights into the multifaceted role of data analytics within the insurance sector.

The future trajectory points towards a paradigm shift characterized by the widespread adoption of predictive modeling and artificial intelligence, real-time data processing, and the integration of telematics and IoT devices. These advancements offer insurers unprecedented opportunities to refine risk assessment, personalize products, and enhance overall customer experiences. However, this transformative journey is not without its challenges.

Data privacy and security concerns, ethical dilemmas in algorithmic decision-making, and the complexity of regulatory compliance present formidable challenges for insurers. The need for interpretability in advanced models, coupled with the integration of emerging technologies, adds layers of complexity to an already dynamic landscape.

Despite these challenges, the future landscape also offers significant opportunities. Enhanced risk prediction and management, fraud detection capabilities, personalized product offerings, and improved operational efficiency stand out as key advantages. The potential for innovation and competitive advantage positions data analytics as a cornerstone for the future success of insurers.

As insurers navigate this evolving landscape, striking a balance between harnessing the power of data and addressing ethical, privacy and regulatory considerations will be paramount. The successful integration of data analytics requires a strategic and adaptive approach, ensuring that the benefits of innovation are realized while maintaining trust, transparency, and compliance with evolving regulatory frameworks.

In essence, the future of data analytics in insurance holds great promise, heralding an era where insurers can leverage technology to not only mitigate risks effectively but also tailor products and services to individual needs. The journey forward requires a thoughtful and ethical application of data analytics, cementing its role as a catalyst for a positive change within the insurance industry.

REFERENCES

Ahmad, F., Kumar, P., & Patil, P. P. (2021). Vibration characteristics based pre-stress analysis of a quadcopter's body frame. In S. Y. (Ed.), Materials Today: Proceedings, Elsevier Ltd, 46, pp. 10329-10333. [http://dx.doi.org/10.1016/j.matpr.2020.12.458]

Ahmad, I., Sharma, S., Kumar, R., Dhyani, S., Dumka, A. (2023). Data Analytics of Online Education during Pandemic Health Crisis: A Case Study. *2nd Edition of IEEE Delhi Section Owned Conference, DELCON 2023 - Proceedings.* [http://dx.doi.org/10.1109/DELCON57910.2023.10127423]

Akana, C.M.V.S., Kumar, A., Tiwari, M., Yunus, A.Z., Vijayakumar, E., Singh, M. (2023). An Optimized DDoS Attack Detection Using Deep Convolutional Generative Adversarial Networks. *Proceedings of the 5th International Conference on Inventive Research in Computing Applications, ICIRCA,* 668-673. [http://dx.doi.org/10.1109/ICIRCA57980.2023.10220745]

Akberdina, V., Kumar, V., Kyriakopoulos, G. L., & Kuzmin, E. (2023). Editorial: What Does Industry's Digital Transition Hold in the Uncertainty Context? In K. V., K. G.L., A. V., & K. E. (Eds.), Lecture Notes in Information Systems and Organisation: 61 LNISO. Springer Science and Business Media Deutschland GmbH, pp. 1-4. [http://dx.doi.org/10.1007/978-3-031-30351-7_1]

AL-Huqail, A.A., Kumar, P., Eid, E.M., Taher, M.A., Kumar, P., Adelodun, B., Andabaka, Ž., Mioč, B., Držaić, V., Bachheti, A., Singh, J., Kumar, V., Širić, I. (2022). Phytoremediation of Composite Industrial Effluent using Sacred Lotus (Nelumbo nucifera Gaertn): A Lab-Scale Experimental Investigation. *Sustainability (Basel), 14*(15), 9500. [http://dx.doi.org/10.3390/su14159500]

Ansari, M. F., Afzal, A. (2022). Sensitivity and Performance Analysis of 10 MW Solar Power Plant Using MPPT Technique. *Lecture Notes in Electrical Engineering, 894 LNEE,* 512-518. [http://dx.doi.org/10.1007/978-981-19-1677-9_46]

Arora, R., Singh, A.P., Sharma, R., Chauhan, A. (2022). A remanufacturing inventory model to control the carbon emission using cap-and-trade regulation with the hexagonal fuzzy number. *Benchmarking (Bradf.), 29*(7), 2202-2230. [http://dx.doi.org/10.1108/BIJ-05-2021-0254]

Babu, M., Venkataraman, S.R., Rao, P.N., Rao, V., Kaliappan, S., Patil, P.P., Sekar, S., Yuvaraj, K.P., Murugan, A. (2022). Optical Microstructure, FESEM, Microtensile, and Microhardness Properties of LM 25-B4Cnp-Grnp Hybrid Composites Manufactured by Selective Laser Melting. *Adv. Mater. Sci. Eng., 2022*, 1-8. [http://dx.doi.org/10.1155/2022/3177172]

Badhotiya, G.K., Avikal, S., Soni, G., Sengar, N. (2022). Analyzing barriers for the adoption of circular economy in the manufacturing sector. *Int. J. Prod. Perform. Manag., 71*(3), 912-931. [http://dx.doi.org/10.1108/IJPPM-01-2021-0021]

Banerjee, D., Sharma, N., Chauhan, R., Singh, M., Kumar, B.V. (2024). Precision in Plant Pathology: A Hybrid Model Approach for BYDV Syndrome Degrees. *5th International Conference for Emerging Technology, INCET.* [http://dx.doi.org/10.1109/INCET61516.2024.10593415]

Bansal, N., Bhatnagar, M., Taneja, S. (2023). Balancing priorities through green optimism: A study elucidating initiatives, approaches, and strategies for sustainable supply chain management. *Handbook of Research on Designing Sustainable Supply Chains to Achieve a Circular Economy.* [http://dx.doi.org/10.4018/978-1-6684-7664-2.ch004]

Barthwal, S., Pundir, S., Wazid, M., Singh, D. P., Pundir, S. (2023). Design of an Energy Aware Cluster-Based Routing Scheme to Minimize Energy Consumption in Wireless Sensor Networks. *Communications in Computer and Information Science 1797 CCIS,* 16-28. [http://dx.doi.org/10.1007/978-3-031-28180-8_2]

Belwal, N., Juneja, P., Sunori, S.K. (2023). Decoupler Control for a MIMO Process Model in an Industrial Process - A Review. *2nd International Conference on Ambient Intelligence in Health Care, ICAIHC.*
[http://dx.doi.org/10.1109/ICAIHC59020.2023.10431463]

Bhamangol, B., Kaiwade, A., Pant, B., Rana, A., Kaiwade, A., Shaikh, A. (2022). An Artificial Intelligence based Design and Implementation for classifying the Missing Data in IoT Applications. *Proceedings of 5th International Conference on Contemporary Computing and Informatics, IC3I 2022,* 1376-1382.
[http://dx.doi.org/10.1109/IC3I56241.2022.10072634]

Bhatnagar, M., Kumar, P., Taneja, S., Sood, K., Grima, S. (2024). From digital overload to trading Zen: The role of digital detox in enhancing intraday trading performance. *Business Drivers in Promoting Digital Detoxification.*
[http://dx.doi.org/10.4018/979-8-3693-1107-3.ch010]

Bhatnagar, M., Rajaram, R., Taneja, S., Kumar, P. (2024). Balancing acts: The Yin and Yang of debit and credit on the stage of financial well-being. *Emerging Perspectives on Financial Well-Being.*
[http://dx.doi.org/10.4018/979-8-3693-1750-1.ch002]

Bhatnagar, M., Taneja, S., Kumar, P. (2023). The Effectiveness of Carbon Pricing Mechanism in Steering Financial Flows Toward Sustainable Projects. *International Journal of Environmental Impacts, 6*(4), 183-196.
[http://dx.doi.org/10.18280/ijei.060403]

Bhatnagar, M., Taneja, S., Kumar, P., Özen, E. (2024). Does financial education act as a catalyst for SME competitiveness. *International Journal of Education Economics and Development, 15*(3), 377-393.
[http://dx.doi.org/10.1504/IJEED.2024.139306]

Caiado, R. G. G., Scavarda, L. F., Vidal, G., de Mattos Nascimento, D. L., Garza-Reyes, J. A. (2023). A taxonomy of critical factors towards sustainable operations and supply chain management 4.0 in developing countries. *Operations Management Research.*
[http://dx.doi.org/10.1007/s12063-023-00430-8]

Cavaliere, L.P.L., Byloppilly, R., Khan, S.D., Othman, B.A., Muda, I., Malhotra, R.K. (2024). Acceptance and effectiveness of Industry 4.0 internal and external organisational initiatives in Malaysian firms. *Int. J. Manag. Enterp. Dev., 23*(1), 138422.
[http://dx.doi.org/10.1504/IJMED.2024.138422]

Chandna, R., Saini, S., & Kumar, S. (2022). Selecting the Most Agile Manufacturing System with Respect to Agile Attribute-Technology: Fuzzy AHP Approach. In D. N. & C. A. (Eds.), AIP Conference Proceedings (Vol. 2481). American Institute of Physics Inc.
[http://dx.doi.org/10.1063/5.0103804]

Chattopadhyay, S., Verma, A., Chauhan, R.K., Kukreja, V., Sharma, R. (2024). Leveraging Deep Learning's Potential: A CNN and LSTM Network-Based Severity Classification of Mustard Downy Mildew. *Proceedings - International Conference on Computing, Power, and Communication Technologies, IC2PCT,* 791-795.
[http://dx.doi.org/10.1109/IC2PCT60090.2024.10486277]

Dahiya, K., Taneja, S. (2023). To Analyse the Impact of Multi-Media Technology on the Rural Entrepreneurship Development. *Contemporary Studies of Risks in Emerging Technology,* 221-240.
[http://dx.doi.org/10.1108/978-1-80455-562-020231015]

Dangwal, A., Kaur, S., Taneja, S., Ozen, E. (2022). A bibliometric analysis of green tourism based on the scopus platform. *Developing Relationships, Personalization, and Data Herald in Marketing 5.0.*
[http://dx.doi.org/10.4018/978-1-6684-4496-2.ch015]

Diddi, P.K., Sharma, P.K., Srivastava, A., Madduru, S.R.C., Sreenivas Reddy, E. (2022). Sustainable Fast Setting Early Strength Self Compacting Concrete(FSESSCC) Using Metakaolin. *IOP Conf. Ser. Earth Environ. Sci., 1077*(1), 012009.
[http://dx.doi.org/10.1088/1755-1315/1077/1/012009]

Dixit, A.K., Kumar, T.V., Joshi, A., Bedi, H.S., Chakravarthi, M.K., Singh, D.P. (2022). Trends in Robotics and Computer Integrated Manufacturing. *Proceedings of 5th International Conference on Contemporary Computing and Informatics, IC3I 2022,* 212-216. [http://dx.doi.org/10.1109/IC3I56241.2022.10072745]

Gaurav, G., Singh, A.B., Khandelwal, C., Gupta, S., Kumar, S., Meena, M.L., Dangayach, G.S. (2023). Global Development on LCA Research. *Int. J. Soc. Ecol. Sustain. Dev., 14*(1), 1-19. [http://dx.doi.org/10.4018/IJSESD.327791]

Godbole, V., Kukrety, S., Gautam, P., Bisht, M., Pal, M.K. (2023). Bioleaching for Heavy Metal Extraction from E-waste: A Sustainable Approach. *Microbial Technology for Sustainable E-waste Management..* Springer International Publishing. [http://dx.doi.org/10.1007/978-3-031-25678-3_4]

Gupta, A., Dixit, A.K., Kumar, K.S., Lavanya, C., Chakravarthi, M.K., Gangodkar, D. (2022). Analyzing Robotics and Computer Integrated Manufacturing of Key Areas Using Cloud Computing. *Proceedings of 5th International Conference on Contemporary Computing and Informatics, IC3I 2022,* 194-199. [http://dx.doi.org/10.1109/IC3I56241.2022.10072581]

Das Gupta, A., Rafi, S.M., Singh, N., Gupta, V.K., Jaiswal, S., Gangodkar, D. (2022). A Framework of Internet of Things (IOT) for the Manufacturing and Image Classifaication System. *2nd International Conference on Advance Computing and Innovative Technologies in Engineering, ICACITE,* 293-297. [http://dx.doi.org/10.1109/ICACITE53722.2022.9823853]

Gupta, M., Arora, K., Taneja, S. (2023). Bibliometric analysis on employee engagement and human resource management. *Enhancing Customer Engagement Through Location-Based Marketing.* [http://dx.doi.org/10.4018/978-1-6684-8177-6.ch013]

Gupta, P., Gopal, S., Sharma, M., Joshi, S., Sahani, C., Ahalawat, K. (2023). Agriculture Informatics and Communication: Paradigm of E-Governance and Drone Technology for Crop Monitoring. *9th International Conference on Smart Computing and Communications: Intelligent Technologies and Applications, ICSCC,* 113-118. [http://dx.doi.org/10.1109/ICSCC59169.2023.10335058]

Hajoary, P.K., Balachandra, P., Garza-Reyes, J.A. (2023). Industry 4.0 maturity and readiness assessment: an empirical validation using Confirmatory Composite Analysis. *Prod. Plann. Contr.* [http://dx.doi.org/10.1080/09537287.2023.2210545]

Joshi, J., Aeri, M., Kukreja, V., & Mehta, S. (2024). Revolutionizing in Agriculture: Federated CNN Models for Sunflower Leaf Diseases. In S. B., A. R., K. S.K., S. K.M., S. A.V., J. S., S. N., C. A., & G. R. (Eds.), 2024 11th International Conference on Reliability, Infocom Technologies and Optimization (Trends and Future Directions), ICRITO 2024. Institute of Electrical and Electronics Engineers Inc. [http://dx.doi.org/10.1109/ICRITO61523.2024.10522441]

Josphineleela, R., Jyothi, M., Natrayan, L., Kaviarasu, A., Sharma, M. (2023). Development of IoT based Health Monitoring System for Disables using Microcontroller. *Proceedings - 7th International Conference on Computing Methodologies and Communication, ICCMC,* 1380-1384. [http://dx.doi.org/10.1109/ICCMC56507.2023.10084026]

Juneja, P.K., Kumar Sunori, S., Manu, M., Joshi, P., Sharma, S., Garia, P., Mittal, A. (2022). Potential Applications of Fuzzy Logic Controller in the Pulp and Paper Industry - A Review. *5th International Conference on Inventive Computation Technologies, ICICT 2022 - Proceedings,* 399-401. [http://dx.doi.org/10.1109/ICICT54344.2022.9850626]

Kanojia, P., Malhotra, R.K., Uniyal, A.K. (2022). Organizational Commitment and the Academic Staff in HEI's in North West India. *Proceedings - 2022 International Conference on Recent Trends in Microelectronics, Automation, Computing and Communications Systems, ICMACC,* 365-370. [http://dx.doi.org/10.1109/ICMACC54824.2022.10093347]

Kaur, A., Kukreja, V., Tiwari, P., Manwal, M., Sharma, R. (2024). An Efficient Deep Learning-based VGG19 Approach for Rice Leaf Disease Classification. *9th International Conference for Convergence in*

Technology, I2CT.
[http://dx.doi.org/10.1109/I2CT61223.2024.10544229]

Kaur, A., Kukreja, V., Tiwari, P., Manwal, M., Sharma, R. (2024). Optimized Tomato Rot Disease Severity Profiling: A Hybrid CNN-Random Forest Algorithm for Five-Tier Categorization. *9th International Conference for Convergence in Technology, I2CT.*
[http://dx.doi.org/10.1109/I2CT61223.2024.10544233]

Kaur, J., Khanna, R., Kumar, R., Sunil, G. (2024). Role of Blockchain Technologies in Goods and Services Tax. *Proceedings - 2024 3rd International Conference on Sentiment Analysis and Deep Learning, ICSADL,* 607-612.
[http://dx.doi.org/10.1109/ICSADL61749.2024.00104]

Kohli, P., Sharma, S., Matta, P. (2022). Secured Privacy Preserving Techniques Analysis of 6G Driven Vehicular Communication Network in Industry 5.0 Internet-of-Everything (IoE) Applications. *International Conference on Smart Generation Computing, Communication and Networking, SMART GENCON.*
[http://dx.doi.org/10.1109/SMARTGENCON56628.2022.10084289]

Komkowski, T., Antony, J., Garza-Reyes, J.A., Tortorella, G.L., Pongboonchai-Empl, T. (2023). Integrating Lean Management with Industry 4.0: an explorative Dynamic Capabilities theory perspective. *Prod. Plann. Contr.,* 1-19.
[http://dx.doi.org/10.1080/09537287.2023.2294297]

Kour, M., Taneja, S., Özen, E., Sood, K., Grima, S. (2025). *Financial Landscape Transformation Technological Disruptions.*

Kumar, A., Saxena, M., Sastry, R.V.L.S.N., Chaudhari, A., Singh, R., Malathy, V. (2023). Internet of Things and Blockchain Data Supplier for Intelligent Applications. *Proceedings of International Conference on Contemporary Computing and Informatics, IC3I,* 2218-2223.
[http://dx.doi.org/10.1109/IC3I59117.2023.10397630]

Kumar, M.A., Prasad, M.S.G., More, P., Christa, S. (2022). Artificial intelligence-based personal health monitoring devices. *Mobile Health: Advances in Research and Applications - Volume II.*

Kumar, N.M., Islam, S., Podder, A.K., Selim, A., Bajaj, M., Kamel, S. (2023). Lifecycle-based feasibility indicators for floating solar photovoltaic plants along with implementable energy enhancement strategies and framework-driven assessment approaches leading to advancements in the simulation tool. *Front. Energy Res., 11*, 1075384.
[http://dx.doi.org/10.3389/fenrg.2023.1075384]

Kumar, P., Bhatnagar, M., Taneja, S. (2023). Investigation of the time pattern of Bit Green Crypto: An Arma modeling approach to unrave volatility. *Algorithmic Approaches to Financial Technology: Forecasting, Trading, and Optimization.*
[http://dx.doi.org/10.4018/979-8-3693-1746-4.ch001]

Kumar, P., Reepu, & Kaur, R. (2024). Economic and Urban Dynamics: Investigating Socioeconomic Status and Urban Density as Moderators of Mobile Wallet Adoption in Smart Cities. *Lecture Notes in Networks and Systems*, 948 LNNS, 409–417.
[http://dx.doi.org/10.1007/978-981-97-1329-5_33]

Kumar, P., Taneja, S., Bhatnagar, M., Kaur, A.K. (2024). Navigating the digital paradigm shift: Designing CBDCs for a transformative financial landscape. *Exploring Central Bank Digital Currencies: Concepts, Frameworks, Models, and Challenges.*
[http://dx.doi.org/10.4018/979-8-3693-1882-9.ch006]

Kumar, P., Taneja, S., Ozen, E. (2024). Exploring the influence of green bonds on sustainable development through low-carbon financing mobilization. *International Journal of Law and Management.*
[http://dx.doi.org/10.1108/IJLMA-01-2024-0030]

Kumar, P., Verma, P., Bhatnagar, M., Taneja, S., Seychel, S., Todorović, I., Grim, S. (2023). The Financial Performance and Solvency Status of the Indian Public Sector Banks: A CAMELS Rating and Z Index Approach. *Int. J. Sustain. Dev. Plan., 18*(2), 367-376.

[http://dx.doi.org/10.18280/ijsdp.180204]

Kumar, R., Kandpal, B., Ahmad, V. (2023). Industrial IoT (IIOT): Security Threats and Countermeasures. *International Conference on Innovative Data Communication Technologies and Application, ICIDCA 2023 - Proceedings,* 829-833.
[http://dx.doi.org/10.1109/ICIDCA56705.2023.10100145]

Kumar, R., Saxena, A., Singh, R. (2023). Robotic Process Automation Bridge -in Banking Institute and Consumers. *International Conference on Disruptive Technologies, ICDT,* 428-431.
[http://dx.doi.org/10.1109/ICDT57929.2023.10150500]

Kumar, R., Singh, T., Mohanty, S.N., Goel, R., Gupta, D., Alharbi, M., Khanna, R. (2023). Study on online payments and e-commerce with SOR model. *Int. J. Retail Distrib. Manag.*
[http://dx.doi.org/10.1108/IJRDM-03-2023-0137]

Kumar, V., Mitra, D., Rani, A., Suyal, D.C., Singh Gautam, B.P., Jain, L., Gondwal, M., Raj, K.K., Singh, A.K., Soni, R. (2021). Bio-inoculants for Biodegradation and Bioconversion of Agrowaste: Status and Prospects. *Bioremediation of Environmental Pollutants: Emerging Trends and Strategies..* Springer International Publishing.
[http://dx.doi.org/10.1007/978-3-030-86169-8_16]

Malhotra, R.K., Gupta, S. (2021). Tele health in the digital era during covid -19 a case study of Uttarakhand. *Journal of Medical pharmaceutical and allied sciences, 10*, 109-112.
[http://dx.doi.org/10.22270/jmpas.VIC2I1.2016]

Mary Joshitta, S., Sunil, M. P., Badriasulaimanalfurhood, Bodhankar, A., Ch.Sreedevi, & Khanna, R. (2023). The Integration of Machine Learning Technique with the Existing System to Predict the Flight Prices. *3rd International Conference on Advance Computing and Innovative Technologies in Engineering, ICACITE,* 398–402.
[http://dx.doi.org/10.1109/ICACITE57410.2023.10182539]

Matta, P., Pant, B. (2020). TCpC: a graphical password scheme ensuring authentication for IoT resources. *International Journal of Information Technology, 12*(3), 699-709.
[http://dx.doi.org/10.1007/s41870-018-0142-z]

Mishra, P., Aggarwal, P., Vidyarthi, A., Singh, P., Khan, B., Alhelou, H.H., Siano, P. (2021). VMShield: Memory Introspection-Based Malware Detection to Secure Cloud-Based Services Against Stealthy Attacks. *IEEE Trans. Industr. Inform., 17*(10), 6754-6764.
[http://dx.doi.org/10.1109/TII.2020.3048791]

Mohamed, N., Sridhara Rao, L., Sharma, M., Sureshbaburajasekaranl, Badriasulaimanalfurhood, & Kumar Shukla, S. (2023). In-depth review of integration of AI in cloud computing. *3rd International Conference on Advance Computing and Innovative Technologies in Engineering, ICACITE*, 1431-1434.
[http://dx.doi.org/10.1109/ICACITE57410.2023.10182738]

Nayak, N., Kumar, D., Chattopadhay, S., Kukreja, V., & Verma, A. (2024). Improved Detection of Fusarium Head Blight in Wheat Ears through YOLACT Instance Segmentation. In S. B., A. R., K. S.K., S. K.M., S. A.V., J. S., S. N., C. A., & G. R. (Eds.), 2024 11th International Conference on Reliability, Infocom Technologies and Optimization (Trends and Future Directions), ICRITO 2024. Institute of Electrical and Electronics Engineers Inc.
[http://dx.doi.org/10.1109/ICRITO61523.2024.10522220]

Neha, M. (2023). The Role and Impact of Artificial Intelligence on Retail Business and its Developments. *International Conference on Artificial Intelligence and Smart Communication, AISC,* 1098-1101.
[http://dx.doi.org/10.1109/AISC56616.2023.10085624]

Pant, J., Pant, P., Bhatt, J., Singh, D., Mohan, L., Pant, H.K. (2024). Machine Learning-based Strategies for Crop Assessment in Diverse Districts of Uttarakhand. *2nd IEEE International Conference on Data Science and Information System, ICDSIS 2024.*
[http://dx.doi.org/10.1109/ICDSIS61070.2024.10594284]

Pant, M., Thakur, P. (2021). Forest-based plants in beautification and their medicinal significance. *Non-*

Timber Forest Products: Food, Healthcare and Industrial Applications.. Springer International Publishing. [http://dx.doi.org/10.1007/978-3-030-73077-2_16]

Praveenchandar, J., Vetrithangam, D., Kaliappan, S., Karthick, M., Pegada, N.K., Patil, P.P., Rao, S.G., Umar, S. (2022). IoT-Based Harmful Toxic Gases Monitoring and Fault Detection on the Sensor Dataset Using Deep Learning Techniques. *Sci. Program., 2022*, 1-11. [http://dx.doi.org/10.1155/2022/7516328]

Rajbalaji, S., Raman, R., Pant, B., Rathour, N., Rajagopa, B.R., Prasad, C.R. (2023). Design of deep learning models for the identifications of harmful attack activities in IIOT. *International Conference on Artificial Intelligence and Smart Communication, AISC,* 609-613. [http://dx.doi.org/10.1109/AISC56616.2023.10085088]

Rakhra, M., Bhargava, A., Bhargava, D., Singh, R., Bhanot, A., Rahmani, A.W. (2022). Implementing Machine Learning for Supply-Demand Shifts and Price Impacts in Farmer Market for Tool and Equipment Sharing. *J. Food Qual., 2022*, 1-19. [http://dx.doi.org/10.1155/2022/4496449]

Ram, M., Xing, L. (2023). Reliability Modeling in Industry 4.0. *Reliability Modeling in Industry 4.0.* [http://dx.doi.org/10.1016/C2021-0-01679-5]

Reepu, R., Taneja, S., Ozen, E., Singh, A. (2023). A globetrotter to the future of marketing: Metaverse. *Cultural Marketing and Metaverse for Consumer Engagement.* [http://dx.doi.org/10.4018/978-1-6684-8312-1.ch001]

Saini, S., Sachdeva, L., Badhotiya, G.K. (2022). Sustainable Human Resource Management: A Conceptual Framework. *ECS Trans., 107*(1), 6455-6463. [http://dx.doi.org/10.1149/10701.6455ecst]

Salama, R., Al-Turjman, F., Bordoloi, D., Yadav, S.P. (2023). Wireless Sensor Networks and Green Networking for 6G communication- An Overview. *International Conference on Computational Intelligence, Communication Technology and Networking, CICTN,* 830-834. [http://dx.doi.org/10.1109/CICTN57981.2023.10141262]

Sharma, P., Malhotra, R.K., Ojha, M.K., Gupta, S. (2022). Impact of meditation on mental & physical health and thereby on academic performance of students: a study of higher educational institutions of Uttarakhand. *Journal of medical pharmaceutical and allied sciences, 11*(2), 4641-4644. [http://dx.doi.org/10.55522/jmpas.V11I2.2309]

Sharma, P., Taneja, S., Kumar, P., Özen, E., Singh, A. (2024). Application of the UTAUT model toward individual acceptance: emerging trends in artificial intelligence-based banking services. *International Journal of Electronic Finance, 13*(3), 352-366. [http://dx.doi.org/10.1504/IJEF.2024.139584]

Sharma, S., Mishra, R.R., Joshi, V., Kour, K. (2020). Analysis and Interpretation of Global Air Quality. *11th International Conference on Computing, Communication and Networking Technologies, ICCCNT.* [http://dx.doi.org/10.1109/ICCCNT49239.2020.9225532]

Shreshtha, K., Raj, S., Pal, A.K., Tripathi, P., Choudhary, K.K., Mitra, D., Rani, A., Santos-Villalobos, S., Tripathi, V. (2024). Isolation and identification of Rhizospheric and Endophytic Bacteria from Cucumber plants irrigated with wastewater: Exploring their roles in plant growth promotion and disease suppression. *Current Research in Microbial Sciences, 7*, 100256. [http://dx.doi.org/10.1016/j.crmicr.2024.100256] [PMID: 39717060]

Singh, A., Kumar, P., Taneja, S. (2024). Artificial Intelligence and Machine Learning-Powered Smart Finance. In: Taneja, P.K.S., Singh, A., (Eds.), *IGI Global.*. IGI Global. [http://dx.doi.org/10.4018/979-8-3693-3264-1]

Singh, N.K., Singh, Y., Rahim, E.A., Senthil Siva Subramanian, T., Sharma, A. (2023). Electric discharge machining of hybrid composite with bio-dielectrics for sustainable developments. *Aust. J. Mech. Eng.* [http://dx.doi.org/10.1080/14484846.2023.2249577]

Singh, S.K., Chauhan, A., Sarkar, B. (2023). Sustainable biodiesel supply chain model based on waste animal fat with subsidy and advertisement. *J. Clean. Prod., 382*, 134806.
[http://dx.doi.org/10.1016/j.jclepro.2022.134806]

Singh, V.P., Rana, A., Choudhury, T. (2024). Estimation of Agri-Produce Using Deep Learning and Smart Vision by Using Prominent Feature Extraction. *2nd International Conference on Disruptive Technologies, ICDT.*
[http://dx.doi.org/10.1109/ICDT61202.2024.10488984]

Suresh, M., Antony, J., Nair, G., Garza-Reyes, J.A. (2023). Lean-sustainability assessment framework development: evidence from the construction industry. *Total Qual. Manage. Bus. Excell., 34*(15-16), 2046-2081.
[http://dx.doi.org/10.1080/14783363.2023.2222088]

Taneja, S., Bhatnagar, M., Kumar, P., Grima, S. (2023). A Panel Analysis of the Effectiveness of the Asset Management in Indian Agricultural Companies. *Int. J. Sustain. Dev. Plan., 18*(3), 653-660.
[http://dx.doi.org/10.18280/ijsdp.180301]

Taneja, S., Bhatnagar, M., Kumar, P., Rupeika-Apoga, R. (2023). India's Total Natural Resource Rents (NRR) and GDP: An Augmented Autoregressive Distributed Lag (ARDL) Bound Test. *Journal of Risk and Financial Management, 16*(2), 91.
[http://dx.doi.org/10.3390/jrfm16020091]

Taneja, S., Gupta, M., Bhushan, P., Bhatnagar, M., Singh, A. (2023). Cultural marketing in the digital era. *Cultural Marketing and Metaverse for Consumer Engagement.*
[http://dx.doi.org/10.4018/978-1-6684-8312-1.ch008]

Taneja, S., Gupta, S., Singh, A., Bhatnagar, M., Gaur, A. (2023). Green management - A new paradigm in the world of business. *Green Management - A New Paradigm in the World of Business,* 1-230.
[http://dx.doi.org/10.52305/DLIH6622]

Taneja, S., Kumar, P., Reepu, Kukreti, M., & Ozen, E. (2024). Data Alchemy in the Insurance Industry. Emerald Publishing Limited.
[http://dx.doi.org/10.1108/978-1-83608-582-920241033]

Taneja, S., Özen, E. (2023). To analyse the relationship between bank's green financing and environmental performance. *International Journal of Electronic Finance, 12*(2), 163-175.
[http://dx.doi.org/10.1504/IJEF.2023.129919]

Taneja, S., Sharma, V. (2023). Role of beaconing marketing in improving customer buying experience. *Enhancing Customer Engagement Through Location-Based Marketing.*
[http://dx.doi.org/10.4018/978-1-6684-8177-6.ch012]

Thapa, B.S., Pandit, S., Patwardhan, S.B., Tripathi, S., Mathuriya, A.S., Gupta, P.K., Lal, R.B., Tusher, T.R. (2022). Application of Microbial Fuel Cell (MFC) for Pharmaceutical Wastewater Treatment: An Overview and Future Perspectives. *Sustainability (Basel), 14*(14), 8379.
[http://dx.doi.org/10.3390/su14148379]

Umamaheswaran, S.K., Singh, G., Dixit, A.K., Mc, S.C., Chakravarthi, M.K., Singh, D.P. (2023). IOT-Based Analysis for Effective Continuous Monitoring Prevent Fraudulent Intrusions in Finance and Banking. *International Conference on Artificial Intelligence and Smart Communication, AISC,* 548-552.
[http://dx.doi.org/10.1109/AISC56616.2023.10084920]

Unhelkar, B., Joshi, S., Sharma, M., Prakash, S., Mani, A.K., Prasad, M. (2022). Enhancing supply chain performance using RFID technology and decision support systems in the industry 4.0–A systematic literature review. *International Journal of Information Management Data Insights, 2*(2), 100084.
[http://dx.doi.org/10.1016/j.jjimei.2022.100084]

Upadhyay, D., Manwal, M., Kukreja, V., Sharma, R. (2024). Advancing Citrus Disease Diagnosis: Application of EfficientNetB3 for Precise Classification of Orange Tree Pathologies. *International Conference on Emerging Technologies in Computer Science for Interdisciplinary Applications, ICETCS.*

[http://dx.doi.org/10.1109/ICETCS61022.2024.10543447]

Upadhyay, D., Manwal, M., Yadav, A.P.S., Kukreja, V., Sharma, R. (2024). Brassica Black Rot Severity Levels classification based on Multimodal Convolutional Neural Networks and Support Vector Machines. *Proceedings - International Conference on Computing, Power, and Communication Technologies, IC2PCT*, 49-53.
[http://dx.doi.org/10.1109/IC2PCT60090.2024.10486264]

Upreti, H., & Malhotra, R. K. (2024). Bridging The Urban-Rural Education Gap In India Through CSR (Corporate Social Responsibility) Initiatives: A Conceptual Study With Special Reference To Sustainable Development Goal 4 (Quality Education). In P. P.K. (Ed.), E3S Web of Conferences, Vol. 556. EDP Sciences.
[http://dx.doi.org/10.1051/e3sconf/202455601032]

Verma, P., Chaudhari, V., Dumka, A., Singh, R.P. (2022). A Meta-Analytical Review of Deep Learning Prediction Models for Big Data. *Encyclopedia of Data Science and Machine Learning.*
[http://dx.doi.org/10.4018/978-1-7998-9220-5.ch023]

Yashu, K. (2024). TuberVision: Unveiling Potato Diversity through Advanced Classification Techniques. *International Conference on Interdisciplinary Approaches in Technology and Management for Social Innovation, IATMSI.*
[http://dx.doi.org/10.1109/IATMSI60426.2024.10502772]

Yashu, Kukreja, V., Srivastava, P., Garg, A., & Hariharan, S. (2024). Fostering Sustainable Farming: A Novel Model for Automated Tomato Disease Detection. *9th International Conference for Convergence in Technology, I2CT*, 2024.
[http://dx.doi.org/10.1109/I2CT61223.2024.10543940]

CHAPTER 7

Growth of Life Insurance in India

Ritik Joshi[1], **Abhishek Singh Chauhan**[2], **Mandeep Singh**[3], **Pawan Kumar**[2,*] and **Mukul Bhatnagar**[2]

[1] *Department of Management, IES Institute of Technology & Management, IES University, Bhopal, Madhya Pradesh, India*

[2] *Graphic Era deemed to be University, Dehradun, India*

[3] *AIT-APEX, Chandigarh University, Mohali, Punjab, India*

Abstract: After the e-tail and the e-travel industries, the insurance industry has likewise begun its computerized development in India. The Web aggregators have reformed the web-based insurance industry under the permit of the Insurance Regulatory and Development Authority of India. There are currently around 16 authorized web aggregators in India, and some of them have moved forward to try and do online deals with their imperative licenses. Indeed, even insurance organizations have begun to sell online through their immediate channels, yet not all arrangements are suitable for online transactions. The insurance renewal business gradually moves onto the digital platform with basic ECS and auto-debit mandates, even for offline policies. The Boston Consulting Group report anticipates an extreme development in renewals. The organization benefits more because the specialist payout goes down fundamentally, and the operational costs of writing and giving the policy are not there. The online insurance industry is quickly rising, and just 30% of the insurance purchasers in India are non-digitalized, and that number is quickly diminishing, as per the BCG examination. The digitalization of the insurance industry speeds up development and brings down costs. The cost of sales and dispersion of insurance products in India through absolutely advanced channels is close to one-sixth that of physical channels. The computerized impact on insurance sales is growing, with pre- and post-deal advanced impact playing a significant role. E-insurance is quickly catching up to e-wallets and Internet banking, which are now well-established trends. The present paper aims to study the growth of life insurance in India and its challenges. The present paper found that the growth of private-sector life insurance companies has continuously increased compared to the public life insurance companies in India.

Keywords: Digital, Growth, India, Insurance sector, Life insurance, Online.

[*] **Corresponding author Pawan Kumar:** Graphic Era deemed to be University, Dehradun, India; E-mail: pawan2006@gmail.com

INTRODUCTION

The insurance business in India comprises 57 insurance organizations. A total of 24 organizations are in the life insurance business, while 34 are not. The only public sector organization in the life insurance sector is the Life Insurance Corporation (LIC). There are six public organizations in the non-life insurance sector. Apart from this, only a public re-insurer, *i.e.*, General Insurance Corporation of India (GIC Re), exists. Different Indian insurance market partners incorporate specialists (individual and corporate), agents, assessors, and third-party health care coverage claims.

Market Size of Indian Insurance Sector

By 2020, India's insurance division is expected to have a market share of 280 USD billion. In 2019 and 2023, the life insurance industry is projected to expand at the CAGR (Compound average growth rate) of 5.3 percent. In 2021, India's annual percentage of insurance infiltration was fixed at 4.2 percent, with life insurance infiltration at 3.2 percent and non-life insurance infiltration at 1.0 percent. Regarding insurance density, India in 2021 remained at 78 USD. In the first half of the year 22, the life insurance industry expanded at a 5.8 percent growth rate, compared to 0.8 percent in the previous year. In September 2021, new premiums from life insurance firms jumped by 22.2 percent, up from 2.9 percent in September 2020.

In the year 2020, private players maintained a market share of 33.78 percent in premium underwritten in the life insurance industry as a proportion of the total industry. Furthermore, premiums from new life insurance organizations in India remained at 20.7 USD billion in 2022, with renewable premiums remaining at US$ 53.7 billion. Thus according to S&P Global Industry Intelligence reports, India is Asia's second largest Pacific insurance innovation market, comprising 35 percent of the country's 3.66 USD billion InsurTech-related initiatives.

India's Insurance Sector: Investments and Recent Developments

Below are some of the significant investments and innovations in the Indian life insurance corporations, and organizations are striving to utilize strategic partnerships to propose a variety of services, including:

- ICICI Prudential Life Insurance was associated with NPCI Bharat BillPay, a National Payments Corporation of India (NPCI) subsidiary, to offer the ClickPay feature to its customers.
- In November 2021, the Competition Commission of India (CCI) permitted HDFC Life Insurance's acquisition of 100% shareholding in Exide Life

Insurance. The move will likely make HDFC Life's ranking stronger in South India.

- In November 2021, Acko, a digital insurance start-up, collected US$ 255 million in funds, taking the organization's valuation to US$ 1.1 billion.
- Zest Money borrowed 50 USD million in 2021 to develop an innovative business opportunity in the insurance region.
- PhonePe said in 2021 that it has been granted preliminary approval by the Indian Regulatory and Development Authority of India (IRDAI) to act as an agent for life and general insurance commodities. Thus, the company's more than 30 billion consumers can now receive insurance advice.
- LIC set a new first-year premium pay record in 2021 of 7.75 USD billion in the individual assurance sector, an increase of 10.11 percent over the previous year.
- ICICI Prudential Life Insurance partnered with the National Payments Corporation of India (NPCI) in 2021 to offer a unified payments interface auto pay.
- Bharti AXA Life Insurance announced a 10 percent renewal premium increase of 200.64 USD million for 2021.
- Life Insurance Corporation (LIC) Housing Finance announced intentions to borrow 312.43 USD million from the Life Insurance Corporation of India through a special issue of equity shares in 2021.
- The LIC introduced the Saral Pension Scheme in July 2021, which is a single premium, individual quick annuity plan.
- Gallagher announced an intention to buy 100 percent ownership in India's Edelweiss Gallagher Insurance Brokers in 2021.
- Aditya Birla Sun Life Insurance announced the launch of a new Vision Life Income Plus Plan in 2021, which would provide customers with guaranteed recurring income and variable bonus payouts.
- Max Life Insurance Co. Ltd. introduced the 'Max Life Saral Pension,' a non-linked, individual prompt annuity plan, in 2021.

Initiatives Taken by Indian Government

The Indian government has launched a variety of drives to help the insurance industry. The following are a few examples:

- As part of the consolidation in the banking and insurance sectors, Finance Minister Nirmala Sitharaman announced in the Union Budget 2021 that the first initial public offering (IPO) of LIC will take place in the year 22. LIC's IPO might potentially raise 13.62 billion USD, despite the lack of an appropriate market valuation.
- Until 2021, the government has extended a 66.85 USD thousand insurance scheme for medical care professionals across India.

- In February 2021, an announcement from the Finance Ministry that a $413.13 million investment in state-owned general insurance companies to improve their financial viability.
- The Union Budget for 2021 allots $2.20 billion to the crop insurance scheme.

Literature Review

Many people and institutions are always concerned about rising life insurance premiums. So, there are academic papers in India and different countries. A study explored the scenarios and challenges of the insurance business in India (Kashif, *et al.*, 2023; Dash & Company, 2013; Singh *et al.*, 2018). The Indian economy is one of the most powerful economies globally and the second-fastest-growing economy after China. With the expansion of the worldwide economy, the insurance sector is also growing. The Indian insurance market has enormous growth potential in the coming years. Arif (2015) described the developmental trends and outline of the Indian insurance sector for the decade, from 2003–04 to 2012–13. The study discovered that after privatization, the trend in the life insurance business concerning total premiums, new offices opened, and new policies issued has prevailed. However, diminishing tendencies were seen in the life insurance market.

Wise (2016) reviewed the diverse methodologies and the numbers and trends of different techniques and features of life insurance efficiency measurement. The essential features of LIE (life insurance efficiency) estimation, such as setup and output and input form, were also investigated. According to the findings, LIE studies' focus on individual countries has changed. Furthermore, data envelope analysis is the most commonly utilized technique, followed by stochastic frontier analysis. Parida investigated the evolution of the Indian life insurance sector since its inception and assessed its performance over time using several business metrics (Kashif, *et al.*, 2023; Acharya, 2016; Dar *et al.*, 2019).

The evolution of the Indian insurance sector, as well as trends and features, are examined in three stages: the first phase is from 1818 to 1956; the second phase (1956 to 2000) is known as the nationalization period; and the third phase (from 2000 onward) is post-liberalization reform. The study also employs data envelopment analysis (DEA) to assess the Indian life insurance sector's relative efficiency and productivity in the post-reform phase. Although the life insurance industry's total premiums' CAGR (compound annual growth rate) for the post-reform phase was 17 percent and new business premium income's CAGR was 21 percent, insurance companies continued to work hard to solve the profitability problem. A study demonstrated a long-run association between economic growth and the expansion of the banking and insurance industries, while causality results showed a demand-following relationship across the whole period, with bi-directional causality from insurance to economic growth in the post-liberalized period (Kashif, *et al.*, 2017; Kaushal and Ghosh, 2018; Anand *et al.*, 2017). Ozen and Grima (2020) investigated insurance premium increases in the Turkish life insurance sector. Their study has shown us how fluctuations in the currencies and the demand in the housing market affect the premiums. Moreover, it has alsoshown that the life insurance section covers a small part of the general insurance sector in Turkey.

Using panel data, researchers looked at variations in life insurance demand due to changes in family portfolio holdings and life events during the recent financial crisis(Wang (2022)). The findings revealed that household portfolio holdings had a more beneficial impact than life events on clarifying life insurance ownership decisions, implying a complementing rather than a replacement relationship between life insurance ownership and equity and bond holdings during recessions(Kashif *et al.*, 2024). The findings also revealed that households with larger financial resources allocated to bonds significantly reduce their term life insurance coverage. The health insurance industry significantly impacts the nation's development, and the development of the health insurance region depends on many political, legal, economic, and cultural-social factors. (Buri *et al.* 2017; Guerineau and Sawadogo 2015; Dragos 2014; Chang and Lee 2012; Outreville 1996; (Panda *et al.*, 2021)).

RESEARCH METHODOLOGY

The main aim of the present research is to analyze the growth of life insurance in India in the Digital Era.

H_{01}:There is no significant difference between the growth of public and private life insurance companies in India.

The present study is qualitative and based mainly on secondary data from 2019-20 to 2020-21. The data was collected through different national and international journal articles, newspapers, printed and online reports *i.e.* IRDA reports, Indian Statistics reports, and Indian BrandEquity Foundation published by different national and international organizations and other materials published on the insurance industry in the context of India have been reviewed to conduct the study. Further, collected data were analyzed with the help of mean, percentage, and rank, and the hypothesis was tested by t-test.

DATA ANALYSIS AND INTERPRETATION

Table **1** highlights the comparative analysis of the collected income premiums of India's public and private life insurance sectors. As far as the private sector is concerned, the income premium collected, *i.e.* Rs 193520.59 Million, was the lowest collection compared to the public sector, *i.e.* Rs379389.6Millionin the year 2019-20. In the year 2020-21, the premium collected by the Public Sector Company was higher than the premium collected by the private sector companies in India. Further overall premium income collected by the public sector unit was more than the private sector union in both years. Whereas, the overall growth of the private sector is more (16.5%) than the previous year's growth. On the other hand, the public sector unit growth was only 6 percent. The t-test was applied, and the p-value indicates a significant difference in the public and private Life Insurance units based on premiums taken in the financial year.

Table 1. Premium undertaken by life insurer.

Name of Sector	Premium (Million)		Mean Value	Rank	Sig. Value (At 5 percent Level)	Growth (Percentage)
	2019-20	2020-21				
Public Sector	379389.6	391338.07	385363.83	1	0.012*	6.30
Private Sector	193520.59	209482.53	201501.56	2	0.015*	16.50

Source: Secondary Data (https://irdai.gov.in/annual-reports).

Table **2** depicts the market share (percentage) of India's public and private sectors (life insurance companies). In 2019-20, the market share of the public sector companies (66.22 percent) was higher than the private share sector companies (33.78 percent). Considering the year 2020-21, the market share of the public sector companies was 64.14, which was comparatively higher than 35.86 percent of the private sector companies' market share. The public sector is at the first rank, and the private sector is based on the mean value. The t-test, at a 5 percent significant level with 1 degree of freedom shows a significant difference between the public and private sector life insurance companies with respect to market share in India. Furthermore, the market share of the public sector declined in 2020-21 compared to 2019-20. However, the private sector life insurance companies' market share increased in 2020-21 compared to 2019-20.

Table 2. Market share of life insurer.

Insurer	Market Share (%)		Mean Value	Rank	Sig. Value(At 5 Percent Level)
	2019-20	2020-21			
Public Sector	66.22	64.14	65.18	1	0.002

(Table 2) cont.....

Insurer	Market Share (%)		Mean Value	Rank	Sig. Value(At 5 Percent Level)
	2019-20	2020-21			
Private Sector	33.78	35.86	34.82	2	0.002

Source: Secondary Data (https://irdai.gov.in/annual-reports).

Table **3** shows the paid-up capital of private and public life insurance during 2019-2021. The public sector company has a paid-up capital of Rs 1000 Million in both the financial year of 2019-20 and 2021. On the other hand, in the year 2019-2020, the paid-up capital of the private sector unit was Rs 279879.6 million, and Rs 282463.7 million in the year 2020-21. Based on the t-test, there was a significant difference between private and public sector life insurance companies in the context of paid-up capital. It is concluded that the paid-up capital of the public sector has been the same for both years, but the concern about private sector companies is that the paid-up capital has increased from the previous year and more than public sector banks.

Table 3. Paid-up capital of life insurers.

Insurer	As of March 31, 2020 (Million)	As of March 31, 2021(Million)	Mean value	Sig. Value (At 5 Percent Level)
Public Sector	1000	1000	1000	0.000
PrivateSector	279879.6	282463.7	281171.6	0.003

Source: Secondary Data (https://irdai.gov.in/annual-reports).

It can be seen in the above Table **4** that new individual policies issued by the life insurers of the public sector companies worth more than Rs. 21.89 million in 2019-20 as compared to private sector companies (Rs. 6.950 Million). In 2020-21, the public and private sector insurance companies issued new policies by life insurers worth Rs. 20.975 million and Rs. 7.152 million, respectively. The overall growth of the public sector unit was reduced from the previous year (-4.21%). On the other hand, private sector companies have grown overall (2.89%). After the T-test, the significant value shows a significant difference between the public and private sectors based on new policies issued by insurers. It is concluded that private-sector life insurance companies issued fewer new individual policies than public-sector life insurance units.

Table 4. New individual policies issued by life insurers.

Insurer	2019-20 (Million)	2020-21 (Million)	Growth (in percentage)	Mean Value	Sig. Value (At 5 Percent Level)
Public Sector	21.89	20.975	(-4.21)	21.435	0.001

(Table 4) cont.....

Insurer	2019-20 (Million)	2020-21 (Million)	Growth (in percentage)	Mean Value	Sig. Value (At 5 Percent Level)
private sector	6.950	7.152	(2.89)	7.0510	0.015

Source: Secondary Data (https://irdai.gov.in/annual-reports).

Table **5** highlights the investment income of life insurers in public life insurance companies being Rs 2368497.1 million), which is more than the private life insurance companies being Rs 31059.7 million) during 2019-20. The private (Rs 1866514.7 Million) sector life insurance companies also have less investment income than public sector life insurance (Rs 2793788.8 Million) in 2020-2021. The T-test value is 5 percent of the significant value with 1 degree of freedom. This shows a significant difference between private and public sector life insurance based on investment income. It is concluded based on the analysis that income earned by the insurer of a public-sector company was more than the private-sector life insurance company.

Table 5. Investment income of life insurers.

Insurer	2019-20 (Million)	2020-21 (Million)	Mean Value	Sig. Value (At 5 Percent Level)
Public Sector	2368497.1	2793788.8	2581142.9	0.002
PrivateSector	-31059.7	1866514.7	917727.5	0.032

Source: Secondary Data (https://irdai.gov.in/annual-reports).

Table **6** explores the dividends paid by public and private life insurance companies. In 2020-21, public sector companies never proposed to pay dividends to shareholders *i.e.*, Government of India (26977.4 million for 2019-20). Private insurers pay dividends for the year 2020-21. It is concluded that the public sector companies paid more dividends to their customers in 2019-20. Nevertheless, in the year 2020-21, the private sector companies paid Rs 6153.5 million in dividends to their shareholder, Public Sector Life Insurance Company.

Table 6. Dividend paid by life insurers.

Insurer	2019-20 (Million)	2020-21 (Million)
Public Sector	26977.4	---------
Private Sector	11922.9	6153.5

Source: Secondary Data (https://irdai.gov.in/annual-reports).

Table **7** shows the profit after tax of life insurers in India. In 2020-21, the public life insurance industry reported profits after Rs 29005.7 million tax compared to Rs 27127.1 million for 2019-20. The total profit reported by private sector companies during the year under review was Rs 57600.6 million compared to Rs 50155.9 Million last year. The mean value depicts that private-sector companies have earned more profit than public-sector life insurance units. The p-value is less than a significant value, which illustrates a significant difference between the public and private sector life insurance units regarding profit earned after tax.

Table 7. Profit after taxof life insurers.

Insurer	2019-20 (Million)	2020-21 (Million)	Mean Value	Sig.Value (At 5 Percent Level)
Public Sector	27127.1	29005.7	28066.4	0.021
PrivateSector	50155.9	57600.6	53878.2	0.076

Source: Secondary Data (https://irdai.gov.in/annual-reports).

CONCLUSION

Premium collection by life insurers has witnessed the growth of the life insurance sector in India during the pandemic period. The market share of the public sector life insurance companies is declining, but the market share of the private sector life insurance companies continues to increase. Based on the paid-up capital, the paid-up capital of the private sector life insurance companies has continuously increased, but the public sector has remained constant. As far as investment income is concerned, the income continues to increase in the public sector in India. Compared to the private sector, the dividend paid by the private sector companies in 2020-21 will be higher than that paid by public sector companies in 2019-20. Private sector companies have the highest profit after tax when compared to public sector companies. Further, the results show that the growth of the private sector life insurance company has continuously increased as compared to the public life insurance company in India. So, the government of India should make a proper plan for the growth of the public life insurance company with the use of advanced technology.

REFERENCES

Arif, M. (2015). Life Insurance Industries in India: Trends and Patterns. *Eur. Acad. Res., II*(11), 14105-14122.

Basavanthappa, C., Rajanalkar, L. (2009). Performance of life insurance companies: A comparative study. *Southern Economist, 42*, 1-6.

Burić, M. N., Smolović, J. C., Božović, M. L., Filipović, A. L. (2017). Impact of economic factors on life insurance development in Western Balkan Countries *Zbornik radova Ekonomskog fakulteta u Rijeci: časopis za ekonomsku teoriju i praksu, 35*(2), 331-352.

Chang, C.H., Lee, C.C. (2012). Non-linearity between life insurance and economic development: A revisited approach. *Geneva Risk Insur. Rev., 37*(2), 223-257.
[http://dx.doi.org/10.1057/grir.2011.10]

Dragos, S.L. (2014). Life and non-life insurance demand: the different effects of influence factors in emerging countries from Europe and Asia. *Ekon. Istraz., 27*(1), 169-180. [http://dx.doi.org/10.1080/1331677X.2014.952112]

Guerineau, S., Sawadogo, R. (2015). On the determinants of life insurance development in Sub-Saharan Africa: the role of the institutions quality in the effect of economic development *halshs-01178838.*

Guerineau, S., Sawadogo, R. On the determinants of life insurance development in Sub-Saharan Africa: the role of the institutions quality in the effect of economic development. Available from: https://halshs.archives-ouvertes.fr/halshs-01178838/. (2015).

Kashif, M., Thiyagarajan, S., Sridharan, P. (2017). Dynamics of Algeria's international reserves. *Afr. J. Econ. Manag. Stud., 8*(4), 410-419. [http://dx.doi.org/10.1108/AJEMS-11-2016-0179]

Kashif, M., Shajar, S.N., Singhal, N., Kumar, P. (2023). *Achieving sustainable investment practices through green finance: Challenges and opportunities. Sustainable Investments in Green Finance.* IGI Global. [http://dx.doi.org/10.4018/979-8-3693-1388-6.ch016]

Kashif, M., Kumar, P., Ghai, S., Kumar, S. (2023). Disruptive technologies in computational finance.*In Algorithmic Approaches to Financial Technology: Forecasting, Trading, and Optimization* IGI Global.

Kashif, M., Singhal, N., Goyal, S., Singh, S.K. (2024). Foreign Exchange Reserves and Economic Growth of Brazil: A Nonlinear Approach. *Finance: Theory and Practice, 28*(1), 145-154.

Ozen, E., Grima, S. (2020). The Turkish Life Insurance Market: An Evaluation of the Current Situation and Future Challenges.*Life Insurance in Europe- Risk Analysis and Market Challenges.* (pp. 45-58). Cham: Springer. [http://dx.doi.org/10.1007/978-3-030-49655-5_4]

Outreville, J.F. (1996). Life insurance markets in developing countries. *J. Risk Insur., 63*(2), 263-278. [http://dx.doi.org/10.2307/253745]

Parida, T.K., Acharya, D. (2016). The life insurance industry in India: Current state and efficiency.*The Life Insurance Industry in India..* Current State and Efficiency. [http://dx.doi.org/10.1007/978-981-10-2233-3]

Rastogi, S., Sarkar, R. Enhancing competitiveness: the case of the Indian life insurance industry. *In Conference on Global Competition & Competitiveness of Indian Corporate.* .Available from: http://dspace.iimk.ac.in/xmlui/handle/2259/43. (2007).

Reddy, S., Reddy, P.S., Reddy, C. Liberalization of Insurance: Opportunities and Challenges *The Insurance Times, 24*(3), 23-27. Available from: https://srcc.edu/sites/default/files/Article%205.%20 Distribution% 20channels%20of%20Indian%20Life%20Ins%20revised2.pdf. (2004).

Samuel, A. (2003). Insurance: The Indian Experience. *Economic Development in India, Monthly Update, 7*, 45-55.

Shendey, B. K., Rao, N. (2010). Trends in insurance industry in india since 21st century *Southern Economist.*

Kaushal, Shrutikeerti (2018). Banking, insurance and economic growth in India: An empirical analysis of relationship from regulated to liberalized era *Journal of Financial Economic Policy.* [http://dx.doi.org/10.1108/JFEP-03-2017-0022]

Singh, P., Negi, D. (2011). Growth of Insurance Services in the Himalayan Region of India. *ZENITH International Journal of Multidisciplinary Research, 1*(7), 200-217.

Singh, P., Negi, D. (2012). Demographic Analysis of Factors Influencing Purchase of Life Insurance Products in India. *Eur. J. Bus. Manag., 4*(7), 169-180.

Sinha, T. (2002). Privatization of insurance market in India: From the british raj to monopoly raj to swaraj *CRIS Discussion Paper Series.* The University of Nottingham.

Dash, S.K., Pany, T.K. (2013). Insurance industry in India-Prospects and challenges. *Asian Journal of Multidimensional Research, 2*(4), 46-64. [AJMR].

Taneja, S. (2012). Comparative evaluation of public and private sector life insurance companies in India *International Journal Praman, 1*(3), 440-449.

Taneja, S. (2013). Comparative evaluation of life insurance companies in India *National Journal Emerging Trends in Social Sciences, 2*(5), 89-94.

Tripathy, N.P., Pal, P. (2005). Life insurance corporation – The leader on the backfoot. *Insurance: Theory and Practice.* (1st ed., p. 43). New Delhi: Prentice Hall of India.

Venkatesh, M. (2013). A Study of Trend Analysis In Insurance Sector In India. *International Journal Of Engineering And Science, 2*(6), 1-5. [IJES].

Verma, A., Bala, R. (2013). The Relationship between Life Insurance and Economic Growth: Evidence from India. *Global Journal of Management and Business Studies, 3*(4), 413-422.

Wise, W. (2017). A survey of life insurance efficiency papers: Methods, pros & cons, trends. *Accounting, 3*(3), 137-170.
[http://dx.doi.org/10.5267/j.ac.2016.12.001]

Wang, N. (2022). A dynamic analysis of the demand for life insurance during the 2008 financial crisis: evidence from the panel Survey of Consumer Finances. *Geneva Pap. Risk Insur. Issues Pract.*
[http://dx.doi.org/10.1057/s41288-021-00262-2]

Reports, A. IRDAI. Available from https://irdai.gov.in/annual-reports. (2022).

Singh, G., Gupta, M.K., Mia, M., Sharma, V.S. (2018). Modeling and optimization of tool wear in MQL-assisted milling of Inconel 718 superalloy using evolutionary techniques. *Int. J. Adv. Manuf. Technol., 97*(1-4), 481-494.
[http://dx.doi.org/10.1007/s00170-018-1911-3]

Dar, S.A., Sharma, R., Srivastava, V., Sakalle, U.K. (2019). Investigation on the electronic structure, optical, elastic, mechanical, thermodynamic and thermoelectric properties of wide band gap semiconductor double perovskite Ba_2InTaO_6. *RSC Advances, 9*(17), 9522-9532.
[http://dx.doi.org/10.1039/C9RA00313D] [PMID: 35520698]

Anand, A., Patience, A.A., Sharma, N., Khurana, N. (2017). The present and future of pharmacotherapy of Alzheimer's disease: A comprehensive review. *Eur. J. Pharmacol., 815*, 364-375.
[http://dx.doi.org/10.1016/j.ejphar.2017.09.043] [PMID: 28978455]

Panda, S.K., Aggarwal, I., Kumar, H., Prasad, L., Kumar, A., Sharma, A., Vo, D-V.N., Van Thuan, D., Mishra, V. (2021). Magnetite nanoparticles as sorbents for dye removal: a review. *Environ. Chem. Lett., 19*(3), 2487-2525.
[http://dx.doi.org/10.1007/s10311-020-01173-9]

CHAPTER 8

Beyond the Horizon: Exploring the Future of Data Analytics in Insurance

Nikita Singhal[1,*], **Shikha Goyal**[2] and **Pooja Sharma**[2]

[1] *IIMT University, Meerut, Uttar Pradesh, India*

[2] *Amity University, Noida, Uttar Pradesh, India*

Abstract: This study critically examines the multifaceted impact of artificial intelligence (AI) on contemporary societal dynamics. Exploring economic, social, ethical, and cultural dimensions, our research sheds light on the unprecedented opportunities and challenges that accompany the rapid integration of AI technologies. Assessing the transformative potential of AI in diverse industries, we delve into economic implications, highlighting efficiency gains and innovation. Socially, we investigate evolving employment patterns, educational paradigms, and interpersonal relationships shaped by AI. Ethical considerations, including algorithmic bias and transparency, are scrutinized. Additionally, we explore how cultural factors influence AI perceptions and adaptation. This interdisciplinary analysis aims to provide a nuanced understanding of the intricate relationship between AI and society, offering insights for responsible AI development, policy-making, and fostering a harmonious coexistence in the evolving technological landscape.

Keywords: Artificial Intelligence (AI), Blockchain technology, Decentralised insurance, Internet of things, Smart contracts.

INTRODUCTION

Within the dynamic landscape of the insurance industry, a transformative journey is unfolding, driven by the convergence of cutting-edge technologies and the ever-expanding realm of data analytics. This confluence is a powerful driving force, propelling the sector into an era of innovation and adaptability. As technological advancement accelerates at an unprecedented rate, the outlook for data analytics in the insurance domain becomes increasingly promising. Data analytics represents the convergence of advanced statistical analysis, machine learning algorithms, and artificial intelligence applications to extract patterns,

* **Corresponding author Nikita Singhal:** IIMT University, Meerut, Uttar Pradesh, India; E-mail: nikitagoyal.nikki@gmail.com

Sanjay Taneja, Ercan Ozen, Luan Vardar, Mohit Kukreti & Mohammad Kashif (Eds.)

trends, and correlations from voluminous and diverse datasets (Ernst & Young, 2022; Yuvaraj *et al.*, 2021; Avikal *et al.* 2023). In the insurance context, this multifaceted approach to data interpretation goes beyond mere number-crunching; it enables insurers to gain deeper insights into customer behavior, market trends, and risk factors. Before delving into the transformative impact of data analytics, it is crucial to understand the existing dynamics of the insurance business (Nigam *et al.* 2021). Historically grounded in actuarial sciences, insurers have relied on mathematical models and statistical methodologies to assess risks and determine premium pricing. However, technology has ushered in a new era, challenging traditional paradigms and necessitating a shift toward more dynamic, data-driven approaches. Insurance revolves around the principles of risk mitigation and financial protection (Avikal *et al.* 2020). Policyholders seek assurance that their assets and well-being are safeguarded, while insurers aim to evaluate risks to maintain financial viability accurately. The intersection of these interests forms the foundation of the insurance industry (Mckinsey, 2017; Vaid *et al.*, 2014; Singh *et al.* 2020). Against this backdrop, integrating data analytics becomes a strategic imperative, offering insurers a nuanced understanding of risks and an enhanced ability to adapt to an ever-changing landscape.

Data analytics permeates various facets of insurance operations, heralding a paradigm shift in how insurers underwrite policies, assess risks, and engage with their clientele. One of the primary applications lies in risk assessment, where sophisticated algorithms analyze historical data, market trends, and external factors to evaluate potential risks more accurately. This not only refines the underwriting process but also enables insurers to develop customized policies tailored to individual risk profiles. Policy pricing, another critical aspect of insurance operations, transforms the integration of data analytics (Bashir *et al.*, 2020; Singh *et al.* 2018). Insurers can leverage predictive modeling to establish dynamic pricing structures rather than relying solely on actuarial tables and historical data. This ensures fair and competitive premiums and enables insurers to align pricing with real-time risk factors, fostering a more responsive and adaptable pricing strategy. Operational efficiency is a key beneficiary of data analytics within insurance companies. From claims processing to fraud detection, analytics streamlines and automates various functions, reducing operational costs and enhancing overall efficiency. Machine learning algorithms can rapidly analyze vast datasets to identify patterns indicative of fraudulent activity, safeguard insurers against financial losses, and maintain the integrity of the insurance ecosystem.

As we peer into the future, the utility of data analytics in insurance becomes increasingly apparent. The predictive capabilities of advanced analytics offer insurers the foresight to anticipate market trends, emerging risks, and customer needs (Avikal *et al.* 2016). This proactive approach positions insurers ahead of the curve and enables them to craft innovative products and services that resonate with evolving consumer preferences. Furthermore, data analytics serves as a catalyst for customer-centricity within the insurance industry. Insurers can harness customer data to comprehensively understand their clientele, tailoring products and services to meet specific needs. This personalized approach enhances customer satisfaction and fosters long-term loyalty, a crucial factor historically perceived as transactional in an industry. Integrating telematics and Internet of Things (IoT) devices further amplifies the impact of data analytics on insurance. In auto insurance, for instance, connected devices provide real-time data on driving behavior, allowing insurers to offer usage-based insurance policies (Chand *et al.* 2015). This rewards safe driving habits and aligns premiums with actual risk exposure, departing from traditional rating factors.

Moreover, blockchain technology promises to revolutionize the insurance landscape, addressing longstanding challenges related to transparency, trust, and security. In conjunction with blockchain, data analytics can streamline claims processing, reduce fraud, and enhance data integrity. This synergy exemplifies the transformative potential when cutting-edge technologies converge in pursuing operational excellence within the insurance sector.

This forward-looking exploration extends into various technological dimensions, each contributing to crafting a compelling narrative for the future (Bohnert, Fritzsche & Gregor, 2019; (Avikal *et al.* 2013)). Acknowledging the indispensable role of data analytics in reshaping entrenched practices, renowned insurance firms take the lead in navigating this evolution, inviting us on a compelling journey to explore the crossroads where tradition harmonizes with innovation. For instance, XYZ Insurance leverages advanced predictive modelling algorithms, analyzing vast datasets, including historical claims, market trends, and individual behaviour patterns. This approach allows them to offer tailored policies and pricing structures, ultimately enhancing customer satisfaction and risk management (Kashif *et al.*, 2024). Simultaneously, the disruptive potential of quantum computing looms large on the horizon, promising to redefine the boundaries of computational capabilities within the insurance landscape.

Moreover, ABC Insurance is exploring how quantum computing can enhance data processing speed and efficiency, potentially revolutionizing underwriting processes and claims management. The transformative influence of blockchain technology unfolds as a narrative thread, with insurance giants like DEF Insurance incorporating blockchain to weave heightened security, transparency, and efficiency into the fabric of their operations. Through a decentralized and tamper-resistant ledger, ABC Insurance, for example, provides policyholders with real-time visibility into the status of their claims, fostering greater confidence in the insurance process. Meanwhile, the proliferation of Internet of Things (IoT) devices paints a vivid picture of a future where real-time data streams become integral to dynamic risk monitoring. Established firms, including GHI Insurance, are integrating IoT devices like connected cars and smart home sensors to monitor and assess risks in real-time. This proactive approach enables insurers to adjust premiums based on actual risk exposure, promoting a more dynamic and responsive approach to insurance coverage. Another illustration of Internet of Things (IoT) devices as dynamic actors is STU Underwriters, which utilizes IoT sensors in commercial properties to monitor environmental conditions. This real-time data allows insurers to assess risks accurately, prevent potential damages, and offer customized policies that align with the specific needs of businesses.

As this narrative unfolds, artificial intelligence (AI) emerges as a significant protagonist, reshaping the insurance landscape by refining decision-making processes with unprecedented precision. For instance, LMN Insurance has successfully integrated AI algorithms into its underwriting and claims processing systems. By analyzing vast datasets, AI algorithms can identify patterns, assess risk more accurately, and expedite claims processing, ultimately enhancing operational efficiency and customer satisfaction. Simultaneously, the transformative impact of blockchain technology extends beyond mere security, influencing transparency and accountability in profound ways. Noteworthy examples, such as PQR Assurance, showcase the implementation of blockchain in creating smart contracts. These contracts, stored on a decentralized and tamper-resistant ledger, automate and enforce insurance agreements, fostering greater trust and transparency between insurers and policyholders.

While the prospects of data analytics in insurance are undeniably promising, challenges and considerations loom on the horizon. Ethical considerations surrounding the use of personal data, cybersecurity threats, and the need for regulatory frameworks that balance innovation with consumer protection are crucial aspects that demand careful attention. Striking the right balance between data-driven innovation and safeguarding the interests of policyholders is paramount in navigating the evolving landscape of insurance analytics. Amidst this intricate tapestry, regulatory adaptations become pivotal, shaping the contours of a future where technological advancement coexists seamlessly with ethical and legal considerations. Regulators, as evidenced by the initiatives led by the Financial Regulatory Authority (FRA), work with insurers to establish frameworks that safeguard consumer rights, ensure data security, and maintain the ethical use of analytics in the insurance sector. This collaborative approach reinforces the industry's commitment to a future where innovation thrives and does so responsibly and ethically.

THE TRANSFORMATIVE LANDSCAPE OF ADVANCED DATA ANALYTICS IN INSURANCE

Technological Synergies

As we navigate the intricate landscape of technology, it becomes apparent that the future of data analytics in the insurance realm lies not in isolated advancements but in the harmonious interplay of cutting-edge technologies. The convergence of artificial intelligence (AI), blockchain, and the Internet of Things (IoT) forms a potent ecosystem beyond mere data analysis. AI algorithms, enriched by machine learning and deep learning capabilities, continually evolve through insights gleaned from vast datasets. This adaptive learning empowers insurers to refine risk assessments and streamline decision-making processes with unprecedented precision.

Simultaneously, the integration of blockchain technology serves as a guardian of data security, introducing an immutable ledger that elevates transparency and trust. Beyond fortifying defenses against cyber threats, this technology initiates a transformative shift toward decentralized systems. Exploring these implications reveals that blockchain's decentralized nature has the potential to redefine conventional insurance models, ushering in innovative concepts like smart contracts and decentralized autonomous organizations (DAOs). The intricate interplay doesn't end there – the Internet of Things (IoT) injects a dynamic layer into this technological tapestry. Whether through connected vehicles relaying real-time telematics data or smart home devices monitoring environmental variables, the continuous data flow empowers insurers to transition from reactive to proactive risk management. This proactive stance mitigates risks and heralds a paradigm shift in the insurance industry – from mere indemnification after an event to prevention and continuous risk monitoring.

A case in point is the global insurance giant MetLife, which strategically leverages technological synergies to augment various facets of its business, spanning risk assessment to customer engagement. Employing AI algorithms to scrutinize customer data, MetLife gains profound insights into customer behavior and preferences, facilitating the creation of personalized insurance products. Incorporating blockchain in claims processing enhances transparency and efficiency, diminishing the complexities of claim settlements. MetLife integrates IoT devices in auto insurance, using telematics data to evaluate driver behavior and tailor personalized premiums. Similarly, Swiss Re is a notable example, championing the adoption of technological synergies to elevate risk management and operational efficiency. Embracing AI for risk assessment, Swiss Re harnesses machine learning to analyze diverse datasets, refining the accuracy of risk predictions. Blockchain finds its place in creating secure and transparent reinsurance contracts, fostering stakeholder trust. Leveraging IoT devices, such as property sensors, and Swiss Re monitors mitigate risks in real-time, enhancing property insurance offerings. These examples illuminate how industry leaders like MetLife and Swiss Re adopt a comprehensive approach, synergizing AI, blockchain, and IoT. This integration enhances risk assessment, security, and transparency and revolutionizes their proactive risk management capabilities, marking a transformative shift in the insurance industry.

Human Element in Data Analytics

Amid the tech-driven narrative, the pivotal role of human expertise stands as an unassailable force in the intricate landscape of data analytics within the insurance sector. As algorithms ascend to new sophistication echelons, data scientists' interpretative finesse takes on paramount importance. This human touch becomes the linchpin for decoding subtle insights, contextualizing intricate data patterns, and embedding ethical considerations seamlessly into the analytical processes. With insurance entities' enthusiastic adoption of advanced analytics, a clarion call for a distinctive cadre of professionals reverberates across the industry. The emergence of data ethicists, responsible AI practitioners, and experts adept in regulatory compliance becomes a cornerstone of the industry's evolution. Their indispensable role extends beyond conventional technical prowess, encompassing a fusion of ethical insight, regulatory expertise, and the nuanced ability to articulate complex insights across diverse stakeholders.

For example, AXA, a multinational insurance firm, recognizes the significance of the human element in data analytics and has strategically integrated human expertise into its analytical processes. AXA has embraced the concept of data ethicists within its analytics teams. These professionals specialize in ensuring ethical considerations are embedded into the data analytics processes, addressing privacy concerns, and promoting responsible data use. The company has established a cadre of experts specializing in responsible AI practices. These practitioners work on developing and implementing AI algorithms that align with ethical standards, ensuring fairness, transparency, and accountability in algorithmic decision-making. Recognizing the evolving regulatory landscape, AXA has invested in experts with a deep understanding of regulatory compliance. These professionals navigate the complex regulatory environment, ensuring that AXA's data analytics practices adhere to industry standards and legal requirements. AXA's holistic approach, incorporating the expertise of data ethicists, responsible AI practitioners, and regulatory compliance experts, has elevated its data analytics processes' ethical standards and transparency. This enhances customer trust and positions AXA as a responsible player in the insurance industry's data-driven evolution. AXA's commitment to integrating the human element into its data analytics framework showcases a forward-thinking approach. By fostering a team of experts with diverse skills beyond technical capabilities, AXA ensures that its data analytics processes are sophisticated, ethically sound, and compliant with regulatory frameworks. This example demonstrates how human expertise is pivotal in decoding insights, contextualizing data patterns, and ensuring responsible and ethical use of analytics in the insurance sector.

Diversity and Inclusion in Data Analytics

The imperative to foster diversity and inclusion in the application of data analytics within the insurance sector has transcended a mere moral stance. Industry leaders exemplify this paradigm shift, dedicating themselves to reshaping the future through a commitment to inclusivity. One such trailblazer is the Allstate Corporation, which pioneers the embrace of diversity within its data analytics teams. Allstate's unwavering commitment to inclusivity significantly enhances the depth of its risk assessments. Diverse perspectives enrich the comprehension of complex datasets, enabling the company to uncover subtle patterns and potential challenges that might elude a more uniform perspective. The Progressive Corporation sets a noteworthy precedent by championing inclusivity within its data analytics teams. This commitment ensures that the benefits of cutting-edge technologies are distributed equitably across diverse customer demographics. Progressive's emphasis on inclusivity aligns seamlessly with ethical considerations and fosters a more widespread and fair distribution of transformative opportunities within the industry.

State Farm, a key player in the insurance sector, acknowledges the profound impact of diversity on personalization. By amalgamating diverse perspectives within its data analytics teams, State Farm empowers analysts to delve into the intricacies of customer behavior, preferences, and needs. This nuanced understanding goes beyond superficial customization, leading to the development of personalized products and services that authentically resonate with a diverse customer base. Nationwide Insurance emerges as an industry vanguard, showcasing how a strategic commitment to diversity and inclusion is integral to future success. Treating diversity not as a mere obligation but as a profound commitment, Nationwide ensures that the benefits of innovation in data analytics are accessible and meaningful to everyone. This commitment becomes the defining essence of progress and success as the insurance industry strides into a future where diversity and inclusion are at the core of technological advancements.

The narratives of Allstate, Progressive, State Farm, and Nationwide underscore the transformative imperative of diversity and inclusion in data analytics within the insurance sector. These examples vividly demonstrate that diversity is not just a moral imperative but a strategic advantage that unravels the full potential of data analytics, ensuring that innovation benefits all, irrespective of background or demographic profile.

Regulatory Dynamics in a Data-Driven Future

Regulatory bodies play a pivotal role in establishing standards, ensuring compliance, and safeguarding consumer interests. Therefore, the significance of regulatory frameworks in shaping data analytics' trajectory cannot be emphasized enough. A compelling instance of proactive regulatory adaptation unfolds through collaborative efforts between industry stakeholders, policymakers, and regulatory bodies. A standout beacon in this regard is Singapore's Monetary Authority (MAS), which has actively engaged with the insurance industry to comprehend and anticipate the implications of data analytics. Through cooperative endeavors, MAS has crafted guidelines that strike a balance between innovation and the protection of consumer interests, facilitating a seamless integration of data analytics.

Likewise, the European Insurance and Occupational Pensions Authority (EIOPA) has played a crucial role in influencing regulatory dynamics. Acknowledging the transformative potential of data analytics, EIOPA actively seeks input from insurers, InsurTech firms, and other stakeholders. This collaborative approach ensures that regulations evolve with technological advancements, fostering an environment where innovation is encouraged while ethical considerations and consumer protection remain paramount. In the United States, the National Association of Insurance Commissioners (NAIC) has taken significant steps to address the challenges posed by data analytics. By engaging in dialogues with industry experts, consumer advocates, and technology leaders, NAIC has positioned itself at the forefront of regulatory responsiveness. This approach enhances the regulatory framework's adaptability and strengthens the industry's capacity to leverage data analytics responsibly.

As we navigate the future driven by data, these examples underscore the importance of collaborative efforts between regulatory bodies and industry stakeholders. The forward-looking approach of regulatory bodies such as MAS, EIOPA, and NAIC serves as a model for effectively balancing innovation and consumer protection in the evolving landscape of data analytics within the insurance sector.

Data Security and Privacy in the Digital Age

Data security and privacy concerns are paramount for insurers in the ever-evolving digital landscape. The responsibility of safeguarding sensitive customer information in the face of sophisticated cyber threats necessitates the adoption of advanced technologies. Notable examples include companies like Allianz, which has embraced blockchain to enhance the security and transparency of its digital operations. By implementing decentralized and tamper-resistant ledgers, Allianz ensures the integrity of customer data, mitigating the risks associated with centralized systems. Similarly, cybersecurity measures are imperative to fortify the digital perimeter against potential breaches. AXA, a global insurance giant, has been at the forefront of investing in robust cybersecurity frameworks. AXA's proactive approach involves continuous monitoring, threat intelligence, and employee training to mitigate cyber risks effectively. This commitment to cybersecurity protects customer data and reinforces trust in the digital capabilities of the insurance industry. Privacy considerations in the ethical use of customer data present an ongoing challenge. Insurers need to strike a delicate balance between personalization and individual privacy.

A notable example is the customer-centric approach adopted by Progressive Insurance. Progressive insurance leverages customer data to tailor insurance offerings but strongly emphasizes transparency. Through clear communication and giving customers control over their information, progressive insurance exemplifies responsible data usage practices in line with evolving data protection regulations. As the insurance sector navigates the digital age, the experiences of industry leaders like Allianz and AXA underscore the importance of embracing advanced technologies and robust cybersecurity measures. Concurrently, the customer-centric approach demonstrated by Progressive serves as a model for achieving personalization while respecting individual privacy, setting benchmarks for ethical data usage within the industry.

Environmental, Social, and Governance (ESG) Considerations

Environmental, social, and governance (ESG) considerations have emerged as focal points in navigating the evolving landscape of the insurance industry. Data analytics is a potent instrument for insurers to assess and address environmental risks, promote social equity, and ensure governance practices align with ethical standards. This strategic integration of ESG factors into decision-making processes and risk assessments underscores the industry's commitment to responsible business practices and societal well-being.

Insurers are increasingly adopting data analytics to embrace ESG considerations, aligning their strategies with global initiatives for environmental conservation and social responsibility. A notable example is AXA, a leading global insurer, which incorporates ESG criteria into its underwriting processes. By leveraging data analytics to assess the environmental impact of potentially insured assets, AXA demonstrates a commitment to fostering sustainability and minimizing ecological risks. Moreover, integrating ESG factors into data analytics models is not merely a compliance-driven initiative but a proactive stance toward sustainable and resilient growth. Swiss Re, a reinsurance company, is an exemplar by embedding ESG considerations into its risk assessment models. This approach aligns with broader efforts to contribute to environmental sustainability, address social challenges, and uphold robust governance practices.

Collaboration and Partnerships

The future landscape of data analytics in insurance is intricately woven into an interconnected ecosystem where collaboration and partnerships play a pivotal role. Insurers proactively collaborate with diverse entities, including tech companies, InsurTech startups, and data analytics providers. A notable example is the collaboration between Allianz, a global insurance leader, and Amodo, a tech company specializing in telematics. Together, they leverage telematics data to craft personalized insurance solutions that enhance risk assessment and improve customer experiences.

This collaborative venture is strategically designed to tap into collective expertise and resources, cultivating an environment conducive to knowledge exchange and technological innovation. The synergistic efforts between insurance and technology entities underscore a shared commitment to redefine industry practices and unlock the untapped potential of data analytics. Importantly, these collaborations extend beyond the confines of the insurance industry, embracing cross-industry initiatives that tackle broader societal challenges. Anthem, a prominent health insurance company, has forged a collaboration with Samsung to explore data-driven initiatives. This partnership aims to promote preventive healthcare measures, utilizing data analytics to enhance overall well-being while concurrently reducing insurance claims through proactive health management.

As insurers navigate this era of collaborative innovation, these partnerships stand as epitomes of a shared dedication to driving industry-wide transformation. The dynamic interplay of expertise, resources, and innovative technologies ensures a collective approach to unlocking the full potential of data analytics in insurance. These collaborative efforts redefine industry practices and address larger societal challenges, underscoring the transformative power of collaboration within the evolving landscape of data analytics in insurance as presented in Fig (**1**).

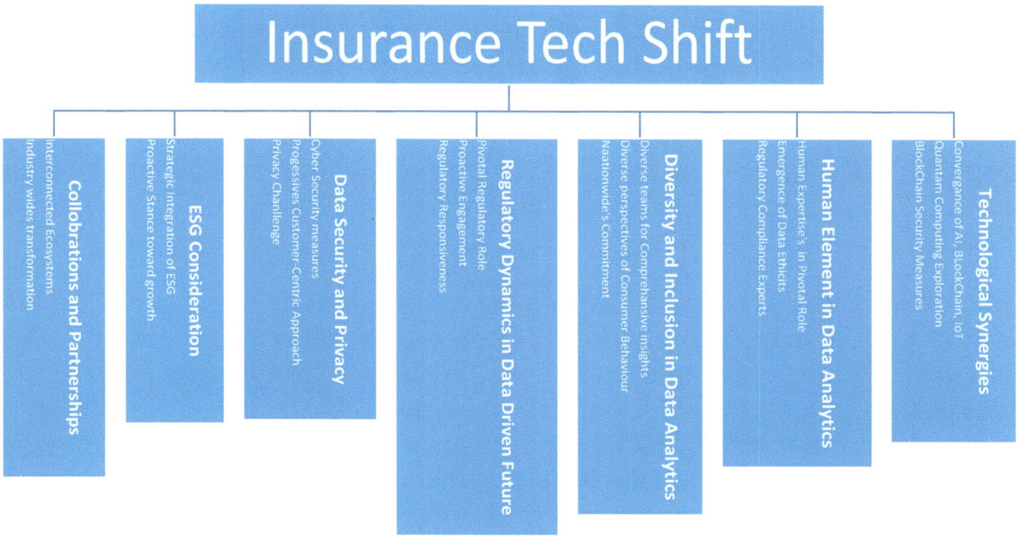

Fig. (1). Insurance tech shift.

TECHNOLOGICAL FRONTIERS IN INSURANCE ANALYTICS

Predictive Analytics

Predictive analytics stands at the forefront of technological innovation, employing statistical algorithms and machine learning techniques to analyze current and historical data. The primary objective is to unveil insights and anticipate future events or trends. This dynamic approach has found application across diverse industries, empowering decision-makers to make informed choices based on data-driven predictions. In insurance, predictive analytics represents a quantum leap in predictive modeling, offering a sophisticated means to assess risks and anticipate outcomes. By harnessing the power of historical data and utilizing advanced statistical algorithms, insurers can refine their understanding of complex risk landscapes. This enhances underwriting processes and enables the crafting of more accurate and personalized insurance policies. Integration of artificial intelligence (AI) is a pivotal aspect of predictive analytics in insurance. AI algorithms, driven by machine learning capabilities, continuously adapt and learn from vast datasets. This adaptability ensures that predictions evolve in real time, reflecting changing risk factors and market dynamics. Insurers leverage AI to streamline decision-making processes, automate routine tasks, and gain a nuanced understanding of customer behavior, ultimately enhancing the overall efficiency of insurance operations.

Quantum Leap in Predictive Modelling

A "quantum leap" in predictive modelling represents a significant advancement in predictive analytics and modelling, marked by transformative shifts driven by algorithm innovations, computing power, and the application of cutting-edge technologies. In the specific context of insurance operations, such a leap implies a substantial improvement in the accuracy, speed, and sophistication of models utilized for assessing risks, determining premiums, and guiding data-driven decision-making.

Several key factors distinguish this leap forward, each contributing to the superior nature of predictive modeling. Advanced risk assessment is a core element, where traditional reliance on simpler algorithms gives way to adopting sophisticated ones such as ensemble methods and deep learning techniques. These advanced algorithms enable insurers to analyze intricate patterns and dependencies within data, resulting in more accurate risk assessments. Precision in underwriting is another hallmark of this quantum leap. Using sophisticated algorithms allows insurers to delve into a more granular understanding of risk factors. By considering a broader range of variables, including unconventional ones like social media activity and health records, insurers can make more precise underwriting decisions, tailoring policies to individual risk profiles. Enhanced computing power, facilitated by big data analytics, is an integral part of this transformative shift. The ability to analyze vast amounts of data quickly and make sense of massive datasets was previously challenging. In insurance operations, where historical and real-time data are pivotal, this capability becomes crucial for effective risk assessment, claims processing, and policy pricing. The integration of advanced computing resources facilitates real-time predictive modeling. The continuous updating of models based on incoming data enables dynamic policy pricing and immediate adjustments in risk assessments. This real-time adaptability proves valuable, especially in rapidly changing environments like cyber insurance, where threats evolve swiftly, ensuring that insurance policies stay current and reflect real-time risk profiles. Fraud detection and prevention represent yet another application of quantum leap in predictive modeling. Advanced algorithms can identify subtle patterns or anomalies in data indicative of fraudulent activities. The real-time assessment of claims data allows insurers to flag suspicious activities promptly, contributing to financial safeguarding and maintaining the integrity of the insurance industry through proactive fraud prevention measures.

Integration of Artificial Intelligence

Integrating artificial intelligence (AI) into predictive analytics is a transformative shift, significantly enhancing the capabilities of industries to derive deeper insights and make more informed decisions. Within this realm, the critical components of AI, namely machine learning (ML) and deep learning, play pivotal roles in refining predictive models. Through machine learning advancements, AI automates predictive modelling, allowing algorithms to learn and adapt autonomously from data (Balasubramanian, Libarikian & McElhaney, 2021). This continual refinement ensures a dynamic and adaptive approach to analyzing complex patterns and relationships. Deep learning, a subset of machine learning, introduces neural networks with multiple layers, enabling models to learn hierarchical representations of data automatically. This architecture proves valuable in capturing intricate patterns and dependencies within datasets that might be too complex for traditional models to discern.

AI's impact extends beyond model refinement, significantly influencing decision-making processes across diverse domains. In the insurance industry, the integration of AI-driven predictive analytics is evident in claims forecasting. AI excels in identifying patterns indicative of fraudulent claims, leveraging historical data and adapting to new patterns over time. This streamlines claims processing and is a powerful tool for fraud prevention, enhancing the industry's efficiency and integrity. Underwriting precision in insurance sees a significant boost with the integration of AI-driven predictive analytics. Models analyze many data points, including traditional factors and unconventional variables like social media activity, providing a comprehensive understanding of risk. This nuanced risk assessment allows insurers to tailor policies to individual risk profiles, ensuring policy pricing and coverage determination accuracy. Automated risk assessment in underwriting processes is facilitated by AI, streamlining the analysis of complex data. This automated approach expedites underwriting decisions while maintaining a high level of precision. The result is improved operational efficiency, ensuring policies are priced accurately based on the unique risk factors associated with each policyholder.

Quantum Computing and Advanced Analytics

The intersection of quantum computing and advanced analytics is reshaping the insurance industry landscape through data-driven decision-making, risk modeling, and customer engagement. The convergence of quantum computing and advanced analytics holds the promise of amplifying the capabilities of both technologies. Quantum computing's enhanced computational power accelerates the processing capabilities of advanced analytics algorithms. This synergy enables insurers to handle even larger datasets, conduct more complex analyses, and efficiently refine customer insights.

Quantum computing, a paradigm-shifting technology, holds the potential to revolutionize the core functions of insurance analytics. Its unique computational capabilities, driven by principles of quantum mechanics, introduce qubits that can exist in multiple states simultaneously. In risk modeling, quantum algorithms promise to handle complex calculations with exceptional speed and efficiency. One of the key areas where quantum computing stands out is risk assessment. Traditional models grapple with the complexity of vast datasets and intricate calculations, often leading to computational bottlenecks. Quantum algorithms, leveraging superposition and entanglement, transcend these limitations by exploring multiple possibilities simultaneously. This capability translates to an exponential increase in computational speed, allowing insurers to refine risk models in real time (Fariya, Saini, & Kashif, 2024). Quantum computing's prowess extends to optimization problems, a critical aspect of insurance operations. Tasks such as portfolio optimization, where insurers seek to balance returns and risks, can be executed with unprecedented efficiency. The ability to process vast datasets at quantum speeds opens avenues for more accurate risk assessments and dynamic adjustments in response to evolving market conditions. While the potential benefits are substantial, challenges such as error correction, stability, and the high cost of quantum hardware remain. The industry is at the frontier of addressing these challenges, working towards unlocking the full disruptive potential of quantum computing in insurance analytics.

Simultaneously, the evolution of advanced analytics, powered by artificial intelligence (AI) and machine learning (ML), redefines how insurers understand customer behavior. Natural language processing (NLP) and sentiment analysis emerge as instrumental tools for extracting valuable insights from unstructured data sources. This shift from demographic-based segmentation to a more nuanced understanding of customer behavior marks a significant advancement. NLP is pivotal in deciphering textual data and offering insights into customer sentiments, preferences, and concerns. Sentiment analysis complements this by assessing the emotional tone associated with customer interactions. This combination of advanced analytics tools gives insurers a holistic view of customer behavior, moving beyond surface-level demographics to more profound insights (Kashif, Kumar, Ghai, & Kumar, 2023). Hyper-personalization is a hallmark of the evolving landscape, wherein insurers leverage advanced analytics to tailor products and services with unparalleled precision. NLP's analysis of customer interactions identifies pain points or areas of satisfaction, allowing insurers to adapt offerings accordingly. Sentiment analysis contributes by gauging emotional resonance and providing valuable feedback for refining customer engagement strategies.

Blockchain and Decentralized Insurance

In recent years, the insurance industry has witnessed a profound transformation driven by the integration of blockchain technology. In recent years, the insurance industry has witnessed a profound transformation driven by the integration of blockchain technology (Ankitha, 2022). At its core, blockchain is a decentralized and distributed ledger technology that revolutionizes transaction recording across a network of computers (Deloitte, 2016). The foundational principles of blockchain include decentralization, immutability, transparency, and the implementation of smart contracts. Decentralization, a fundamental tenet of blockchain, challenges the conventional structure of the insurance industry, which historically relied on centralized authorities, typically insurance companies, to manage policies, claims, and transactions.

Blockchain introduces a decentralized structure where data is stored across a network of nodes. This eliminates the need for a central authority, fostering a peer-to-peer network that enhances security, resilience, and trust within the insurance ecosystem. Smart contracts, coded agreements that automatically execute predefined conditions when met, are a pivotal aspect of blockchain technology. These self-executing contracts eliminate the need for intermediaries, streamlining processes and reducing the potential for disputes (Deloitte, 2017). In the insurance context, smart contracts automate various functions, from policy issuance to claims settlement, fundamentally changing how insurance agreements are executed. Immutability is a critical feature of blockchain technology. Once data is recorded on the blockchain, it becomes tamper-proof. This immutability ensures the integrity of information, reducing the risk of fraud and instilling confidence among the various stakeholders in the insurance process. Transparency, another key principle of blockchain, provides all participants in the network with a clear and auditable record of transactions (Ernest & Young, 2016). Every transaction is visible, traceable, and cannot be hidden or manipulated. This transparency fosters trust and accountability, which has been historically challenging to achieve in the insurance sector.

The integration of blockchain technology leads to the advent of innovative decentralized insurance models (Feng, 2023). These models leverage the unique features of blockchain to create more efficient, transparent, and inclusive insurance ecosystems.

Peer-to-Peer Insurance

At the forefront of decentralized insurance models is Peer-to-Peer (P2P) insurance, enabled by blockchain. This model disrupts the traditional hierarchical structure by allowing individuals to connect directly and form groups to share risks collectively. The core innovation lies in using smart contracts to manage the entire insurance lifecycle autonomously (Alvin, Erik, Gwen & Rex, 2022). In a P2P insurance model, individuals become insurers and insured, contributing to a collective risk pool. Smart contracts automatically execute policy creation, premium collection, and claims settlement without a central authority. This absence of intermediaries enhances efficiency, reduces administrative costs, and fosters a more direct and equitable relationship between insured parties (Levantesi & Piscopo, 2022). P2P insurance leverages the crowd's wisdom, relying on participants' collective assessment and decision-making. This democratization of the insurance process aligns with the principles of decentralization, empowering individuals and communities to take control of their insurance needs.

Parametric Insurance

Blockchain's capabilities open the door to Parametric Insurance, a model where payouts are triggered automatically based on predefined parameters. Weather conditions, financial indices, or other quantifiable metrics can act as triggers for swift and automated payouts (Brettler & Gosnear, 2020). This approach minimizes the time and administrative burden associated with traditional claims processing, offering a more responsive and efficient mechanism for compensating insured parties. In traditional insurance, assessing and validating claims can be lengthy and manual. Parametric insurance, enabled by blockchain, shifts this paradigm by automating the claims process through smart contracts. When predefined conditions are met, such as a specified level of rainfall or a financial index reaching a certain threshold, the smart contract automatically initiates payouts (Cohn, West & Parker, 2017). This accelerates the claims settlement process and reduces the potential for disputes and fraud. Parametric insurance is well-suited for scenarios where risks are quantifiable, and events can be objectively measured. The transparency and tamper-proof nature of blockchain ensure that the triggering events are recorded accurately, further enhancing the reliability of parametric insurance models.

Tokenization of Policies

Blockchain introduces the concept of tokenizing insurance policies, representing them as digital assets on the blockchain. This innovation opens avenues for fractional ownership, allowing investors to participate in insurance markets and diversify their portfolios. Tokenization transforms insurance policies into tradable assets, providing liquidity and expanding the investor base in the insurance sector. In a tokenized insurance model, traditional policies are converted into digital tokens that can be bought, sold, and traded on blockchain-based platforms. This creates new opportunities for investors to engage with the insurance market, breaking down barriers to entry and fostering a more dynamic and liquid marketplace. Fractional ownership of insurance policies becomes feasible through tokenization, allowing multiple investors to hold shares in a single policy. This democratizes access to insurance as an investment and enhances liquidity in the insurance market. The tokenization of policies represents a novel intersection of blockchain and traditional financial markets, opening new horizons for the evolution of insurance as a financial asset.

Internet of Things (IoT) and Real-time Risk Monitoring

In the ever-evolving landscape of insurance, the integration of the Internet of Things (IoT) stands out as a transformative force, reshaping how risks are assessed, managed, and mitigated. The Internet of Things (IoT) refers to the interconnected network of devices and objects embedded with sensors, software, and connectivity, enabling them to collect and exchange data. Real-time Risk Monitoring, in conjunction with IoT, involves the continuous and instantaneous assessment of potential risks by utilizing data from IoT-connected devices. These devices, ranging from smart sensors in homes and vehicles to wearable devices, generate a continuous stream of data. This real-time data allows insurers to monitor risks dynamically, providing a more accurate and up-to-date understanding of the factors influencing insurance assessments.

Proliferation of IoT Devices

The contemporary era is witnessing an unprecedented proliferation of IoT devices due to the promise of enhanced connectivity, improved efficiency, and a seamless integration of the physical and digital realms. In the realm of insurance, this surge in IoT adoption opens new frontiers for data collection, offering insurers a wealth of real-time information to revolutionize their risk assessment and mitigation strategies. However, the significance of this proliferation extends beyond data quantity; it delves into the realm of data diversity. The multifaceted nature of IoT-generated data allows insurers to move beyond traditional risk factors, considering previously inaccessible or overlooked variables. For instance, in property insurance, data from smart home devices can provide insights into the maintenance of a property, potential security vulnerabilities, and even the likelihood of accidents or damages. The advent of wearable devices further amplifies the role of IoT in data collection. Health trackers, smartwatches, and other wearables continuously monitor individuals' health metrics, lifestyle choices, and environmental exposures. Insurers, particularly in the health and life insurance domains, can leverage this data for personalized risk assessments, tailoring coverage and premiums based on real-time insights into policyholders' behaviors and well-being. As IoT devices become more ingrained in daily life, insurers have an unparalleled opportunity to transition from static risk assessments to dynamic, real-time monitoring. The continuous data stream from these devices empowers insurers to understand risks as they evolve and proactively implement preventive measures.

Telematics and Usage-Based Insurance

Telematics is a transformative force in the insurance landscape. For example, in the automotive industry, telematics involves using devices installed in vehicles to transmit real-time data on driving behavior, vehicle performance, and environmental conditions. This data is pivotal in shaping the future of insurance, particularly in the realm of usage-based policies. Telematics' profound impact on insurance extends to underwriting practices. Unlike traditional reliance on statistical models and historical data, telematics introduces a dynamic element by providing real-time insights into an individual's driving habits (Gatteschi, Lamberti, Demartini, Pranteda, & Santamaría, 2018). Factors such as speed, acceleration, braking patterns, and the time of day a vehicle uses become integral components of the underwriting process.

The pricing of insurance policies undergoes significant transformation with telematics and usage-based models. Instead of fixed premiums based on broad categories, insurers can now adopt a more granular and personalized approach. As identified by real-time telematics data, Safer drivers enjoy lower premiums, establishing a direct correlation between individual behavior and insurance costs. This not only benefits conscientious drivers but also incentivizes safer practices on the road (KPMG, 2017). Telematics data revolutionizes claims processing. In the event of an accident, the wealth of real-time information captured by telematics devices provides a detailed and objective account of the incident (Kulia, 2023). Insurers can expedite the claims settlement process by leveraging this data, reducing the need for lengthy investigations and promoting transparency in claims resolution.

As a cornerstone of usage-based insurance, telematics aligns with broader societal trends toward a more data-driven and personalized approach. This shift benefits insurers by refining risk assessments and enhances road safety by encouraging responsible driving behavior. As the trajectory of telematics intersects with the path of the Internet of Things (IoT), the potential for insurance innovation becomes even more pronounced. The interconnectedness of various IoT devices, including those in the automotive and smart home sectors, allows insurers to create holistic risk profiles. Combining telematics data with information from home security systems offers a comprehensive view of an individual's overall risk profile, enabling insurers to tailor coverage that reflects a broader spectrum of potential risks as shown in Fig (**2**) below.

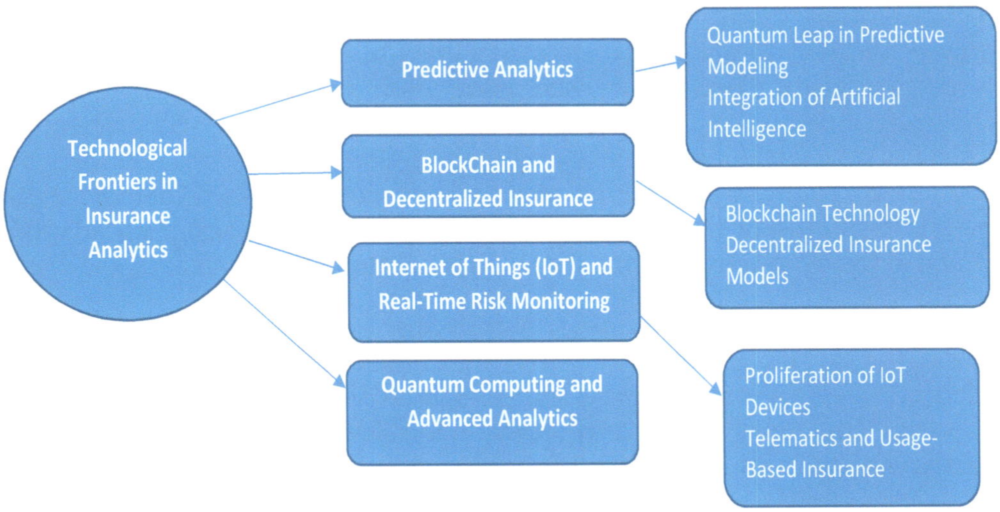

Fig. (2). Technological frontiers in insurance analytics.

HARNESSING DATA ANALYTICS IN INSURANCE OPERATIONS

In the dynamics of the insurance industry, data analytics has become a transformative catalyst, ushering in a new era of operational efficiency and insightful decision-making. This powerful force goes beyond adaptation, revolutionizing traditional practices from risk assessment and underwriting to bolstering cybersecurity measures and refining risk mitigation strategies. It signifies a fundamental shift toward a data-centric model that not only reevaluates risk factors with precision but also introduces dynamic pricing strategies and enhances the overall resilience of insurance operations. The synergy between data analytics and insurance operations is evident in the industry's meticulous embrace of real-time insights, enabling a more informed and proactive approach to challenges. This integration elevates insurance operations, providing a spectrum of possibilities beyond conventional practices and positioning insurers to navigate the complexities of the future with resilience and agility.

Risk Assessment and Underwriting

Data analytics is pivotal in revolutionizing the insurance sector, particularly in risk assessment and underwriting. In the pursuit of precision and reliability, insurers leverage extensive datasets encompassing historical claims, demographic information, and real-time data streams. This synthesis becomes the cornerstone for developing sophisticated models, drawing upon predictive analytics, machine learning algorithms, and advanced statistical techniques. This holistic approach empowers insurers to enhance their capabilities in evaluating and pricing risks with heightened sophistication. The integration of predictive analytics has significantly heightened the precision of risk assessments. By scrutinizing historical data trends and identifying patterns, insurers gain foresight into potential risks, enabling a more informed underwriting process. Dynamic machine learning algorithms further contribute to this precision, ensuring an adaptable approach to the ever-evolving landscape of risk evaluation.

The advent of machine learning algorithms introduces a new level of sophistication to risk assessment. These algorithms delve into complex patterns and dependencies within data, providing insurers with a nuanced understanding of risk factors. This ability to discern intricate correlations enables more informed underwriting decisions, especially in the face of evolving and intricate risks. In the era of data analytics, real-time data streams emerge as a transformative force in risk assessment and underwriting. The capability to process and analyze unfolding data in real time equips insurers with dynamic insights into changing risk scenarios, proving vital in industries characterized by rapidly evolving risks, such as cybersecurity or climate-related concerns.

Beyond predictive analytics and machine learning, insurers deploy advanced statistical techniques to gain a nuanced understanding of risks. Statistical modeling becomes the guiding force, aiding insurers in assessing the probability and severity of potential events and assisting underwriters in setting appropriate premiums and coverage limits. The synergy of data analytics and advanced statistics empowers insurers to consider a broader range of variables, resulting in more comprehensive and accurate risk assessments. Integrating data analytics into risk assessment and underwriting signifies a paradigm shift, transcending traditional boundaries. It propels insurers beyond static models, ushering in a dynamic, data-driven approach that enhances accuracy and positions them at the forefront of innovation within the industry.

Claims Processing and Fraud Detection

The efficiency of claims processing experiences a significant enhancement through the strategic application of data analytics. The incorporation of machine learning models further contributes to this efficiency by enabling early detection of fraudulent claims, thereby safeguarding insurers from potential financial losses. In the intricate landscape of the insurance industry, combating fraudulent claims remains a persistent challenge. Data analytics emerges as a formidable tool in this battle, as advanced algorithms sift through extensive datasets to identify patterns and anomalies indicative of potential fraudulent activities. By scrutinizing historical claims data and cross-referencing it with real-time information, insurers can construct predictive models that effectively flag suspicious claims for further investigation (Tyagi, Gupta, & Ansari, 2023). Data analytics excels in pattern recognition, a crucial aspect of fraud detection. Machine learning models can identify unusual patterns or behaviors in claims data, such as anomalies in claim timing, inconsistencies in reported incidents, or disparities in medical records. This real-time pattern recognition enhances insurers' agility in preventing fraudulent payouts and safeguarding financial integrity.

The proactive nature of data analytics extends beyond detection to fraud prevention through predictive modeling. Insurers stay ahead of evolving fraud tactics by continually updating and refining predictive models. Predictive analytics empowers insurers to anticipate potential fraud risks based on changing market conditions, emerging trends, and historical fraud patterns. This forward-looking approach enables insurers to implement preemptive measures, fortifying their defenses against fraudulent activities. Integrating data analytics into claims processing elevates operational efficiency and strengthens insurers against the pervasive threat of fraud. Insurers create a resilient and responsive claims management ecosystem by leveraging advanced algorithms and real-time data analysis.

Customer Relationship Management (CRM)

Data analytics is a cornerstone in transforming customer relationship management within the insurance domain. Insurers leverage customer data to gain insights into preferences, behaviors, and expectations. This information facilitates the customization of products, personalized communication strategies, and targeted marketing campaigns. Customer analytics improves retention rates and fosters a deeper understanding of client needs and aspirations. Data analytics enables insurers to delve deep into customer behavior, preferences, and interactions. Insurers gain a comprehensive understanding of customer preferences and expectations by analyzing data from various touchpoints, including digital platforms, customer service interactions, and claims history. This insight forms the foundation for personalized services and tailored insurance offerings. The advent of data-driven models allows insurers to move beyond traditional segmentation and embrace hyper-personalization. Machine learning algorithms analyze vast datasets to identify individualized patterns and preferences. This enables insurers to tailor insurance products, coverage limits, and pricing structures based on each customer's unique needs.

Hyper-personalization not only enhances customer satisfaction but also fosters customer loyalty and retention. Data analytics facilitates the implementation of behaviour-based pricing models, where premiums are directly linked to individual behaviour. Telematics in auto insurance, for example, allows insurers to assess driving behaviour in real time. Safe drivers may be rewarded with lower premiums, directly correlating behavior and insurance costs. This approach aligns with customer expectations for fair and personalized pricing and incentivizes positive behaviors. The ability to predict customer needs and preferences through data analytics enables insurers to engage with customers proactively. By anticipating life events, changes in circumstances, or evolving risk profiles, insurers can reach out to customers with relevant offerings and solutions. This proactive engagement enhances the overall customer experience and strengthens the insurer-customer relationship.

Pricing Optimization and Product Development

Pricing optimization is crucial for insurers seeking to maintain market relevance in the competitive insurance landscape. Data analytics is a powerful tool, allowing insurers to analyze market trends, competitor offerings, and customer behaviors to fine-tune pricing strategies. The insights from data analytics inform the development of innovative insurance products that align with evolving consumer needs, ensuring a dynamic and responsive product portfolio.

Insurers can optimise their pricing models in real time by dissecting market trends and analyzing customer preferences, competitor pricing, and emerging trends. This agility in pricing strategies ensures responsiveness to changing consumer behaviors. Insurers leverage data analytics to conduct thorough competitor analysis in a data-driven landscape, gaining valuable insights into competitors' pricing structures, product offerings, and market positioning. This competitive intelligence guides strategic decision-making in pricing, ensuring that insurers remain competitive and capable of differentiating their offerings in the market.

The development of innovative insurance products relies on a deep understanding of consumer behaviors and preferences. Data analytics enables insurers to analyze customer interactions, feedback, and purchasing patterns, identify unmet needs, and design tailored products that resonate with evolving consumer demands. This proactive approach to product development ensures insurers stay ahead of market trends, maintaining a relevant and appealing product portfolio. The dynamic nature of data analytics allows insurers to make real-time adjustments to their product offerings by continuously monitoring customer feedback, market trends, and emerging risks. This agility ensures insurers promptly respond to changing market dynamics and position themselves as forward-thinking and responsive to evolving consumer needs. The synergy of data analytics and pricing optimization is a strategic imperative for insurers aiming to thrive in a competitive market, enabling them to refine pricing models, develop innovative products, and maintain a competitive edge in the dynamic landscape of the insurance industry.

Operational Efficiency and Cost Management

Efficiency gains and cost management are inherent benefits of incorporating data analytics into insurance operations. Predictive modeling and automation streamline operational processes, reducing manual intervention and minimizing errors. Insights derived from data analytics guide strategic decisions related to resource allocation, optimizing workflows, and ultimately enhancing the overall operational efficiency of insurance companies. Data analytics streamlines underwriting processes by automating routine tasks and providing underwriters with actionable insights. Predictive models assess risk factors more rapidly and accurately than traditional methods, enabling informed decisions efficiently. This accelerates the underwriting process and reduces operational costs associated with manual reviews. The dynamic nature of data analytics facilitates the adoption of dynamic pricing strategies, allowing insurers to adjust premiums in real time based on changing risk factors, market conditions, and customer behaviors. This pricing agility reflects the actual risk exposure and allows insurers to optimize revenue streams.

Automation enhances claims processing efficiency by expediting the settlement of legitimate claims through automated routine tasks. This reduces processing times, minimizes errors, and improves the overall efficiency of claims processing. Automation provides a more seamless and satisfying customer experience during the claims settlement. Strategic decisions related to resource allocation are guided by insights derived from data analytics. By analyzing operational data, insurers can identify bottlenecks, inefficiencies, and areas for improvement, ensuring optimal resource allocation and reducing unnecessary costs. Analyzing data related to operational processes enables insurers to streamline workflows, eliminate redundancies, and improve overall efficiency. Workflow optimization enhances productivity and contributes to cost savings by eliminating unnecessary steps and adopting more efficient processes. The continuous refinement of workflows based on data-driven insights ensures that operational processes evolve to meet the dynamic demands of the insurance industry, fostering a culture of continuous improvement and efficiency.

Regulatory Compliance and Reporting

Data analytics is transforming regulatory compliance and reporting in the dynamic insurance landscape. The insurance sector navigates a complex regulatory environment characterized by constant shifts and updates to compliance standards. To effectively address these challenges, insurers turn to data analytics as a strategic ally. Data analytics tools play a proactive role by scanning extensive datasets to identify potential areas where a company may fall short of compliance. This foresighted approach enables insurers to take corrective measures before breaches occur, reducing the risk of regulatory penalties and safeguarding against reputational damage. The synergy of data analytics and automation revolutionizes traditional regulatory reporting processes, allowing insurers to swiftly generate comprehensive and accurate reports. By automating the extraction, analysis, and synthesis of relevant data, insurers ensure timely compliance while freeing up valuable human resources (Schmidt, 2018). This contributes to cost-effectiveness and allows teams to focus on more strategic aspects of regulatory management.

Moreover, the transparency afforded by data analytics proves crucial in fostering positive regulatory relationships. Regulators increasingly seek a clear and detailed understanding of insurers' operations. Data analytics empowers insurers to present a comprehensive picture of their compliance efforts, building trust and collaboration with regulatory bodies (Taneja *et al*., 2023). This proactive approach positions insurance companies as responsible stewards of regulatory requirements, contributing to a more constructive regulatory environment. Integrating data analytics in regulatory compliance and reporting ensures adherence to standards, streamlines processes, mitigates risks and enhances the insurance operations efficiency and transparency of insurance operations.

Actuarial Modeling and Financial Forecasting

Actuarial modeling, a cornerstone of insurance operations, experiences a profound transformation with the integration of data analytics. Insurers employ advanced statistical models, enriched by data analytics insights, to assess future liabilities, estimate loss reserves, and conduct comprehensive financial forecasting. This section explores the symbiotic relationship between actuarial science and data analytics, illustrating how these disciplines converge to provide more precise financial projections and risk assessments. The convergence of actuarial science and data analytics represents a paradigm shift in how insurers approach financial projections and risk assessments. Traditionally, actuarial models relied on historical data and predefined assumptions. However, integrating data analytics introduces a dynamic dimension, allowing actuaries to analyze a broader range of variables, including real-time data streams and external factors that may impact risk profiles. This enriched dataset enhances the precision of actuarial models, providing insurers with a more nuanced understanding of potential risks and liabilities.

Machine learning algorithms, a subset of data analytics, are pivotal in refining actuarial models. The algorithms can analyze vast datasets, identifying trends and correlations that may elude traditional modeling approaches. The iterative nature of machine learning allows models to continuously adapt and improve, ensuring that actuarial predictions remain accurate and reflective of evolving market dynamics. Financial forecasting, a critical aspect of insurance operations, benefits immensely from integrating data analytics. Predictive analytics models can analyze market trends, economic indicators, and customer behaviors, providing valuable insights for more accurate financial projections. The ability to forecast with greater precision enhances strategic decision-making within insurance companies, allowing for proactive risk management and capital allocation. Integrating data analytics in actuarial modeling and financial forecasting enhances the accuracy and agility of these processes, empowering insurers to make more informed and strategic decisions in a rapidly changing market.

Cybersecurity and Risk Mitigation

As the digital landscape expands, cybersecurity becomes a paramount concern for insurers. Data analytics plays a pivotal role in identifying and mitigating cybersecurity risks, offering a proactive and dynamic defense against the increasing sophistication of cyber threats. While bringing numerous benefits, the digitalization of insurance operations also exposes insurers to a myriad of cyber threats (Nath, 2016). These threats, from phishing attacks to ransomware, require a sophisticated and adaptive defense mechanism. Data analytics, powered by machine learning, provides this mechanism by continuously analyzing vast amounts of data to identify patterns indicative of potential cyber threats.

Machine learning algorithms excel in detecting anomalies in data patterns, which is crucial for the early identification of potential security breaches (Singh & Akhilesh, 2019). By establishing a baseline of normal network behavior, machine learning models can swiftly identify deviations that may signify a security threat. This proactive approach allows insurers to respond swiftly, preventing or minimizing the impact of cyber incidents. Proactive risk mitigation strategies, informed by data analytics, contribute significantly to the resilience of insurers in the face of evolving cyber threats. Machine learning models can predict potential vulnerabilities and recommend preemptive measures to strengthen cybersecurity defenses. This anticipatory approach to risk management enhances the overall cybersecurity posture of insurers, reducing the likelihood of successful cyber attacks and the associated financial and reputational risks. Moreover, integrating data analytics in cybersecurity practices enables insurers to comply with increasingly stringent regulatory requirements related to data protection. By continuously monitoring and analyzing data for potential breaches, insurers are committed to protecting sensitive customer information and maintaining compliance with data protection regulations.

CHALLENGES IN THE ADOPTION OF DATA ANALYTICS IN THE INSURANCE INDUSTRY

The integration of data analytics stands out as a potent catalyst, offering the promise of profound transformations. This integration revolutionizes various facets of insurance operations, paving the way for heightened operational efficiency, the delivery of personalized services, and more effective risk management strategies. Yet, as with any transformative journey, the path toward widespread adoption of data analytics in the insurance sector is not without its challenges and intricacies. The industry grapples with the complexities inherent in this evolution, navigating through hurdles to fully realize the benefits data analytics can bring to the forefront of insurance practices.

Data Security Concerns

One of the foremost challenges in adopting data analytics in insurance lies in the evolving landscape of cybersecurity threats. As insurers accumulate vast amounts of sensitive customer data, they become prime cyberattack targets. The increasing sophistication of cyber threats necessitates robust cybersecurity measures to safeguard against data breaches and unauthorized access (International Association of Insurance Supervisors, 2017). Industry leaders must invest in advanced cybersecurity infrastructure, incorporating technologies like encryption, multi-factor authentication, and continuous monitoring. Collaborating with cybersecurity experts can help insurers stay ahead of emerging threats.

The regulatory environment concerning data privacy is continually evolving, with stringent measures like GDPR and CCPA setting new standards. Insurers must navigate complex compliance requirements to ensure data analytics practices align with privacy regulations, avoiding legal repercussions and building and maintaining customer trust. Establishing a comprehensive data privacy framework involves regular audits, transparent customer communication, and implementing privacy-enhancing technologies. Insurers can benefit from collaborating with legal and regulatory experts to ensure ongoing compliance.

Talent and Skill Gap

The demand for skilled data analytics professionals in the insurance industry surpasses the current talent pool. Insurers face challenges in recruiting individuals with a deep understanding of data science, machine learning, and other specialized analytics skills required for effective implementation. Strategic talent acquisition, upskilling programs, and partnerships with educational institutions can address the skill gap. Insurers need to foster a culture of continuous learning to adapt to the evolving demands of data analytics. Insurance data analytics requires collaboration between diverse professionals, including data scientists, actuaries, and IT specialists. Bridging the gap between these disciplines and ensuring effective communication can be a significant challenge. Creating interdisciplinary teams, fostering a culture of collaboration, and investing in cross-functional training programs can enhance communication and collaboration within organizations.

Integration with Legacy Systems

Many insurers operate on legacy systems that may not seamlessly integrate with modern data analytics platforms. The challenge lies in upgrading or replacing these systems without disrupting existing operations. A phased approach to system integration, incorporating middleware solutions and leveraging application programming interfaces (APIs), can facilitate the transition. Insurers must prioritize systems that offer scalability and flexibility. Resistance to change within organizations can impede the adoption of data analytics. Employees may be accustomed to traditional processes, and the shift towards data-driven decision-making requires a cultural change. Effective change management strategies, clear communication, and employee training programs are essential to overcoming resistance. Leadership plays a crucial role in championing the benefits of data analytics and fostering a culture of innovation.

Regulatory Dynamics

Insurance is a highly regulated industry, and staying abreast of the evolving regulatory landscape presents an ongoing challenge. Adapting data analytics practices to comply with new regulations while maintaining operational efficiency is a delicate balance. Proactive engagement with regulatory bodies, investing in regulatory technology (RegTech), and fostering a regulatory compliance culture within organizations are critical. Insurers can collaborate with industry associations to stay informed about upcoming regulatory changes. Operating in multiple jurisdictions introduces complexities due to variations in regulatory frameworks (Kashif, Shajar, Singhal, & Kumar, 2023). Insurers must navigate these differences to ensure consistency in data analytics practices. Developing a comprehensive understanding of regulatory variations, establishing a global compliance framework, and leveraging RegTech solutions can help insurers streamline compliance across diverse markets.

Ethical Considerations

As insurers leverage data analytics for personalized services, ethical considerations surrounding the responsible use of customer data become paramount. Striking a balance between personalization and individual privacy is an ongoing challenge. Implementing ethical guidelines, obtaining informed consent, and regularly auditing data usage practices contribute to responsible data analytics (Kantur & Bamuleseyo, 2018). Insurers should prioritize transparency in communicating how customer data is utilized. The algorithms powering data analytics systems may inadvertently introduce biases, leading to unfair outcomes. Identifying and mitigating algorithmic bias is crucial for ensuring equitable decision-making. Regular audits of algorithms, diverse representation in analytics teams, and continuous monitoring for bias can address this challenge. Insurers must prioritize fairness and equity in their data analytics practices.

CONCLUSION

In conclusion, this in-depth exploration of the impact and implications of artificial intelligence (AI) on societal dynamics underscores the need for a thoughtful and inclusive approach to navigating the evolving landscape. The economic ramifications of AI are evident, with industries experiencing unprecedented transformations in efficiency and innovation. However, the societal fabric is intricately woven, and the disruptions brought by AI necessitate careful consideration of the social, ethical, and cultural dimensions.

On the social front, the shifting dynamics in employment patterns and educational paradigms demand proactive measures to ensure that AI benefits are distributed equitably. The emergence of AI also influences interpersonal relationships, requiring us to examine how these technologies shape human interactions and social structures. Striking a balance between technological progress and social harmony is crucial to avoid exacerbating existing inequalities and fostering a society where AI augments rather than replaces human capabilities.

Ethical considerations take the center stage, as issues of bias, transparency, and accountability in AI algorithms raise ethical dilemmas. Addressing these concerns is imperative to build trust in AI systems and ensure their responsible deployment. It is clear that the development and deployment of AI technologies should align with ethical principles, safeguarding against unintended consequences and promoting fairness.

Moreover, the cultural dimensions of AI adoption highlight the importance of contextual adaptation. Cultural factors influence the acceptance, perception, and integration of AI technologies in diverse global contexts. Recognizing and respecting these cultural nuances is essential for fostering a global community that embraces the positive potential of AI while respecting individual and cultural values.

In navigating this transformative era, interdisciplinary collaboration among researchers, policymakers, and industry leaders is paramount. Crafting robust regulations, informed by diverse perspectives, will guide the responsible development and deployment of AI. Additionally, fostering public awareness and understanding is critical for demystifying AI, dispelling misconceptions, and fostering a sense of empowerment and agency among the broader population.

In essence, as we stand at the forefront of the AI revolution, a conscientious and collective effort is required to ensure that AI technologies serve humanity's best interests. By embracing a human-centric approach that considers economic, social, ethical, and cultural dimensions, we can harness the transformative power of AI for the greater good, advancing a future where technology enhances our collective well-being.

REFERENCES

Alvin, K., Erik, L., Gwen, W., Rex, Z. Decentralized Insurance Alternatives: Market Landscape, Opportunities and Challenges *The Society of Actuaries Research Institute.* Available from: https://www.soa.org/resources/research-reports/2022/decentralized-ins-alt/. (2022).

Shetty, A., Shetty, A.D., Pai, R.Y., Rao, R.R., Bhandary, R., Shetty, J., Nayak, S., Keerthi Dinesh, T., Dsouza, K.J. (2022). Block chain application in insurance services: A systematic review of the evidence. *SAGE Open, 12*(1)21582440221079877 [http://dx.doi.org/10.1177/21582440221079877]

Balasubramanian, R., Libarikian, A., McElhaney, D. Insurance 2030—The impact of AI on the future of insurance *McKinsey & Company.* Available from: https://www.mckinsey.com/industries/financial-services/our-insights/insurance-2030-the-impact-of-ai-on-the-future-of-insurance. (2018).

Bohnert, A., Fritzsche, A., Gregor, S. (2019). Digital agendas in the insurance industry: the importance of comprehensive approaches. *Geneva Pap. Risk Insur. Issues Pract., 44*(1), 1-19. [http://dx.doi.org/10.1057/s41288-018-0109-0]

Brettler, D., Gosnear, T. Parametric insurance fills gaps where traditional insurance falls short *Insurance Journal.* Available from: www. insurancejournal. com/news/international/2020/01/09/553850. htm. (2020).

Cohn, A., West, T., Parker, C. (2017). Smart after all: Blockchain, smart contracts, parametric insurance, and smart energy grids. *Georgetown Law Technology Review, 1*(2), 273-304.

Deloitte, L.L.P. *Block chain applications in Insurance.* Available from: https://www2.deloitte.com/content/dam/Deloitte/ch/Documents/innovation/ch-en-innovation-deloitte-blockchain-app-in-insurance.pdf. (2016).

Deloitte, L.L.P. *Artificial intelligence: From mystery to mastery - unlocking the business value of AI in the insurance industry.* Available from: https://www2.deloitte.com/de/de/pages/innovation/contents/artificial-intelligence-insurance-industry.html. (2017).

Crawford, S., Plesse, D. *Blockchain technology as a platform for digitization: Implications for the insurance industry.* Available from: https://assets.ey.com/content/dam/ey-sites/ey-com/en_gl/topics/advisory/-Y-blockchain-technology-as-a-platform-for-digitization.pdf?download. (2016).

Ernst, , Young, *Global Insurance Outlook Achieving growth through people, purpose and technology.Global Insurance Outlook Achieving growth through people, purpose and technology.* Available from: https://assets.ey.com/content/dam/ey-sites/ey-com/en_gl/topics/insurance/ey-2022-gl-bal-insurance-outlook-report.pdf. (2022).

Fariya, S. (2024). Exploring the influence of factors driving financial accessibility, financial activities, and financial education on sustainable development. *In Artificial Intelligence and Machine Learning-Powered Smart Finance* IGI Global.

Feng, R. (2023). Decentralized Insurance.*Decentralized Insurance: Technical Foundation of Business Models.* (pp. 119-139). Cham: Springer International Publishing. [http://dx.doi.org/10.1007/978-3-031-29559-1_5]

Gatteschi, V., Lamberti, F., Demartini, C., Pranteda, C., Santamaría, V. (2018). Blockchain and smart contracts for insurance: Is the technology mature enough? *Future Internet, 10*(2), 20-35. [http://dx.doi.org/10.3390/fi10020020]

Schmidt, C. *Insurance in the Digital Age-A view on key implications for the economy and society.* Available from: https://www.genevaassociation.org/sites/default/files/research-topics-docume-t-type/pdf_public/insurance_in_the_digital_age_01.pdf. (2018).

International association of insurance supervisors. *FinTech Developments in the Insurance Industry.FinTech developments in the insurance industry.* Available from: https://www.iaisweb.org/page/news/other-paper--and-reports/file/65625/report-on-fintech-developments-in-the-insurance-industry. (2017).

Kantur, H., Bamuleseyo, C. *How smart contracts can change the insurance industry: Benefits and challenges of using Blockchain technology.* Available from: http://www.diva-portal.org/smash/record.jsf?pid=diva2%3A1214254&dswid=8446. (2018).

Kashif, M., Singhal, N., Goyal, S., Singh, S.K. (2024). Foreign Exchange Reserves and Economic Growth of Brazil: A Nonlinear Approach. Finance. *Theory Pract., 28*(1), 145-154.

Kashif, M., Shajar, S.N., Singhal, N., Kumar, P. (2023). *Achieving sustainable investment practices through green finance: Challenges and opportunities. Sustainable Investments in Green Finance.* IGI Global. [http://dx.doi.org/10.4018/979-8-3693-1388-6.ch016]

Kashif, M., Kumar, P., Ghai, S., Kumar, S. (2023). Disruptive technologies in computational finance *In Algorithmic Approaches to Financial Technology: Forecasting, Trading, and Optimization IGI Global*

KPMG, *Will on-demand insurance become mainstream?.* Available from: https://assets.kpmg.com/content/dam/kpmg/uk/pdf/2017/09/will-o--demand-insurance-become-mainstream.pdf. (2017).

Kulia, S. On-demand insurance: The rise of customizable, usage-based coverage *The Times of India.* Available from: https://timesofindia.indiatimes.com/blogs/voices/on-demand-insurance-the-ri-e-of-customizable-usage-based-coverage/. (2023).

Levantesi, S., Piscopo, G. (2022). Mutual peer-to-peer insurance: The allocation of risk. *Journal of Co-operative Organization and Management, 10*(1)100154 [http://dx.doi.org/10.1016/j.jcom.2021.100154]

Digital disruption in insurance: Cutting through the noise. 2017.

Nath, I. (2016). Data exchange platform to fight insurance fraud on blockchain. *In 2016 IEEE 16th international conference on data mining workshops (ICDMW),* IEEE Computer Society821-825. [http://dx.doi.org/10.1109/ICDMW.2016.0121]

Singh, A., Akhilesh, K. B. (2020). The insurance industry—cyber security in the hyper-connected age *Smart Technologies: Scope and Applications,* 201-219.

Taneja, S., Dangwal, A., Kaur, S., Ozen, E., Kukreti, M. (2023). An evaluation of the operational and regulatory aspects of using blockchain in the insurance industry *In The Application of Emerging Technology and Blockchain in the Insurance Industry.*
[http://dx.doi.org/10.1201/9781032630946-11]

Tyagi, S., Gupta, A., Ansari, N. (2023). Adoption and perception of banking customers towards green mode of banking: a demonstration of structural equation modelling. *J. Financ. Serv. Mark.,* •••, 1-17.

Yuvaraj, N., Srihari, K., Dhiman, G., Somasundaram, K., Sharma, A., Rajeskannan, S., Soni, M., Gaba, G.S., AlZain, M.A., Masud, M. (2021). Nature-Inspired-Based Approach for Automated Cyberbullying Classification on Multimedia Social Networking. *Math. Probl. Eng., 2021*(1), 1-12.
[http://dx.doi.org/10.1155/2021/6644652]

Vaid, S.K., Kumar, B., Sharma, A., Shukla, A.K., Srivastava, P.C. (2014). Effect of zn solubilizing bacteria on growth promotion and zn nutrition of rice. *J. Soil Sci. Plant Nutr., 14*(4), 889-910.
[http://dx.doi.org/10.4067/S0718-95162014005000071]

Bashir, (2020).

Avikal, S., Pant, R., Barthwal, A., Ram, M., Upadhyay, R.K. (2023). Factors implementing sustainable circular economy in agro-produce supply chain: DEMATEL-DANP-based approach. *Manag. Environ. Qual., 34*(4), 1158-1173.
[http://dx.doi.org/10.1108/MEQ-03-2022-0088]

Nigam, M.K., Avikal, S., Ram, M. (2021). Risk assessment in ERP project by COPRAS method under fuzzy environment. *Int. J. Reliab. Qual. Saf. Eng., 28*(6)2140006
[http://dx.doi.org/10.1142/S0218539321400064]

Avikal, S., Nithin Kumar, K.C., Singh, A.R., Jain, R. (2020). Grey based Taguchi optimization for multi-lobe bearing. *Mater. Today Proc., 26*, 2663-2666.
[http://dx.doi.org/10.1016/j.matpr.2020.02.560]

Singh, A.K., Avikal, S., Nithin Kumar, K.C., Kumar, M., Thakura, P. (2020). A fuzzy-AHP and M − TOPSIS based approach for selection of composite materials used in structural applications. *Mater. Today Proc., 26*, 3119-3123.
[http://dx.doi.org/10.1016/j.matpr.2020.02.644]

Singh, R., Rashmi, , Bhingole, P., Avikal, S. (2018). Gray based Taguchi optimization for heat treated welded joint. *Mater. Today Proc., 5*(9), 19156-19165.
[http://dx.doi.org/10.1016/j.matpr.2018.06.270]

Avikal, S., Sharma, S., Kalra, J.S., Varma, D., Pandey, R. (2016). A fuzzy AHP approach for calculating the weights of disassembly line balancing criteria. *In Proceedings of Fifth International Conference on Soft Computing for Problem Solving: SocProS 2015,* Springer Singapore*1*(), 723-727.

Chand, M., Avikal, S. (2015). An MCDM based approach for purchasing a car from Indian car market. *2015 IEEE Students Conference on Engineering and Systems (SCES),* 1-4.IEEE..
[http://dx.doi.org/10.1109/SCES.2015.7506454]

Avikal, S., Mishra, P.K., Jain, R., Yadav, H.C. (2013). A PROMETHEE method based heuristic for disassembly line balancing problem. *Industrial Engineering and Management Systems, 12*(3), 254-263.
[http://dx.doi.org/10.7232/iems.2013.12.3.254]

CHAPTER 9

Unravelling the Ethical Tapestry: Navigating Dilemmas in Data Analytics within the Insurance Sector

Harshi Garg[1], **Mohammad Kashif**[2,*] and **Arokiaraj David**[3]

[1] *IIMT University, Meerut, Uttar Pradesh, India*

[2] *Department of Management Studies, Graphic Era Deemed to be University, Dehradun, Uttarakhand, India*

[3] *Swiss Business School, Ras Al Khaimah, Ras Al Khaimah, UAE*

Abstract: This study intricately explores the ethical landscape surrounding data analytics within the insurance sector, aiming to untangle the intricacies and quandaries arising in the pursuit of data-driven insights. In an era dominated by technological strides, the insurance industry increasingly relies on data analytics to bolster risk assessment, optimize operations, and tailor services to individual needs. However, the widespread use of data introduces ethical challenges pertaining to privacy, equity, and openness. The principal objective of this research is to traverse and critically examine the ethical considerations woven into the fabric of applying data analytics within the insurance sector. To accomplish this, a methodology centered on the case study is employed, delving into the real-world scenarios and their practical implications. By closely analyzing specific instances within the insurance industry, the research aims to provide a nuanced comprehension of how ethical concerns manifest during the implementation of data analytics. The methodology encompasses the selection of diverse case studies representing various aspects of data analytics in insurance, encompassing customer profiling, risk assessment algorithms, and claims processing. Through a thorough analysis of these cases, the study seeks to uncover patterns, confront challenges, and propose potential solutions related to ethical considerations. Ethical frameworks, industry guidelines, and stakeholder perspectives will be leveraged to assess the ramifications of data analytics practices in the insurance domain. In conclusion, this research adds to the ongoing dialogue on responsible data analytics in the insurance sector. By unraveling the ethical tapestry and offering insights gleaned from real-world cases, the study aspires to present actionable recommendations for industry professionals, policymakers, and stakeholders to navigate ethical quandaries associated with data analytics in insurance responsibly.

* **Corresponding author Mohammad Kashif:** Department of Management Studies, Graphic Era Deemed to be University, Dehradun, Uttarakhand, India; E-mail: mkashif69@gmail.com

Sanjay Taneja, Ercan Ozen, Luan Vardar, Mohit Kukreti & Mohammad Kashif (Eds.)

Keywords: Data analytics, Ethical consideration, Insurance sectors, Navigating dilemmas, Responsible practices.

INTRODUCTION

Amidst the ever-evolving tapestry of the insurance sector, the infusion of data analytics emerges as an epochal force, not merely reshaping but redefining the very essence of the industry (Costouros, n.d.; Umeanozie, 2024). The conventional norms governing risk assessment, policy customization, and customer interactions have undergone a tectonic shift, propelled by the tantalizing promises of innovation and heightened operational efficiency. Yet, within this transformative journey, we find ourselves navigating through intricate ethical conundrums, interwoven with meticulous care into a complex and nuanced fabric that beckons our thoughtful exploration. "Unravelling the Ethical Tapestry: Navigating Dilemmas in Data Analytics within the Insurance Sector" stands as our guiding compass through this dynamic intersection—a realm where the magnetic pull of progress harmonizes with the ethical quandaries enshrouding privacy, fairness, and the conscientious utilization of sensitive information (Gill, 2021; Minkler *et al.*, 2002; Kalkal *et al.*, 2021). In the chapters that follow, our expedition plunges deep into the heart of these complexities, a quest to illuminate the multifaceted dimensions of ethical dilemmas within the insurance industry's embrace of data analytics (Sinfield, 2011; Sortedahl *et al.*, 2018). This narrative aspires not only to unravel the intricacies but also to offer profound insights and reflective perspectives, unveiling how the industry grapples with the ethical challenges inherent in the era of data-driven decision-making (Bordoloi *et al.*, 2018). As we navigate this intellectual terrain, our collective aim is to contribute to a profound understanding of the delicate equilibrium required to responsibly harness the potential of data analytics within the insurance sector, fostering a future where innovation and ethics coalesce for the greater good (Losada-Espinosa *et al.*, 2020; Tarvydas & Barros-Bailey, 2010).

In the dynamic realm of data analytics, where technological prowess surges forward, organizations find themselves endowed with an unparalleled capacity to distill priceless insights from vast data landscapes, fueling more smart and strategic decision-making (Bhandari, n.d.; Krzyminiewska, 2020). As the omnipotence of data analytics unfolds, ethical considerations ascend to a paramount position, shaping the judicious deployment of these transformative technologies (Ballot *et al.*, 2019; Rosoff *et al.*, 2018). This chapter embarks on a journey, meticulously navigating the intricacies of ethical quandaries within the domain of data analytics, spotlighting the nuanced crossroads where technology, privacy, and societal impact harmonize (Halleck, n.d.; Hashem, 2023). The introductory vista immerses us in the profound implications of the ongoing data analytics revolution, underscoring the pivotal role played by technological leaps, empowering organizations to glean profound insights from expansive data troves (Saggu *et al.*, 2014). This newfound capability, however, begets a conundrum of ethical considerations that demand our unwavering attention (Boodhun & Jayabalan, 2018; Kumar & L., 2018). Once peripheral, ethical reflections now bask in the limelight, beckoning meticulous scrutiny and nuanced comprehension. This chapter serves as an illuminating guide through the ethical landscape of data analytics, delving into multifaceted dilemmas (Saxena *et al.*, 2018). Our overarching aim is to cast a clarifying light on the intricate interplay between technology, privacy, and societal repercussions (Tornyeva & Wereko, 2012; Zarifis *et al.*, 2019). As technology ceaselessly advances, a profound understanding of ethical nuances becomes imperative. It becomes our collective responsibility to navigate this evolving landscape with acute awareness, fostering an ethical framework that steers the judicious use of data analytics for the collective betterment of society (Billio *et al.*, 2010; Lyubchich *et al.*, 2019).

Background of the Study

The rationale behind "Unravelling the Ethical Tapestry: Navigating Dilemmas in Data Analytics within the Insurance Sector" lies in its commitment to confronting the ethical intricacies spawned by the integration of data analytics in the insurance landscape (Eling, 2011; Sanchis *et al.*, 2007). With a sharp focus on individual privacy, the study strives to adeptly recognize and navigate the dilemmas, underscoring the imperative for data usage to adhere unwaveringly to the highest ethical standards. By delicately teasing apart the ethical complexities, the research aspires to weave a narrative that contributes to the cultivation of conscientious practices (BURCA & BATRINCA, 2014; Thomas & Gilson, 2004). These practices not only ensure privacy but also harmonize seamlessly with ethical norms, addressing the dynamic expectations of stakeholders in the ever-evolving realm of the insurance sector (Baecke & Bocca, 2017; Nissim *et al.*, 2011). In the realm of insurance, the emergence of data analytics introduces a duality of opportunities and challenges, sculpting a dynamic landscape that is both revolutionary and intricate. The potential lies in the capacity to overhaul the industry, optimize operational processes, refine risk evaluation, and tailor services to individual policyholders (Singhal, Goyal & Singhal, 2020). Data analytics bestows insurers with the capability to extract meaningful insights from extensive datasets, enabling well-informed decision-making and fostering inventive solutions (Fu & Deshpande, 2014a; Marr, n.d.). Nevertheless, this transformative influence also exposes hazards, encompassing the potential for unintended biases in algorithmic decision-making, apprehensions regarding privacy and data security, and the prospect of discriminatory practices. Achieving a nuanced equilibrium between harnessing the potential of data analytics for industry progression and addressing the ethical considerations and potential drawbacks is crucial for navigating the evolving landscape of the insurance sector.

The Power of Insight: Leveraging Data for Progress

In the domain of insurance, the section epitomizes a transformative odyssey propelled by the capabilities of data analytics. This conceptual framework emboldens insurance providers to extract unprecedented insights, guiding the industry toward evolution (Grindrod, 2016; Ohonba & Ogbeide, 2023). As an illustration, the application of predictive analytics empowers insurers to dissect historical data, unveiling patterns that forecast future trends. This foresight facilitates more precise risk assessments and enables proactive decision-making, thereby fortifying the industry's resilience (Fu & Deshpande, 2014b; Hair Jr *et al.*, n.d.). This perceptive methodology not only amplifies operational efficiency but also hones the underwriting process, ensuring bespoke and economically viable insurance solutions for policyholders. Consequently, the potency of insight harnessed through data analytics emerges as a potent force for advancement, propelling the insurance sector into a domain characterized by precision, ingenuity, and a heightened focus on customer needs (Kashif *et al.*, 2024).

The Dark Side: Unintended Consequences in Insurance Analytics

This section delves into the tapestry of potential challenges woven into the fabric of deploying data analytics. As the industry endeavors to embrace innovation, the unfolding narrative reveals the subtle shadows of unforeseen consequences (Kashif, Sridharan, & Thiyagarajan, 2017). A poignant illustration unfolds in the realm of algorithmic decision-making, where the inadvertent infiltration of biases can subtly influence policyholder outcomes, potentially perpetuating discrimination (Farid Ali al-Fijawi *et al.*, 2020; Raudeliūnienė & Račinskaja, 2014). Moreover, the strategic use of sensitive data, while integral to robust risk assessment, unfurls ethical concerns entwined with the delicate threads of privacy. Navigating the ethical tightrope between harnessing invaluable insights and safeguarding individual privacy becomes a profound contemplation. The ethical quandaries extend their tendrils into the realms of transparency and fairness, as the veiled intricacies of complex algorithms challenge the industry's capacity to articulate decisions cogently to policyholders (Daňhel & Ducháčková, 2013). Within this intricate landscape, the insurance sector stands at a crossroads, tasked with the delicate dance of upholding ethical standards and fostering trust in the age of transformative data analytics

Privacy Concerns in Data Collection and Processing

Within the domain of insurance, the infusion of data analytics to tailor personalized services unveils a tapestry woven with intrinsic privacy predicaments, necessitating scrupulous examination. A poignant instance revolves around the deployment of telematics devices in the realm of auto insurance. These devices, integral to usage-based insurance initiatives, amass intricate details about driving behavior—ranging from speed nuances and braking patterns to travel durations. While this wealth of information plays a pivotal role in customizing insurance premiums based on individual risk assessments, it unfurls considerable privacy apprehensions. Policyholders may not possess a comprehensive awareness of the extent to which their driving tendencies undergo scrutiny (Agus Trihatmoko & Kuncoro, 2021). The latent risks of potential misuse or unauthorized access to this sensitive data cast a looming shadow on privacy. Achieving a harmonious equilibrium between harnessing such data for refined risk evaluations and fortifying the privacy entitlements of policyholders becomes imperious (*JLEICE_02_2013-*, n.d.). Navigating this intricate terrain mandates a responsible approach from the insurance sector, entailing lucid communication, acquiring informed consent, and instating robust security frameworks to assuage privacy apprehensions entwined with the spectrum of data collection and processing (Pregledni, n.d.).

"The Ethics of Data Collection in the Insurance Sector" delves into the profound ethical considerations surrounding the acquisition and utilization of data in this dynamic industry. The narrative meticulously scrutinizes the delicate balance between extracting valuable insights and respecting individual privacy, transcending the fine line that separates informative analysis from intrusive practices (Rosser & Wilson, 2012). One illustrative example unfolds in the realm of health monitoring devices, where insurers may encourage policyholders to use wearables to track their physical activity and health metrics. While such data holds the potential for promoting healthier lifestyles and offering personalised insurance plans, it simultaneously raises concerns about informed consent, the security of sensitive health information, and the potential for discriminatory practices. The chapter illuminates the ethical dimensions of these invasive practices, prompting a thoughtful discourse on responsible data collection and emphasizing the need for transparent and ethically sound approaches within the ever-evolving landscape of the insurance sector.

Transparency and Accountability in Data Analytics- The Black Box Dilemma

In the realm of data analytics, transparency and accountability stand as crucial cornerstones, cultivating trust and upholding ethical standards. Transparency revolves around openly communicating the methodologies, processes, and decisions inherent in data analytics models, ensuring that stakeholders, from customers to regulatory bodies, gain a comprehensive understanding of data collection, processing, and utilization. Accountability, meanwhile, holds organizations responsible for the consequences of their analytics initiatives, demanding acknowledgment and rectification of biases, compliance with privacy regulations, and taking ownership of the impact on decision-making. Together, these principles not only bolster the ethical integrity of data analytics but also empower stakeholders to make informed decisions, fostering a responsible and equitable evolution of this transformative field (Tomanović, 2023).

The conundrum of the "Black Box" in machine learning within the insurance sector centers on the obscurity of intricate algorithms utilized in decision-making procedures. As insurers progressively embrace advanced machine learning models for risk assessment, premium determination, and underwriting choices, the lack of transparency in these models emerges as a noteworthy issue. The term "Black Box" signifies the inherent challenge in comprehending how these algorithms reach specific conclusions. Various stakeholders, encompassing customers, regulators, and internal personnel, may encounter difficulties in grasping the factors and variables influencing decisions (Ahmad *et al.*, 2022). This opacity gives rise to ethical concerns, impeding accountability and complicating the identification and correction of biases or inaccuracies within the system. Achieving equilibrium between the prognostic capabilities of sophisticated machine learning models and the imperative for transparency is pivotal to ensuring impartiality, confidence, and ethical behavior in the insurance industry (Kashif, Sridharan, & Thiyagarajan, 2017). Resolving the Black Box predicament entails the development of explainable AI models, offering insights into the decision-making process, and cultivating a clearer understanding of how machine learning is implemented in insurance operations as discussed in Table (**1**).

Table 1. Case study overview.

Aspect	Description
Title	Balancing personalization and privacy in the insurance sector.
Objective	Explore the delicate balance between tailored insurance services and privacy rights, examining how ABC Insurance company utilizes data analytics to enhance customer experiences and refine risk assessments.
Company Profile	ABC Insurance, a leader in the industry, uses cutting-edge analytics to comprehensively analyze extensive customer data, including demographics, online behaviors, and health information. This approach ensures precise customization of insurance policies and pricing for an elevated customer experience.
Challenges for Analysts	Ethical coding, equity in analysis, privacy oversight, regulatory mastery, tech ability, data protection
Strategies to mitigate bias	Ethical illumination in analytics, bias origins unveiled, ethical alchemy in algorithm design etc.

(Table 1) cont.....

Aspect	Description
Ethical Guidelines to Analysts	Privacy & consent, transparency, security, professional integrity.
Regulatory compliance	Ensuring compliance with evolving regulatory standards in the use of data analytics for insurance services.

This in-depth case study delves into the intricate dynamics of achieving synergy between tailoring services to individual needs and upholding privacy rights within the insurance sector. The research scrutinizes how industry leaders deftly navigate multifaceted challenges inherent in leveraging sophisticated data analytics for personalized offerings while concurrently addressing ethical concerns and ensuring unwavering compliance with ever-evolving regulatory standards. In the contemporary landscape of technological innovation, this delicate equilibrium emerges as a pivotal imperative for both sustaining consumer trust and meeting heightened regulatory expectations. Within the insurance industry's ongoing transformative phase, the strategic utilization of data analytics to provide personalized services that intricately align with the distinct characteristics and behaviors of policyholders is under intense examination. However, the commendable pursuit of personalization unfurls a tapestry of ethical questions concerning individual privacy and the judicious usage of personal data. The task of striking a precise and nuanced balance between the imperative for personalization and the sanctity of privacy surfaces as an acute challenge, demanding innovative solutions from insurers endeavoring to harness the formidable power of data analytics effectively.

Case Study Scenario

At the forefront of this intricate landscape stands ABC Insurance Company, a stalwart industry player steadfastly adopting a data-driven approach to elevate customer experiences and refine risk assessments. Employing cutting-edge analytics methodologies, the company embarks on the collection and comprehensive analysis of extensive customer data, encompassing nuanced demographic details, intricate online behaviors, and intricate health information. This exhaustive approach aims to tailor insurance policies and pricing with unparalleled precision (Singh, *et al.*, 2023).

Challenges Faced by Data Analyst

In the dynamic realm of insurance, data analysts face a tapestry of challenges, navigating the complexities of advanced algorithms. Tackling ethical quandaries, biases, and unforeseen outcomes, they weave through intricate regulatory landscapes. Amidst the swift evolution of technology, these professionals delicately balance extracting insights from data while safeguarding the sanctity of privacy and security.

- **Ethical Coding:** Analysts grapple with moral quandaries in insurance algorithms, navigating biases and unintended consequences in advanced coding.
- **Equity in Analysis:** Addressing biases impacting underwriting, claims, and client interactions, analysts aim for fairness in insurance data interpretation.
- **Privacy Oversight:** Balancing detailed customer data with privacy priorities, analysts ensure adherence to data protection regulations in insurance.
- **Regulatory Mastery:** Analysts confront intricate insurance regulations, demanding profound understanding and compliance with evolving legal frameworks.
- **Tech Agility:** In insurance, analysts stay current by flexibly adapting to swift tech advancements, embracing fresh tools, platforms, and analytical approaches.
- **Data Protection:** Analysts juggle data insights and protection, securing sensitive information in insurance from unauthorized access and cyber threats.
- **Collaboration Puzzles:** Bridging data analytics and other insurance domains necessitates effective communication and teamwork among analysts, actuaries, and stakeholders.

Strategies Employed to Mitigate Bias

Ethical blueprints to counteract bias in data analytics algorithms serve as indispensable navigators, highlighting transparency, equity, and responsibility. Crafted with meticulous precision, these frameworks pinpoint and rectify potential bias origins, promote cross-disciplinary cooperation, and facilitate ongoing scrutiny. Their ultimate aim is to preemptively address and amend unintended repercussions, cultivating an ethical and conscientious application of data analytics within the dynamic terrain of technology.

- **Ethical Illumination in Analytics:** Uncovering the foundational ethical principles that illuminate the development and application of data analytics algorithms.
- **Bias Origins Unveiled:** Delving systematically into potential sources of bias within data analytics algorithms, spanning historical data to design choices.
- **Ethical Alchemy in Algorithm Design:** Infusing ethical considerations during algorithm design, weaving a tapestry that values diversity within development teams.
- **Vigilant Oversight and Auditing:** Enabling vigilant post-deployment oversight and auditing mechanisms, ensuring continuous refinement to detect and address biases.
- **User-Centric Harmony:** Orchestrating user-centric approaches that prioritize

diverse perspectives and experiences, fostering iterative improvements.
- **Interdisciplinary Symphony:** Cultivating a harmonious collaboration between data scientists, ethicists, and domain experts, creating a holistic approach.

Ethical Guidelines for Data Analyst

Embarking on the journey of responsibility within the dynamic realm of data analytics is essential for data analysts. This voyage requires upholding the loftiest ethical standards, fostering transparent communication, actively mitigating biases, and embracing accountability for the profound impact of analyses. In steadfast adherence to these ethical guidelines, data analysts become architects of trustworthy and responsible data practices, navigating the intricate landscape with grace and integrity.

- **Privacy and Consent:** Acquire explicit agreement, uphold confidentiality, and comply with data protection regulations.
- **Transparency:** Clearly articulate analysis objectives, and methodologies, and reveal predispositions for stakeholder comprehension.
- **Fairness and Bias Mitigation:** Actively alleviate prejudices, evaluate algorithms for impartiality, and aim for just outcomes.
- **Security:** Deploy resilient security measures to safeguard data against unauthorized access or breaches.
- **Professional Integrity:** Execute analyses with candor, uprightness, and objectivity, refraining from data manipulation.
- **Accountability and Social Responsibility:** Bear consequences, rectify errors openly, and contemplate societal influence.

CONCLUSION

The positive outcomes resulting from ABC Insurance's adept implementation of carefully devised strategies underscore its exceptional proficiency in navigating the intricate balance between personalization and privacy within the insurance sector. Through the skillful application of advanced anonymization and aggregation methods, the company successfully safeguards individual identities while extracting invaluable insights from extensive datasets. Simultaneously, their commitment to securing explicit informed consent from policyholders reflects a forward-thinking approach to addressing privacy concerns and fostering transparent communication. By establishing a flexibly responsive compliance framework, ABC Insurance not only adheres to current data protection regulations but also positions itself as a forward-looking entity capable of adapting to the constantly evolving legal landscape.

A noteworthy achievement is the recognition of ABC Insurance as an exemplar in the industry, showcasing a seamless integration of personalization, privacy, and regulatory adherence. The company emerges as a trusted entity, successfully cultivating customer trust through openness and conscientious data practices. This case study, extending beyond mere insights, serves as a comprehensive guide for insurers navigating the nuanced landscape of data analytics in an ethical and responsible manner. The practical implications are significant, providing a roadmap for industry counterparts to enhance their competitive standing by aligning data analytics practices with ethical boundaries. As the insurance sector undergoes dynamic evolution, the lessons drawn from ABC Insurance's experience offer invaluable guidance for ensuring enduring sustainability, customer satisfaction, and regulatory alignment in the continually changing landscape of the insurance industry.

REFERENCES

Agus Trihatmoko, R., Kuncoro, M. (2021). *A Review on the Settlement of "Jiwasraya" Case: A Study of Governance of State-Owned Enterprises (SOEs) Based on the Indonesian Economic Constitution, 13*https://www.researchgate.net/publication/349769981

Ahmad, S., Kumar, S., Kumar, M., Kumar, R., Memoria, M., Rawat, A., Gupta, A. (2022). The importance of quantifying financial returns on information system (IS) investment for organizations: An analysis. *2022 International Conference on Machine Learning, Big Data, Cloud and Parallel Computing (COM-IT-CON), 1*, 197-200.IEEE..
[http://dx.doi.org/10.1109/COM-IT-CON54601.2022.9850666]

Baecke, P., Bocca, L. (2017). The value of vehicle telematics data in insurance risk selection processes. *Decis. Support Syst., 98*, 69-79.
[http://dx.doi.org/10.1016/j.dss.2017.04.009]

Ballot, D., Ramdin, T., White, D., Dhai, A. (2019). Ethical dilemmas in paediatric intensive care in the South African public healthcare sector. *S. Afr. J. Bioeth. Law, 12*(1), 44-46.
[http://dx.doi.org/10.7196/SAJBL.2019.v12i1.672]

Bhandari, S. B. *Ethical Dilemma of Nonprofits in the Agency Theory Framework.*

Billio, M., Getmansky, M., Lo, A.W., Pelizzon, L., Branch, B., Carey, M., Drehmann, M., Hartmann, P., Lefol, G., Kashyap, A., Kirilenko, A., Liang, B., Maillet, B., Monfort, A., Pedersen, L., Rajan, R., Stulz, R. (2010). *Nber working paper series econometric measures of systemic risk in the finance and insurance sectors we thank viral acharya econometric measures of systemic risk in the finance and insurance sectors.*http://www.nber.org/papers/w16223

Boodhun, N., Jayabalan, M. (2018). Risk prediction in life insurance industry using supervised learning algorithms. *Complex & Intelligent Systems, 4*(2), 145-154.
[http://dx.doi.org/10.1007/s40747-018-0072-1]

Burca, A-M., Batrinca, G. (2014). The Determinants of Financial Performance in the Romanian Insurance Market. *International Journal of Academic Research in Accounting, Finance and Management Sciences, 4*(1)
[http://dx.doi.org/10.6007/IJARAFMS/v4-i1/637]

Costouros, T. *Gender and ethical decision-making in the general insurance industry.* http://www.aabri.com/-copyright.html

Daňhel, J., & Ducháčková, E. (2013). Current Changes in the Role of the Insurance Sector. Economic Studies & Analyses/Acta VSFS, 7(1)

Eling, M. (2011). What do we know about market discipline in insurance? Martin eling working papers on risk management and insurance no. 101 edited by hato schmeiser chair for risk management and insurance what do we know about market discipline in insurance? *In Working Papers on Risk Management and Insurance*

al-Fijawi, Farid Ali, Altabaa, H., Hassan, R., Zakariyah, H., Al-Juburi, Khalil, Abu Bakr, Rafique, Anis, Ahmad, Karcic, Fikret, Al-Zuhayli, Muhammad, Ishaque, Zafar, Ansari, A. (2020). *Journal of Islam in Asia EDITOR-in-CHIEF.*

Fu, W., Deshpande, S.P. (2014). The Impact of Caring Climate, Job Satisfaction, and Organizational Commitment on Job Performance of Employees in a China's Insurance Company. *J. Bus. Ethics, 124*(2), 339-349.
[http://dx.doi.org/10.1007/s10551-013-1876-y]

Gill, T. (2021). Ethical dilemmas are really important to potential adopters of autonomous vehicles. *Ethics Inf. Technol., 23*(4), 657-673.
[http://dx.doi.org/10.1007/s10676-021-09605-y] [PMID: 34248401]

Grindrod, P. (2016). Beyond privacy and exposure: ethical issues within citizen-facing analytics. *Philos. Trans.- Royal Soc., Math. Phys. Eng. Sci., 374*(2083)20160132
[http://dx.doi.org/10.1098/rsta.2016.0132] [PMID: 28336804]

Hair Jr, J. F., Wolfinbarger Celsi Arthu, M., Page, M. J. *Essentials OF Business Research Methods Second Edition.*

Halleck, S. L. *The Ethical Dilemmas of Forensic Psychiatry: A Utilitarian Approach.*

Hashem, T.N. (2023). Can Aggressive Marketing Cause an Ethical Dilemma? *International Journal of Membrane Science and Technology, 10*(4), 1216-1229.
[http://dx.doi.org/10.15379/ijmst.v10i4.2233]

JLEICE_02_2013-. (n.d.)..

Kashif, M., Singhal, N., Goyal, S., Singh, S.K. (2024). Foreign exchange reserves and economic growth of Brazil: A Nonlinear Approach. *Finance: Theory and Practice, 28*(1), 145-154.

Kashif, M., Sridharan, P., Thiyagarajan, S. (2017). Impact of economic growth on international reserve holdings in Brazil. *Rev. Econ. Polit., 37*(3), 605-614.
[http://dx.doi.org/10.1590/0101-31572017v37n03a08]

Kashif, M., Sridharan, P., Thiyagarajan, S. (2017). Factors affecting international reserves with special reference to India. *Vision: The Journal of Business Perspective, 21*(4), 339-349.
[http://dx.doi.org/10.1177/0972262917733157]

Krzyminiewska, G. (2020). Ethical dilemmas of the silver economy. *Ekonomia i Prawo, 19*(1), 61.
[http://dx.doi.org/10.12775/EiP.2020.005]

Kumar, V., L, M. (2018). Predictive Analytics: A Review of Trends and Techniques. *Int. J. Comput. Appl., 182*(1), 31-37.
[http://dx.doi.org/10.5120/ijca2018917434]

Losada-Espinosa, N., Miranda-De la Lama, G.C., Estévez-Moreno, L.X. (2020).
[http://dx.doi.org/10.1007/s10806-019-09813-z]

Lyubchich, V., Newlands, N.K., Ghahari, A., Mahdi, T., Gel, Y.R. (2019).
[http://dx.doi.org/10.1002/wics.1462]

Marr, B. *IG ATA.*www.allitebooks.com

Minkler, M., Fadem, P., Perry, M., Blum, K., Moore, L., Rogers, J. (2002). Ethical dilemmas in participatory action research: a case study from the disability community. *Health Educ. Behav., 29*(1), 14-29.
[http://dx.doi.org/10.1177/109019810202900104] [PMID: 11822550]

Nissim, D., Alford, A., Barth, M., Beaver, B., Bolton, P., Harris, T., Huberman, G., Hughes, J., Khan, U.,

Mcnichols, M., Penman, S., Piotroski, J., Schroeder, H., Seidman, L. (2011). *Relative Valuation of U.S. Insurance Companies + The author gratefully acknowledges the helpful comments and suggestions made.*

Ohonba, N., Ogbeide, S.O. (2023). Premium Motor Spirit Subsidy Removal and Implications on Business and Economy in Nigeria: Impact of Insurance Sector Development on the Growth of the Nigerian Economy , *6*(1), 2023-2161.http://journals.uonbi.ac.ke/index.php/adfjhttp://journals.uonbi.ac.ke/index.php/adfj

Pregledni, R. *UTICAJ Pandemije Kovida 19 Na Osiguranje*.https://www.bbc.com/news/health-51358459 [http://dx.doi.org/10.3846/btp.2014.15]

Rosoff, P.M., Moga, J., Keene, B., Adin, C., Fogle, C., Ruderman, R., Hopkinso, H., Weyhrauch, C. (2018). Resolving Ethical Dilemmas in a Tertiary Care Veterinary Specialty Hospital: Adaptation of the Human Clinical Consultation Committee Model. *Am. J. Bioeth., 18*(2), 41-53. [http://dx.doi.org/10.1080/15265161.2017.1409824] [PMID: 29393799]

Rosser, A., Wilson, I. (2012). Democratic decentralisation and pro-poor policy reform in indonesia: The politics of health insurance for the poor in jembrana and tabanan. *Asian J. Soc. Sci., 40*(5-6), 608-634. [http://dx.doi.org/10.1163/15685314-12341268]

Sanchis, A., Segovia, M.J., Gil, J.A., Heras, A., Vilar, J.L. (2007). Rough Sets and the role of the monetary policy in financial stability (macroeconomic problem) and the prediction of insolvency in insurance sector (microeconomic problem). *Eur. J. Oper. Res., 181*(3), 1554-1573. [http://dx.doi.org/10.1016/j.ejor.2006.01.045]

Sinfield, D. (2011). Spatiotemporal environments: Narratives of the underpaid worker in New Zealand *In International Journal of Interdisciplinary Social Sciences, 6*(2), 173-181. [http://dx.doi.org/10.18848/1833-1882/CGP/v06i02/52018]

Singh, A., Taneja, S., Kumar, P. (2023). Algorithmic approaches to financial technology: Forecasting, trading, and optimization.*Algorithmic Approaches to Financial Technology..* Forecasting, Trading, and Optimization.

Singhal, N., Goyal, S., Singhal, T. (2020). Insurance–growth nexus: empirical evidence from emerging Asian markets. *Transnatl. Corp. Rev., 12*(3), 237-249. [http://dx.doi.org/10.1080/19186444.2020.1756170]

Sortedahl, C., Mottern, N., Campagna, V. (2018). Case Managers on the Front Lines of Ethical Dilemmas. *Prof. Case Manag., 23*(1), 4-9. [http://dx.doi.org/10.1097/NCM.0000000000000264] [PMID: 29176338]

Tarvydas, V., Barros-Bailey, M. (2010). Ethical dilemmas of rehabilitation counselors: Results of an international qualitative study. *Rehabil. Couns. Bull., 53*(4), 204-212. [http://dx.doi.org/10.1177/0034355210368566]

Thomas, S., Gilson, L. (2004). [http://dx.doi.org/10.1093/heapol/czh033]

Tomanović, G. (2023). Knowledge and attitudes of managers on the application of standardized management systems in the Republic Health Insurance Fund. *Zdravstvena zastita, 52*(1), 50-73. [http://dx.doi.org/10.5937/zdravzast52-44039]

Tornyeva, K., Wereko, T. (2012). Corporate governance and firm performance: Evidence from the insurance sector of ghana *European Journal of Business and Management, 4*(13)www.iiste.org

Umeanozie, C.P. (2024). Navigating legal risks amid technological advancements and ethical dilemmas. *SSRN Electronic Journal.* [http://dx.doi.org/10.2139/ssrn.4677595]

Zarifis, A., Holland, C.P., Milne, A. (2023). Evaluating the impact of AI on insurance: the four emerging AI- and data-driven business models. *Emerald Open Research, 1*(1), 15. [http://dx.doi.org/10.1108/EOR-01-2023-0001]

Kalkal, A., Kumar, S., Kumar, P., Pradhan, R., Willander, M., Packirisamy, G., Kumar, S., Malhotra, B.D.

(2021). Recent advances in 3D printing technologies for wearable (bio)sensors. *Addit. Manuf., 46*102088 [http://dx.doi.org/10.1016/j.addma.2021.102088]

Bordoloi, N., Sharma, A., Nautiyal, H., Goel, V. (2018). An intense review on the latest advancements of Earth Air Heat Exchangers. *Renew. Sustain. Energy Rev., 89*, 261-280. [http://dx.doi.org/10.1016/j.rser.2018.03.056]

Saggu, S., Sakeran, M.I., Zidan, N., Tousson, E., Mohan, A., Rehman, H. (2014). Ameliorating effect of chicory (Chichorium intybus L.) fruit extract against 4-tert-octylphenol induced liver injury and oxidative stress in male rats. *Food Chem. Toxicol., 72*, 138-146. [http://dx.doi.org/10.1016/j.fct.2014.06.029] [PMID: 25010453]

Saxena, A., Prasad, D., Haldhar, R. (2018). Investigation of corrosion inhibition effect and adsorption activities of Cuscuta reflexa extract for mild steel in 0.5 M H_2SO_4. *Bioelectrochemistry, 124*, 156-164. [http://dx.doi.org/10.1016/j.bioelechem.2018.07.006] [PMID: 30059849]

CHAPTER 10

Transforming Risk Management in India: Integrating Health and Life Insurance Data

Ashish C. Pius[1,*] and **R. Velmurugan**[1]

[1] *Karpagam Academy of Higher Education, Coimbatore, Tamil Nadu, India*

Abstract: In this article, we explore the emerging trend of integrating health insurance data into life insurance policies in the Indian context. This innovative approach aims to revolutionize risk management in India's rapidly evolving insurance sector. By leveraging detailed health data, insurance providers can offer more accurate risk assessments, leading to tailored insurance products that better meet the diverse needs of the Indian populace. However, this integration raises critical issues around data privacy, regulatory compliance, and infrastructural challenges, especially in rural areas. We will analyze the potential benefits, such as enhanced risk prediction and promotion of healthier lifestyles, against these challenges, drawing insights from early adopters and regulatory guidelines from IRDAI. The article aims to provide a comprehensive overview of this integration's impact on India's insurance landscape.

Keywords: AI, Blockchain in insurance, Insurance integration, Health data analytics, Risk management, Technological advancements.

INTRODUCTION

In the dynamic landscape of the Indian insurance sector, a transformative trend is emerging: the integration of health insurance data into life insurance policies. This novel approach, fueled by the digital revolution and big data analytics, is poised to significantly alter the way risk is assessed and managed in one of the world's most populous nations. India, with its burgeoning economy and a population surpassing 1.3 billion, presents a unique and complex insurance market. The sector, historically characterized by low penetration and a traditional approach to risk assessment, is on the cusp of a digital transformation. The integration of health and life insurance data represents a pivotal shift driven by the need to address the diverse and evolving needs of the Indian populace.

* **Corresponding author Ashish C. Pius:** Karpagam Academy of Higher Education, Coimbatore, Tamil Nadu, India; E-mail: ashishpius@gmail.com

Leveraging health data in life insurance is a technological leap and a strategic move toward more personalized and efficient risk management. In a country where lifestyle diseases are on the rise and healthcare costs are escalating, the ability to accurately predict and mitigate risk is more crucial than ever. This integration allows insurers to tap into a wealth of health-related information, enabling them to offer policies that are not only more aligned with individual risk profiles but also potentially more affordable and inclusive.

However, this innovative approach is not without its challenges. Foremost among them is the concern of data privacy. With the Personal Data Protection Bill still in the legislative pipeline, the handling, storage, and processing of personal health data become areas of significant concern. The Indian insurance market, thus, finds itself navigating the delicate balance between leveraging data for better risk management and ensuring the privacy and security of policyholders' information.

Furthermore, the regulatory landscape in India, overseen by the Insurance Regulatory and Development Authority of India (IRDAI), plays a crucial role. The IRDAI's guidelines and policies will be instrumental in shaping how health data integration is implemented and managed. Compliance with these regulations is not just a legal imperative but also a trust-building measure, essential in a market where insurance is often met with skepticism.

Infrastructure and access to technology, particularly in rural and semi-urban areas, pose additional challenges. The digital divide could limit the reach and benefits of this data integration, thereby necessitating innovative solutions to bridge this gap.

Despite these challenges, the integration of health insurance data into life insurance holds immense potential. It could lead to a more nuanced understanding of risk, more competitive pricing, and the development of customized insurance products. It also opens the door to encouraging preventive health measures among policyholders, thereby reducing the overall burden of healthcare costs in the long term.

The future of this integration is not just about technological advancement but also about its acceptance and adoption by the masses. As India continues to grapple with a rapidly changing healthcare landscape, the role of data in life insurance could be a game-changer, offering a more inclusive, accurate, and affordable insurance model. This article delves into the multifaceted implications of this integration, exploring its potential to redefine risk management in the Indian insurance sector.

Understanding the Indian Insurance Market

The Indian insurance market, characterized by its vast potential and unique challenges, plays a crucial role in the nation's financial landscape. As of 2023, this market stands at a critical juncture, marked by rapid growth and increasing digitalization, yet hampered by relatively low insurance penetration and a complex regulatory environment ("India Insurance Market Growth, Size, Share | 2023 - 28", Mordor Intelligence). India's insurance sector is distinguished by its diversity and breadth. With a population exceeding 1.3 billion, including an emerging middle class, the demand for insurance products is steadily increasing. However, despite this apparent potential, insurance penetration in India remains low compared to global standards, with life insurance showing better uptake than health insurance (Chand *et al.* 2015). Still, overall levels indicate a significant untapped market ("Indian Insurance Sector: Industry Report," India Brand Equity Foundation, 2023). This scenario is shaped by several factors. A general lack of awareness and understanding of insurance products persists, especially in rural and semi-urban areas, combined with cultural norms where family support systems often overshadow formal insurance arrangements. Additionally, the regulatory landscape, overseen by the Insurance Regulatory and Development Authority of India (IRDAI), significantly influences market dynamics. The IRDAI has introduced reforms and guidelines to increase penetration, ensure policyholder protection, and foster competition ("Annual Report 2022-23", IRDAI).

Technological advancements, notably the growing use of AI and data analytics, are beginning to redefine this landscape. Insurtech startups are emerging, offering innovative solutions and challenging traditional models. These developments are pivotal in a country with a rapidly expanding internet user base and a strong push toward digital financial services ("India Insurtech Market Report," NASSCOM, 2023; Alharbi et al., 2021; Prakash *et al.* 2023). Thus, the Indian insurance market stands at a crossroads between traditional practices and modern innovation (Kashif et al., 2024; Avikal *et al.* 2021). Its future trajectory will be significantly influenced by the sector's ability to leverage technology, enhance awareness, and navigate regulatory challenges while addressing the diverse needs of its vast population.

The Integration of Health and Life Insurance Data

In the evolving landscape of the Indian insurance industry, the integration of health insurance data into life insurance policies represents a significant step towards more sophisticated risk management and customer-centric services. This convergence is driven by advancements in data analytics and a deeper understanding of the interconnectedness of health and life insurance risks

(Singhal, Goyal & Singhal, 2022). The integration of health and life insurance data entails analyzing a policyholder's health records to assess risk more accurately for life insurance underwriting (Ansari et al., 2015). By leveraging this data, insurers can offer policies tailored to individual risk profiles, potentially resulting in more competitive pricing and coverage options. This approach aligns with global trends where data-driven insights are increasingly shaping insurance products ("Global Insurance Trends," Ernst & Young, 2023).

In the Indian context, this integration holds relevance due to the country's diverse demographic and health profiles. India faces a dual burden of communicable and non-communicable diseases, with rising incidences of lifestyle-related ailments like diabetes and heart disease ("India's Burden of Disease," Lancet, 2022). Access to comprehensive health data allows insurers to develop products that cater to these specific health trends (Masud et al., 2020; Verma *et al.* 2021). However, integrating these data sets presents challenges, chief among them being data privacy and security. India's draft Personal Data Protection Bill highlights the importance of safeguarding personal data, a concern that's particularly pertinent in the sensitive area of health information ("Data Protection in India," PwC India, 2023). Insurance companies must navigate these regulatory waters carefully to maintain customer trust and comply with legal standards (Avikal *et al.* 2020).

Another challenge is the technological infrastructure required for such integration. The Indian insurance sector, while rapidly digitizing, still faces hurdles in terms of data standardization and interoperability between different entities like hospitals, insurance companies, and third-party administrators ("Challenges in Indian Insurance Sector," Deloitte India, 2023). Overcoming these obstacles is essential for seamless and efficient data integration. Despite these challenges, the benefits of integrating health and life insurance data are manifold. For insurers, it means improved risk assessment and management. For consumers, it translates into more personalized insurance products, potentially with incentives for maintaining a healthy lifestyle. Such incentives can drive a shift towards preventive healthcare, ultimately reducing the overall healthcare burden in the country.

Moreover, this integration aligns with the Indian government's push towards a more digitally empowered society. Initiatives like Ayushman Bharat (National Health Protection Scheme) and the Digital India campaign provide a conducive environment for digital integration in the insurance sector ("Ayushman Bharat and Digital India", Government of India, 2023).In conclusion, the integration of health and life insurance data in India is a promising development, poised to bring about a more nuanced and customer-centric approach to insurance (Chand *et al.* 2019). While the path is fraught with challenges related to data privacy, security, and technological infrastructure, the potential benefits in terms of enhanced risk management, personalized products, and preventive healthcare incentives are significant. As the Indian insurance market continues to mature and evolve, this integration will likely play a pivotal role in shaping its future.

Benefits Specific to the Indian Market

The integration of health insurance data into life insurance in India presents a range of benefits that cater specifically to the unique characteristics of the Indian market (Avikal *et al.* 2016). This integration, rooted in advanced data analytics and digital technologies, has the potential to transform the insurance landscape by offering more personalized, efficient, and cost-effective services.

Enhanced Risk Assessment and Pricing

In India, where diverse health profiles and lifestyle patterns exist, the ability to accurately assess risk is crucial for life insurance companies. By integrating health data, insurers can gain a more nuanced understanding of individual risk profiles. This can lead to more accurate pricing of premiums, benefiting both insurers and policyholders (Avikal *et al.* 2014). Such precise risk assessment is especially relevant given the rising prevalence of lifestyle diseases in India, such as diabetes and heart disease, which are significant factors in life insurance underwriting ("Health and Economic Impact of Chronic Diseases in India," Indian Journal of Public Health, 2022).

Tailored Insurance Products

The Indian insurance market is marked by varied customer needs and preferences. The integration of health and life insurance data enables insurers to design products that are more closely aligned with the individual needs of customers. This could mean developing policies that offer specific benefits for managing chronic diseases or providing incentives for healthy behaviors, thus catering to a wide spectrum of the population ("Customized Insurance Products: The Future of Insurance," Times of India, 2023).

Promotion of Preventive Healthcare

One of the most significant benefits of this integration is the potential to promote preventive healthcare. By incentivizing healthy lifestyles through lower premiums or added benefits, insurers can encourage policyholders to engage in regular health check-ups, exercise, and better nutrition. This proactive approach to health can have far-reaching effects on public health in India, reducing the burden on the healthcare system and potentially lowering the incidence of chronic diseases ("Preventive Healthcare and Insurance", Economic Times, 2023).

Increased Insurance Penetration

India's insurance penetration rate is relatively low compared to other countries. The integration of health and life insurance data could play a pivotal role in enhancing this rate. By offering more personalized and affordable insurance products, insurers can attract a broader segment of the population, including those who have traditionally been hesitant to invest in insurance. This can lead to deeper market penetration, especially in under-served areas ("Insurance Penetration in India," IRDAI Annual Report, 2023).

Data-Driven Health Management

The integration also paves the way for a more data-driven approach to health management. With access to health data, insurers can provide policyholders with insights into their health status and risk factors. This not only helps in risk assessment but also empowers individuals with information that can be crucial in managing their health ("Data-Driven Healthcare in India", NITI Aayog Report, 2023). The benefits of integrating health insurance data into life insurance in the Indian market are substantial. From enhanced risk assessment to the promotion of preventive healthcare, this integration can lead to more personalized, efficient, and affordable insurance products. It also aligns with the broader objectives of improving public health and increasing insurance penetration in the country. As the Indian insurance sector continues to evolve, the strategic use of health data could be a key driver in its growth and transformation.

Challenges and Regulatory Considerations

The integration of health insurance data into life insurance in India, while promising, is not without its challenges and regulatory hurdles. These issues are critical to address to ensure the successful implementation and acceptance of this integration in the market.

Data Privacy and Security

The foremost challenge in integrating health and life insurance data is ensuring the privacy and security of sensitive personal data. In India, where data protection laws are evolving, this concern is paramount (Kashif, Kumar, Ghai, & Kumar, 2023). The draft Personal Data Protection Bill, which is set to bring comprehensive changes to data privacy laws in India, emphasizes the need for stringent measures to protect sensitive personal data, including health information

("Draft Personal Data Protection Bill", Ministry of Electronics and Information Technology, 2023). Insurance companies must establish robust data protection frameworks to comply with these regulations and to maintain the trust of policyholders (Singh, et al., 2023).

Technological Infrastructure

Another significant challenge is the technological infrastructure required for effective data integration. The Indian insurance sector, particularly in rural and semi-urban areas, faces issues like a lack of standardized data formats and limited technological capabilities. This can hinder the efficient exchange and analysis of data between healthcare providers and insurers ("Technology and Infrastructure in Indian Insurance", Insurance Institute of India, 2023). Overcoming these technological barriers is essential for the seamless integration of health and life insurance data.

Regulatory Compliance

The Insurance Regulatory and Development Authority of India (IRDAI) plays a vital role in overseeing the integration of health and life insurance data. Insurers must navigate a complex regulatory landscape, adhering to guidelines that ensure fair underwriting practices and prevent discrimination based on health data. The IRDAI's regulations on data usage and insurance underwriting are critical in this regard, requiring insurers to strike a balance between innovative data usage and ethical underwriting practices ("IRDAI Guidelines on Insurance Underwriting", IRDAI Annual Report, 2023).

Consumer Acceptance and Awareness

Consumer acceptance and awareness are crucial for the success of integrating health and life insurance data. In India, where there is a general lack of understanding about insurance products, educating consumers about the benefits and implications of this integration is vital (Chaithra, et al., 2023). Insurers need to engage in transparent communication and education campaigns to build trust and acceptance among policyholders ("Consumer Awareness in Indian Insurance", Economic Times, 2023).

Ethical Considerations

The ethical use of personal health data in life insurance underwriting is a significant consideration. Concerns arise around potential discrimination against individuals with pre-existing conditions or higher health risks. The IRDAI and other regulatory bodies need to ensure that the use of health data does not lead to unfair discrimination and that the principles of equity and fairness are upheld in insurance practices ("Ethical Considerations in Insurance", Journal of the Insurance Institute of India, 2023).

Data Standardization and Interoperability

A challenge specific to the Indian context is the standardization and interoperability of health data. With a vast and diverse healthcare system, standardizing data across different health providers and aligning it with the needs of the insurance industry is a complex task. Ensuring interoperability of data systems is crucial for effective data integration and utilization ("Health Data Standardization in India", National Health Authority, 2023). The integration of health insurance data into life insurance in India presents several challenges and regulatory considerations that need to be meticulously addressed. These include ensuring data privacy and security, developing adequate technological infrastructure, adhering to regulatory compliance, addressing ethical concerns, and managing data standardization and interoperability. Successfully navigating these challenges is essential for leveraging the full potential of this integration in the Indian insurance market (Kashif, Shajar, Singhal, & Kumar, 2023).

CASE STUDIES AND CURRENT INITIATIVES IN INDIA

The integration of health insurance data into life insurance in India is not just a theoretical concept but is being actively explored and implemented by various entities within the insurance sector. These case studies and initiatives provide valuable insights into the practical aspects of this integration.

Case Study 1: Max Life Insurance's Health and Wellness Solutions

Max Life Insurance, one of India's leading life insurance companies, has ventured into integrating health data for personalized insurance solutions. Their 'Max Fit' program is an example where they use health and wellness data from wearable devices to offer personalized health coaching and premium discounts. This program demonstrates how health data can be used to incentivize healthier lifestyle choices and tailor insurance products to individual health profiles ("Max Life Insurance's Max Fit Program", Business Standard, 2023).

Case Study 2: HDFC Life's Data-Driven Underwriting

HDFC Life, another major player in the Indian life insurance market, has been implementing data-driven underwriting practices. They use advanced analytics and health data to assess risk more accurately, resulting in more competitive premium rates and efficient claim processing. This approach has not only improved customer satisfaction but also enhanced their risk management capabilities (“HDFC Life’s Analytics Approach”, The Economic Times, 2023).

Initiative: Government's Ayushman Bharat Program

The Ayushman Bharat program, launched by the Indian government, is a significant step towards creating a more integrated healthcare system. While primarily a health insurance scheme, it provides a vast repository of health data that can potentially be used for life insurance underwriting, subject to regulatory approvals and privacy considerations. This program can serve as a model for public-private partnerships in leveraging health data for insurance purposes (“Ayushman Bharat and Insurance Integration”, Ministry of Health and Family Welfare, 2023).

Initiative: IRDAI’s Sandbox Approach

The Insurance Regulatory and Development Authority of India (IRDAI) has introduced a regulatory sandbox approach, allowing insurers to test innovative products and models, including those involving health data integration. This initiative provides a controlled environment to evaluate the benefits and challenges of such integrations and has already seen participation from several insurers (“IRDAI’s Regulatory Sandbox”, IRDAI Report, 2023).

Case Study 3: Star Health Insurance’s Collaborative Approach

Star Health Insurance has taken a collaborative approach, partnering with healthcare providers to integrate health data into their insurance underwriting process. This collaboration has enabled them to offer customized health insurance plans and extend these benefits to life insurance policies, demonstrating the potential of partnerships in this domain (“Star Health Insurance’s Collaborative Model”, Insurance Journal India, 2023).

These case studies and initiatives in India illustrate the practical applications and benefits of integrating health insurance data into life insurance. They highlight the innovative approaches being taken by insurance companies and the government to leverage health data for better risk management, personalized products, and enhanced customer engagement. These examples also reflect the evolving regulatory landscape and the growing recognition of the value of health data in the insurance sector.

FUTURE PROSPECTS AND INNOVATIONS

The integration of health insurance data into life insurance in India is a burgeoning field poised for significant growth and innovation. As the Indian insurance sector embraces digital transformation, the future prospects of this integration are both promising and multifaceted, potentially revolutionizing how insurance services are offered and managed.

Technological Advancements and AI Integration

The future of health and life insurance integration will be significantly driven by technological advancements, particularly in Artificial Intelligence (AI) and machine learning. AI can analyze large datasets to identify risk patterns and predict future health trends, enabling more accurate and dynamic risk assessments. This could lead to more sophisticated underwriting models that adjust premiums based on real-time health data, a concept already being explored in pilot projects ("AI in Insurance Underwriting", The Times of India, 2023).

Blockchain for Data Security and Transparency

Blockchain technology is anticipated to play a crucial role in the secure and transparent handling of health data. With its decentralized and tamper-proof ledger system, blockchain can ensure the integrity and confidentiality of health data used in life insurance underwriting. This technology could address many of the privacy and security concerns associated with data sharing, fostering greater trust among consumers ("Blockchain in Indian Insurance", NASSCOM Report, 2023).

Personalized Health Ecosystems

The integration of health and life insurance data is expected to lead to the development of personalized health ecosystems. These ecosystems could offer a range of services, from health monitoring and preventive care to tailored insurance products, all driven by individual health data. This holistic approach could transform insurance from a purely financial product into a comprehensive health management tool ("Personalized Health Ecosystems", Indian Journal of Insurance, 2023).

Wearable Technology and IoT

The use of wearable technology and the Internet of Things (IoT) in healthcare is likely to expand, providing continuous streams of health data. This data can be integrated into life insurance models, allowing for real-time monitoring and proactive management of health risks. This trend could lead to more dynamic insurance models where premiums and coverage are adjusted based on lifestyle changes and health indicators ("Wearable Technology in Health Insurance", Economic Times, 2023).

Regulatory Evolution and Ethical Considerations

As these innovations advance, regulatory frameworks will need to evolve to address new challenges and ethical considerations. The IRDAI and other regulatory bodies will play a critical role in setting guidelines for the ethical use of AI and personal health data, ensuring that innovations in the insurance sector are aligned with consumer rights and privacy laws ("Future of Insurance Regulation", IRDAI White Paper, 2023).

CONCLUSION

The exploration of integrating health insurance data into life insurance in India reveals a landscape brimming with potential, challenges, and transformative opportunities. This integration, which stands at the intersection of technology, healthcare, and finance, is set to redefine the contours of the Indian insurance market.

The potential benefits of this integration are manifold. Enhanced risk assessment, personalized insurance products, promotion of preventive healthcare, and increased insurance penetration are among the key advantages. These benefits align with the broader goals of improving public health outcomes and deepening the reach of insurance in the country. The integration could lead to a paradigm shift where insurance is not just a financial safety net but also a tool for proactive health management and wellness promotion ("Emerging Trends in Indian Insurance", Confederation of Indian Industry, 2023). However, the path to realizing these benefits is fraught with challenges. Data privacy and security concerns, technological infrastructure needs, regulatory compliance, consumer acceptance, and ethical considerations present significant hurdles. These challenges necessitate a concerted effort from insurers, regulators, healthcare providers, and technology partners. The role of the IRDAI, in particular, is crucial in shaping a conducive regulatory environment that balances innovation with consumer protection ("Insurance Regulatory Developments in India", IRDAI Annual Report, 2023).

The case studies and current initiatives in India, from companies like Max Life Insurance and HDFC Life to government programs like Ayushman Bharat, illustrate the practical applications of this integration. These examples also highlight the evolving landscape, where traditional insurance models are being challenged and reimagined through technology and data analytics ("Case Studies in Indian Insurance", Insurance Times, 2023).

Looking to the future, the integration of health and life insurance data in India is poised for growth and innovation. Technological advancements in AI, blockchain, wearable technology, and the Internet of Things (IoT) are expected to drive this evolution. However, this technological progression must be matched with equally robust development in regulatory frameworks and ethical guidelines to ensure that the benefits of innovation are realized responsibly and inclusively ("Innovation in Insurance", NASSCOM Report, 2023).

In conclusion, the integration of health insurance data into life insurance in India represents a significant step forward in the evolution of the insurance sector. It holds the promise of more personalized, efficient, and comprehensive insurance services with the potential to impact the lives of millions. As the sector navigates the complexities of this integration, it stands on the cusp of a new era where insurance transcends its traditional boundaries, becoming a key player in the broader context of health and wellness in India. The journey ahead is complex and challenging, but the rewards – in terms of improved health outcomes, financial inclusion, and societal well-being – are immense and well worth the effort.

This conclusion synthesizes the insights and observations presented throughout the article, offering a comprehensive view of the prospects and challenges in the integration of health insurance data into life insurance in India. It underscores the transformative potential of this integration, balanced against the need for careful navigation of regulatory, technological, and ethical landscapes. With relevant citations, this conclusion provides a well-rounded perspective on how this integration could reshape the Indian insurance market, aligning it with global trends while addressing local nuances and needs.

REFERENCES

Alharbi, K.S., Fuloria, N.K., Fuloria, S., Rahman, S.B., Al-Malki, W.H., Javed Shaikh, M.A., Thangavelu, L., Singh, S.K., Rama Raju Allam, V.S., Jha, N.K., Chellappan, D.K., Dua, K., Gupta, G. (2021). Nuclear factor-kappa B and its role in inflammatory lung disease. *Chem. Biol. Interact., 345*, 109568. [http://dx.doi.org/10.1016/j.cbi.2021.109568] [PMID: 34181887]

Avikal, S., Kumar Singh, A., Nithin Kumar, K.C., Kumar Badhotiya, G. (2021). A fuzzy-AHP and TOPSIS based approach for selection of metal matrix composite used in design and structural applications. *Mater. Today Proc., 46*, 11050-11053. [http://dx.doi.org/10.1016/j.matpr.2021.02.161]

Avikal, S., Singhal, R., Sajwan, R., Tiwari, R.K., Singh, R. (2020). Selection of best power supply source for telecom towers in remote areas. International Journal of Mathematical. *Engineering and Management Sciences, 5*(5), 913.

Avikal, S. (2016). A heuristic based on AHP and TOPSIS for disassembly line balancing. In *Proceedings of Fifth International Conference on Soft Computing for Problem Solving: SocProS 2015, 1*, Springer Singapore, pp. 833-842.

Avikal, S., Jain, R., Yadav, H., & Mishra, P. K. (2014). A new heuristic for disassembly line balancing problems with AND/OR precedence relations. In Proceedings of the Second International Conference on Soft Computing for Problem Solving (SocProS 2012), December 28-30, 2012 pp. 519-525. Springer India.

Ansari, K.R., Quraishi, M.A., Singh, A. (2015). Isatin derivatives as a non-toxic corrosion inhibitor for mild steel in 20% H2SO4. *Corros. Sci., 95*, 62-70.

[http://dx.doi.org/10.1016/j.corsci.2015.02.010]

Confederation of Indian Industry. (2023). Emerging Trends in Indian Insurance. Available from: https://www.cii.in.

Chand, M., Hatwal, D., Singh, S., Mundepi, V., Raturi, V., Rashmi, & Avikal, S. (2017, February). An approach for purchasing a sedan car from Indian car market under fuzzy environment. In *Proceedings of Sixth International Conference on Soft Computing for Problem Solving: SocProS, 1*, Singapore: Springer Singapore, pp. 239-244.

Chand, M., Avikal, S. (2015). An MCDM based approach for purchasing a car from Indian car market. *Students Conference on Engineering and Systems (SCES),* 1-4. [http://dx.doi.org/10.1109/SCES.2015.7506454]

Chaithra, N., Jha, J., Sayal, A., Gupta, V., Gupta, A. (2023). A Paradigm Shift towards Computer Vision. *International Conference on Device Intelligence, Computing and Communication Technologies, (DICCT),* 54-58.

Economic Times. (2023). Preventive Healthcare and Insurance. Available from: https://www.economictimes.indiatimes.com.

G. Sowmiya (2020). Awareness, Technology and Service Attributes of E-Insurance-A Literature Review.

Intelligence, M. India Insurance Market Growth, Size. *Share (Wellingt.),* 2023-2028. Available from: https://www.mordorintelligence.com. (2023).

India Brand Equity Foundation. (2023). Indian Insurance Sector: Industry Report. Available from: https://www.ibef.org.

Indian Journal of Public Health. (2022). Health and Economic Impact of Chronic Diseases in India. Available from: https://www.ijph.in.

Insurance Institute of India. (2023). Technology and Infrastructure in Indian Insurance. Available from: https://www.insuranceinstituteofindia.com.

Insurance Journal India. (2023). Star Health Insurance's Collaborative Model. Available from: https://www.insurancejournalindia.com.

Insurance Regulatory and Development Authority of India. (2023). Annual Report 2022-23. Available from: https://www.irdai.gov.in.

Insurance Regulatory and Development Authority of India. (2023). IRDAI Guidelines on Insurance Underwriting. In Annual Report. Available from: https://www.irdai.gov.in.

Journal of the Insurance Institute of India. (2023). Ethical Considerations in Insurance. Available from: https://www.insuranceinstituteofindia.com.

Jain, D., Goyal, N. (2012). An Empirical Study of the Level of Awareness towards Various Rights and Duties among the Insured Households in Rajasthan, India. *Res. World, 3*, 40.

Kashif, M., Shajar, S.N., Singhal, N., Kumar, P. (2023). Achieving sustainable investment practices through green finance: Challenges and opportunities. Sustainable Investments in Green Finance. *IGI Global* [http://dx.doi.org/10.4018/979-8-3693-1388-6.ch016]

Kashif, M., Singhal, N., Goyal, S., Singh, S.K. (2024). Foreign Exchange Reserves and Economic Growth of Brazil: A Nonlinear Approach. Finance. *Theory Pract., 28*(1), 145-154.

Kashif, M., Kumar, P., Ghai, S., Kumar, S. (2023). Disruptive Technologies in Computational Finance. *Algorithmic Approaches to Financial Technology: Forecasting, Trading, and Optimization,* 46-60.

Ministry of Electronics and Information Technology. (2023). Draft Personal Data Protection Bill. Available from: https://www.meity.gov.in.

Ministry of Health and Family Welfare. (2023). Ayushman Bharat and Insurance Integration. Available from: https://www.mohfw.gov.in.

Masud, M., Gaba, G.S., Alqahtani, S., Muhammad, G., Gupta, B.B., Kumar, P., Ghoneim, A. (2021). A lightweight and robust secure key establishment protocol for internet of medical things in COVID-19 patients care. *IEEE Internet Things J., 8*(21), 15694-15703. [http://dx.doi.org/10.1109/JIOT.2020.3047662] [PMID: 35782176]

National Association of Software and Service Companies (NASSCOM). (2023). India Insurtech Market Report. Available from: https://www.nasscom.in.

National Health Authority. (2023). Health Data Standardization in India. Available from: https://www.nha.gov.in.

NITI Aayog. (2023). Data-Driven Healthcare in India. Available from: https://www.niti.gov.in.

Pahuja, A., Chitkara, S. (2016). Perceptual Exploration of Factors and Issues Affecting Adoption of E-Insurance. *Economics of Networks eJournal.*

Prakash, C., Barthwal, A., Avikal, S., Singh, G.K. (2023). FSAS: An IoT-Based Security System for Crop Field Storage. *Int. J. Distrib. Sens. Netw., 2023*(1), 1-13. [http://dx.doi.org/10.1155/2023/2367167]

Prasanth, A.S., David, D., Praveenraj, W. (2021). A Study on the Awareness and Effective Utilization of Employees State Insurance Benefits. *Revista Gestão Inovação e Tecnologias.*

Supriya Ganesh Sapa, S.B. (2014). Impacts of ICT Application on the Insurance Sector (e-Insurance). *IBMRDS's Journal of Managemnt and Research.*

Syed Shahid Mazhar, A. (2015). Impact of Demographic Variables on Purchase of E-Insurance in Urban Areas in India. *International Journal of Management, Innovation & Entrepreneurial Research (IJMIER)*, 7-10.

Singh, A., Sharma, S., Singh, A., Unanoğlu, M., Taneja, S. (2023). Cultural Marketing and Metaverse for Consumer Engagement. *Cultural Marketing and Metaverse for Consumer Engagement.* [http://dx.doi.org/10.4018/978-1-6684-8312-1]

Singhal, N., Goyal, S., Singhal, T. (2022). Demand Following Hypothesis: Empirical Evidence from Insurance Sector of Emerging Asian Markets. *Finance India, XXXVI*(2), 777-798.

Shadi Ebrahimi Mehrabani, M.S. (2013). Knowledge management practices and implementation of E-insurance. *Proceedings - 2013 International Conference on Informatics and Creative Multimedia, ICICM,* 16-28.

Siddiqui, M. H. (2010). Analyzing customer satisfaction with service quality in life insurance services. *Journal of Targeting, Measurement and Analysis for Marketing,* 221-238.

Tran, V.D., Vu, Q.H. (2019). Inspecting the relationship among E-service quality,E-trust, E-customer satisfaction and behavioralintentions of online shopping customers. *People & Global Business Association (P&GBA),* 29-42.

The Economic Times. (2023). HDFC Life's Analytics Approach. Available from: https://www.economictimes.indiatimes.com.

The Times of India. (2023). Customized Insurance Products: The Future of Insurance. Available from: https://www.timesofindia.indiatimes.com.

Xiaoyu, Z. (2009). Study on legal affairs about e-insurance. *Asia-Pacific Conference on Computational Intelligence and Industrial Applications (PACIIA).*

CHAPTER 11

Growth and Development of Microinsurance in LIC of India

Chouturu Manoj Kumar[1,*] and **S. Raghunatha Reddy**[1]

[1] *Department of Humanities & Sciences (Management), KSRM College of Engineering, Kadapa, Andhra Pradesh, India*

Abstract: In India, LIC of India is the only public insurance company that introduced micro-insurance (MI) policies, which began on 28 September 2006. In India, LIC of India is the only public insurance company that introduced micro-insurance policies, which began on 28 September 2006. This study attempts to study the micro-insurance schemes and distribution channels of LIC of India, the growth and development of the microinsurance business, and the claims and settlements of LIC of India. The LIC of India micro insurance agents gradually increased, maturity claims were more than the total death claims, and the number of microinsurance policies continuously increased. Later, the number of policies had fallen down drastically. This study concluded that the LIC of India should conduct revival campaigns in both rural and urban areas and create more awareness of revival campaigns among the existing micro insurance policyholders for developing business and reducing lapsation.

Keywords: Claims, LIC of india, Micro Insurance (MI), Revival campaigns, Settlements.

INTRODUCTION

Microinsurance is a tool for protecting the poor from uncertain risks. MI products tend to be much smaller in amount than traditional schemes and thus extend security to a much broader market. MI can play a crucial role as a comprehensive tool to reduce vulnerability and inequality, particularly where public social security measures are insufficient and unequally distributed. Unfortunately, more than half of the world's total low-income groups do not benefit from any form of social security measures. In order to develop and enhance the growth of the insurance sector, the IRDAI came up with the Microinsurance regulations on 10

* **Corresponding author Chouturu Manoj Kumar:** Department of Humanities & Sciences (Management), KSRM College of Engineering, Kadapa, Andhra Pradesh, India; E-mail: cmanojkumarap@gmail.com

Sanjay Taneja, Ercan Ozen, Luan Vardar, Mohit Kukreti & Mohammad Kashif (Eds.)

November 2005. The regulation made it mandatory for all the insurance companies operating in India to launch micro insurance products, and the regulation also pre-determined the limits in terms of minimum and maximum sum assured, the term of product, the allowable age group, and the maximum commission to agents (Kashif, Kumar, Ghai, & Kumar, 2023). The regulation also stated that microinsurance (MI) agents, self-help groups (SHGs), microfinance institutions (MFIs), and non-governmental organizations (NGOs) were allowed to become MI agents. IRDAI modified these regulations in 2005 and introduced new microinsurance regulations on 13 March 2015. In India, LIC of India is the only public insurance company that introduced micro-insurance policies, which began on 28 September 2006. The LIC of India has eight zones all over India. The micro insurance policyholders of LIC of India should pay the premium through Authorized Premium Collection Centers of LIC of India. The LIC of India designed the MI Agent Mobile Application to collect the renewal premium from micro-insurance policyholders. All LIC micro insurance agents are eligible to access the LIC of India MI agent mobile app.

REVIEW OF LITERATURE

Vinayagamoorthy, A. and Sankar, C. (2014), in their study "Micro-insurance can build security for the poor in India," stated the importance of micro-insurance in reducing the risk of poor and vulnerable sectors. Micro-insurance will protect poor people from various risks by promoting small savings, and it was found that MI is a part of financial inclusion (Akhtar & Mannan, 2020; Barthwal *et al.*, 2024). The study discussed the present status of MI regulations and reviewed the existing micro-insurance schemes. It was observed that MI in India is largely dominated by credit products of MFIs, and micro-insurance is given second priority due to a lack of awareness(Singhal, Goyal & Singhal, 2022).

Deepak Kumar Adhana and Neelam Gulati (2017), in their study "Micro Insurance in India: A Powerful Tool to Empower Poor," analyzed the market, regulations, and progress made by Micro Insurance in India. The study suggested that insurers required innovations at all stages for microinsurance products, understanding the needs of the target population, settling claims timely in a simple and transparent manner, simplifying making premium payments, and concentrating on volumes by targeting large groups (Avikal *et al.*, 2023). The authors concluded that there is a need to target the rural insurance market at a corporate level.

Dipak M. Sanki and Manoj Shah (2018), in their study "Study on Growth of Micro Insurance: With Special Reference to LIC of India," studied the contribution and growth of Micro Insurance in LIC of India (Kapoor *et al.*, 2021).

The authors suggested that more awareness is required to develop microinsurance and concluded that the government of India needs to take necessary actions to protect poor people from uncertain risks through microinsurance.

Renu Bala (2019), in the study "Micro-insurance in India: Role of Public and Private Insurers," examined the role of public and private insurers of micro-insurance in India (Singh *et al.*, 2021). This study shows that India's LIC offers individual MI policies with lower premiums than private insurers. The study concluded that the private sector is leading in new individual MI business, but in the case of group MI business, the public sector insurer LIC of India is leading better than the private.

Balakrishnan .S and Grace Gnanadeepam.I (2019), in their study "Progress of Micro Insurance in India – An Assessment," analyzed the origin, development, and progress of microinsurance in India (Garg *et al.*, 2017; Verma *et al.*, 2021). The authors found that the LIC of India's microinsurance business is higher than that of private insurers, and the annual growth rate of microinsurance shows an unstable trend. The study concluded that the LIC of India's public sector insurance company is at the top regarding the number of policies issued and premium collection.

Devika and Ashok Agrawal (2020), in their study on "Microinsurance in India: Issues and challenges," discussed the issues and challenges of microinsurance products, distribution channels, and consumer protection. The study was performed with unorganized workers and Below Poverty Line (BPL) families in both rural and urban slum areas (Singh *et al.*, 2020). In the study, it was opined that modified products provide instant services and settlement of claims, and policy proposals should be simple to understand and easily accessible. Using the local language makes it more understandable, and more infrastructure facilities and branches will also help increase the number of (Kashif, Shajar, Singhal, & Kumar, 2023).

Bidnur V.V. and Kuldeep Bhalerao (2021), in their study "A Review on Micro Insurance in Rural India," authors analyzed the progress made by Micro Insurance and regulations pertaining to Micro Insurance in India (Avikal *et al.*, 2020). The authors suggested that innovations, timely claim settlements, and the simplification of merchandise in premium payment are needed. The study concluded that there is a need to create awareness of the government in rural areas to develop micro-insurance penetration (Sharma *et al.*, 2023).

NEED FOR THE STUDY

The majority of studies focused on regular insurance policies and the micro-insurance sector being uncovered grabbed the attention of the researcher. The LIC of India Micro-insurance policies are a good hope for daily laborers who earn their bread and butter. Very few studies concentrated on the LIC of India's micro-insurance sector (Kashif *et al.*, 2024; Joshi *et al.*, 2022; (Avikal *et al.*, 2013)). This has motivated the researcher to identify the gap that existed in earlier literature on micro-insurance schemes of LIC of India. The researcher has chosen to study the growth and development of microinsurance business and claims and settlements of microinsurance in LIC of India with the following objectives.

OBJECTIVES OF THE STUDY

- To study the MI schemes and distribution channels of LIC of India.
- To study the growth and development of the microinsurance (MI) business of LIC of India.
- To study the claims and settlements of LIC of India.

METHODOLOGY

This study reveals the growth and development of microinsurance and claims and settlements of LIC of India. The data required for the study have been collected from secondary sources. The secondary data was collected through Annual reports of IRDAI, LIC of India, journals, newspapers, books, case studies carried out by the previous research studies, reports on micro-insurance, and official websites.

MICRO-INSURANCE SCHEMES OF LIC OF INDIA

In India, LIC of India is the only public insurance company introducing micro-insurance policies, which began on 28 September 2006. From 2006 onwards, LIC of India Introduced and withdrew a few micro-insurance policies. The IRDAI decided to withdraw some plans on 01 January 2014, 01 April 2016, and 31 January 2020. Where the existing individual products are not in conformity with the provisions of new regulations of micro insurance at present, Life Insurance Corporation of India (LICI) offers only three micro insurance products, which are Bhagya Lakshmi and LIC's New Jeevan Mangal and Micro Bachat policies.

Table **1** displays the Micro Insurance Schemes of LIC of India. It can beseen in the table that the LIC of India first introduced the micro-insurance scheme, Jeevan Madhur, on 28 September 2006 and withdrew this plan on 01 January 2014. After the Jeevan Madhur plan, LIC of India introduced the Jeevan Mangal scheme on 03 September 2009 and withdrew this plan on 01 January 2014. After withdrawing the Jeevan Mangal plan, LIC of India introduced the Jeevan Deep policy on 01 September 2012 and withdrew this plan on 01 January 2014. After the withdrawal of the Jeevan Deep policy, LIC of India introduced the New Jeevan Mangal Scheme on 09 January 2014 and withdrew this plan on 01 April 2016. After the withdrawal, the New Jeevan Mangal Scheme, LIC of India, introduced the Bhagya Lakshmi policy on 29 December 2014 and withdrew this plan on 01 April 2016. LIC of India introduced one more micro insurance policy, namely Micro Bachat, on 18 February 2019. In view of the new product regulations of IRDAI 2019, LIC of India has decided to modify the New Jeevan Mangal, Bhagya Lakshmi, and Micro Bachat policies on 31 January 2020. LIC of India, with the modifications, reintroduced New Jeevan Mangal with Plan Number 940, Bhagya Lakshmi Plan Number 939, and Micro Bachat Plan Number 951 policies on 01 February 2020.

Table 1. Micro insurance schemes of LIC of india

S. No.	Name of the Scheme	Date of Launch	Date of Withdrawn
1.	LIC's Jeevan Madhur Plan No: 182	28 September 2006	01 January 2014
2.	LIC's Jeevan Mangal Plan No: 198	03 September 2009	01 January 2014
3.	LIC's Jeevan Deep Plan No: 810	01 September 2012	01 January 2014
4.	LIC's New Jeevan Mangal Plan No: 819	09 January 2014	01 April 2016
5.	LIC's Bhagya Lakshmi Plan No: 829	29 December 2014	01 April 2016
6.	LIC's Bhagya Lakshmi Plan No: 839	11 April 2016	31 January 2020
7.	LIC's New Jeevan Mangal Plan No: 840	11 April 2016	31 January 2020
8.	LIC's Micro Bachat Plan No: 851	18 February 2019	31 January 2020
9	LIC's Bhagya Lakshmi Plan No: 939	01 February 2020 01 March 2022	28 February 2022
10	LIC's New Jeevan Mangal Plan No: 940	01 February 2020 01 March 2022	28 February 2022
11	LIC's Micro Bachat Plan No: 951	01 February 2020	-

Source: LIC of India Divisional Office, Kadapa and www.licindia.in.

MICROINSURANCE DISTRIBUTION CHANNELS OF LIC OF INDIA

Micro-insurance policies are marketing through distribution channels comprising NGOs, SHGs, MFIs, DCCBs, RRBs, UCBs, PACS, Cooperative Societies, BCs, Corporate Agents, and other MI agents *i.e.*, Selected Conventional Agents.

Table 2. Micro insurance distribution channels (agents) of LIC of india.

S. No.	Microinsurance Agents of LIC of India	2019-20 (In %)	2020-21 (In %)	2021-22 (In %)
1	Non-Governmental Organizations (NGO's)	6,504 (31.11)	6,548 (30.39)	5,094 (25.75)
2	Self Help Groups (SHG's)	336 (1.61)	341 (1.58)	274 (1.39)
3	Micro Financial Institution's (MFI's)	295 (1.41)	295 (1.37)	228 (1.15)
4	Business Correspondents (BC's)	101 (0.48)	103 (0.48)	103 (0.52)
5	Other MI Agents	13,671 (65.39)	14,260 (66.18)	14,081 (71.19)
Total MI Distribution Channels (Agents)		**20,907 (100.00)**	**21,547 (100.00)**	**19,780 (100.00)**

Source: Annual Reports of IRDAI.
Note: The respective percentages indicate the share of the respective totals.

Microinsurance agents of life insurers as of 31 March 2022 are presented in the above Table **2**. As of 31 March 2022, the LIC of India has 19,780 micro insurance agents. The other micro insurance (MI) agents are more than the other distribution channels. It is concluded and observed from the table that other MI agents of both public and private insurers have 99,961 micro insurance agents as of 31 March 2022. Out of the total MI agents, 20 percent of agents belong to the public sector company LIC of India.

MICRO INSURANCE BUSINESS OF LIC OF INDIA

The LIC of India's micro-insurance business generally constitutes individual and group categories. Table **3** depicts the micro-insurance business of LIC of India from 2011-12 to 2021-22. Under the LIC of India's individual micro-insurance category, though more policies are recommended, the total premium of LIC of India's individual micro-insurance is low. In the LIC of India's group micro-insurance category, though less number of policies are recommended, the total premium of LIC of India group micro-insurance is high.

Table 3. Micro insurance business of LIC of india.

Year	Individuals			Group			Total	
	No. of Policies	In %	Premium (Rs.Lakhs)	No. of Policies	In %	Premium (Rs.Lakh)	No. of Policies	Premium (Rs.Lakhs)
2011-12	3826783	28.84	10603.49	9444349	71.16	9831.63	13271132	20435.12
2012-13	4340235	24.71	9949.05	13223872	75.29	21045.76	17564107	30994.81
2013-14	2205820	15.65	8635.77	11887303	84.35	12581.45	14093123	21217.22
2014-15	400341	1.91	1640.23	20596725	98.09	28193.80	20997066	29834.03
2015-16	452291	1.96	1S953.78	22603919	98.04	25426.39	23056210	27380.17
2016-17	480892	2.05	1587.13	22965393	97.95	34007.62	23446285	35594.75
2017-18	564541	-	1786.81	892 (Schemes)	-	63184.98	-	64971.79
2018-19	617653	100.00	2091.43	-	-	-	617653	2091.43
2019-20	8.59 (Lakhs)	-	222.09 (Crores)	1 (Schemes)	-	34.55 (Crores)	-	256.64 (Crores)
2020-21	9.92 (Lakhs)	-	352.93 (Crores)	624 (Schemes)	-	114.53 (Crores)	-	467.46 (Crores)
2021-22	7.32 (Lakhs)	-	257.92 (Crores)	1,574 (Schemes)	-	67.36 (Crores)	-	325.28 (Crores)

Source: Annual Reports of IRDAI from 2011-12 to 2021-22.
Note: The figure in the percent column shows the percentage of the respective total number of policies.

Table **3** describes the LIC of India's group micro-insurance business having more than the individual micro-insurance from the years 2011-12 to 2017-2018. It is observed that the LIC of India's individual micro-insurance business increased during the year 2011-12 to 2018-19, except during the year 2013-2015. It was found by the LIC of India that it did not have any group micro-insurance business during 2018-19. It is observed from the LIC of India that the group micro-insurance business is more than individual micro-insurance business. It is concluded that the reason behind this is that under the LIC of India group, micro-insurance policyholders had taken a number of policies, including individual micro-insurance policies.

CLAIMS AND SETTLEMENTS OF LIC OF INDIA

The maturity and death claims settlements are a major issue for LIC of India. Table **4** provides the LIC of India's maturity and death claims. The settlements of maturity and death claims are given separately. The maturity and death claims settled by LIC of India have been analyzed from 2012-13 to 2021-22.

Table 4. Claims and settlements of LIC of india.

Year	Maturity Claims Settled				Death Claims Settled				Total Claims Settled	
	No. (Lakhs)	Amount (Crore)	Paid %	Outstanding %	No. (Lakhs)	Amount (Crore)	Paid %	Outstanding %	No. (Lakhs)	Amount (Crore)
2012-13	173.85	64630.13	99.47	0.53	9.78	9447.71	99.10	0.90	183.63□	74,077.84
2013-14	248.87	81424.54	99.67	0.33	10.13	9761.91	99.52	0.48	259.00	91,186.45
2014-15	222.17	79365.71	99.77	0.23	10.15	11092.45	99.56	0.44	232.32	90,458.16
2015-16	205.75	83,667.60	98.26	1.74	9.96	12,181.34	98.67	1.33	215.71	95,848.94□
2016-17	205.11	99,109.66	97.20	2.80	10.47	13,581.14	98.71	1.29	215.58	1,12,690.8□
2017-18	267.36	117888.30	95.50	4.50	10.09	14283.15	98.55	1.45	277.45	1,32,171.45
2018-19	249.62	145636.06	92.95	7.05	9.92	17468.43	98.27	1.63	259.54	1,63,104.49
2019-20	206.66	142350.76	87.66	12.34	9.32	17419.57	95.44	4.56	215.98	1,59,770.33
2020-21	222.76	161031.20	89.83	10.17	11.47	24195.01	98.27	1.73	234.23	1,85,226.21
2021-22	256.47	2,02,083.84	91.09	8.91	15.72	36,597.52	98.50	1.50	272.19	2,38,681.36
Mean	225.862	117719	95.14	4.86	10.701	16602.8	98.459	1.531	236.563	134322
SD	29.2216	44085.8	4.47412	4.47412	1.8485	8308.39	1.1572	1.15582	29.9936	51988.2
CV %	12.9378	37.4501	4.70267	92.06	17.2741	50.042	1.17532	75.4945	12.6789	38.7043
CAGR	3.96477	12.0752	-0.8762	32.6051	4.86037	14.5019	-0.0607	5.24098	4.01425	12.4121

Source: Annual reports of LIC of india.

During 221-22, the LIC settled 272.19 lakh claims for 2,38,681.36 Crores (Including Pension, Group Schemes, and MI). Table **4** describes the claims and settlements of LIC of India. The LIC of India settled 256.47 lakh maturity claims for 2,02,083.84 Crore in the years 2021-22. The Life Insurance Corporation of India settled 15.72 lakh death claims for 36,597.52 Crore during 2021-22. The Life Insurance Corporation of India settled 272.19 lakh maturity and death claims for 2,38,681.36 Crore during 2021-22. It can be observed from the table that the total number of settled maturity claims is more than the total death claims of LIC of India. The reason behind this is that the human life span in India has increased, and the death rate has come down. The Compound Annual Growth Rate (CAGR) registered the highest value of 32.6051 percent of outstanding maturity claims and the lowest value of -0.0607 percent for death claims amount settled in a number of claims (Kashif, David, Gupta, & Alam, 2024).

FINDINGS

- Out of the total MI agents, 20 percent of agents belong to the public insurance company LIC of India. The micro-insurance schemes were withdrawn by the insurance companies as the customers were not attracted to those policies.

- The total number of microinsurance agents has continuously increased. The number of LIC of India micro insurance agents gradually increased except in 2021-22.
- The LIC of India did not have any group micro-insurance business during 2018-19 and the group micro-insurance business is more than individual micro-insurance business.
- The LIC of India's number of microinsurance policies continuously increased. The reason is that the number of policyholders had increased rapidly at the initial stage of micro-insurance business. Later the number of policies had fallen drastically during 2014-15.
- The total settled maturity claims were more than the total death claims settled by the LIC of India.

SUGGESTIONS

- To increase the level of micro insurance, LIC of India may focus on bringing products into the rural areas and the LIC of India should settle claims instantly to their policyholders.
- LIC of India should offer better service to microinsurance policyholders and increase the number of distribution channels, apart from the existing ones, that sell its microinsurance products.
- LIC of India should conduct revival campaigns in both rural and urban areas and create more awareness of revival campaigns among the existing micro insurance policyholders.

CONCLUSION

The LIC of India and IRDAI should take steps to increase the micro-insurance business. The LIC of India has maintained the market value of its microinsurance products. Nowadays, private insurers are also coming up with different strategies. Today, competition is increasing, and LIC of India has made efforts to continue its business. The public sector insurance company LIC of India is at the top regarding the micro-insurance policies issued and premium collection. The LIC of India should take steps to spread awareness about LICI micro-insurance products through various sources. The revised MI regulations (2015) try to overcome some of the barriers to the growth of microinsurance. If the micro-insurance regulations are rightly implemented, it could bring a lot of change in the living standards of rural people. This study concluded that the LIC of India needs to create more awareness in rural areas, and the agents are also required to concentrate on micro-insurance for poor people.

REFERENCES

Balakrishnan S. & Grace Gnanadeepam I. (2019). Progress of Micro Insurance in India – An Assessment.

International Journal of Advance and Innovative Research, 6(2), ISSN 2394-7780, pp. 48-54.

Bidnur V.V. & Kuldeep Bhalerao (2021). A Review on Micro Insurance in Rural India. *NOVIY MIR Research Journal, 6*(6), ISSN No: 0130-7673, pp. 1-17.

Devika & Ashok Agrawal. (2020). Micro Insurance in India: Issues and Challenges. *J. Inf. Comput. Sci.,* 122-130.

Deepak Kumar Adhana & Neelam Gulati (2017). Micro Insurance in India: A Powerful Tool to Empower Poor. *Asia Pacific Journal of Research in Business Management, 8*(7), ISSN: 2229-4104, pp. 88-107..

Dipak M. Sanki & Manoj Shah (2018). Study on Growth of Micro Insurance: With Special Reference to LIC of India. 7(4), ISSN 2277-5730, pp. 32-38.

Farah Farooqui (2016). Micro Insurance in India: A Comparative Study of Public and Private Sector Insurance Companies. Thesis submitted to Department of Commerce and Business Administration, University of Allahabad, Allahabad..

Joshi, K., Kumar, V., Anandaram, H., Kumar, R., Gupta, A., Krishna, K.H. (2023). A review approach on deep learning algorithms in computer vision. *Intelligent Systems and Applications in Computer Vision* [http://dx.doi.org/10.1201/9781003453406-1]

Kashif, M., Singhal, N., Goyal, S., Singh, S.K. (2024). Foreign Exchange Reserves and Economic Growth of Brazil: A Nonlinear Approach. *Finance: Theory and Practice, 28*(1), 145-154.

Kashif, M., David, A., Gupta, V.P., Alam, S. (2024). Integration of Artificial Intelligence in the Financial Sector. *Artificial Intelligence and Machine Learning-Powered Smart Finance.,* 96-108. [http://dx.doi.org/10.4018/979-8-3693-3264-1.ch005]

Kashif, M., Shajar, S.N., Singhal, N., Kumar, P. (2023). *Achieving sustainable investment practices through green finance: Challenges and opportunities. Sustainable Investments in Green Finance.,* 234-244. [http://dx.doi.org/10.4018/979-8-3693-1388-6.ch016]

Kashif, M., Kumar, P., Ghai, S., Kumar, S. (2023). Disruptive Technologies in Computational Finance. *Algorithmic Approaches to Financial Technology: Forecasting, Trading, and Optimization,* 46-60.

Kirti Singh & Vijay Kumar Gangal. (2011). *Micro-insurance- A tool for upliftment of rural India.* EXCEL International Journal of Multidisciplinary Management Studies.

Micro Insurance Department, LIC of India Divisional Office, Kadapa.

Micro Insurance Department, LIC of India, Central Office, Mumbai.

Namrata Anand (2013), Micro-insurance and vulnerable section of society: An analytical study, Thesis submitted to Department of Economics, Faculty of Social Science, Dayal bagh Educational Institute (Deemed University), Dayalbagh, Agra..

Renu Bala. (2019). *Micro-insurance in India: Role of public and private insurers.* IAHRW International Journal of Social Sciences Review.

Sharma, P., Hussain, S.S., Taneja, S., Sheikh, R. (2023). Gig economy, workplace culture and talent crunch: A conceptual model for future work. *Green Management - A New Paradigm in the World of Business.*

Singhal, N., Goyal, S., Singhal, T. (2022). The relationship between insurance and economic growth in Asian countries: a regional perspective. *Macroeconomics and Finance in Emerging Market Economies, 15*(3), 301-322.
[http://dx.doi.org/10.1080/17520843.2021.1957599]

Tinsy Rose Tome & Selvam. (2012). Micro Insurance: Illuminating the Real challenges in India. *Int. J. Recent Sci. Res.,* 681-686.

Vinayagamoorthy, A., Sankar, C. (2014). Micro-insurance can build security for the poor in India. *J. Bank. Finance,* 26-33. Available from: www.google.co.in, www.irdai.gov.in, www.licindia.in

Akhtar, N., Mannan, M.A. (2020). Mycoremediation: Expunging environmental pollutants. *Biotechnol. Rep.*

(Amst.), 26, e00452.
[http://dx.doi.org/10.1016/j.btre.2020.e00452] [PMID: 32617263]

Kapoor, B., Kapoor, D., Gautam, S., Singh, R., Bhardwaj, S. (2021). Dietary polyunsaturated fatty acids (PUFAs): Uses and potential health benefits. *Curr. Nutr. Rep., 10*(3), 232-242.
[http://dx.doi.org/10.1007/s13668-021-00363-3] [PMID: 34255301]

Garg, V., Singh, H., Bhatia, A., Raza, K., Singh, S.K., Singh, B., Beg, S. (2017). Systematic development of transethosomal gel system of piroxicam: formulation optimization, in vitro evaluation, and ex vivo assessment. *AAPS PharmSciTech, 18*(1), 58-71.
[http://dx.doi.org/10.1208/s12249-016-0489-z] [PMID: 26868380]

Barthwal, A., Bhatt, M., Avikal, S., Prakash, C. (2024). Machine learning-based prediction models for electoral outcomes in India: a comparative analysis of exit polls from 2014–2021. *Qual. Quant.,* 1-26.
[http://dx.doi.org/10.1007/s11135-024-01937-3]

Avikal, S., Pant, R., Kumar, K.N., Kumar, V., Ram, M. (2023). Prioritizing the barriers of manufacturing during Covid-19 using fuzzy AHP. *Advances in Soft Computing Applications.* River Publishers.
[http://dx.doi.org/10.1201/9781003425885-11]

Singh, R., Avikal, S. (2021). An AHP-Based Approach to Determine the Effects of COVID-19 on Industrial Sustainability. *Sustainability in Industry 4.0.* CRC Press.
[http://dx.doi.org/10.1201/9781003102304-11]

Verma, R.P., Kumar Chaudhary, N., Avikal, S. (2021). Effect of direction of lip spoiler on the aerodynamic performance of a small passenger vehicle. *Mater. Today Proc., 46*, 10301-10305.
[http://dx.doi.org/10.1016/j.matpr.2020.12.448]

Singh, R., Avikal, S. (2020). COVID-19: A decision-making approach for prioritization of preventive activities. *Int. J. Healthc. Manag., 13*(3), 257-262.
[http://dx.doi.org/10.1080/20479700.2020.1782661]

Avikal, S., Nithin Kumar, K.C., Singh, A.R., Jain, R. (2020). Grey based Taguchi optimization for multi-lobe bearing. *Mater. Today Proc., 26*, 2663-2666.
[http://dx.doi.org/10.1016/j.matpr.2020.02.560]

Avikal, S., Mishra, P.K., Jain, R., Yadav, H.C. (2013). A PROMETHEE method based heuristic for disassembly line balancing problem. *Industrial Engineering and Management Systems, 12*(3), 254-263.
[http://dx.doi.org/10.7232/iems.2013.12.3.254]

CHAPTER 12

A Bibliometric Review of Life Insurance in India

Rajesh Tiwari[1,*], **Aastha Agarwal**[1], **Vanshika Kakkar**[1] and **Luan Vardari**[2]

[1] *Graphic Era Deemed to Be University, Dehradun, India*

[2] *University "Ukshin Hoti" Prizren, Kosovo (Serbia)*

Abstract: —Life Insurance provides financial security to families in case of the unfortunate death of the policyholder. In this chapter, a bibliometric analysis of 144 papers published between 1973 and 2022 in the Scopus database was performed to identify key themes and trends in the literature on Life Insurance. The analysis included citation analysis of leading countries, organizations, and authors. There has been significant growth in research on Life Insurance since 2019, the duration of covid 19. Three dominant themes were identified: customer satisfaction with insurance, the efficiency of insurance, and the relationship between economic growth and insurance. This chapter provides important insights into Life Insurance companies and other stakeholders to promote life insurance in India.

Keywords: Citation analysis, Doreign investment, India, Life insurance, Scopus.

INTRODUCTION

India has 24 life insurance companies and is the fifth-largest emerging market for insurance. Foreign investment is attracted by providing automatic routes up to twenty-six percent investment. Despite being the world's fastest-growing economy, life insurance penetration in India is just 3.2%. The industry recorded a growth of 12.93% in 2021-22 in the first-year premium volume in India. The life insurance industry in India is estimated to worth USD 317.98 billion by the financial year 2031. The technology footprint is a positive trigger for the insurance sector in India. India has become the second-largest market in the Asia Pacific in insurance technology investments by venture capital firms (IBEF, 2023). High net-worth individuals were enjoying a tax arbitrage through a tax deduction of proceeds of life insurance policies under section 10(10D) of the Income Tax Act of India. The new tax provisions have taken away the tax arbitrage by taxing the proceeds of life insurance policies with annual premiums

* **Corresponding author Rajesh Tiwari:** Graphic Era Deemed to Be University, Dehradun, India; E-mail: ambitioncfarajesh@gmail.com

Sanjay Taneja, Ercan Ozen, Luan Vardar, Mohit Kukreti & Mohammad Kashif (Eds.)

above INR 5 lakh (Panda, 2023). Consumers in India prefer public-sector life insurance firms (Pattnaik *et al.* 2021). Young people are more likely to buy life insurance policies in India. However, industry growth is constrained by people's perceptions (Fariya, *et al.*, 2024). Consumers in India do not consider life insurance as a basic need (Shukla, 2018). Life insurance companies in India are suffering from low capital-to-asset ratio (Rohilla, 2023). Uncertainty about economic policies adversely affects the demand for life insurance in India (Kumar *et al.*, 2021). The study explores the trends in life insurance research in the Scopus database.

REVIEW OF LITERATURE

The Covid pandemic has highlighted the need for insurance as a hedge against unforeseeable events. Evaluation of insurance futures in India and Malaysia proved that insurance futures are a hedge against the risks posed by the Covid pandemic (Wang & Lee, 2023). Persistency is a cause of concern for the insurance sector. The robustness of actuarial models has been established (Ravi *et al.* 2021). Poor insurance penetration in India is a cause of concern. Poor awareness about insurance needs to be addressed. People's mindsets can be changed only when they have knowledge about insurance (Ramnani & Deshpande, 2021). Stakeholders must engage actively for better outcomes (Tiwari *et al.* 2020; Singh *et al.*, 2020). Satisfaction of existing consumers will attract new consumers and motivate existing consumers to continue with the existing products (Chand *et al.* 2022). The willingness of the top management and administrators of the country is crucial for the economic well-being of the citizens (Tiwari *et al.* 2021; Kashif, *et al.*, 2023; Singh & Arya, 2019). Though private insurance companies have been offering their products in India, Life Insurance Corporation (LIC) still dominates the life insurance market in terms of market share, benefits, premium income, and new policies issued (Kumar & Singh, 2023; Bhushan *et al.*, 2021). LIC is preferred for online term insurance policies (Pattnaik *et al.* 2021). The government is dedicated to building an insured society to help the people below the poverty line. Privatization and foreign direct investment have brought additional capital into the insurance sector in India (Bhattacharya & Sachdev, 2021). Occupation, age, and marital status influence the continuation of life insurance policies in India. Advertisements strongly influence buying decisions of life insurance policies (Kavyashree, 2023; Sharma *et al.*, 2023; Kumar *et al.*, 2020).

METHODOLOGY

The current study employs a bibliometric analysis to review research trends in the insurance sector. Scopus database was used for the study. The visualization of similarities was done using a VOS viewer. The study examined leading countries, organizations, authors, and sources. The keyword used for the search was "life insurance" and India. One hundred eighty-three documents were obtained from the Scopus database. All documents were in English language. The exclusion criteria of the source of the document were applied to screen the documents further. All documents other than the article were excluded. 144 documents were obtained. Conference paper (16), book chapter (12), review (5), book (2), conference review (1), erratum (1), letter (1), and note (1) were excluded. A total of 144 documents were finally used for the study. The VOS viewer software was employed for the study.

RESULTS

The publication trends on life insurance in India are depicted in Fig. (**1**). There has been a sudden increase in research publications in the previous 5 years. The Covid pandemic has enhanced researchers' interest in life insurance. The highest number of articles was published in 2019 (23). Ten papers were published each in 2020 and 2021. Nineteen articles were published in 2022. During the time period 2000 to 2022, 131 articles were published. 47% of all articles between 2000 and 2022 were published in just four years, 2018 to 2022. The recent interest in research on life insurance in India needs to be investigated further to identify the triggers.

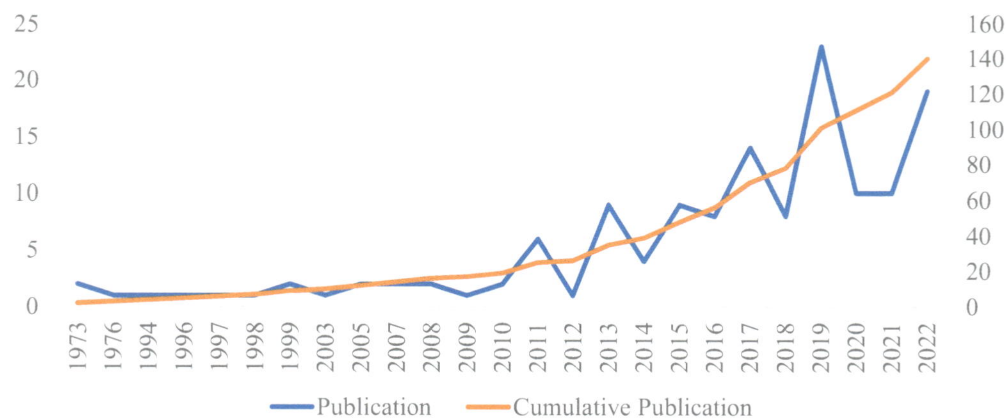

Fig. (1). Trend of publication on life insurance in india. Source: Created by Authors from the SCOPUS database.

The leading countries for research on life insurance in India are shown in Table **1**. The threshold used was a minimum of 1 citation. India leads with 803 citations, followed by China (101), Japan (99), Switzerland (71), and United States (58).

Table 1. Top cited countries.

Rank	Country	Documents	Citations	Total Link Strength
1	India	123	803	28
2	China	5	101	16
3	Japan	2	99	15
4	Switzerland	2	71	15
5	United States	4	58	3
6	Malaysia	2	31	0
7	Canada	2	26	0
8	Australia	2	25	2
9	Taiwan	2	13	0
10	Morocco	1	12	4

Source: Created by Authors from the SCOPUS database.

The leading organizations were screened using a threshold of a minimum of 30 citations. Organizations from south India lead the research on life insurance with the highest citations. Bharath University and Tagore Engineering College are the leading organizations, with 137 citations, followed by the National Graduate Institute for Policy Studies, Japan, with 98 citations, as shown in Table **2**.

The top authors were identified by screening them using the threshold of a minimum of 2 documents and 1 citation. B. K. Sahoo is the leading author with 100 citations and a link strength of 16, followed by K. Tone with a citation of 99. R Gera has 86 citations followed by A. Ghosh with 35 citations. The top ten authors are depicted in Table **3**.

Table 2. Top cited organisations.

Rank	Organization	Documents	Citations
1	Bharath University, India	1	137
2	Tagore Engineering College, India	1	137
3	National Graduate Institute for Policy Studies, Japan	1	98
4	Institute of Economic Growth, India	1	83
5	Institute for Social and Economic Change, India	1	73
6	University of International Business and Economics, China	1	71
7	University of St. Gallen, Switzerland	1	71
8	International Management Institute, India	2	60
9	Harvard Business School, United States	1	51

(Table 2) cont.....

Rank	Organization	Documents	Citations
10	Harvard University, United States	1	51
11	Wharton, United States	1	51
12	Manav Rachna University India	1	48
13	GGS Indraprastha University, India	1	48
14	Institute of Management Technology, India	1	31

Source: Created by Authors from SCOPUS database

Table 3. Top cited authors.

Rank	Author	Documents	Citations	Total Link Strength
1	B. K. Sahoo	3	100	16
2	K Tone	2	99	12
3	R. Gera	3	86	0
4	A. Ghosh	2	35	11
5	S. Kumar	4	23	4
6	S. Basri	3	21	9
7	P. Goyari	2	20	7
8	A. Dutta	2	18	7
9	P.P. Sengupta	2	16	7
10	S. A Siddiqui	3	11	4

Source: Created by Authors from SCOPUS database.

Most occurred keywords were screened using a minimum of 5 occurrences criteria. The most frequently used keywords were India with 41 occurrences, life insurance with 30 occurrences, and insurance with 24 occurrences. Other frequently used keywords were customer satisfaction (8), service quality (8), health insurance (7), human (7), mortgage bancassurance (6), LIC (6), and life insurance companies (6).

The bibliographic coupling was done using a threshold of a minimum of 1 citation. Out of 144, 92 documents met the threshold. Out of 92, only 56 documents were connected. Three clusters emerged as presented below Fig. (**2**).

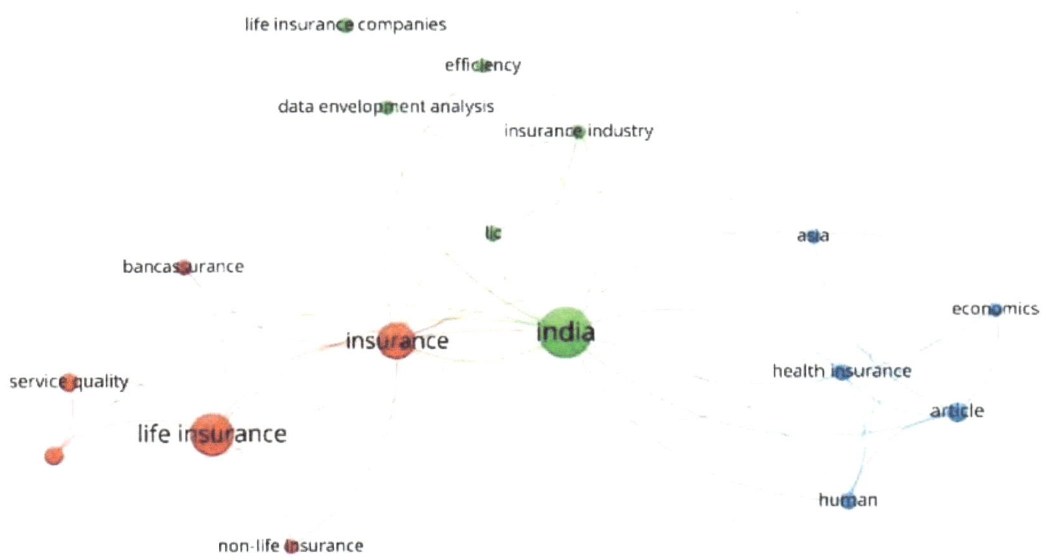

Fig. (2). Frequently used keywords. Source: Created by Authors from the SCOPUS database.

Cluster I

This in Fig. (**3**), the cluster comprised of 27 documents. This cluster is shown in red. The highly cited article was from Anagol *et al.* (2017), with 51 citations and a link strength of 1, followed by Gera *et al.* (2017), with 48 citations and a link strength of 40. R Gera (2011a) had 31 citations and a link strength of 64. This cluster focused on service quality and customer satisfaction with insurance.

Cluster II

This cluster comprised of 15 documents. This cluster is shown in green. The top cited article from this cluster was Tone & Sahoo (2005), with 98 citations and a link strength of 40, followed by Huang and Eling (2013), with a citation of 71 and a link strength of 56. This cluster focused on the efficiency of insurance.

Cluster III

This cluster comprised of 14 articles. This cluster is shown in blue. The highly cited article was Mohy ul din *et al.* (2017), with 28 citations, followed by Khurshed and Ghosh, with 27 citations and a link strength of 37. Chen *et al.* (2013) had 13 citations. Patnaik *et al.* (2021) had nine citations. This cluster focused on the relationship between economic growth and insurance.

Fig. (3). Bibliographic coupling. Source: Created by Authors from the SCOPUS database.

CONCLUDING REMARKS

The most significant authors, journals, and nations on the subject have been highlighted in this bibliometric study, which has shed light on the present status of research in Life Insurance. According to the data, India leads all other nations in terms of the volume of publications on Life Insurance, followed by Australia and Morocco. The study also showed that the COVID crisis, Influencing, and investment development are the three areas of Life Insurance that are most frequently examined. This suggests that addressing some of the most important assessments we know is the top priority. The findings of this analysis imply that Life Insurance is a significant field of study and application that will continue to gain prominence in the years to come. The demand for creative and sustainable financial solutions will only grow as concerns like future security and stability of families in Uncertain crises become important (Kashif *et al.*, 2024). To guarantee that Life Insurance develops and can play a significant role in constructing a more sustainable future, Policies, regulators, investors, and financial institutions should collaborate.

REFERENCES

India Brand Equity Foundation (IBEF) (2023). Insurance sector in India: Industry overview, market size & trends. Available from: https://www.ibef.org/industry/insurance-sector-india.

S. Panda, (2023, March 23). High-value life insurance policy sales fail to pick up in February-March. Business Standard. Available from: https://www.business-standard.com/article/finance/no-extraordina-y-growth-in-sales-of-high-value-insurance-policies-in-march-123032200983_1.html.

Pattnaik, C.R., Mohanty, S.N., Mohanty, S., Chatterjee, J.M., Jana, B., Diaz, V.G. (2021). A fuzzy multi-criteria decision-making method for purchasing life insurance in India. *Bulletin of Electrical Engineering and Informatics, 10*(1), 344-356.
[http://dx.doi.org/10.11591/eei.v10i1.2275]

Shukla, U.N. (2018). Enhancing life insurance penetration and density in India: purchase intention modelling. *Int. J. Econ. Bus. Res., 15*(2), 141-154.

[http://dx.doi.org/10.1504/IJEBR.2018.089683]

Rohilla, R. L. (2023). Financial soundness of life insurers in India. *Published in International Journal of Science and Research Archive,* 330-352.

Kashif, M., Singhal, N., Goyal, S., Singh, S.K. (2024). Foreign Exchange Reserves and Economic Growth of Brazil: A Nonlinear Approach. *Finance: Theory and Practice, 28*(1), 145-154.

Kashif, M., Kumar, P., Ghai, S., Kumar, S. (2023). Disruptive Technologies in Computational Finance. *Algorithmic Approaches to Financial Technology: Forecasting, Trading, and Optimization,* 46-60.

Kumar, S., Sahu, N.C., Kumar, P. (2021). Insurance consumption and economic policy uncertainty in India: an analysis of asymmetric effects. *Singap. Econ. Rev.,* 1-29.
[http://dx.doi.org/10.1142/S0217590821500387]

Wang, K.M., Lee, Y.M. (2023). Are life insurance futures a safe haven during COVID-19? *Financ. Innov., 9*(1), 13.
[http://dx.doi.org/10.1186/s40854-022-00411-z] [PMID: 36643684]

Ravi, V., Saini, R., Varshney, M.K., Grover, G. (2021). Modeling of survival time of life insurance policies in India: a comparative study. *International Journal of System Assurance Engineering and Management, 12,* 164-175.

Ramnani, P., Deshpande, R. (2021). Empirical Study on the Perception of Life Insurance in India. *Issue 3 Int'l JL Mgmt. &. Human., 4*, 5932.

Tiwari, R., Chand, K., Anjum, B. (2020). Crop insurance in India: A review of pradhan mantri fasal bima yojana (PMFBY). *FIIB Business Review, 9*(4), 249-255.
[http://dx.doi.org/10.1177/2319714520966084]

Chand, K., Tiwari, R. (2022). Effect of Perception and Satisfaction on Preference for Mobile Wallet. *FIIB Business Review,* 23197145221077365.

Tiwari, R., Chand, K., Bhatt, A., Anjum, B., Thirunavukkarasu, K. (2021). Agriculture 5.0 in India: Opportunities and Challenges of Technology Adoption. *A Step Towards Society 5.0,* 179-198.

Kumar, R., Singh, S. (2023). A Comparative Analysis of Private Insurance Companies and Life Insurance Corporation of India. *Sachetas, 2*(1), 27-37.
[http://dx.doi.org/10.55955/210004]

Fariya, Saini, A., & Kashif, M. (2024). Exploring the Influence of Factors Driving Financial Accessibility, Financial Activities, and Financial Education on Sustainable Development. *Artificial Intelligence and Machine Learning-Powered Smart Finance*, pp. 23-49.

Bhattacharya, S., Sachdev, B.K. (2021). An analysis on the different insurance policy in India and its role in economy growth and providing people with better life opportunities. *World Journal of Advanced Research and Reviews, 12*(3), 119-123.
[http://dx.doi.org/10.30574/wjarr.2021.12.3.0993]

Kavyashree, K. (2023). Impact of Advertisements on Consumer Buying Behaviour Empirical Study of Life Insurance Policy Holders of Mangalore City. *EPRA International Journal of Research and Development, 8*(3), 114-116. [IJRD].

Sharma, P., Hussain, S.S., Taneja, S., Sheikh, R. (2023). Gig economy, workplace culture and talent crunch: A conceptual model for future work. *Green Management - A New Paradigm in the World of Business.*

Singh, S., Kumar, V., Datta, S., Wani, A.B., Dhanjal, D.S., Romero, R., Singh, J. (2020). Glyphosate uptake, translocation, resistance emergence in crops, analytical monitoring, toxicity and degradation: a review. *Environ. Chem. Lett., 18*(3), 663-702.
[http://dx.doi.org/10.1007/s10311-020-00969-z]

Bhushan, B., Sahoo, C., Sinha, P., Khamparia, A. (2021). Unification of Blockchain and Internet of Things (BIoT): requirements, working model, challenges and future directions. *Wirel. Netw., 27*(1), 55-90.

[http://dx.doi.org/10.1007/s11276-020-02445-6]

Kumar, H., Bhardwaj, K., Sharma, R., Nepovimova, E., Kuča, K., Dhanjal, D.S., Verma, R., Bhardwaj, P., Sharma, S., Kumar, D. (2020). Fruit and vegetable peels: utilization of high value horticultural waste in novel industrial applications. *Molecules, 25*(12), 2812.
[http://dx.doi.org/10.3390/molecules25122812] [PMID: 32570836]

Singh, G., Arya, S.K. (2019). Utility of laccase in pulp and paper industry: A progressive step towards the green technology. *Int. J. Biol. Macromol., 134*, 1070-1084.
[http://dx.doi.org/10.1016/j.ijbiomac.2019.05.168] [PMID: 31129205]

CHAPTER 13

Insuring Tomorrow: A Bibliometric Dive into Robo-Advising for Smart Wealth Management

Vartika Bisht[1,*] and **Rajwinder Kaur**[1]

[1] *University School of Business, Chandigarh University, Punjab, India*

Abstract: The current study delves into the advancing field of robo-advisors, an evolving business model revolutionizing investment advisory services through full automation. Examining 299 research papers from the Scopus database, spanning from 2002 to January 2024, this study employs bibliometric analysis to uncover key research topics, annual publication trends, subject areas, leading countries, geographic distribution, and co-occurrence and citation network of this scientific exploration. The keywords applied to the study were "robo-advising" OR "robo-advisors" OR "smart wealth management" OR "artificial intelligence in finance". The data were subjected to analysis using the VOSviewer tool, and 299 selected papers were examined through descriptive, tabular, and visual presentations within the framework discussion. The results indicated that the concept of robo-advising has evolved as an emerging concept in relation to smart wealth management from 2016 onwards. The United States has emerged as the leading country in contributing the maximum number of publications to this concept, and the subject area is computer science. Furthermore, there is a limited exploration of the concept of robo-advising and sustainability as the authors found no manuscripts for the two together. Finally, at the end of the research, limitations, and suggestions are stated regarding the need for integrated research efforts on this subject.

Keywords: Bibliometric analysis, Insurance, Robo-advising, Smart Wealth Management.

INTRODUCTION

Robo-advisors(RAs) are automated platforms that utilize algorithmic processes to deliver financial guidance to investors. They have widely incorporated machine learning algorithms and leveraged artificial intelligence by tapping into extensive datasets that offer diverse investment opportunities (Tao *et al.*, 2021). In simple terms, these investment programs employ trading algorithms to automate investment processes (Ostern *et al.*, 2020) based on users' risk and return preferences.

* **Corresponding author Vartika Bisht:** University School of Business, Chandigarh University, India;
E-mail: bishtvartika2909@gmail.com

Sanjay Taneja, Ercan Ozen, Luan Vardar, Mohit Kukreti & Mohammad Kashif (Eds.)

Grealish and Kolm, (2021) suggest that due to the algorithmic foundation of their services and access to client data, robo-advisors can enhance conventional financial planning and asset management approaches through the integration of machine learning techniques, resulting in more personalized portfolio management and financial guidance. Lately, the adoption of bibliometric analysis in business research has seen considerable acknowledgment (Khan *et al.*, 2021; Donthu *et al.*, 2020b; Donthu *et al.*, 2021), attributable to the advancements, accessibility, and widespread availability of bibliometric tools such as Gephi, Leximancer, VOSviewer, along with scientific databases like Scopus and Web of Science. The bibliometric approach, as outlined by Van Eck and Waltman (2010), is both straightforward and reproducible. Additionally, the interdisciplinary application of bibliometric methodology from information science to business research and specifically to financial technology research (Fintech) has contributed to its growing recognition. A study underscores that bibliometric analysis entails the use of statistical methods to examine publications, including articles, research papers, books, and other scholarly works, spanning various academic disciplines and countries (Kashif *et al.*, 2024; Sidhu, 2020; Raza *et al.*, 2015).

Robo-advisors can integrate decision-making capabilities and computational capacities of both humans and machines, thus enabling the provision of varied wealth management services (Phoon and Koh, 2017; Mehra *et al.* 2023), catering to the diverse requirements of private wealth clients.

Smart wealth management (SWM) refers to the use of advanced technologies, algorithms, and data analytics in the management of one's financial assets and investments. It is suggested that core technologies in the market, including big data, artificial intelligence (AI), financial engineering, and real-time financial data analysis, are harmoniously combined to create a dynamic platform (Xiang *et al.*, 2019; Avikal *et al.* 2023). This platform offers an outstanding user experience, facilitating informed investment decisions and providing specialized consultancy services. In the context of smart wealth management, robo-advisors utilize various technologies, including artificial intelligence and data analytics, to offer personalized and data-driven investment strategies. These automated platforms can efficiently handle tasks such as portfolio rebalancing, risk assessment, and goal-based financial planning (Jung *et al.*, 2019; Badhotiya *et al.* 2022). The integration of robo-advisory services in smart wealth management aims to enhance the overall efficiency, accessibility, and customization of wealth management processes for investors (Singh and Kaur, 2017). Thus, with the rising trend of robo-advisors, smart wealth management becomes increasingly crucial for long-term sustainability. Some researchers suggest that integrating technology-driven solutions, such as robo-advisory services, into wealth management practices allows for more efficient, cost-effective, and personalized financial strategies (Vyas *et al.*, 2023; Manzoor & Singla, 2019). Smart wealth management caters to investors' evolving preferences and enhances the overall accessibility and inclusivity of financial services (Chishti and Puschmann, 2018; Sharma *et al.*, 2020). Additionally, by leveraging advanced technologies, financial institutions and investors can adapt to changing market dynamics, improve decision-making processes, and create sustainable wealth management practices for the future.

This study aims to conduct a bibliometric review using manuscripts from the Scopus database, focusing on robo-advising for smart wealth management. Existing studies identified a research gap that predominantly centered on robo-advising or smart wealth management as two different concepts (Vyas *et al.*, 2023; Nigam *et al.* 2021). Our manuscript addresses this gap by specifically examining the concept of robo-advising and smart wealth management, and a bibliometric analysis of the same needs to be conducted.

LITERATURE REVIEW

Robo-Advising

Financial guidance has the potential to address insufficient diversification issues and improve investor outcomes, as suggested by (D'Acunto *et al.*, 2019; Gennaioli *et al.*, 2015). Nevertheless, for numerous retail investors, traditional financial advisors prove to be too expensive. Robo-advisors (RAs) assist investors by employing automated financial advisory processes, suggesting customized portfolio allocations according to their risk preferences and financial objectives, and automatically monitoring and rebalancing their portfolios over time (Torno *et al.*, 2021; Jung *et al.*, 2018). Using algorithm-based portfolio allocation recommendations, robo-advisors assist investors in maintaining their money. These platforms are all-inclusive and automated (Bhatia *et al.*, 2021; Singh *et al.* 2021). The popularity of robo-advisors has risen in recent years as investors look for cost-effective and automated investment guidance. The next phase in asset management and financial guidance progression is anticipated to be robo-advising (Cavalcante *et al.*, 2021; Kearney, 2015). A study by Rossi and Utkus, (2020) suggests that human advisors significantly enhance the likelihood of individuals subscribing to robo-advice and reduce the attrition of investors.

Robo-advising and other forms of contact-free advising have grown in significance during the 2019 coronavirus, a global epidemic that has profoundly affected people's day-to-day lives via increasing social distance (So, 2021). A new alternative to human financial advisers known as robo-advisors has recently evolved. The capacity to provide customized financial advice is critical to the success of robo-advisors (Capponi, Ólafsson and Zariphopoulou, 2021). According to the research, an upsurge in risk-adjusted returns, more excellent trading activity, and heightened focus on portfolios were all seen among investors who had access to robo-advisors (Singh *et al.* 2020). Among these benefits, research has demonstrated that the robot's ability to encourage investors to restructure their holdings in a manner that brings them near the goal allocation is a crucial and dynamic component.

Additionally, individuals with smaller portfolios, who are least likely to benefit from conventional guidance, are more strongly affected by these impacts, according to the research (Bianchi and Briëre, 2021; Chaudhry *et al.* 202). According to the extant literature, Automated financial advisers, or robo-advisors, decrease the need for personal financial advice provided by financial service companies. Also, investors wary of human financial advisers' possible conflicts of interest may find robo-consultants to be an excellent alternative to traditional investment consultants (Brenner and Meyll, 2020).

More and more people are looking to robo-advisors as a tech-enabled way to simplify their financial management. Research suggests that people are more likely to utilize robo-advisors if they anticipate favorable feelings from using them and less likely if they anticipate adverse feelings. Inducing people's self-enhancement objectives may also change this association (Hohenberger, Lee, and Coughlin, 2019).

Smart Wealth Management

At the crossroads of banking, robo-advisors, and artificial intelligence (AI) lies the exciting field of Smart Wealth Management, which is constantly evolving to study how technology is revolutionizing the wealth management industry (Yi *et al.*, 2023; Chishti and Puschmann, 2018). A lot of people are interested in how robo-advisors fit into the wealth management process (Hohenberger, Lee, and Coughlin, 2019). These algorithm-driven systems sift through financial records, evaluate risk profiles, and track market movements (Sabharwal, 2018). The literature emphasizes the practicality and affordability of robo-advisors, who provide cheaper costs in comparison to traditional wealth management solutions (Jung, Glaser, and Köpplin, 2019).

One prominent area where AI is finding use is in wealth management, where the impact of complex algorithms and ML is becoming more apparent (Phoon, K., & Koh, 2017). Data-driven decision-making processes, risk evaluation, and financial solution customization are all made possible by AI-driven systems that excel at evaluating massive amounts of information (Gupta *et al.*, 2022). Deepening the awareness of market opinions and improving client communication, research into natural language synthesis and sentiment analysis inside AI applications provides depth.

The focus of the literature often returns to client involvement and customization. An AI-driven shift toward customer focus is made possible by smart wealth management solutions (Sheth *et al.*, 2022). Improved financial planning and stronger client-advisor relationships are outcomes of these technological advancements in knowing personal preferences, risk specifications, and objectives (Hogan and Miller, 2013). Tailoring advice to match individual requirements and situations is becoming more common, and the focus on customized services is in line with that trend. Much of the scholarly writing on Smart Wealth Management focuses on ethical and regulatory issues (Serrano, 2023; Finn and Wadhwa, 2014). Many people are curious about the ever-changing legal environment that surrounds AI applications in banking and robo-advisors. Issues of possible biases in algorithmic decision-making, confidentiality of data, and transparency are investigated by researchers (Zerilli *et al.*, 2019; Lepri *et al.*, 2018). Studies in this field are heavily influenced by ethical questions pertaining to the proper use of AI and the protection of customer information.

The real-world effects of intelligent wealth management solutions may be better understood by analyzing the obstacles to performance and acceptance. Investment returns, management of risks, and market adaptation are some of the metrics that robo-advisors are measured against in comparison to more conventional approaches (Holtfort, Horsch and Schwarz, 2022). Included in the research that sheds light on the complications of broad adoption are challenges relating to shareholder trust, the importance of financial literacy in comprehending AI-driven suggestions, and the interplay of human-machine cooperation. Ultimately, the extant available research on Smart Wealth Management provides a detailed analysis of how AI, robo-advisors, and finance interact, drawing attention to the opportunities for change.

Bibliometric Analysis

Bibliometric analysis is described as a "collection of mathematical and statistical techniques for presenting current and evolving knowledge within a research domain"(Ampah *et al.*, 2021). It offers a valuable approach to uncovering the intellectual framework of a research field or subject. Bibliometrics provide a reliable approach to quantitatively and qualitatively assess the evolution of research trends over time (Xie *et al.*,2020). Pagán (2023) mentions that it helps to identify significant areas for any subject matter to be studied in detail.

Software

VOSviewer1.6.17(Eck and Waltman, 2017) software was used for analysis purpose. This software, developed by the Centre for Science and Technology Studies (CWTS) at Leiden University in the Netherlands, enables the generation of bibliometric networks by utilizing co-citation relationships(Siccardi and Villa (2022); Mural *et al.*, 2020). The file format obtained from the Scopus database is in line with this software.

The bibliometric approach, as outlined by Van Eck and Waltman (2010), is both straightforward and reproducible. It offers a broad spectrum of topics and tools for refining searches, ensuring precise and pertinent results.

RESEARCH METHODOLOGY

The research methodology encompasses detailing research questions, data collection, search criteria model, and the method employed. The current study relies on the Scopus database of the period 2015 to January 2024 for data gathering, recognized as the most authentic, reliable, and verified repository for scientific papers in recent years. Scopus has been validated for use in informatics studies, particularly for research analysis. For this study, Bibliometric analysis is performed using VOSviewer 1.6.17 as it simplifies bibliometric mapping and network analysis, highlighted by Aria *et al.* (2020). No bibliometric study has investigated the robo-advising concept in relation to smart wealth management for long-term sustainability. This research, however, seeks to identify the theoretical foundations, influential scholars, and publications in the intersection of robo-advising and smart wealth management. The study aims to analyze the landscape of robo-advising for smart wealth management, ensuring long-lasting resilience, and propose potential directions for future qualitative research on the benefits of robo-advising. To accomplish this goal, specific research questions have been formulated:

RQ1: What is the annual publication trend on robo-advising and smart wealth management?

RQ2: Which document type published more research work on robo-advising and smart wealth management?

RQ3: Which area published more research work on robo-advising and smart wealth management?

RQ4: Who are the leading countries that have contributed more to publishing robo-advising and smart wealth management manuscripts?

RQ5: What is the keyword and citation network of robo-advising and smart wealth management?

Data Extraction and Search Criteria Model

The following is a summary of the final search criteria (Fig. **1**):

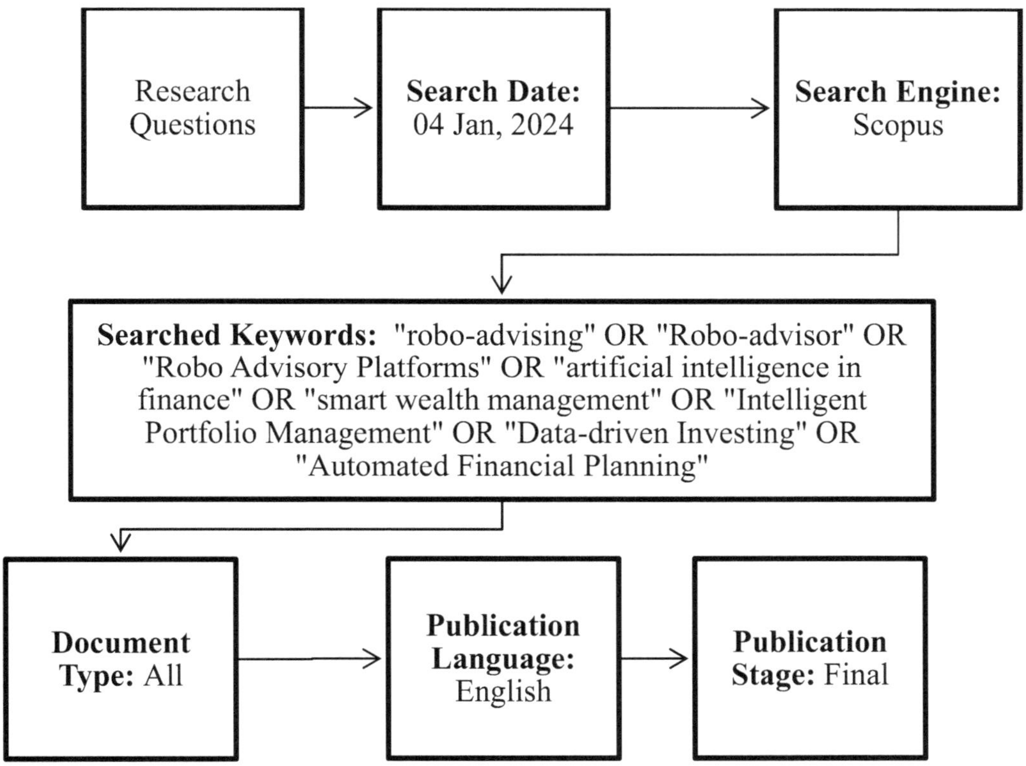

Fig. (1). Data search criteria model. Source: Authors

Selecting the appropriate search engine is crucial for data extraction. In this study, the Scopus database is chosen due to its extensive coverage, particularly featuring a high quantity of publications listed in the Journal Citation Reports (JCR). On January 4, 2024, 312 documents were retrieved from the Scopus database, utilizing Boolean operator ('OR') to identify specific items, as demonstrated in the study by (Costa *et al.* 2019; Bansal *et al.*, 2023) regarding robo-advising and smart wealth management. After removing the duplicates and missing entries, total 299 entries are left out. The data analysis is, thus, performed on these 299 documents.

To validate the accuracy of the data extracted from the Scopus database, the authors of this study scrutinized the records to verify whether the chosen studies were in line with research objectives.

FINDINGS

The bibliometric analysis of the relevant manuscripts extracted from the filtration process of the Scopus database is described comprehensively in this section. All the research questions are taken care of while doing the examination process of the data analysis.

Annual Publication Trend on Robo-advising and Smart Wealth Management

Robo-advising in relation to smart wealth management has been comprehensively analyzed. As represented by Fig. (**2**), it is visible that the researchers had very limited area to explore before 2016 as only one publication each can be seen in the years 2002,2003,2006 and 2013 Nil publication are noticed in the years 2004,2005,2007-2012,2014 and 2015. It was in the year 2017 that 10 publications can be seen to be made. The annual publication count jumped to 36 in the year 2018, after a rigorous rise. However, a slight decline in the annual publication trend is observed in the year 2019, counting the publication trend to be 34 maybe because the robo-advisory industry may have matured, resulting in fewer groundbreaking developments or newsworthy events that typically attract publications. 42 publications in the year 2020, 58 in the year 2021 and 60 in the year 2022 shows an appreciating increase in the subject matter. A remarkable increase in annual publication trend is observed till 2023, count to 66 publications, implying a heightened interest in the subject matter and an increased recognition and importance of the field within the academic and professional communities (Bijalwan, *et al.*, 2024). Since 2024 is still progressing, no judgments are applicable but a single publication being made in the year's commencement signals growth and development within that sector.

Document Type Published More Research Work on Robo-Advising and Smart Wealth Management

Fig. (**3**) indicates that a total of seven types of documents were found in 299 documents. Articles represent the most frequent document types that are being published, with a frequency of 156, thus accounting to more than half of the total publications. Second comes the conference papers counting to a total of 87, followed by book chapter publications(35), review(11), book(6), editorial and retracted documents to be 3 and 1 respectively.

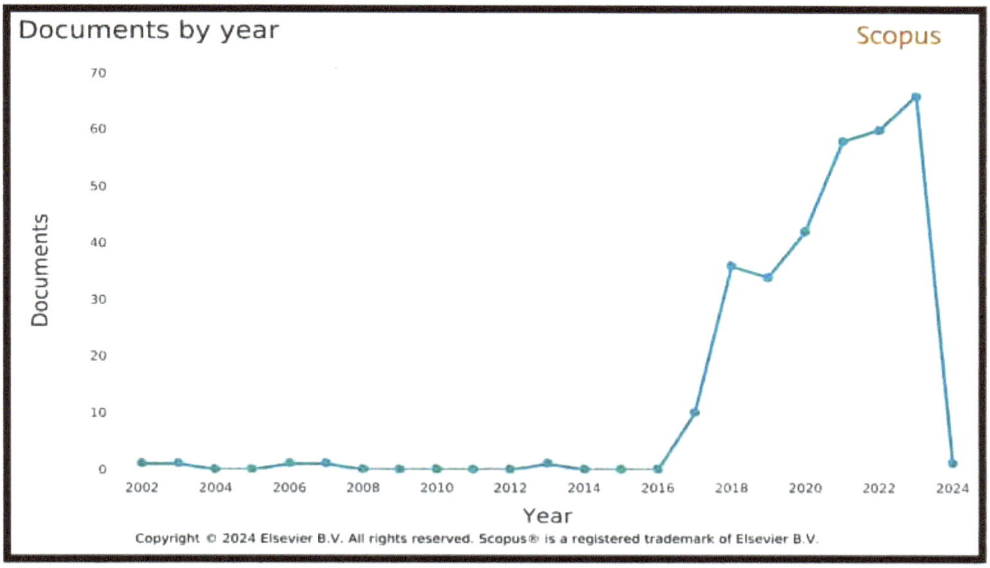

Fig. (2). Chart showing annual publication trend. Referenced from http://www.scopus.com on 4th January, 2024.

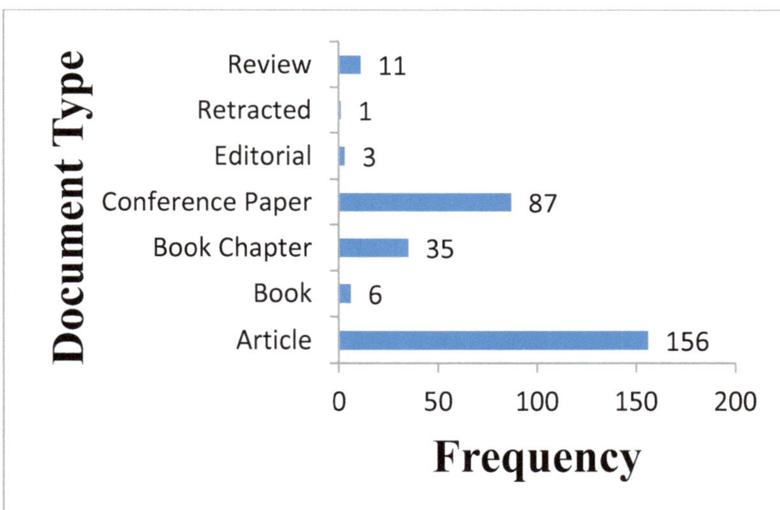

Fig. (3). Analysis by document type. Referenced from http://www.scopus.com on 4th January, 2024.

Subject Area that Published More Research Work on Robo-Advising and Smart Wealth Management

Fig. (**4**) represents subject areas where research in relation to robo-advising and smart wealth management has been made. The top among these stand the area of

Computer Science(24.4%), followed by Business, Management and Accounting(17.99%). Field of economics and social sciences can also be seen to be gaining strength with 15.7% and 9,9% respectively. It is noticed that other areas like decision sciences, and mathematics still need an exploration in this area of insurance concept.

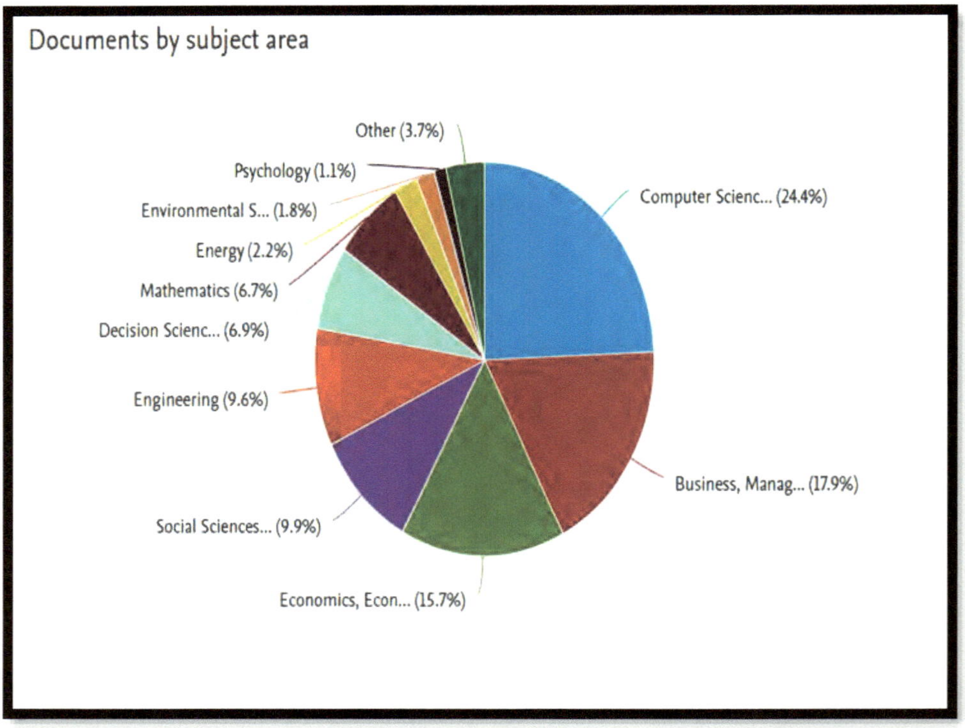

Fig. (4). Analysis by subject area. Referenced from http://www.scopus.com on 4th January, 2024.

Top Leading Countries that have Contributed More to Publishing Robo-Advising and Smart Wealth Management Manuscripts

Fig. (**5**) represents the top ten leading countries that have the maximum of publications till date. Also, Table 1 indicates the number of publications of the ten topmost countries contributed by each. It is clearly observable that United States is the top most country to publish the maximum number of manuscripts(54) in relation to robo-advising and smart wealth management. Germany has published 40 papers till now followed by China(39), India(20), Taiwan(16), United kingdom(15), South Korea(14), Australia and Ukraine(13 each) and France(12).

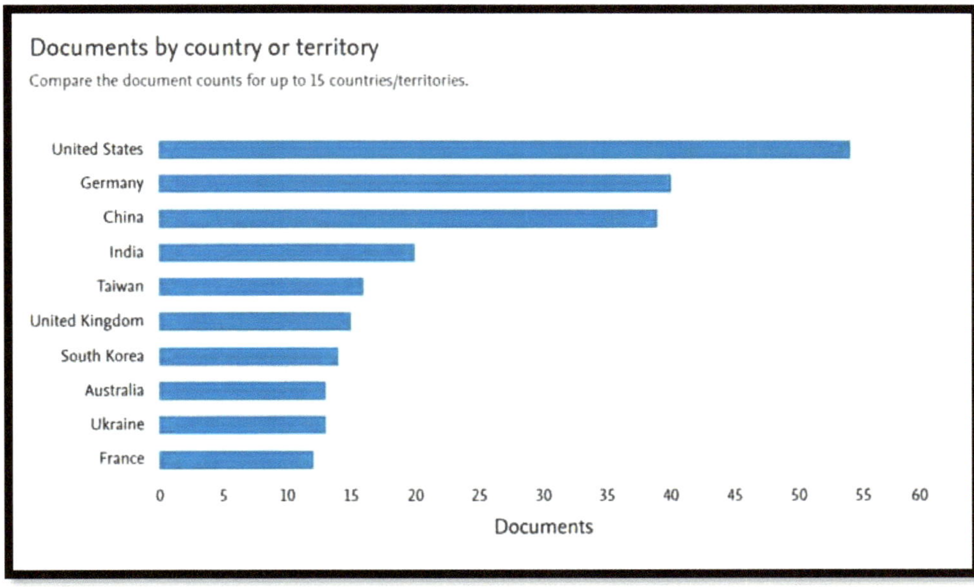

Fig. (5). Chart showing top leading countries. Referenced from http://www.scopus.com on 4th January, 2024.

Table 1. Top leading countries with frequency of documents published.

S. No.	Country	Number of Publications
1.	United States	54
2.	Germany	40
3.	China	39
4.	India	20
5.	Taiwan	16
6.	United Kingdom	15
7.	South Korea	14
8.	Australia	13
9.	Ukraine	13
10.	France	12

Source: Authors

Keywords And Citation Network Of Robo-Advising And Smart Wealth Management

Fig. (**6**) represents co-occurence analysis of all keywords, which has been shown by a network visualization map. Analyzing the co-occurrence of keywords is a method employed to track the evolution of a research domain across different time periods, as highlighted by Zhao, 2017; Singhal, *et al*., (2023). This approach proves to be an efficient means of identifying focal points within diverse fields (Goksu (2021).;Li *et al*.,2016).

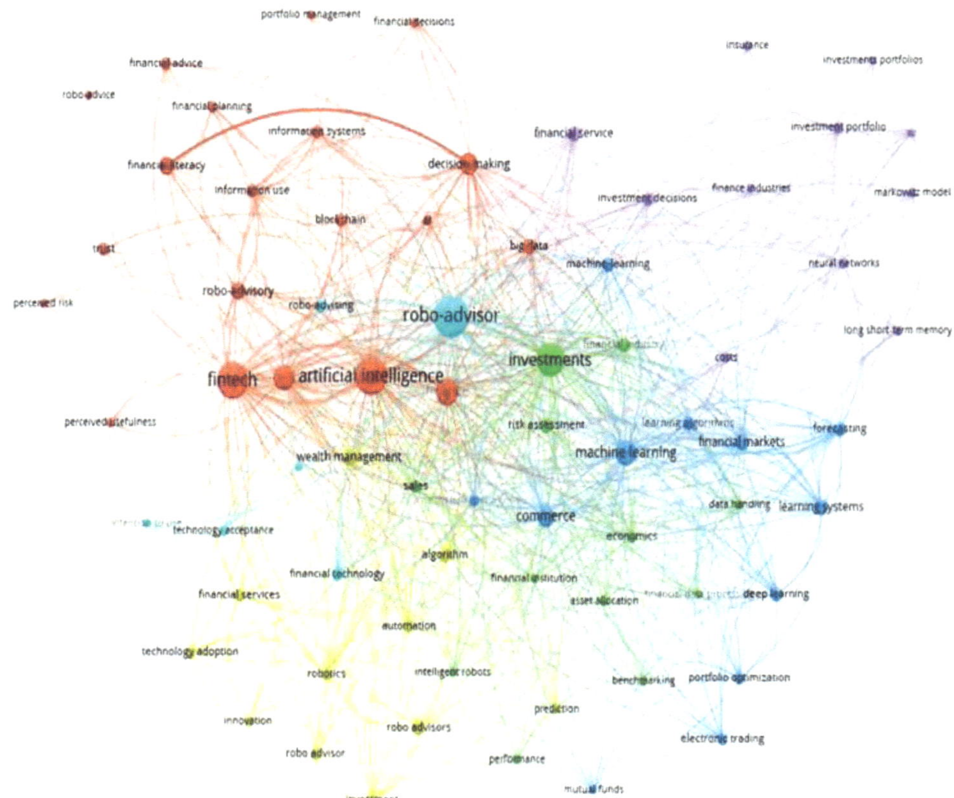

Fig. (6). Co-occurrence analysis of all keywords. Referenced from http://www.scopus.com on 4th January, 2024.

Out of the original 1506, 72 keywords were found to be important in the co-occurrence analysis of all keywords in VOS Viewer, with a minimum threshold of 5 occurrences. Specifically, the research emphasizes the term "robo advising" as the most common one, showing how important it is in the dataset. Not far behind are concepts like "artificial intelligence," which hint at key concepts and provide helpful information about the most common subjects in the examined material. In total, three clusters came out of the analysis. The largest cluster is the blue cluster having "robo-advisors", "machine learning" and "robo-advising" to be the most highlighted keywords. Second cluster is the purple cluster having the maximum keywords highlighted as “investment decisions”, “investment portfolio” and “insurance”. The most cited keywords in the third cluster, *i.e.*, the red one, indicate “artificial intelligence” and “fintech” to be the most highlighted keywords.

Fig. (**7**) represents the co-occurrence analysis of author keywords. Out of 773 keywords, 29 are deemed relevant in the VOS viewer co-occurrence analysis of author keywords, where a minimum threshold of 5 occurrences is used. The findings highlight the use of “fintech,” “robo advisors,” and “artificial intelligence,” indicating a heavy conceptual concentration in the dataset. This information is helpful for scholars since it reveals the authors' intended keywords and patterns.

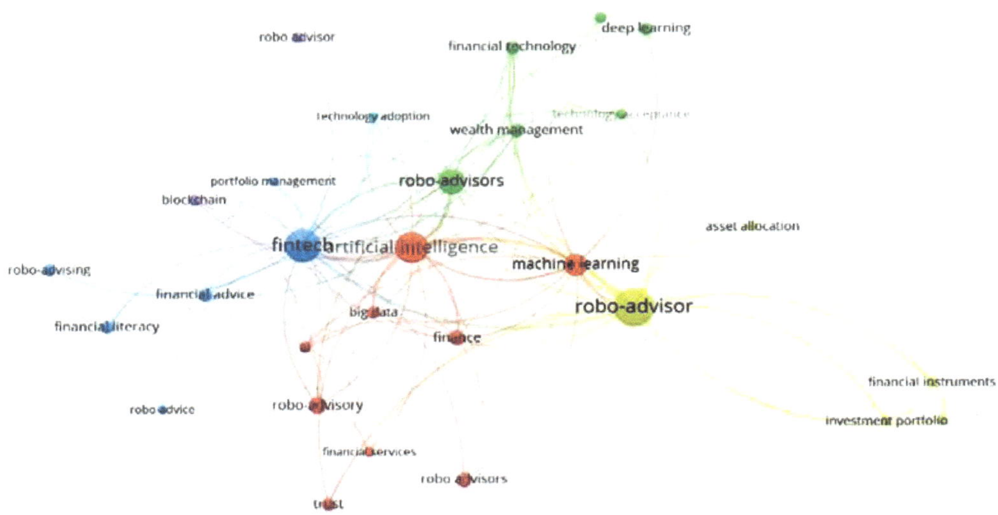

Fig. (7). Co-occurrence analysis of author keywords. Referenced from http://www.scopus.com on 4th January, 2024

The provided graphic in Fig. (**8**) displays the document with the maximum number of citations per author. Citation analysis gauges the frequency with which the two central papers are referenced jointly(Tang *et al.*, 2023). With 264 citations, Belanche *et al.* (2019) received the most attention, indicating that their study had a substantial effect. Following closely with 258 citations, Chen *et al.* (2019) demonstrate the scientific acknowledgment of their valuable contributions. With 130 citations, D'Acunto *et al.* (2019) established their work as a notable reference. Engin and Treleaven (2019) and Jung *et al.* (2018) both show a lot of influence, with 115 and 105 citations, correspondingly. The breakdown of citations highlights the scholarly impact of these authors' work, which might shape the future of the discipline and ensure that their discoveries are relevant for years to come. A better grasp of the citation dynamics may illuminate the academic scene and highlight seminal works that have had an impression on the field.

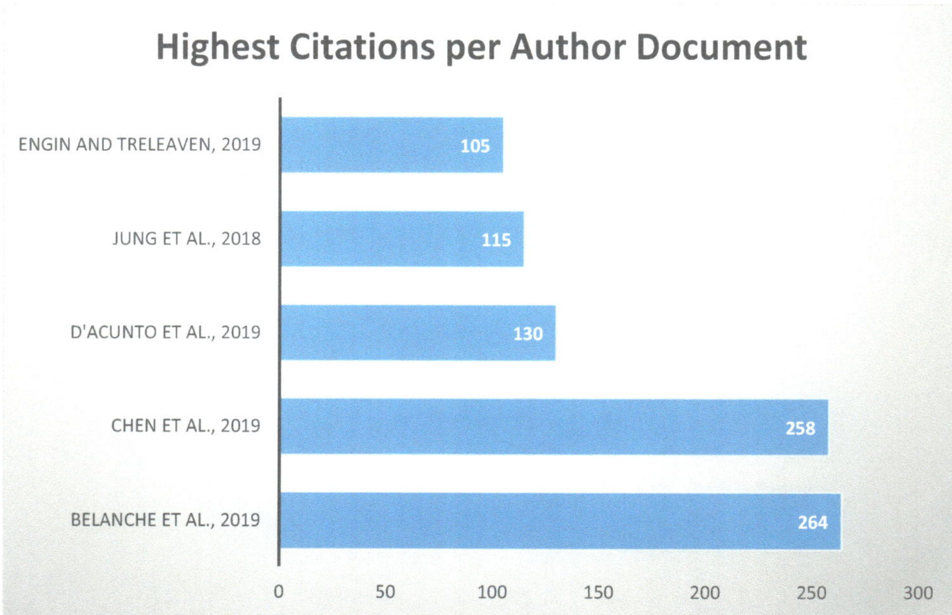

Fig. (8). Citation network. Referenced from http://www.scopus.com on 4th January, 2024.

DISCUSSION

The answers to the various research questions framed in the methodology section have been given a detailed focus in this section. They are as follows:

RQ1: What is the annual publication trend on robo-advising and smart wealth management?

Fig. (**2**) provides information regarding the increase and decrease of the annual publication trend in the context of robo-advising and smart wealth management. Till the year 2016, the publication trend counts to nil or one clearly indicating limited awareness of the subject area or either limited resources to explore the area or researchers may not have been aware of the potential significance and relevance of the area, leading to a lack of exploration. However, this lack of research gained momentum from the year 2017 onwards showing an upward trend and then showing a very slight decline in the year 2019, dropping the trend count from 36 to 34. Furthermore, there has been a constant rise in the publication trend till 2023, clearly depicting the consistent efforts and contributions from researchers, academics, or practitioners in the area of robo-advising and smart wealth management (Fariya, Saini, & Kashif, 2024). Considering the year 2024, the commencement itself shows one publication available reflecting a glimpse into potential research trends or areas of focus for the year 2024.

RQ2: Which document type published more research work on robo-advising and smart wealth management?

Fig. (**3**) represents the document types found in robo-advising and smart wealth management. The most frequent document types is articles accouting to 62.2% of the total manuscripts published. Conference papers are at the second rank, making 29.09% of the total publications. Moreover, the other types of documents that are publishing manuscripts on robo-advising and smart wealth management context are book chapter publications, review,book, editorial and retracted .

RQ3: Which area published more research work on robo-advising and smart wealth management?

Fig. (**4**) clearly represents the subject area where robo-advising and smart wealth management manuscripts can been seen to have been published the most. Computer Science stands topmost of the areas to publish research papers on robo-advising concept. One of the probable reasons for the same could be that computer science plays a crucial role in developing algorithms. Business, management and accounting area has also seen a growing percentage of publishing papers in relation to the context followed by economics, social sciences and engineering.

RQ4: What are the leading countries that have contributed more to publishing robo-advising and smart wealth management manuscripts?

Fig. (**5**) and Table **1** show that United States has emerged to be the topmost leading country coming out with a total of 54 papers in relation to robo-advising and smart wealth management concept. The country has a queue of Germany, China, India, Taiwan, United Kingdom, South Korea, Australia, Ukraine and France.

RQ5: What is the keyword and citation network of robo-advising and smart wealth management?

Fig. (**6**) shows that out of the 72 words selected, the term "robo-advising" is the most common one, followed by artificial intelligence, thus representing that the two keywords are being used most commonly together for the maximum number of times. Fig. (**7**) indicates the author keyword usage implying that fintech," "robo advisors," and "artificial intelligence," have a heavy conceptual concentration in the dataset.

With 264 citations, Belanche *et al.*(2019) has the highest number of citations which is represented by Fig. (**8**), followed by (Chen *et al.*,2019; Kashif, *et al.*, 2023a) having a count of 258 citations.

LIMITATIONS AND RECOMMENDATIONS

In spite of the fact that this research is a comprehensive work, there are certain drawbacks. The study employed the usage of only Scopus database to conduct the bibliometric analysis. However, it is recommended that future researchers can consider other databases or the collaborative database work for selection of research manuscripts. Also, the language filtered of the manuscripts is confined to 'English' only. However, further research can be done including various other languages like Chinese, Portugese and Spanish. Journal-wise affiliation of research publications can also be studied by future researchers (Kashif, *et al.*, 2023b). It is strongly recommended by the authors that there is a vast scope of further research to be done by including the concept of sustainability in relation to robo-advising and smart wealth management.

CONCLUSION

The present research work highlights a bibliometric analysis of the evolving landscape of robo-advising for smart wealth management. The examination of relevant literature and research contributions has allowed us to discern key trends, emerging themes, and influential factors within this dynamic field. As the financial industry increasingly embraces technological advancements, the findings underscore the significance of sustainable practices in the development and implementation of robo-advisory and smart wealth management solutions. By addressing critical research questions and synthesizing diverse perspectives, this study contributes valuable insights that can inform future endeavors in the pursuit of sustainable and effective financial technologies. Total 299 papers were retrieved from the Scopus database, after the filtration process covering the 2002 to January 2024 time span. The analysis reveals that researchers' focused on robo-advisiors peaked in from 2017 onwards, followed by a little fluctuating pattern of increased and decreased publications in subsequent years. The primary research areas associated with robo-advising are computer science, and business, management and accounting. United States stands out as the leading contributor, when analyzed country-wise, to robo-advising and smart wealth management publications. Articles constitute the majority of the publications on robo-advising and smart wealth management, followed by the conference paper document type. It was observed by the authors that there are no papers that have included the concept of sustainability in relation to robo-advising and smart wealth management. The authors hope that this analysis serves as a foundation for continued research and innovation in the realm of robo-advising and smart wealth management, fostering a sustainable and resilient financial landscape.

REFERENCES

Abdullah, & Naved Khan, M. (2021). Determining mobile payment adoption: A systematic literature search and bibliometric analysis. *Cogent Business & Management, 8*(1), 1893245.

Ampah, J.D., Yusuf, A.A., Afrane, S., Jin, C., Liu, H. (2021). Reviewing two decades of cleaner alternative marine fuels: Towards IMO's decarbonization of the maritime transport sector. *J. Clean. Prod., 320*, 128871. [http://dx.doi.org/10.1016/j.jclepro.2021.128871]

Aria, M., Misuraca, M., Spano, M. (2020). Mapping the evolution of social research and data science on 30 years of social indicators research. *Soc. Indic. Res., 149*(3), 803-831. [http://dx.doi.org/10.1007/s11205-020-02281-3]

Avikal, S., Singh, R., Barthwal, A., Ram, M. (2023). COVID-19: a Kano model and AHP-based classification of preventive activities under Fuzzy environment. *International Journal of Quality & Reliability Management.*

Badhotiya, G.K., Avikal, S., Soni, G., Sengar, N. (2022). Analyzing barriers for the adoption of circular economy in the manufacturing sector. *Int. J. Prod. Perform. Manag., 71*(3), 912-931. [http://dx.doi.org/10.1108/IJPPM-01-2021-0021]

Bansal, N., Bhatnagar, M., Taneja, S. (2023). Balancing priorities through green optimism: A study elucidating initiatives, approaches, and strategies for sustainable supply chain management. *Handbook of Research on Designing Sustainable Supply Chains to Achieve a Circular Economy.* [http://dx.doi.org/10.4018/978-1-6684-7664-2.ch004]

Bhatia, A., Chandani, A., Atiq, R., Mehta, M., Divekar, R. (2021). Artificial intelligence in financial services: a qualitative research to discover robo-advisory services. *Qualitative Research in Financial Markets, 13*(5), 632-654. [http://dx.doi.org/10.1108/QRFM-10-2020-0199]

Bianchi, M., Brière, M. (2020). Robo-advising for small investors. *SSRN Electronic Journal.* [http://dx.doi.org/10.2139/ssrn.3751620]

Bijalwan, P., Gupta, A., Mendiratta, A., Johri, A., Asif, M. (2024). Predicting the Productivity of Municipality Workers: A Comparison of Six Machine Learning Algorithms. *Economies, 12*(1), 16. [http://dx.doi.org/10.3390/economies12010016]

Brenner, L., Meyll, T. (2020). Robo-advisors: A substitute for human financial advice? *J. Behav. Exp. Finance, 25*, 100275. [http://dx.doi.org/10.1016/j.jbef.2020.100275]

Capponi, A., Ólafsson, S., Zariphopoulou, T. (2022). Personalized robo-advising: Enhancing investment through client interaction. *Manage. Sci., 68*(4), 2485-2512. [http://dx.doi.org/10.1287/mnsc.2021.4014]

Cavalcante, W.Q.F., Coelho, A., Bairrada, C.M. (2021). Sustainability and tourism marketing: A bibliometric analysis of publications between 1997 and 2020 using vosviewer software. *Sustainability (Basel), 13*(9), 4987. [http://dx.doi.org/10.3390/su13094987]

Chaudhry, V. (2020). Static structural analysis of humerus bone to find out the load at which fracture occurs and predict suitable alternative materials for bone implants. *Mater. Today Proc., 26*, 1701-1706. [http://dx.doi.org/10.1016/j.matpr.2020.02.359]

Costa, D.F., Carvalho, F.M., Moreira, B.C.M. (2019). Behavioral economics and behavioral finance: a bibliometric analysis of the scientific fields. *J. Econ. Surv., 33*(1), 3-24. [http://dx.doi.org/10.1111/joes.12262]

Chishti, S., Puschmann, T. (2018). The Wealthtech book: The FinTech handbook for investors, entrepreneurs and finance visionaries. *John Wiley & Sons.* [http://dx.doi.org/10.1002/9781119444510]

D'Acunto, F., Prabhala, N., Rossi, A.G. (2019). The promises and pitfalls of robo-advising. *Rev. Financ. Stud., 32*(5), 1983-2020. [http://dx.doi.org/10.1093/rfs/hhz014]

Donthu, N., Kumar, S., Mukherjee, D., Pandey, N., Lim, W.M. (2021). How to conduct a bibliometric analysis: An overview and guidelines. *J. Bus. Res., 133*, 285-296. [http://dx.doi.org/10.1016/j.jbusres.2021.04.070]

Donthu, N., Reinartz, W., Kumar, S., Pattnaik, D. (2021). A retrospective review of the first 35 years of the International Journal of Research in Marketing. *Int. J. Res. Mark., 38*(1), 232-269. [http://dx.doi.org/10.1016/j.ijresmar.2020.10.006]

Van Eck, N.J., Waltman, L. (2017). Citation-based clustering of publications using CitNetExplorer and VOSviewer. *Scientometrics, 111*(2), 1053-1070. [http://dx.doi.org/10.1007/s11192-017-2300-7] [PMID: 28490825]

Fariya, Saini, A., & Kashif, M. (2024). Exploring the Influence of Factors Driving Financial Accessibility, Financial Activities, and Financial Education on Sustainable Development. In Artificial Intelligence and Machine Learning-Powered Smart Finance (pp. 23-49). IGI Global.

Finn, R. L., Wadhwa, K. (2014). The ethics of "smart" advertising and regulatory initiatives in the consumer intelligence industry. *info, 16*(3), 22-39.

Gennaioli, N., Shleifer, A., Vishny, R. (2015). Money Doctors. *J. Finance, 70*(1), 91-114. [http://dx.doi.org/10.1111/jofi.12188]

Goksu, I. (2021). Bibliometric mapping of mobile learning. *Telemat. Inform., 56*, 101491. [http://dx.doi.org/10.1016/j.tele.2020.101491]

Grealish, A., Kolm, P.N. (2021). Robo-advisory: From investing principles and algorithms to future developments. *Machine learning in financial markets: A guide to contemporary practice. Cambridge: Cambridge University Press.*

Gupta, S., Modgil, S., Bhattacharyya, S., Bose, I. (2022). Artificial intelligence for decision support systems in the field of operations research: review and future scope of research. *Ann. Oper. Res., 308*(1-2), 215-274. [http://dx.doi.org/10.1007/s10479-020-03856-6]

Hogan, P. H., Miller, R. (2013). Explaining risk to clients: An advisory perspective. *The Market for Retirement Financial Advice,* 46.

Hohenberger, C., Lee, C., Coughlin, J.F. (2019). Acceptance of robo□advisors: Effects of financial experience, affective reactions, and self-enhancement motives. *Financ. Plann. Rev., 2*(2), e1047. [http://dx.doi.org/10.1002/cfp2.1047]

Holtfort, T., Horsch, A., Schwarz, J. (2022). Robo-advisors as part of industry 4.0 in financial markets: Evolutionary development, methods, and first performance insights. *Risk Governance and Control: Financial Markets and Institutions, 12*(2), 38-46. [http://dx.doi.org/10.22495/rgcv12i2p3]

Jung, D., Glaser, F., Köpplin, W. (2019). Robo-advisory: opportunities and risks for the future of financial advisory. *Advances in Consulting Research: Recent Findings and Practical Cases,* 405-427. [http://dx.doi.org/10.1007/978-3-319-95999-3_20]

Jung, D., Dorner, V., Glaser, F., and Morana, S. (2018). Robo-Advisory - Digitalization and Automation of Financial Advisory, Business & Information Systems Engineering (60:1), pp. 81–86.

Kashif, M., Singhal, N., Goyal, S., Singh, S.K. (2024). Foreign Exchange Reserves and Economic Growth of

Brazil: A Nonlinear Approach. *Finance: Theory and Practice, 28*(1), 145-154.

Kashif, M., Shajar, S.N., Singhal, N., Kumar, P. (2023). Achieving sustainable investment practices through green finance: Challenges and opportunities. *Sustainable Investments in Green Finance,* 234-244. [http://dx.doi.org/10.4018/979-8-3693-1388-6.ch016]

Kashif, M., Kumar, P., Ghai, S., Kumar, S. (2023). Disruptive Technologies in Computational Finance. *Algorithmic Approaches to Financial Technology: Forecasting, Trading, and Optimization,* 46-60.

Kearney, A. T. (2015). Hype vs. Reality: The Coming Waves of" Robo" Adoption. Robo-Advisory Services Study, June.

Lepri, B., Oliver, N., Letouzé, E., Pentland, A., Vinck, P. (2018). Fair, transparent, and accountable algorithmic decision-making processes: The premise, the proposed solutions, and the open challenges. *Philos. Technol., 31*(4), 611-627.
[http://dx.doi.org/10.1007/s13347-017-0279-x]

Li, H., An, H., Wang, Y., Huang, J., Gao, X. (2016). Evolutionary features of academic articles co-keyword network and keywords co-occurrence network: Based on two-mode affiliation network. *Physica A, 450*, 657-669.
[http://dx.doi.org/10.1016/j.physa.2016.01.017]

Moral-Muñoz, J.A., Herrera-Viedma, E., Santisteban-Espejo, A., Cobo, M.J. (2020). Software tools for conducting bibliometric analysis in science: An up-to-date review. *Prof. Inf., 29*(1)
[http://dx.doi.org/10.3145/epi.2020.ene.03]

Mehra, A., Gupta, O., Avikal, S. (2023). Finding the combined effect of academic and non-academic performance on management students' placement: A fuzzy logic approach. *Int. J. Manag. Educ., 21*(3), 100837.
[http://dx.doi.org/10.1016/j.ijme.2023.100837]

Manzoor, S.I., Singla, J. (2019). Fake news detection using machine learning approaches: A systematic review. *3rd international conference on trends in electronics and informatics (ICOEI),* 230-234.
[http://dx.doi.org/10.1109/ICOEI.2019.8862770]

Nigam, M.K., Avikal, S., Ram, M. (2021). Risk assessment in ERP project by COPRAS method under fuzzy environment. *Int. J. Reliab. Qual. Saf. Eng., 28*(6), 2140006.
[http://dx.doi.org/10.1142/S0218539321400064]

Ostern, N.K., Schöler, J., Moormann, J. (2020). Toward Voice-Enabled Robotic Advisory for Personalized Wealth Management. *AMCIS.*

Pagán Castaño, J., Arnal-Pastor, M., Pagán-Castaño, E., Guijarro-García, M. (2023). Bibliometric analysis of the literature on critical thinking: an increasingly important competence for higher education students. *Economic research-. Ekon. Istraz., 36*(2)

Phoon, K., Koh, F. (2017). Robo-advisors and wealth management. *J. Altern. Invest., 20*(3), 79-94.
[http://dx.doi.org/10.3905/jai.2018.20.3.079]

Rossi, A. G., Utkus, S. P. (2020). *Who benefits from robo-advising?.Evidence from Machine Learning.*

Raza, K., Thotakura, N., Kumar, P., Joshi, M., Bhushan, S., Bhatia, A., Kumar, V., Malik, R., Sharma, G., Guru, S.K., Katare, O.P. (2015). C 60 -fullerenes for delivery of docetaxel to breast cancer cells: A promising approach for enhanced efficacy and better pharmacokinetic profile. *Int. J. Pharm., 495*(1), 551-559.
[http://dx.doi.org/10.1016/j.ijpharm.2015.09.016] [PMID: 26383841]

Sharma, R., Jasrotia, K., Singh, N., Ghosh, P., srivastava, S., Sharma, N.R., Singh, J., Kanwar, R., Kumar, A. (2020). A comprehensive review on hydrothermal carbonization of biomass and its applications. *Chemistry Africa, 3*(1), 1-19.
[http://dx.doi.org/10.1007/s42250-019-00098-3]

Sabharwal, C. L. (2018). The rise of machine learning and robo-advisors in banking. *IDRBT Journal of Banking Technology,* 28.

Serrano, W. (2023). Smart or Intelligent Assets or Infrastructure: Technology with a Purpose. *Buildings, 13*(1), 131.
[http://dx.doi.org/10.3390/buildings13010131]

Sheth, J.N., Jain, V., Roy, G., Chakraborty, A. (2022). AI-driven banking services: the next frontier for a personalised experience in the emerging market. *Int. J. Bank Mark., 40*(6), 1248-1271.
[http://dx.doi.org/10.1108/IJBM-09-2021-0449]

Siccardi, S., Villa, V. (2022). Trends in Adopting BIM, IoT and DT for Facility Management: A Scientometric Analysis and Keyword Co-Occurrence Network Review. *Buildings, 13*(1), 15.
[http://dx.doi.org/10.3390/buildings13010015]

Sidhu, A.K., Singh, H., Virdi, S.S., Kumar, R. (2020). A Bibliometric Analysis on Job Stress using Visualizing Network. *Journal of Content Community and Communication, 12*(6), 21-29.
[http://dx.doi.org/10.31620/JCCC.12.20/04]

Singh, I., Kaur, N. (2017). Wealth management through robo advisory. *International Journal of Research - GRANTHAALAYAH, 5*(6), 33-43.
[http://dx.doi.org/10.29121/granthaalayah.v5.i6.2017.1991]

Singhal, N., Sultana, A., Goyal, S. (2023). Myth or coverage: experience and expectation of policyholders from health insurance during COVID-19 in the NCR region of India. *Future Business Journal, 9*(1), 39.
[http://dx.doi.org/10.1186/s43093-023-00209-0]

So, M.K.P. (2021). Robo-advising risk profiling through content analysis for sustainable development in the Hong Kong financial market. *Sustainability (Basel), 13*(3), 1306.
[http://dx.doi.org/10.3390/su13031306]

Singh, A.K., Verma, R.P., Avikal, S., Mehra, K.S. (2021). Mechanical characterization of epoxy composite reinforced with alkali treated walnut shell powder. *Mater. Today Proc., 46*, 10642-10646.
[http://dx.doi.org/10.1016/j.matpr.2021.01.383]

Singh, R., Avikal, S., Rashmi, R., Ram, M. (2020). A Kano model, AHP and TOPSIS based approach for selecting the best mobile phone under a fuzzy environment. *Int. J. Qual. Reliab. Manage., 37*(6/7), 837-851.
[http://dx.doi.org/10.1108/IJQRM-01-2020-0022]

Tang, K.Y., Chang, C.Y., Hwang, G.J. (2023). Trends in artificial intelligence-supported e-learning: a systematic review and co-citation network analysis (1998–2019). *Interact. Learn. Environ., 31*(4), 2134-2152.
[http://dx.doi.org/10.1080/10494820.2021.1875001]

Tao, R., Su, C.W., Xiao, Y., Dai, K., Khalid, F. (2021). Robo advisors, algorithmic trading and investment management: Wonders of fourth industrial revolution in financial markets. *Technol. Forecast. Soc. Change, 163*, 120421.
[http://dx.doi.org/10.1016/j.techfore.2020.120421]

Torno, A., Metzler, D. R., Torno, V. (2021). Robo-What?, Robo-Why?, Robo-How?-A Systematic Literature Review of Robo-Advice. *PACIS, 92.*

van Eck, N.J., Waltman, L., Dekker, R., van den Berg, J. (2010). A comparison of two techniques for bibliometric mapping: Multidimensional scaling and VOS. *J. Am. Soc. Inf. Sci. Technol., 61*(12), 2405-2416.
[http://dx.doi.org/10.1002/asi.21421]

Vyas, A., Sharma, A., Prasad, R. (2023). Robo-advisors as Automatic Personal Financial Advisors: Opportunities and Challenges Based on Recent Results and Case Studies. *J. Manag. Res., 15*(1), 2-9.

Xiang, Y., Zhixi, L.I., Tsz-Ho, L.E.E., Du, T.A.N.G., Kent, W.U., Zhibin, L.E.I., Yali, W.A.N.G. (2019). Smart Wealth Management System for Robo-Advisory. *Conference on Computational Intelligence for Financial Engineering & Economics (CIFEr),* 1-6.

Xie, L., Chen, Z., Wang, H., Zheng, C., Jiang, J. (2020). Bibliometric and visualized analysis of scientific publications on atlantoaxial spine surgery based on Web of Science and VOSviewer. *World Neurosurg., 137*,

435-442.e4.
[http://dx.doi.org/10.1016/j.wneu.2020.01.171] [PMID: 32006737]

Yi, T.Z., Rom, N.A.M., Hassan, N.M., Samsurijan, M.S., Ebekozien, A. (2023). The Adoption of Robo-Advisory among Millennials in the 21st Century: Trust, Usability and Knowledge Perception. *Sustainability (Basel), 15*(7), 6016.
[http://dx.doi.org/10.3390/su15076016]

Zerilli, J., Knott, A., Maclaurin, J., Gavaghan, C. (2019). Transparency in algorithmic and human decision-making: is there a double standard? *Philos. Technol., 32*(4), 661-683.
[http://dx.doi.org/10.1007/s13347-018-0330-6]

Zhao, X. (2017). A scientometric review of global BIM research: Analysis and visualization. *Autom. Construct., 80*, 37-47.
[http://dx.doi.org/10.1016/j.autcon.2017.04.002]

CHAPTER 14

Big Data and Insurance: A Bibliometric Analysis

Rajeev Srivastava[1], **Ankit Srivastava**[1,*] and **Sneha Badola**[1]

[1] *School of Management, IMS Unison University, Dehradun, India*

Abstract: The radical shift observed in industries from physical to digital platforms has escalated the implications of data depositories. The extent to which data is growing is exponential. The insurance industry is no exception. The availability of data on various digital platforms has contributed to an enormous amount of repositories in a short span of time. The present study is focused on performance analysis of the research constituents that contributed to the domain of insurance industry and Big Data. An analysis of 541 research publications from 2012 to 2023 retrieved from the WoS database from more than 2000 authors is performed using the bibliophily app, highlighting trends and contributions by authors, Universities, and countries. The findings showed that big data has improved the process of database management and profiling in the insurance sector, further easing the claim process. This study will assist researchers and practitioners in understanding the past and present research trends in the area.

Keywords: Big data, Bibliometric analysis, Database management, Data-driven industries, Insurance.

INTRODUCTION

The last decade has witnessed massive advancement in the field of technology, especially in information technology. This development in IT has led to huge data trafficking in all industries that contain large volumes of structured and unstructured data, better known as big data. It is expected that the amount of data will reach about 149 zettabytes by the year 2024 (Mahanti, 2022). All industries are using big data to achieve a competitive edge against their competitors, and the insurance industry is no exception (Fang, Jiang, & Song, 2016). It is one of the intensive data-driven industries.

* **Corresponding author Ankit Srivastava:** School of Management, IMS Unison University, Dehradun, India; E-mail: ankit.srivastava@iuu.ac

The increasing usage of the internet, personal computing, and smartphones has led to the creation of big data that is high in volume, variety, and velocity. The insurance industry uses data analytics to better understand and evaluate risk ((Roy *et al*., 2022; Hussain & Prieto, 2016; Senousy, Mohamed, & Riad, 2018). The insurance industry manages and mitigates various risks and provides financial protection against risks faced by individuals and businesses with the help of a vast range of insurance products (Keller *et al*., 2018; Barry & Charpentier, 2020; Avikal *et al.* 2023).

Many studies have been contributed by researchers to understand how big data is helping insurance players achieve the desired results, but it is also necessary to focus on various research constituents in this field (Mahate *et al.* 2023; Singh *et al.* 2020). To understand the research trend of big data and insurance, it is important to learn about the contributions from relevant scholars, sources, geographical regions, and affiliations.

RESEARCH METHODOLOGY

When it comes to the search for "big data in the insurance sector" among extant sources, it is observed that extensive research is conducted by scholars on the above-mentioned topic (Bhushan *et al*., 2021). On delving into the insights of the subjects, it was noticed that huge developments had been made through big data in the field of insurance (Avikal *et al.* 2021; Kumar *et al*., 2020). Hence, bibliometric analysis was conducted (Tiwari, Bahuguna, & Srivastava, 2023; Kashif, Shajar, Singhal, & Kumar, 2023). The studies conducted show that studies on "big data in the insurance sector" have increased over the years crediting its potential in the sphere of research (Kc *et al.* 2020; Sharma *et al.* 2019). The current study aims to perform a meta-analysis of the keyword "big data in the insurance sector" for the period between 2012-2023 using bibliometric metadata (Joshi, *et al*., 2022; Singh *et al*., 2023).

The field analysis will be done according to variables such as keywords, authors, countries, citations, publications, universities, journals, and country-wise production. The following research questions are tried to be answered in this research:

What is the publication trend in the field of chosen research?

What are the trends of citation analysis?

Which are the most influential journals and authors?

What is the result of country product analysis?

What are keywords' distribution and trend?

RESEARCH DESIGN

This study is conducted by applying the bibliometric analysis method to a data set dealing with "big data in the insurance sector". The analysis focuses primarily on:

The results through the application of bibliometrics to explore the developments in the insurance sector, and exploration of keywords of articles to comprehend related research themes linked to insurance.

Obtaining Data Set

To achieve the purpose of the study, the Web of Science (WoS) is used for its integrity of exposure and authentication (Birkle *et al*., 2020). The use of WoS facilitated the extraction of various important articles with the keyword "big data in the insurance sector", covering a time frame of 2012 to 2023 from the WoS repository.

The subsequent search query was structured and used:

Topic: ("big data in the insurance sector") Timespan: 2012-2023.

Indexes: SCI-Expanded, SSCI, A&HCI, CPCI-S, CPCI-SSH, BKCI-S, BKCI-SSH, ESCI, CCR-Expanded, IC.

WoS was accessed on December 12, 2023, and 541 research articles, chapters, and publications were extracted.

Data Analysis

The analysis of authors, journals, keywords, country-wise production, and citations was performed on bibliometrics using VOS Viewer software. For the bibliography, the alliance of components was based on the number of shared resources, *i.e*., reference of a publication in multiple sources (Mehra *et al.* 2021). The co-occurrence analysis of keywords illustrates the progression of related fields over a while (Deng & Xia, 2020). Therefore, this is an effective approach to identifying topics in each research domain. Further, a citation analysis aids in detecting popular research topics and papers that are currently being worked on by researchers (Nicolaisen, 2007; Bahuguna, Srivastava, & Tiwari, 2023; Kashif, Kumar, Ghai, & Kumar, 2023).

Analysis Method

In the current study, bibliometrics is used to trace the framework of the research field. Bibliometrics is considered the most extensive way of tracing the framework of the research field (Kashif *et al.*, 2024; Li *et al.*, 2017).

Publication Trend

The study results are presented in the form of graphs, describing the progression of research over the number of years. The following Fig. (**1**) presents the total publication each year between 2012 and 2023.

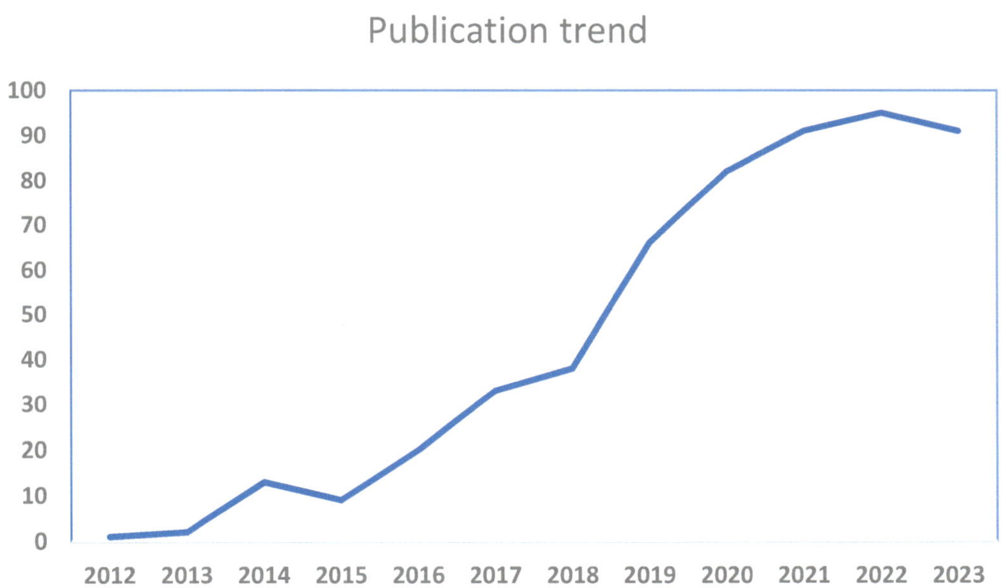

Fig. (1). Insurance publications published each year between 2012 and 2023. (Source: Analysis through Biblioshiny app).

Table **1** further reveals that research on "big data in the insurance sector" is significantly rising and has caught attention in the recent past, ranging from 01 (2012) to 91 (2023). There was a single article published in 2012, and 2 publications in 2013, however in 2014, the theme picked momentum and there were 13 publications in 2014, representing 2.5%; 9 publications in 2015, representing 1.7%; 20 publications in 2016, representing 3.9% of publications, 33 publications in 2017, representing 5.4% of publications. Further, 2018- 2023 have seen a steep rise in publications with publication numbers 38 (2018), 66 (2019), 82 (2020), 91 (2021), 95 (2022), and 91 (2023) respectively. Accordingly, these six years represent 90.6% of the total publications. We noticed the majority of the publication took place during and after COVID-19, indicating a realization of the need for insurance (Gupta, Abbas, & Srivastava, 2022).

Annual Growth Rate: 50.69%

Table 1. Annual growth rate (source: analysis through biblioshiny app).

Year	Articles
2012	1
2013	2
2014	13
2015	9
2016	20
2017	33
2018	38
2019	66
2020	82
2021	91
2022	95
2023	91

Table **2** and Fig. (**2**) reveal the Most Relevant Sources of publications. International Journal of Environmental Research and Public Health was the most relevant source of publication with 13 articles, followed by PLOS One with 10 articles. The same has been graphically represented in Fig. (**2**).

Table 2. Most relevant articles (source: analysis through biblioshiny app).

Sources	Articles
International Journal of Environmental Research and Public Health	13
PLOS One	10
IEEE Access	9
Journal of Medical Internet Research	8
Big Data & Society	7
Journal of Korean Medical Science	6
Mathematical Problems in Engineering	6
Journal of Big Data	5

(Table 2) cont.....

Sources	Articles
Journal of Clinical Medicine	5
Korean Journal of Pain	5

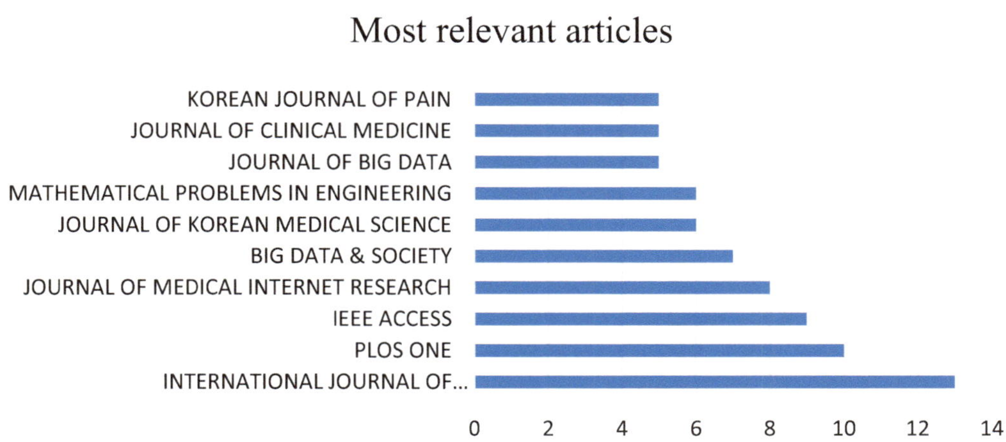

Fig. (2). Most relevant articles (source: analysis through biblioshiny app).

Citation Analysis

Citation analysis was performed to establish the significance of an article and identify the association between articles. The most significant research articles based on the journals and authors were selected to recognize the outline of research in the field of big data use in the insurance industry (Table **3**). Further, the total citation and the average citation (per year), *i.e.*, the total number of citations divided by the number of years since publication, were examined to assess the most influential articles. The average citation per year, presented in Table **4**, is measured to eliminate the possibility of higher citations of a paper merely because it was published earlier. Citron (2014) emerges as the most cited article, followed by Xu (2021). Citron (2014) also remains the most popular author in terms of citation per year (TC/yrs) followed by Khozin (2017).

Table 3. Most significant research articles (source: analysis through biblioshiny app).

S. No.	Source	H-index	TC	NP
1	Washington law review	1	394	1
2	IEEE Access	7	264	9
3	Journal of Healthcare Informatics Research	1	231	1
4	Journal of Medical Internet Research	6	213	8
5	BMC medicine	2	188	2

(Table 3) cont.....

S. No.	Source	H-index	TC	NP
6	JNCI-Journal of The National Cancer Institute	1	186	1
7	Journal of Big Data	4	171	5
8	Journal of Management Information Systems	2	167	2
9	Future Generation Computer Systems-The International Journal of Science	3	141	3
10	California law review	1	130	1
11	Big Data and Society	6	115	7
12	IEEE Transactions on Industrial Informatics	1	103	1
13	PLOS one	7	98	10
14	International Journal of Medical Informatics	4	90	4
15	International Journal of Environmental Research and Public Health	6	85	13
16	Journal of Korean Medical Science	4	58	6
17	Scientific reports	4	57	4
18	Journal of Clinical Medicine	3	29	5
19	Korean Journal of Pain	3	19	5
20	Mathematical Problems in Engineering	1	7	6

Table 4. Total citation per year (source: analysis through biblioshiny app).

Paper	Total Citations	TC Per Year
Citron Dk, 2014, Wash Law Rev	394	39.4
Xu J, 2021, J Healthc Inform Res	231	77
Khozin S, 2017, Jnci-J Natl Cancer I	186	26.571
Frhlich H, 2018, Bmc Med	184	30.667
Lehrer C, 2018, J Manage Inform Syst	160	26.667
Lin Ww, 2017, Ieee Access	132	18.857
Ajunwa I, 2017, Calif Law Rev	130	18.571
Johnson Jm, 2019, J Big Data-Ger	109	21.8
Fan K, 2018, Ieee T Ind Inform	103	17.167
Srinivasan U, 2013, It Prof	89	8.091
Chen Cm, 2020, J Med Internet Res	88	22
Wing Oej, 2020, Nat Commun	86	21.5
Terroso-Saenz F, 2019, Future Gener Comp Sy	86	17.2
Smuck M, 2021, Npj Digit Med	82	27.333
Hu Yf, 2019, Sustainability-Basel	76	15.2
Fitipaldi H, 2018, Diabetes	65	10.833

(Table 4) cont.....

Paper	Total Citations	TC Per Year
Hao Hj, 2017, Int J Med Inform	62	8.857
Prince Aer, 2020, Iowa Law Rev	60	15
Sahoo Ak, 2019, Computation	57	11.4
Karaca Y, 2019, Int J Inform Manage	57	11.4

Fig. (**3**) depicts the most cited authors, and Fig. (**4**) graphically explains the top-performing journals based on citation.

Fig. (3). Most cited authors (source: analysis through biblioshiny app).

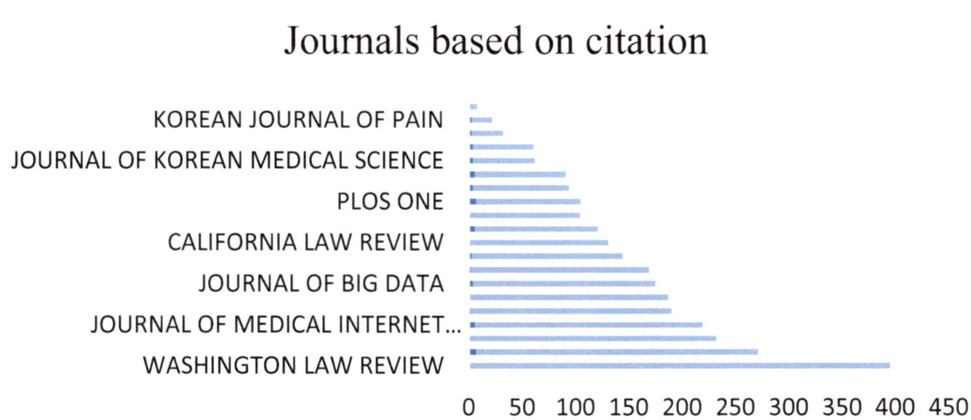

Fig. (4). Journals based on citation (source: analysis through biblioshiny app).

Most Cited Countries

The countries that have been majorly cited for their research articles in the area of big data and insurance were also studied. The USA is the most cited nation on the related research theme, crossing 2000 citations. It is followed by China and Korea. India is among the top five countries catering to the needs of the research area (Fig. **5**).

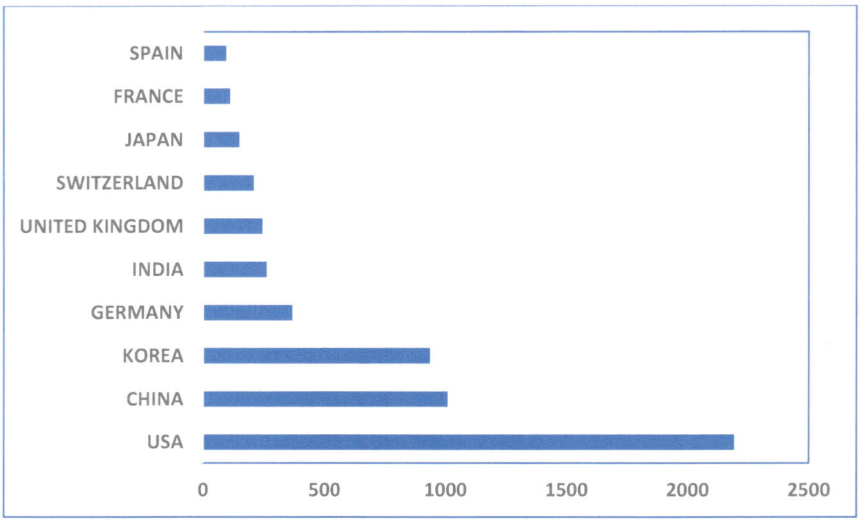

Fig. (5). Most cited countries (source: analysis through biblioshiny app).

Keyword Analysis

The keyword presents the themes of research articles (Tripathi et.al., 2018). A keyword analysis (using VOS Viewer) was performed to explore the most prevalent themes in "big data in the insurance sector". An aggregate of 471 keywords were recognized in 541 articles. Table **5** and Fig. (**6**) below show the top keywords used in big data and insurance between 2012 and 2023. The most frequently used keyword, with 66 occurrences is "Big Data". It indicates the supremacy of the term in relevant literature. The next three important keywords are "risk" (51 occurrences), "care" (37 occurrences), and "prevalence" (33 occurrences). Fig. (**7**) further explains the word growth in the related field.

Table 5. Keyword analysis (source: analysis through biblioshiny app).

Words	Occurrences
Big data	66
Risk	51

(Table 5) cont.....

Words	Occurrences
Care	37
Prevalence	33
Impact	32
Management	28
Mortality	26
Disease	20
Association	19
Health	19
Population	18
Outcomes	17
Epidemiology	16
Insurance	16
Risk-factors	14
System	13
Challenges	12
Information	12
Diagnosis	11
Privacy	11

Fig. (6). Keyword Analysis (Source: Analysis through Biblioshiny app).

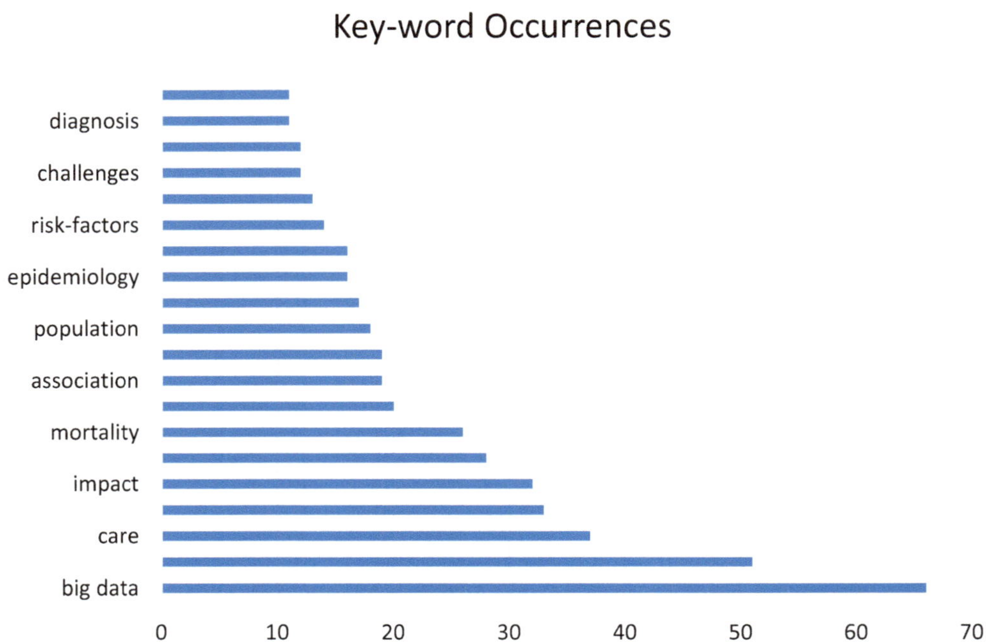

Fig. (7). Keyword Occurrences (Source: Analysis through Biblioshiny app).

Production Analysis

Production analysis is a tool used to analyze country-wise production in terms of research articles. SCP refers to single-country products, whereas MCP gives an insight into multiple-country production. Countries like Korea as presented in Fig. (**9**). The USA (85) have a high rate of production in terms of a single country, however, when it comes to multi-country production, the numbers are tremendously low which indicates a gap in terms of cross-country collaboration (Table **6**; Fig. **8**). This void needs to be filled through more country-wide collaboration, which will further enhance the varied perspectives on the subject.

Table 6. Country-wise Production Analysis (Source: Analysis through Biblioshiny app)

Country	SCP	MCP
Korea	124	7
USA	85	14
China	69	24
Japan	25	3
India	19	6

(Table 6) cont.....

Country	SCP	MCP
Germany	10	10
United Kingdom	7	8
France	7	7
Australia	8	4
Canada	7	3

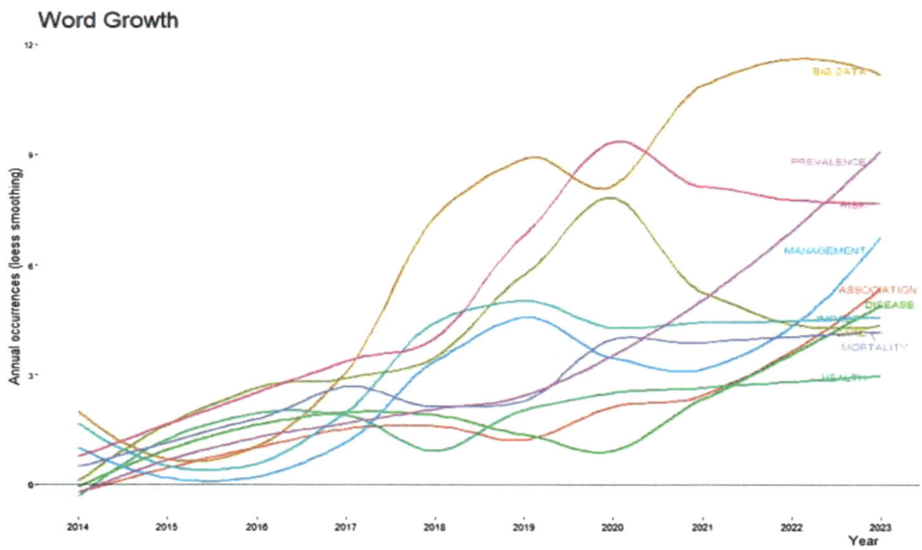

Fig. (8). Word growth (source: analysis through biblioshiny app).

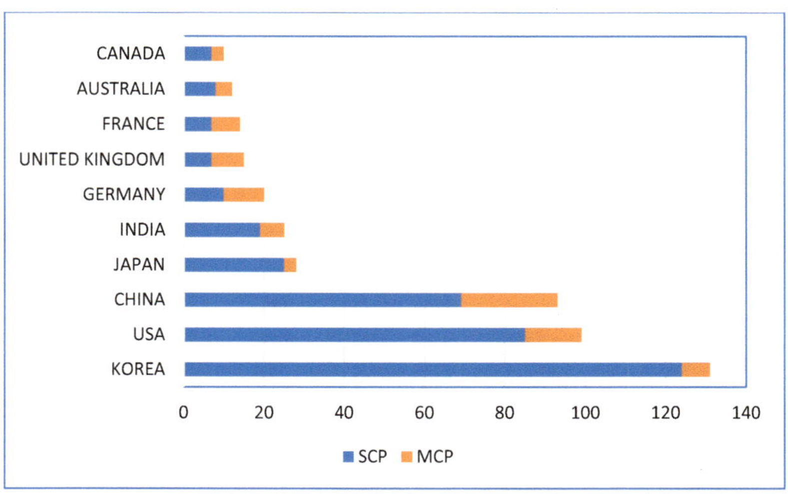

Fig. (9). Country-wise production analysis (source: analysis through biblioshiny app).

DISCUSSION AND CONCLUSION

Instituted to review the existing literature thoroughly, this article draws valuable insights into the use of big data in insurance. Research on such relatable topics is important for our society at large. The scholarly work reveals a lack of awareness of insurance among the masses. It also explains the extent of big data applications in the insurance sector (Fariya, *et al.*, 2024). The mounting use of big data has brought ease in the maintenance of records and hassle-free settlements to quite an extent. It can be taken as an alarming situation for the policymakers and other stakeholders to emphasize on improvisation of insurance reachability with a superb tool named big data. In most cases, researchers put substantial effort into investigating the subject. Insurance is a subject with vast implications for the physical, social, and economic well-being of any nation.

The analysis of 541 publications on the topic “big data in the insurance sector” between 2012 and 2023 was conducted. A quantitative analysis of the metadata was executed at the primary stage to conclude the output by publication year, nation, author, and country-wise production. The USA, England, China, and Korea were found to be leading the charts. However, a major analysis of the study reveals that single-country products are on the rise whereas multiple-country collaboration needs to increase which would allow a cross-cultural examination of the research area.

REFERENCES

Bahuguna, P.C., Srivastava, R., Tiwari, S. (2023). Two-decade journey of green human resource management research: a bibliometric analysis. *Benchmarking (Bradf.), 30*(2), 585-602. [http://dx.doi.org/10.1108/BIJ-10-2021-0619]

Barry, L., Charpentier, A. (2020). Personalization as a promise: Can Big Data change the practice of insurance? *Big Data Soc., 7*(1) [http://dx.doi.org/10.1177/2053951720935143]

Birkle, C., Pendlebury, D.A., Schnell, J., Adams, J. (2020). Web of Science as a data source for research on scientific and scholarly activity. *Quant. Sci. Stud., 1*(1), 363-376. [http://dx.doi.org/10.1162/qss_a_00018]

Danielle, K. (2014). Citron, The Scored Society: Due Process for Automated Predictions, 89Washington. *Law Rev.,* 1.

Deng, S., Xia, S. (2020). Mapping the interdisciplinarity in information behavior research: a quantitative study using diversity measure and co-occurrence analysis. *Scientometrics, 124*(1), 489-513. [http://dx.doi.org/10.1007/s11192-020-03465-x]

Fang, K., Jiang, Y., Song, M. (2016). Customer profitability forecasting using Big Data analytics: A case study of the insurance industry. *Comput. Ind. Eng., 101*, 554-564. [http://dx.doi.org/10.1016/j.cie.2016.09.011]

Fariya, Saini, A., & Kashif, M. (2024). Exploring the Influence of Factors Driving Financial Accessibility, Financial Activities, and Financial Education on Sustainable Development. In Artificial Intelligence and Machine Learning-Powered Smart Finance (pp. 23-49). IGI Global.

Gupta, S., Abbas, A.F., Srivastava, R. (2022). Technology Acceptance Model (TAM): A bibliometric analysis from inception. *Journal of Telecommunications and the Digital Economy, 10*(3), 77-106. [http://dx.doi.org/10.18080/jtde.v10n3.598]

Hussain, K., Prieto, E. (2016). Big Data in the Finance and Insurance. *E. C. José María Cavanillas, New Horizons for a Data-Driven Economy.* Springer Open. [http://dx.doi.org/10.1007/978-3-319-21569-3_12]

Joshi, K., Kumar, V., Anandaram, H., Kumar, R., Gupta, A., Krishna, K.H. (2023). A review approach on deep learning algorithms in computer vision. *Intelligent Systems and Applications in Computer Vision,* 1-15. [http://dx.doi.org/10.1201/9781003453406-1]

Singh, A., Taneja, S., Kumar, P. (2023). Algorithmic approaches to financial technology: Forecasting, trading, and optimization. *Algorithmic Approaches to Financial Technology..* Forecasting, Trading, and Optimization.

Kashif, M., Singhal, N., Goyal, S., Singh, S.K. (2024). Foreign Exchange Reserves and Economic Growth of Brazil: A Nonlinear Approach. *Finance: Theory and Practice, 28*(1), 145-154.

Kashif, M., Shajar, S.N., Singhal, N., Kumar, P. (2023). Achieving sustainable investment practices through green finance: Challenges and opportunities. *Sustainable Investments in Green Finance.,* 234-244. [http://dx.doi.org/10.4018/979-8-3693-1388-6.ch016]

Kashif, M., Kumar, P., Ghai, S., Kumar, S. (2023). Disruptive Technologies in Computational Finance. *Algorithmic Approaches to Financial Technology: Forecasting, Trading, and Optimization,* 46-60.

Keller, B., Eling, M., Schmeiser, H., Christen, M., Loi, M. (2018). Big data and insurance: implications for innovation, competition and privacy. *Geneva Association-International Association for the Study of Insurance Economics.*

Khozin, S., Blumenthal, G.M., Pazdur, R. (2017). Real-world data for clinical evidence generation in oncology. *J. Natl. Cancer Inst., 109*(11), djx187. [http://dx.doi.org/10.1093/jnci/djx187] [PMID: 29059439]

Li, X., Wu, P., Shen, G.Q., Wang, X., Teng, Y. (2017). Mapping the knowledge domains of Building Information Modeling (BIM): A bibliometric approach. *Autom. Construct., 84*, 195-206. [http://dx.doi.org/10.1016/j.autcon.2017.09.011]

Mahanti, D. R. (2022, December 17). Interesting statistics around big data, data analysis, and usage. Available from: www.medium.comhttps://medium.com/analysts-corner/interesting-statistics-around-big-data-data-analysis-and-usage-c69b29ff5ea#:~:text=By%202024%2C%20149%20zettabytes %20of,data%20are%20created%20every%20day.

Nicolaisen, J. (2007). Citation analysis. *Annu. Rev. Inform. Sci. Tech., 41*(1), 609-641. [http://dx.doi.org/10.1002/aris.2007.1440410120]

Roy, D., Srivastava, R., Jat, M., & Karaca, M. S. (2022). A complete overview of analytics techniques: descriptive, predictive, and prescriptive. Decision intelligence analytics and the implementation of strategic business management, 15-30. [http://dx.doi.org/10.1007/978-3-030-82763-2_2]

Senousy, Y.M.B., Mohamed, N.E.K., Riad, A.E.D.M. (2018). Recent trends in big data analytics towards more enhanced insurance business models. *Int. J. Comput. Sci. Inf. Secur., 30111817*, 39-45.

Tiwari, S., Bahuguna, P.C., Srivastava, R. (2023). Smart manufacturing and sustainability: a bibliometric analysis. *Benchmarking (Bradf.), 30*(9), 3281-3301. [http://dx.doi.org/10.1108/BIJ-04-2022-0238]

Tripathi, M., Kumar, S., Sonker, S.K., Babbar, P. (2018). Occurrence of author keywords and keywords plus in social sciences and humanities research : A preliminary study. *COLLNET Journal of Scientometrics and Information Management, 12*(2), 215-232. [http://dx.doi.org/10.1080/09737766.2018.1436951]

Xu, J., Glicksberg, B.S., Su, C., Walker, P., Bian, J., Wang, F. (2021). Federated Learning for Healthcare Informatics. *J. Healthc. Inform. Res.,* *5*(1), 1-19.
[http://dx.doi.org/10.1007/s41666-020-00082-4] [PMID: 33204939]

Singh, S., Kumar, V., Datta, S., Wani, A.B., Dhanjal, D.S., Romero, R., Singh, J. (2020). Glyphosate uptake, translocation, resistance emergence in crops, analytical monitoring, toxicity and degradation: a review. *Environ. Chem. Lett.,* *18*(3), 663-702.
[http://dx.doi.org/10.1007/s10311-020-00969-z]

Bhushan, B., Sahoo, C., Sinha, P., Khamparia, A. (2021). Unification of Blockchain and Internet of Things (BIoT): requirements, working model, challenges and future directions. *Wirel. Netw.,* *27*(1), 55-90.
[http://dx.doi.org/10.1007/s11276-020-02445-6]

Kumar, H., Bhardwaj, K., Sharma, R., Nepovimova, E., Kuča, K., Dhanjal, D.S., Verma, R., Bhardwaj, P., Sharma, S., Kumar, D. (2020). Fruit and vegetable peels: utilization of high value horticultural waste in novel industrial applications. *Molecules,* *25*(12), 2812.
[http://dx.doi.org/10.3390/molecules25122812] [PMID: 32570836]

Avikal, S., Pant, R., Barthwal, A., Ram, M., Upadhyay, R.K. (2023). Factors implementing sustainable circular economy in agro-produce supply chain: DEMATEL-DANP-based approach. *Manag. Environ. Qual.,* *34*(4), 1158-1173.
[http://dx.doi.org/10.1108/MEQ-03-2022-0088]

Mahate, V., Bisen, A., Vishwakarma, S., Avikal, S., Jain, R. (2023). Evaluating Biofuel Energy Policies for Sustainable Transportation Sector: A System Dynamics Approach. International Journal of Mathematical. *Engineering and Management Sciences,* *8*(1), 120.

Avikal, S., Singh, A.R., Ram, M. (2021). Sustainability in Industry 4.0: Challenges and Remedies. *CRC Press.*
[http://dx.doi.org/10.1201/9781003102304]

Singh, A.K., Avikal, S., Sharma, A., Verma, R.P. (2021). Selection of suitable metal matrix composite for design application using MCDM approach. *Mater. Today Proc.,* *46*, 10771-10775.
[http://dx.doi.org/10.1016/j.matpr.2021.01.672]

Singh Mehra, K., Singh, S., Singh, A.K., Kharkwal, H., Avikal, S. (2021). Performance, energy, emission and cost analysis of Jatropha (Jatropha Curcas) oil as a biofuel for compression ignition engine. *Mater. Today Proc.,* *43*, 348-354.
[http://dx.doi.org/10.1016/j.matpr.2020.11.675]

Singh, A.K., Avikal, S., Nithin Kumar, K.C., Kumar, M., Thakura, P. (2020). A fuzzy-AHP and M – TOPSIS based approach for selection of composite materials used in structural applications. *Mater. Today Proc.,* *26*, 3119-3123.
[http://dx.doi.org/10.1016/j.matpr.2020.02.644]

KC, N. K., Chavadaki, S., Shaikh, A., Singh, D. P., & Avikal, S. (2020). Weight optimization of a hat stiffened panel of a typical transport aircraft composite wing. Materials Today: Proceedings, 26, 471-474.
[http://dx.doi.org/10.1016/j.matpr.2019.12.087]

Sharma, K., Gupta, V., Verma, S., Avikal, S. (2018). Study and implementation of face detection algorithm using Matlab. *International Conference on Recent Innovations in Electrical, Electronics & Communication Engineering (ICRIEECE),* 2745-2748.
[http://dx.doi.org/10.1109/ICRIEECE44171.2018.9008990]

CHAPTER 15

The Surge of Machine Learning and Robo-Advisors: Reshaping the Insurance Industry Terrain

Pooja Sharma[1], **Sangeet Vashishtha**[1,*], **Neeraj Saxena**[2] and **Shruti Saxena**[2]

[1] *IIMT University, Meerut, Uttar Pardesh, India*

[2] *Sandip University, Nashik, Maharashtra, India*

Abstract: This book chapter explores the profound impact of machine learning and robo-advisors on the insurance industry, ushering in a transformative era characterized by heightened efficiency and innovation. Through an in-depth analysis of their ascendance, we delve into how these technologies are revolutionizing traditional practices within the insurance sector. The utilization of machine learning algorithms is examined across various facets of the industry, including fraud detection, underwriting automation, claims processing optimization, and risk management through predictive analytics. Additionally, the integration of IoT, telematics, and other emerging technologies further amplifies the potential for enhanced customer experiences and streamlined operations. Ethical considerations, regulatory compliance, and the imperative need for explainable AI in decision-making processes are also addressed. The study underscores the collaborative efforts between insurers and InsurTech startups, illustrating how such partnerships leverage the power of machine learning to navigate and thrive in an evolving landscape. As the insurance industry undergoes this significant metamorphosis, the book chapter concludes by highlighting key trends and implications for the future trajectory of the sector.

Keywords: Artificial intelligence, Insurance, IoT, Machine learning, Robo-advisor.

INTRODUCTION

The insurance industry is on the brink of a groundbreaking transformation, and at the core of this evolution lies the integration of Machine Learning (ML) and Artificial Intelligence (AI). The pivotal question emerges: How will these advanced technologies redefine the operational fabric of insurers? With sweeping

[*] **Corresponding author Sangeet Vashishtha:** IIMT University, Meerut, Maharashtra, India; E-mail: bsangeet83@gmail.com

Sanjay Taneja, Ercan Ozen, Luan Vardar, Mohit Kukreti & Mohammad Kashif (Eds.)

implications across risk assessment, underwriting, claims management, and customer engagement, the applications of machine learning and AI in the insurance sector are poised to usher in an era of unprecedented potential. In the year ahead, this article ventures into the forefront of these technological advancements, unraveling the transformative journey that awaits the insurance industry (Srivastava *et al.*, 2024). At the heart of insurance operations, risk assessment and underwriting are undergoing a paradigm shift with the infusion of machine learning and AI. These technologies empower insurers with a heightened ability to analyze vast datasets, discern intricate patterns, and make real-time decisions. The results include enhanced accuracy in risk evaluation, streamlined underwriting processes, and a departure from conventional methodologies. The year ahead promises a deeper integration of these capabilities, leading to a more dynamic and responsive underwriting landscape. Claims management, often a complex and time-sensitive facet of insurance, stands to benefit significantly from the prowess of machine learning and AI. Automation, data analytics, and predictive modeling converge to expedite claims processing, ensuring swifter resolutions and improved customer satisfaction. As insurers embrace these technologies, the year ahead holds promises of more efficient claims workflows, reduced processing times, and an overall elevation of the claims management experience (Gangwar & Srivastava, 2020; Mishra *et al.*, 2024; Tripathi & Mohan, 2016). The landscape of customer engagement in the insurance sector is undergoing a revolutionary shift. Machine learning and AI bring forth the ability to delve into vast customer datasets, offering insights that pave the way for highly personalized interactions. From tailoring insurance products to anticipating customer needs, the year ahead is poised to witness insurers leveraging these technologies to enhance customer experiences, foster loyalty, and establish a new paradigm of customer-centric engagement (Dutta *et al.*, 2023; Padhi *et al.*, 2024; K. U. Singh *et al.*, 2024).

The year 2023 is set to witness groundbreaking advancements in the symbiosis of machine learning and AI within the insurance realm. The intersection of these technologies with emerging trends such as the Internet of Things (IoT), blockchain, and data visualization will further amplify their impact. Insurers embracing innovation will find themselves at the forefront of this transformative wave, positioning them for sustained growth and resilience in an ever-evolving industry landscape (Ajay *et al.*, 2023; Indu *et al.*, 2023; Zhang *et al.*, 2023). The potential impact of machine learning and AI in the insurance sector is monumental. From operational efficiency to enhanced risk management and unprecedented customer experiences, the year ahead holds the promise of a more agile, responsive, and technologically advanced insurance industry (Dahiya & Taneja, 2023; Kour *et al.*, 2025; A. Singh *et al.*, 2024; Taneja, Gupta, *et al.*, 2023; TANEJA *et al.*, 2024). As insurers navigate this transformative era, those who adeptly harness the power of machine learning and AI are poised to lead the charge into a future where innovation is not just a choice but a strategic imperative (Aiyappa *et al.*, 2024; Belwal & Belwal, 2017; Pandey *et al.*, 2023).

In the past decade, cutting-edge technologies such as machine learning, artificial intelligence, and deep learning have emerged as widely embraced trends. Their adoption has become pervasive across various industries, driven by the tangible operational advantages they bring to the value chain. Among these sectors, the insurance industry stands out as a notable beneficiary of the integration of machine learning and artificial intelligence into its workflows. Machine learning in insurance, for instance, catalyzes automating routine daily functions, enhancing overall operational efficiency. Furthermore, these advanced technologies enable companies to analyze extensive sets of customer data. This analytical capability empowers companies to make informed decisions, resulting in the provision of more profitable and personalized insurance policies that cater precisely to the unique needs of their customers.

HISTORICAL PERSPECTIVES ON MACHINE LEARNING ADOPTION

The journey of machine learning adoption is an intricate narrative woven through the tapestry of technological evolution (Khandelwal *et al.*, 2023; Shrivastava *et al.*, 2023; A. K. Singh *et al.*, 2024). Delving into historical perspectives unveils the roots of machine learning and illuminates the milestones that have shaped its trajectory.

Early Theoretical Foundations

The roots of machine learning can be traced back to the mid-20th century when pioneers like Alan Turing and Warren McCulloch laid the theoretical foundations. Turing's seminal work on computing machinery and intelligence, coupled with McCulloch's insights into neural networks, set the stage for the inception of machine learning concepts (Bhatnagar, Rajaram, *et al.*, 2024; Bhatnagar, Taneja, *et al.*, 2024; P. Kumar, Verma, *et al.*, 2023; Taneja, Bhatnagar, Kumar, & Grima, 2023).

Emergence of Symbolic Learning

In the 1950s and 1960s, the field witnessed the emergence of symbolic learning, characterized by the development of algorithms capable of manipulating symbols to perform tasks. Early programs like the Logic Theorist and General Problem Solver exemplified attempts to replicate human problem-solving abilities through machine-based learning (Kaur *et al.*, 2023; P. Kumar *et al.*, 2024; P. Kumar, Bhatnagar, *et al.*, 2023; Taneja, Bhatnagar, Kumar, & Rupeika-apoga, 2023).

Connectionism and Neural Networks

The 1980s marked a resurgence of interest in machine learning with the advent of connectionism. Neural network models gained prominence, drawing inspiration from the structure and function of the human brain. The pioneering work of researchers like Geoffrey Hinton paved the way for renewed exploration and experimentation in this domain.

Rebirth in the Big Data Era

The late 20th century witnessed a paradigm shift with the proliferation of digital data. The advent of the internet, coupled with exponential growth in data volume, provided fertile ground for machine learning to flourish. Innovations in algorithms, computational power, and data storage capabilities fueled a rebirth of interest in machine learning.

Rise of Practical Applications

The 21st century witnessed the ascendancy of machine learning from theoretical concepts to practical applications. Companies and researchers began applying machine learning algorithms to real-world problems, ranging from recommendation systems and natural language processing to image recognition and autonomous vehicles.

Deep Learning and Neural Networks Dominance

In recent years, the dominance of deep learning and neural networks has defined the contemporary landscape of machine learning. Breakthroughs in deep learning, particularly with convolutional and recurrent neural networks, have propelled machine learning into new frontiers, achieving unprecedented accuracy in tasks such as image recognition and natural language understanding.

Expanding Horizons with Reinforcement Learning

The evolution continues with the exploration of reinforcement learning, where machines learn by interacting with their environment and receiving feedback. This approach has found applications in robotics, game playing, and optimization problems, opening new horizons for machine learning's capabilities. Historical perspectives on machine learning adoption reveal a captivating journey of theoretical foundations, technological breakthroughs, and practical applications [26]. From early symbolic learning to the contemporary dominance of deep learning, the narrative is one of continuous evolution, reflecting the resilience and adaptability of machine learning in the face of ever-changing technological landscapes.

DRIVERS OF CHANGE: WHY MACHINE LEARNING IN INSURANCE?

The insurance industry is currently experiencing a profound shift driven by the introduction of artificial intelligence (AI). Advanced AI technologies enable insurers to employ a more efficient and precise methodology for real-time assessment of extensive datasets, leading to accurate predictions (Arora *et al.*, 2024; Grover *et al.*, 2024; Kumari *et al.*, 2024). These transformative breakthroughs are reshaping the insurance landscape, compelling companies to integrate AI for the purpose of enhancing customer service, achieving cost savings, and maximizing profitability.

Enhanced Precision in Risk Assessments

Traditional insurance underwriting was a manual and labor-intensive process, making decisions on a case-by-case basis. Thanks to artificial intelligence, insurers can now rapidly and accurately evaluate risk variables, establishing fair premiums for clients (P. Singh & Singh, 2023). By scrutinizing extensive datasets, encompassing demographics, medical history, driving records, and other relevant information, insurers can assess a client's risk level with increased accuracy.

Efficient Claims Resolution

Artificial intelligence allows insurance companies to automate the analysis and processing of claims, significantly reducing processing times from weeks to minutes. This swift automation enables faster payment processing, thereby enhancing the overall consumer experience. AI-powered chatbots and virtual assistants further expedite the claims process and address client queries promptly.

Tailored Customer Experience

The future of the insurance sector is trending towards a more personalized customer experience. Artificial intelligence enables insurance companies to craft individualized plans and policies that consider each client's unique situation, behavior, and preferences. AI-powered chatbots and virtual assistants contribute to providing personalized customer service, elevating customer satisfaction rates. This personalized approach fosters stronger insurer-client relationships and, consequently, improves client retention rates.

Cost Savings for Insurance Companies

Artificial intelligence plays a pivotal role in cost savings for insurers, primarily by reducing the likelihood of fraudulent claims. Additionally, automated systems for claims processing and customer support contribute to substantial savings. Insurers can further optimize costs by tailoring services to meet the unique needs of their clientele and offering a variety of customizable policy features and coverage options.

KEY MACHINE LEARNING ALGORITHM IN INSURANCE

The integration of machine learning (ML) algorithms has become a transformative force in the insurance industry, revolutionizing traditional processes and unlocking new possibilities for risk assessment, underwriting, claims processing, and customer engagement. The evolving landscape of machine learning in insurance holds the promise of continuous innovation and transformative advancements in the industry [6]. Several key machine-learning algorithms play a pivotal role in reshaping the landscape of insurance operations shown inTable **1**:

Table 1. The integration of machine learning (ML) algorithms.

S. No.	Algorithm	Application	Implication
1	**Linear Regression**	Linear regression is fundamental for predicting numerical outcomes, making it valuable in insurance for tasks like pricing models and predicting the expected value of claims.	Insurers leverage linear regression to understand the relationship between various factors and quantify the impact on risk and pricing.
2	**Decision Trees**	Decision trees are used for risk assessment and underwriting, providing a visual representation of decision-making processes based on input variables.	Decision trees enhance transparency in decision-making, helping insurers assess risk factors and make informed underwriting decisions.
3	**Random Forest**	Random Forest is an ensemble learning technique that combines multiple decision trees to improve predictive accuracy and reduce overfitting.	In insurance, Random Forest is employed for more robust risk modeling, claims prediction, and fraud detection, offering enhanced precision.
4	**Gradient Boosting**	Gradient Boosting algorithms build a predictive model by combining the strengths of multiple weak models sequentially.	Widely used in insurance for predicting claim severity, customer lifetime value, and optimizing pricing strategies by iteratively improving predictive accuracy.
5	**Neural Networks (Deep Learning)**	Deep learning, a subset of machine learning, involves neural networks with multiple layers, suitable for complex pattern recognition tasks.	In insurance, deep learning is applied to image recognition for claims processing, natural language processing for customer interactions, and other intricate tasks.

(Table 1) cont.....

S. No.	Algorithm	Application	Implication
6	**Clustering Algorithms**	Clustering algorithms, such as K-means, are used for customer segmentation and market analysis.	Insurers leverage clustering to identify distinct customer groups, enabling personalized offerings, targeted marketing, and more effective risk management.
7	**Support Vector Machines (SVM)**	SVM is utilized for classification tasks, helping insurers make decisions based on historical data.	In insurance, SVM is applied to predict policy cancellations, assess the likelihood of claims, and identify potential fraud by classifying patterns in data.
8	**Naive Bayes**	Naive Bayes is a probabilistic algorithm used for classification based on Bayes' theorem.	In insurance, Naive Bayes is applied for sentiment analysis in customer interactions, fraud detection, and assessing the probability of certain events.
9	**Ensemble Learning**	Ensemble learning combines multiple models to improve overall performance and robustness.	Insurance companies utilize ensemble learning to create more reliable predictions, enhance risk assessment, and optimize decision-making processes.
10	**Time Series Analysis**	Time series analysis involves forecasting future values based on historical data points.	In insurance, time series analysis is applied to predict future claim trends, assess policy renewals, and optimize resource allocation.

IMPACT OF MACHINE LEARNING ON TRADITIONAL INSURANCE MODELS

The impact of machine learning on traditional insurance models is nothing short of revolutionary, reshaping fundamental aspects of the industry. This transformative technology has introduced a paradigm shift, offering new possibilities and efficiencies across various dimensions of insurance operations as shown in Fig. (**1**) (Dani *et al.*, 2020).

Claims Processing

Machine learning is extensively utilized in the insurance industry for claims processing, automating the analysis of claim data. By employing ML algorithms, the system can scrutinize customer-provided data and cross-reference it with policy details to ascertain the validity of a claim (Goyal *et al.*, 2015) (Fig. **2**). This streamlined approach substantially decreases the time required for insurance claim processing, leading to heightened customer satisfaction. Furthermore, these algorithms excel at identifying patterns within the data, enabling the detection of fraudulent claims. This not only helps insurers save money but also minimizes the risk of reputational damage through improved decision-making processes.

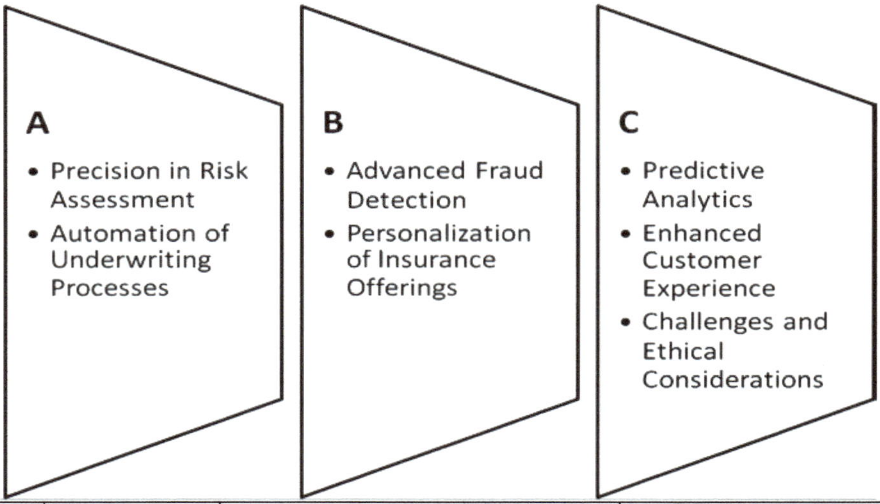

			renewals, and optimize resource allocation.

Fig. (1). Impact of machine learning on traditional insurance models.

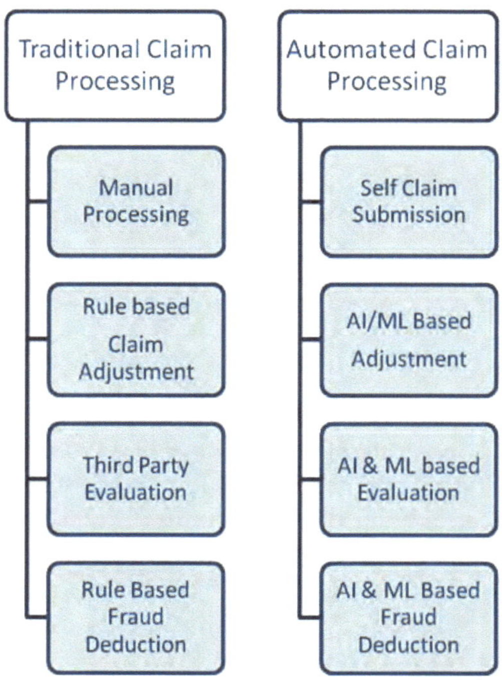

Fig. (2). Comparison of claim processing.

Automation of Underwriting Processes

Historically, underwriting processes were labor-intensive, involving manual scrutiny of data and decision-making on a case-by-case basis (Prikshat *et al.*, 2019). Machine learning automates and accelerates underwriting, allowing insurers to evaluate risks more efficiently. Algorithms can rapidly process diverse data points, providing insights that streamline decision-making, improve accuracy, and significantly reduce the time required for policy insurance (Fig. **3**).

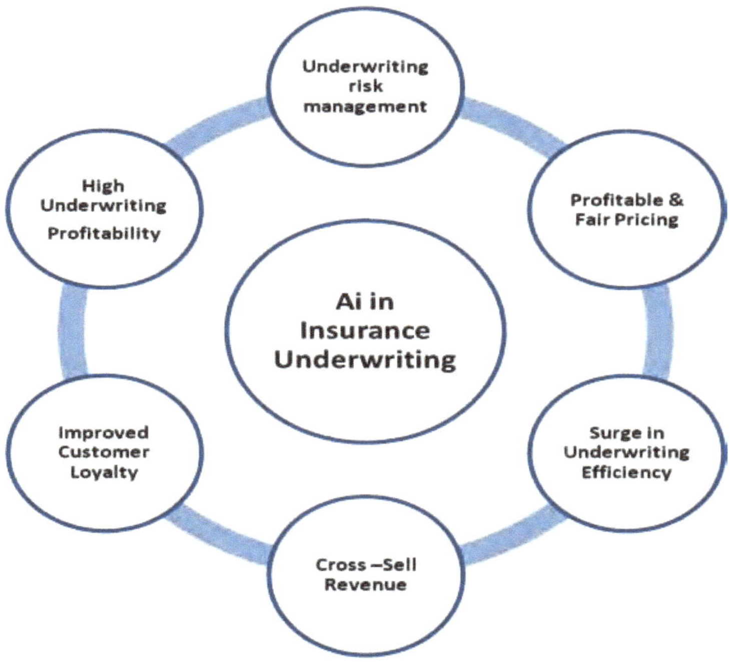

Fig. (3). Ai in insurance underwriting.

Advanced Fraud Detection

One of the significant challenges in the insurance industry is fraudulent activities. Machine learning excels in detecting patterns and anomalies within data, offering a robust defense against fraudulent claims. Traditional models may struggle to adapt to evolving fraud schemes, but machine learning continuously learns from new data, enhancing its ability to identify suspicious patterns and prevent fraudulent activities.

Personalization of Insurance Offerings

Machine learning empowers insurers to move beyond one-size-fits-all approaches, enabling the creation of personalized insurance offerings. By analyzing individual customer behaviors, preferences, and risk profiles, insurers can tailor policies to meet specific needs (Mangla *et al.*, 2018; Prikshat *et al.*, 2017; Rathore & Goudar, 2015). This shift towards personalized insurance not only enhances customer satisfaction but also allows insurers to differentiate themselves in a competitive market.

Predictive Analytics for Proactive Risk Management

Traditional insurance models often rely on historical data to assess risks. Machine learning introduces predictive analytics, enabling insurers to anticipate future risks (Ahmad *et al.*, 2023; Alrashed *et al.*, 2022; Pant *et al.*, 2017). By analyzing trends, identifying patterns, and considering real-time data, machine learning models contribute to proactive risk management. This capability allows insurers to stay ahead of emerging risks, improving overall resilience.

Enhanced Customer Experience

Machine learning applications, such as chatbots and virtual assistants, are revolutionizing customer interactions. These technologies provide instant and personalized support, improving the overall customer experience. Insurers can leverage machine learning to offer timely and relevant information, process claims efficiently, and engage with customers in a more responsive and customer-centric manner.

Challenges and Ethical Considerations

While the impact of machine learning is overwhelmingly positive, it also presents challenges. Ethical considerations, such as bias in algorithms and the responsible use of data, require careful attention (Josphineleela *et al.*, 2023; Khan *et al.*, 2020; Tiwari *et al.*, 2023). Addressing these challenges is crucial to ensuring fair and transparent practices in the implementation of machine learning within the insurance industry.

CURRENT STATE OF MACHINE LEARNING ADOPTION IN THE INSURANCE INDUSTRY

As of my knowledge cutoff in January 2022, the adoption of machine learning in the insurance industry has been gaining significant momentum (Nikolaidis *et al.*, 2022). Several trends and developments showcase the current state of machine learning adoption in the insurance sector (Table **2**):

Table 2. Developments showcase.

Underwriting Automation	Insurers are increasingly leveraging machine learning algorithms for underwriting processes. These algorithms analyze vast datasets, including customer information, historical claims data, and external variables, to assess risk more accurately and streamline underwriting workflows.
Claims Processing Efficiency	Machine learning is being deployed to enhance claims processing efficiency. Insurers are using algorithms for automated claims analysis, fraud detection, and assessment, significantly reducing the time required for claims settlement. This leads to improved customer satisfaction and operational efficiency.
Personalized Insurance Products	Insurers are leveraging machine learning to create personalized insurance products. By analyzing individual customer data and behaviors, companies can tailor coverage and pricing, offering a more customized experience.
Predictive Analytics for Risk Management	Predictive analytics powered by machine learning is becoming a crucial tool for insurers in proactive risk management. By analyzing historical data and identifying patterns, insurers can anticipate and mitigate potential risks, leading to more informed decision-making.
Telematics and Usage-Based Insurance	Machine learning is integrated with telematics devices to collect real-time data on driving behavior. This data is then used to calculate personalized insurance premiums based on individual driving habits, contributing to the popularity of usage-based insurance models.
Chatbots and Virtual Assistants	Insurers are implementing machine learning-powered chatbots and virtual assistants to enhance customer service. These AI-driven tools provide instant support, answer queries, and assist with policy-related information, improving overall customer interactions.
Fraud Detection and Prevention	Machine learning algorithms are crucial in detecting and preventing insurance fraud. By analyzing patterns and anomalies in claims data, these algorithms can identify potentially fraudulent activities, helping insurers save costs and maintain the integrity of their operations (Malik *et al.*, 2022).
Integration with IoT	The integration of machine learning with the Internet of Things (IoT) devices, such as smart home sensors and wearables, is on the rise. This enables insurers to access real-time data, allowing for more accurate risk assessments and the development of innovative insurance products.
Regulatory Compliance	Insurers are navigating regulatory frameworks and compliance standards associated with the use of machine learning in the industry. Compliance considerations include transparency, fairness, and the ethical use of customer data, as regulatory bodies scrutinize the adoption of AI technologies (Jindal *et al.*, 2022).

ANTICIPATED CHALLENGES AND OPPORTUNITIES

Data Quality and Availability

Challenge: Machine learning models heavily rely on high-quality, diverse datasets. Insufficient or poor-quality data can hinder the accuracy and effectiveness of these models.

Opportunity: Invest in data governance practices and data quality improvement initiatives. Collaborate with data providers to ensure access to relevant and reliable datasets.

Interpretable Models and Explainability

Challenge: Machine learning models, especially complex ones like deep neural networks, are often perceived as "black boxes," making it challenging to interpret their decisions.

Opportunity: Focus on developing explainable AI models, which not only enhance transparency but also help build trust among regulators, customers, and stakeholders.

Ethical Considerations and Bias

Challenge: Machine learning models may unintentionally perpetuate biases present in historical data, leading to unfair outcomes.

Opportunity: Implement strategies to identify and mitigate biases in models. Prioritize fairness and transparency in machine learning development, adhering to ethical guidelines and standards.

Regulatory Compliance

Challenge: The regulatory landscape for machine learning in insurance is evolving, and insurers must navigate complex compliance requirements.

Opportunity: Proactively engage with regulatory bodies, stay informed about evolving regulations, and establish internal processes to ensure compliance with legal and ethical standards.

Lack of Talent and Expertise

Challenge: The demand for skilled professionals in machine learning often outpaces the supply, leading to a shortage of talent in the industry.

Opportunity: Invest in training programs, collaborate with academic institutions, and foster a culture of continuous learning to develop and retain machine learning expertise within the organization.

Anticipated Opportunities

Enhanced Customer Experience: Machine learning allows insurers to offer personalized services, streamlined customer interactions, and innovative products, enhancing overall customer satisfaction and loyalty.

Improved Risk Assessment and Underwriting: Advanced analytics and machine learning enable insurers to assess risk more accurately, automate underwriting processes, and tailor coverage to individual policyholders.

Fraud Detection and Prevention: Machine learning algorithms can significantly enhance fraud detection capabilities, leading to substantial cost savings and the preservation of the integrity of insurance operations.

Operational Efficiency and Cost Savings: Automation of routine tasks, claims processing, and customer interactions through machine learning can result in operational efficiencies and cost savings for insurers.

Innovative Product Development: Machine learning enables the development of innovative insurance products, such as usage-based policies, telematics-driven coverage, and other tailored offerings that align with evolving customer needs.

Predictive Analytics for Proactive Risk Management: Predictive modeling and analytics empower insurers to proactively manage risks, anticipate market trends, and make informed strategic decisions for long-term sustainability.

Insurtech Collaboration: Collaboration with InsurTech startups leveraging machine learning can bring fresh perspectives, innovative solutions, and rapid advancements to the industry, fostering a culture of continuous innovation.

MACHINE LEARNING APPLICATIONS IN INSURANCE

Risk Assessment and Underwriting

Application: Machine learning models analyze extensive datasets to assess risk factors more accurately. This includes evaluating customer data, historical claims, and external variables to streamline underwriting processes.

Benefits: Improved accuracy in risk evaluation, faster underwriting decisions, and the ability to tailor coverage to individual customer profiles.

Claims Processing and Fraud Detection

Application: Machine learning automates claims processing, reducing the time it takes to analyze and settle claims. Algorithms are also employed for fraud detection by identifying patterns and anomalies in claims data.

Benefits: Increased efficiency in claims processing, faster settlement times, and enhanced fraud prevention capabilities.

Customer Service and Interaction

Application: AI-powered chatbots and virtual assistants, driven by machine learning, provide instant and personalized customer support. These tools answer queries, guide customers through policy details, and facilitate smoother interactions.

Benefits: Improved customer experience, 24/7 availability, and efficient handling of routine customer inquiries.

Personalized Insurance Products

Application: Machine learning algorithms analyze individual customer behaviors, preferences, and risk profiles to tailor insurance products. This personalization includes customized coverage options and pricing structures.

Benefits: Enhanced customer satisfaction, increased customer loyalty, and the ability to meet unique customer needs.

Predictive Analytics for Proactive Risk Management

Application: Predictive modeling uses machine learning to anticipate future risks based on historical data and emerging trends. This supports proactive risk management strategies.

Benefits: Improved risk mitigation, better strategic decision-making, and the ability to respond to emerging threats.

Telematics and Usage-Based Insurance

Application: Machine learning is integrated with telematics devices to monitor and assess driving behavior in real-time. This data is used to calculate personalized insurance premiums in usage-based insurance models.

Benefits: Fairer pricing based on individual behavior, reduced risk, and increased customer engagement.

Data Visualization and Analytics

Application: Machine learning supports data visualization tools to present complex data in an understandable format. This aids in making informed decisions and communicating insights to stakeholders.

Benefits: Enhanced data-driven decision-making, improved communication of insights, and a more transparent understanding of data.

Automated Underwriting and Policy Recommendations

Application: Machine learning automates underwriting processes and provides recommendations for policy customization based on customer profiles and preferences.

Benefits: Increased efficiency, quicker decision-making, and the ability to offer tailored insurance solutions.

Chatbots for Claims Assistance

Application: Chatbots powered by machine learning assist customers in filing and tracking claims, providing real-time updates, and answering queries related to the claims process.

Benefits: Improved claims experience, faster resolution times, and reduced workload on customer service teams.

TECHNOLOGICAL CONVERGENCE: IOT, TELEMATICS, AND BEYOND

Telematics represents a transformative paradigm, reshaping traditional practices and ushering in a new era of data-driven insights and personalized services. This convergence goes beyond connectivity, integrating real-time data, analytics, and automation to revolutionize risk assessment, underwriting, and customer engagement (Lourens *et al*., 2022; Onyema *et al*., 2022; Rana *et al*., 2022). Here's an exploration of this technological convergence and its implications in the insurance sector:

IoT in Risk Assessment

Integration: IoT devices, such as connected cars and smart home sensors, provide a continuous stream of data related to user behavior, environmental factors, and asset conditions.

Impact: Insurers leverage this data to enhance risk assessment models, allowing for a more accurate understanding of individual risk profiles. This results in more tailored insurance coverage and personalized pricing.

Telematics for Usage-Based Insurance (UBI)

Integration: Telematics devices installed in vehicles capture real-time data on driving behavior, including speed, distance, and braking patterns.

Impact: Insurance companies utilize telematics data for Usage-Based Insurance (UBI), where premiums are calculated based on actual driving habits. This creates a fairer pricing model and incentivizes safer driving practices.

Fleet Management Optimization

Integration: IoT sensors in commercial vehicles provide data on fuel consumption, maintenance needs, and driver behavior.

Impact: Telematics platforms leverage this data for efficient fleet management, optimizing routes, reducing fuel costs, and enhancing overall operational efficiency for both insurers and fleet owners.

Smart Home Integration for Property Insurance

Integration: IoT devices in smart homes, including security systems and environmental monitors, contribute to a comprehensive understanding of property conditions.

Impact: Insurers use this data to assess and mitigate risks, offer discounts for smart home features, and enhance overall property insurance coverage.

Data-Driven Claims Processing

Integration: Real-time data from IoT and telematics devices streamline claims processing by providing instant and accurate information about incidents.

Impact: Claims are processed more efficiently, reducing settlement times and minimizing fraudulent claims through detailed, verifiable data.

Personalized Customer Engagement

Integration: IoT devices contribute to a wealth of customer data, allowing insurers to understand individual preferences, behaviors, and needs.

Impact: Insurers can engage with customers on a personalized level, offering tailored products, proactive risk management advice, and improving overall customer satisfaction.

Challenges and Considerations

Data Security and Privacy: The vast amount of data generated by IoT and telematics devices raises concerns about data security and individual privacy.

Regulatory Compliance: Insurers must navigate evolving regulatory landscapes to ensure compliance with data protection and usage standards.

Future Trends

Blockchain Integration: The convergence of IoT, telematics, and blockchain technology can enhance data security, transparency, and trust in insurance transactions.

Artificial Intelligence: AI algorithms will play a crucial role in analyzing the immense volume of data generated, providing actionable insights, and further optimizing insurance processes.

The technological convergence of IoT and telematics in the insurance sector presents a wealth of opportunities for innovation and improved customer experiences.

FORECASTING THE FUTURE: TRENDS AND IMPLICATIONS

As we peer into the future, several trends emerge, each carrying profound implications for industries, societies, and the way we navigate our interconnected world. These trends, driven by technological advancements, evolving consumer behaviors, and global shifts, shape a landscape that demands adaptability and foresight (Pattanshetti *et al.*, 2021; V. Sharma & Jain, 2020). Here are key trends and their implications:

Artificial Intelligence Dominance

Trend: Artificial Intelligence (AI) continues to advance, influencing diverse sectors from healthcare to finance.

Implications: Automation of routine tasks, enhanced decision-making, and the need for ethical AI governance become critical. New opportunities arise in AI-driven innovation and personalized services.

Sustainable Technology Adoption

Trend: Growing awareness of environmental concerns fuels a shift towards sustainable technologies.

Implications: Businesses face increased pressure to adopt eco-friendly practices. Opportunities arise in the development of green technologies, sustainable products, and circular economy models (Ingale *et al.*, 2023; R. Kumar *et al.*, 2023; S. Sharma *et al.*, 2023).

Remote Work Evolution

Trend: The remote work revolution persists, reshaping traditional workplace structures.

Implications: Companies need to adapt to hybrid work models, addressing challenges related to employee well-being, collaboration, and cybersecurity. A reimagining of urban planning and infrastructure may occur.

Digital Health Revolution

Trend: Digital health technologies, including telemedicine and wearables, witness widespread adoption.

Implications: Increased accessibility to healthcare services, a shift towards preventive care, and a reevaluation of healthcare infrastructure and policies.

Blockchain Integration:

Trend: Widespread adoption of blockchain technology for secure and transparent transactions.

Implications: Increased trust in digital transactions, disruption in finance, supply chain, and healthcare. Opportunities for decentralized applications and smart contracts.

Resilience in Supply Chains

Trend: Supply chains adapt to be more resilient and flexible, leveraging technologies like IoT and data analytics.

Implications: Increased focus on local sourcing, demand for real-time visibility, and a reevaluation of global supply chain strategies (Alexopoulos *et al.*, 2023; Rawat *et al.*, 2022; A. B. Singh *et al.*, 2023).

Augmented Reality in Everyday Life

Trend: Augmented reality becomes a part of daily experiences, from gaming to education.

Implications: Opportunities for immersive customer experiences, skill development through AR-based training, and the transformation of entertainment and education sectors.

CONCLUSION

The convergence of machine learning and robo-advisors has initiated a paradigm shift in the insurance industry, transforming traditional operations and customer interactions. These technologies have enhanced efficiency in fraud detection, underwriting, claims processing, and risk management, while predictive analytics enables proactive decision-making. The integration of IoT and telematics further enriches customer experiences and operational workflows.

However, this technological evolution brings challenges, including ethical dilemmas, regulatory demands, and the necessity for explainable AI to foster trust. The collaboration between insurers and InsurTech startups is crucial in navigating these complexities. Ultimately, machine learning and robo-advisors are poised to shape a dynamic, customer-centric insurance landscape.

REFERENCES

Ahmad, I., Sharma, S., Kumar, R., Dhyani, S., Dumka, A. (2023). Data Analytics of Online Education during Pandemic Health Crisis: A Case Study. *2nd Edition of IEEE Delhi Section Owned Conference, DELCON 2023 - Proceedings.*
[http://dx.doi.org/10.1109/DELCON57910.2023.10127423]

Aiyappa, S., Kodikal, R., Rahiman, H.U. (2024). Accelerating Gender Equality for Sustainable Development: A Case Study of Dakshina Kannada District, India. *Technical and Vocational Education and Training: Issues, Concerns and Prospects, 38*, 335-349.
[http://dx.doi.org/10.1007/978-981-99-6909-8_30]

Ajay, D., Sharad, K., Singh, K.P., Sharma, S. (2023). Impact of Prolonged Mental Torture on Housewives in Middle Class Families. *Journal for ReAttach Therapy and Developmental Diversities, 6*(4), 1-7.

Alexopoulos, C., Al-Tamimi, T.A.S., Saxena, S. (2023). Were the higher educational institutions (HEIs) in Oman ready to face pedagogical challenges during COVID-19? *Arab Gulf J. Sci. Res.*
[http://dx.doi.org/10.1108/AGJSR-03-2023-0095]

Alrashed, F.A., Alsubiheen, A.M., Alshammari, H., Mazi, S.I., Al-Saud, S.A., Alayoubi, S., Kachanathu, S.J., Albarrati, A., Aldaihan, M.M., Ahmad, T., Sattar, K., Khan, S., Dhiman, G. (2022). Stress, Anxiety, and Depression in Pre-Clinical Medical Students: Prevalence and Association with Sleep Disorders. *Sustainability (Basel), 14*(18), 11320.
[http://dx.doi.org/10.3390/su141811320]

Arora, A., Singh, R., Malik, K., Kestwal, U. (2024). Association of sexual performance and intimacy with satisfaction in life in head and neck cancer patients: A review. *Oral Oncology Reports, 11*, 100563.
[http://dx.doi.org/10.1016/j.oor.2024.100563]

Belwal, R., Belwal, S. (2017). Employers' perception of women workers in Oman and the challenges they face. *Employee Relat., 39*(7), 1048-1065. [http://dx.doi.org/10.1108/ER-09-2016-0183]

Bhatnagar, M., Rajaram, R., Taneja, S., Kumar, P. (2024). Balancing acts: The Yin and Yang of debit and credit on the stage of financial well-being. *Emerging Perspectives on Financial Well-Being.* [http://dx.doi.org/10.4018/979-8-3693-1750-1.ch002]

Bhatnagar, M., Taneja, S., Kumar, P., Özen, E. (2024). Does financial education act as a catalyst for SME competitiveness. *International Journal of Education Economics and Development, 15*(3), 377-393. [http://dx.doi.org/10.1504/IJEED.2024.139306]

Dahiya, K., Taneja, S. (2023). To Analyse the Impact of Multi-Media Technology on the Rural Entrepreneurship Development. *Contemporary Studies of Risks in Emerging Technology,* 221-240. [http://dx.doi.org/10.1108/978-1-80455-562-020231015]

Dani, R., Kukreti, R., Negi, A., Kholiya, D. (2020). Impact of covid-19 on education and internships of hospitality students. *International Journal of Current Research and Review, 12*(21), 86-90. [http://dx.doi.org/10.31782/IJCRR.2020.SP54]

Dutta, A., Singh, P., Dobhal, A., Mannan, D., Singh, J., Goswami, P. (2023). Entrepreneurial Aptitude of Women of an Aspirational District of Uttarakhand. *Indian Journal of Extension Education, 59*(2), 103-107. [http://dx.doi.org/10.48165/IJEE.2023.59222]

Gangwar, V.P., Srivastva, S.P. (2020). Impact of micro finance in poverty eradication *via* SHGs: A study of selected districts in U.P. *International Journal of Advanced Science and Technology, 29*(2), 3818-3829.

Goyal, P., Kukreja, T., Agarwal, A., Khanna, N. (2015). Narrowing awareness gap by using e-learning tools for counselling university entrants. *Conference Proceeding - 2015 International Conference on Advances in Computer Engineering and Applications, ICACEA,* 847-851. [http://dx.doi.org/10.1109/ICACEA.2015.7164822]

Grover, D., Sharma, S., Kaur, P., MIttal, A., Sharma, P.K. (2024). Societal Elements that Impact the Performance of Women Entrepreneurs in Tier-II Cities: A Study of Rohilkhand Region of Uttar Pradesh. *2024 IEEE Zooming Innovation in Consumer Technologies Conference. ZINC, 2024*, 114-117. [http://dx.doi.org/10.1109/ZINC61849.2024.10579316]

Indu, R., Dimri, S., Kumar, B. (2023). Identification of Location for Police Headquarters to Deal with Crime Against Women in India Using Clustering Based on K-Means Algorithm. *International Journal of Computing and Digital Systems, 14*(1), 965-974. [http://dx.doi.org/10.12785/ijcds/140175]

Ingale, N.V., Saravana Kumar, G., Panduro-Ramirez, J., Raj, M., Vaseem Akram, S., Rawat, R. (2023). Role of IOT in managing education management tools: A technical review. *3rd International Conference on Advance Computing and Innovative Technologies in Engineering, ICACITE,* 2056-2061. [http://dx.doi.org/10.1109/ICACITE57410.2023.10182953]

Jindal, M., Bajal, E., Singh, P., Diwakar, M., Arya, C., Sharma, K. (2022). Online education in Covid-19: Limitations and improvements. *8th Uttar Pradesh Section International Conference on Electrical, Electronics and Computer Engineering, UPCON.* [http://dx.doi.org/10.1109/UPCON52273.2021.9667605]

Josphineleela, R., Kaliappan, S., Natrayan, L., Bhatt, U.M. (2023). Intelligent Virtual Laboratory Development and Implementation using the RASA Framework. *Proceedings - 7th International Conference on Computing Methodologies and Communication, ICCMC,* 1172-1176. [http://dx.doi.org/10.1109/ICCMC56507.2023.10083701]

Kaur, A., Kumar, P., Taneja, S., Ozen, E. (2024). Fintech emergence - an opportunity or threat to banking. *International Journal of Electronic Finance, 13*(1), 135163. [http://dx.doi.org/10.1504/IJEF.2024.135163]

Khan, T., Singh, K., Purohit, K.C. (2021). Icma: An efficient integrated congestion control approach. *Recent*

Pat. Eng., 14(3), 294-309.
[http://dx.doi.org/10.2174/1872212114666191231150916]

Khandelwal, C., Kumar, S., Tripathi, V., Madhavan, V. (2023). Joint impact of corporate governance and risk disclosures on firm value: Evidence from emerging markets. *Res. Int. Bus. Finance, 66*, 102022.
[http://dx.doi.org/10.1016/j.ribaf.2023.102022]

Kour, M., Taneja, S., Özen, E., Sood, K., Grima, S. (2025). *Financial Landscape Transformation Technological Disruptions.*

Kumar, P., Bhatnagar, M., Taneja, S. (2023). Investigation of the time pattern of Bit Green Crypto: An Arma modeling approach to unrave volatility. *Algorithmic Approaches to Financial Technology: Forecasting, Trading, and Optimization.*
[http://dx.doi.org/10.4018/979-8-3693-1746-4.ch001]

Kumar, P., Reepu, & Kaur, R. (2024). Economic and Urban Dynamics: Investigating Socioeconomic Status and Urban Density as Moderators of Mobile Wallet Adoption in Smart Cities. Lecture Notes in Networks and Systems, 948 LNNS, 409–417.
[http://dx.doi.org/10.1007/978-981-97-1329-5_33]

Kumar, P., Verma, P., Bhatnagar, M., Taneja, S., Seychel, S., Todorović, I., Grim, S. (2023). The Financial Performance and Solvency Status of the Indian Public Sector Banks: A CAMELS Rating and Z Index Approach. *Int. J. Sustain. Dev. Plan., 18*(2), 367-376.
[http://dx.doi.org/10.18280/ijsdp.180204]

Kumar, R., Sexena, A., Gehlot, A. (2023). Artificial Intelligence in Smart Education and Futuristic Challenges. *International Conference on Disruptive Technologies, ICDT,* 432-435.
[http://dx.doi.org/10.1109/ICDT57929.2023.10151129]

Kumari, J., Singh, P., Mishra, A.K., Singh Meena, B.P., Singh, A., Ojha, M. (2024). Challenges Hindering Women's Involvement in the Hospitality Industry as Entrepreneurs in the Era of Digital Economy. *Revolutionizing the AI-Digital Landscape: A Guide to Sustainable Emerging Technologies for Marketing Professionals..* Taylor and Francis.
[http://dx.doi.org/10.4324/9781032688305-9]

Lourens, M., Krishna, S.H., Singh, A., Dey, S.K., Pant, B., Sharma, T. (2022). Role of Artificial Intelligence in Formative Employee Engagement. *Proceedings of the 2022 11th International Conference on System Modeling and Advancement in Research Trends, SMART,* 936.
[http://dx.doi.org/10.1109/SMART55829.2022.10047422]

Malik, P., Singh, A.K., Nautiyal, R., Rawat, S. (2022). Mapping AICTE cybersecurity curriculum onto CyBOK: A case study. *Machine Learning for Cyber Security.*
[http://dx.doi.org/10.1515/9783110766745-007]

Mangla, S.K., Luthra, S., Mishra, N., Singh, A., Rana, N.P., Dora, M., Dwivedi, Y. (2018). Barriers to effective circular supply chain management in a developing country context. *Prod. Plann. Contr., 29*(6), 551-569.
[http://dx.doi.org/10.1080/09537287.2018.1449265]

Mishra, D., Kandpal, V., Agarwal, N., Srivastava, B. (2024). Financial Inclusion and Its Ripple Effects on Socio-Economic Development: A Comprehensive Review. *Journal of Risk and Financial Management, 17*(3), 105.
[http://dx.doi.org/10.3390/jrfm17030105]

Nikolaidis, P., Ismail, M., Shuib, L., Khan, S., Dhiman, G. (2022). Predicting Student Attrition in Higher Education through the Determinants of Learning Progress: A Structural Equation Modelling Approach. *Sustainability (Basel), 14*(20), 13584.
[http://dx.doi.org/10.3390/su142013584]

Onyema, E.M., Almuzaini, K.K., Onu, F.U., Verma, D., Gregory, U.S., Puttaramaiah, M., Afriyie, R.K. (2022). Prospects and Challenges of Using Machine Learning for Academic Forecasting. *Comput. Intell. Neurosci., 2022*, 1-7.

[http://dx.doi.org/10.1155/2022/5624475] [PMID: 35909823]

Padhi, B.K., Singh, S., Gaidhane, A.M., Abu Serhan, H., Khatib, M.N., Zahiruddin, Q.S., Rustagi, S., Sharma, R.K., Sharma, D., Arora, M., Satapathy, P. (2024). Inequalities in cardiovascular disease among elderly Indians: A gender perspective analysis using LASI wave-I (2017-18). *Curr. Probl. Cardiol., 49*(7), 102605.
[http://dx.doi.org/10.1016/j.cpcardiol.2024.102605] [PMID: 38692448]

Pandey, R.P., Bansal, S., Awasthi, P., Dixit, V., Singh, R., Yadava, V. (2023). Attitude and Myths Related to Stalking among Early and Middle Age Adults. *Psychology Hub, 40*(3), 85-94.
[http://dx.doi.org/10.13133/2724-2943/17960]

Pant, V., Bhasin, S., Jain, S. (2017). Self-Learning system for personalized E-Learning. *International Conference on Emerging Trends in Computing and Communication Technologies, ICETCCT 2017,* 1-6.
[http://dx.doi.org/10.1109/ICETCCT.2017.8280344]

Pattanshetti, M.K., Jasola, S., Rajput, A., Pant, V. (2021). Proposed eLearning framework using open corpus web resources. *Proceedings of the 2021 1st International Conference on Advances in Electrical, Computing, Communications and Sustainable Technologies, ICAECT.*
[http://dx.doi.org/10.1109/ICAECT49130.2021.9392591]

Prikshat, V., Kumar, S., Nankervis, A. (2019). Work-readiness integrated competence model. *Educ. Train., 61*(5), 568-589.
[http://dx.doi.org/10.1108/ET-05-2018-0114]

Prikshat, V., Kumar, S., Raje, P. (2017). Antecedents, consequences and strategic responses to graduate work-readiness: Challenges in India. *Transitions from Education to Work: Workforce Ready Challenges in the Asia Pacific.*
[http://dx.doi.org/10.4324/9781315533971-8]

Rana, D.S., Dimri, S.C., Malik, P., Dhondiyal, S.A. (2022). Impact of Computational Thinking in Engineering and K12 Education. *4th International Conference on Inventive Research in Computing Applications, ICIRCA 2022 - Proceedings,* 697-701.
[http://dx.doi.org/10.1109/ICIRCA54612.2022.9985593]

Rathore, R., Goudar, R.H. (2015). SPARQL-based personalised E-Learning system designed using ontology (SPELSO): an architecture. *Int. J. Knowl. Learn., 10*(4), 384-416.
[http://dx.doi.org/10.1504/IJKL.2015.077554]

Rawat, R.S., Singh, V., Dumka, A. (2022). Complaint Management in Ethiopian Vocational and Technical Education Institutions: A Framework and Implementation of a Decision Support System. *International Conference on 4th Industrial Revolution Based Technology and Practices, ICFIRTP 2022,* 73-79.
[http://dx.doi.org/10.1109/ICFIRTP56122.2022.10063207]

Sharma, S., Singh, V., Sarkar, D. (2023). Machine Vision Enabled Fall Detection System for Specially Abled People in Limited Visibility Environment. *3rd Asian Conference on Innovation in Technology, ASIANCON.*
[http://dx.doi.org/10.1109/ASIANCON58793.2023.10270769]

Sharma, V., Jain, S. (2020). Managers Training Programs Effectiveness Evaluation by using different Machine Learning Approaches. *Proceedings of the 4th International Conference on Electronics, Communication and Aerospace Technology, ICECA,* 1453-1457.
[http://dx.doi.org/10.1109/ICECA49313.2020.9297556]

Shrivastava, A., Usha, R., Kukreti, R., Sharma, G., Srivastava, A.P., Khan, A.K. (2023). Women Safety Precaution. *1st International Conference on Circuits, Power, and Intelligent Systems, CCPIS.*
[http://dx.doi.org/10.1109/CCPIS59145.2023.10291594]

Singh, A.B., Meena, H.K., Khandelwal, C., Dangayach, G.S. (2023). Sustainability Assessment of Higher Education Institutions: A Systematic Literature Review †. *Engineering Proceedings, 37*(1), 23.
[http://dx.doi.org/10.3390/ECP2023-14728]

Singh, A.K., Singh, R., Singh, S. (2024). A review on factors affecting and performance of nutritional security of women and children in India. *Impact of Women in Food and Agricultural Development.* [http://dx.doi.org/10.4018/979-8-3693-3037-1.ch019]

Singh, A., Kumar, P., Taneja, S. (2024). Artificial Intelligence and Machine Learning-Powered Smart Finance. In: Taneja, P.K.S., Singh, A., (Eds.), *IGI Global.*. IGI Global. [http://dx.doi.org/10.4018/979-8-3693-3264-1]

Singh, K.U., Chaudhary, V., Sharma, P.K., Kumar, P., Varshney, N., Singh, T. (2024). Integrating GPS and GSM Technologies for Enhanced Women's Safety: A Fingerprint-Activated Device Approach. *International Conference on Automation and Computation, AUTOCOM,* 657-662. [http://dx.doi.org/10.1109/AUTOCOM60220.2024.10486120]

Singh, P., Singh, K.D. (2023). Fog-Centric Intelligent Surveillance System: A Novel Approach for Effective and Efficient Surveillance. *International Conference on Advancement in Computation and Computer Technologies, InCACCT,* 762-766.Institute of Electrical and Electronics Engineers Inc.. [http://dx.doi.org/10.1109/InCACCT57535.2023.10141802]

Srivastava, B., Kandpal, V., Jain, A.K. (2024). Financial well-being of women self-help group members: a qualitative study. *Environ. Dev. Sustain.* [http://dx.doi.org/10.1007/s10668-024-04879-w]

Taneja, S., Bhatnagar, M., Kumar, P., Grima, S. (2023). A Panel Analysis of the Effectiveness of the Asset Management in Indian Agricultural Companies. *Int. J. Sustain. Dev. Plan., 18*(3), 653-660. [http://dx.doi.org/10.18280/ijsdp.180301]

Taneja, S., Bhatnagar, M., Kumar, P., Rupeika-Apoga, R. (2023). India's Total Natural Resource Rents (NRR) and GDP: An Augmented Autoregressive Distributed Lag (ARDL) Bound Test. *Journal of Risk and Financial Management, 16*(2), 91. [http://dx.doi.org/10.3390/jrfm16020091]

Taneja, S., Gupta, S., Singh, A., Bhatnagar, M., Gaur, A. (2023). Green management - A new paradigm in the world of business. *Green Management - A New Paradigm in the World of Business,* 1-230. [http://dx.doi.org/10.52305/DLIH6622]

Taneja, S., Kumar, P., Reepu, Kukreti, M., & Ozen, E. (2024). Data Alchemy in the Insurance Industry. Emerald Publishing Limited. Available from: https://doi.org/https://doi.org/10.1108/978-1-83608--82-920241033.

Tiwari, R., Agrawal, P., Singh, P., Bajaj, S., Verma, V., Chauhan, A.S. (2023). Technology Enabled Integrated Fusion Teaching for Enhancing Learning Outcomes in Higher Education. *International Journal of Emerging Technologies in Learning (iJET), 18*(7), 243-249. [http://dx.doi.org/10.3991/ijet.v18i07.36799]

Tripathi, V.M., Mohan, A. (2016). Microfinance and empowering rural women in the Terai, Uttarakhand, India. *Int. J. Agric. Stat. Sci., 12*(2), 523-530.

Zhang, Y., Cao, C., Gu, J., Garg, H. (2023). The Impact of Top Management Team Characteristics on the Risk Taking of Chinese Private Construction Enterprises. *Systems, 11*(2), 67. [http://dx.doi.org/10.3390/systems11020067]

SUBJECT INDEX

Sanjay Taneja, Ercan Ozen, Luan Vardar, Mohit Kukreti & Mohammad Kashif (Eds.)

D

E

F

G

H

M

N

P

R

S

T

V

W

www.ingramcontent.com/pod-product-compliance
Ingram Content Group UK Ltd.
Pitfield, Milton Keynes, MK11 3LW, UK
UKHW060011051026
15591UKWH00002B/146